Sustainable Development and Free Trade

Sustainable Development and Free Trade examines the interrelationship between trade-induced economic growth and the environment, and its impact on the global quest for sustainable development. It particularly focuses on the interests and concerns of developing countries. The book argues that environmental protection issues are inextricably linked with the economic development of developing countries and also explores the skewing of international environmental policies into justifications for trade protectionism.

The author of this book treats the subject area on an institutional basis. In this sense, he examines the ways in which these issues are addressed in a variety of international legal instruments, ranging from the UN Charter to regional free trade agreements. Despite the seemingly insurmountable problems with the global *status quo* that are presented throughout its chapters, *Sustainable Development and Free Trade* maintains a sense of optimism that the necessary changes can still be made within existing trade and environment paradigms. The book scrutinizes the principles of 'common but differentiated responsibilities' and 'special and differential treatment' and concludes that the merit of such principles has become an increasingly persuasive justification for the instigation of radical changes to the global regulation of trade and environment issues. Proceeding beyond in-principle adherence to the key tenets of sustainable development, a significantly expanded role for the United Nations and its various trade and environment bodies, the immediate abandonment of North/South protectionist trade measures that are currently disguised by a thin veil of purported environmentalism and a truly open rules-based multilateral trading system are all identified as key steps on the pathway to sustainable development.

This book is primarily aimed at academics and university students in areas such as international environmental law, international trade law, international development, sustainable development, international relations and international organizations but will also be beneficial to all areas of economics, law and politics.

Shawkat Alam is Lecturer in the Department of Law at Macquarie University, Sydney, Australia.

Routledge studies in development economics

1 **Economic Development in the Middle East**
Rodney Wilson

2 **Monetary and Financial Policies in Developing Countries**
Growth and stabilization
Akhtar Hossain and Anis Chowdhury

3 **New Directions in Development Economics**
Growth, environmental concerns and government in the 1990s
Edited by Mats Lundahl and Benno J. Ndulu

4 **Financial Liberalization and Investment**
Kanhaya L. Gupta and Robert Lensink

5 **Liberalization in the Developing World**
Institutional and economic changes in Latin America, Africa and Asia
Edited by Alex E. Fernández Jilberto and André Mommen

6 **Financial Development and Economic Growth**
Theory and experiences from developing countries
Edited by Niels Hermes and Robert Lensink

7 **The South African Economy**
Macroeconomic prospects for the medium term
Finn Tarp and Peter Brixen

8 **Public Sector Pay and Adjustment**
Lessons from five countries
Edited by Christopher Colclough

9 **Europe and Economic Reform in Africa**
Structural adjustment and economic diplomacy
Obed O. Mailafia

10 **Post-apartheid Southern Africa**
Economic challenges and policies for the future
Edited by Lennart Petersson

11 **Financial Integration and Development**
Liberalization and reform in sub-Saharan Africa
Ernest Aryeetey and Machiko Nissanke

12 **Regionalization and Globalization in the Modern World Economy**
Perspectives on the Third World and transitional economies
Edited by Alex E. Fernández Jilberto and André Mommen

13 **The African Economy**
Policy, institutions and the future
Steve Kayizzi-Mugerwa

14 **Recovery from Armed Conflict in Developing Countries**
Edited by Geoff Harris

15 **Small Enterprises and Economic Development**
The dynamics of micro and small enterprises
Carl Liedholm and Donald C. Mead

16 **The World Bank**
New agendas in a changing world
Michelle Miller-Adams

17 **Development Policy in the Twenty-first Century**
Beyond the post-Washington consensus
Edited by Ben Fine, Costas Lapavitsas and Jonathan Pincus

18 **State-owned Enterprises in the Middle East and North Africa**
Privatization, performance and reform
Edited by Merih Celasun

19 **Finance and Competitiveness in Developing Countries**
Edited by José María Fanelli and Rohinton Medhora

20 **Contemporary Issues in Development Economics**
Edited by B.N. Ghosh

21 **Mexico Beyond NAFTA**
Edited by Martín Puchet Anyul and Lionello F. Punzo

22 **Economies in Transition**
A guide to China, Cuba, Mongolia, North Korea and Vietnam at the turn of the twenty-first century
Ian Jeffries

23 **Population, Economic Growth and Agriculture in Less Developed Countries**
Nadia Cuffaro

24 **From Crisis to Growth in Africa?**
Edited by Mats Lundal

25 **The Macroeconomics of Monetary Union**
An analysis of the CFA franc zone
David Fielding

26 **Endogenous Development**
Networking, innovation, institutions and cities
Antonio Vasquez-Barquero

27 Labour Relations in Development
Edited by
Alex E. Fernández Jilberto and Marieke Riethof

28 The Crisis of Rural Poverty and Hunger
An essay on the complementarity between market and government-led land reform for its resolution
M. Riad El-Ghonemy

29 Globalization, Marginalization and Development
Edited by S. Mansoob Murshed

30 Programme Aid and Development
Beyond conditionality
Howard White and Geske Dijkstra

31 Competitiveness Strategy in Developing Countries
A manual for policy analysis
Edited by Ganeshan Wignaraja

32 The African Manufacturing Firm
An analysis based on firm surveys in sub-Saharan Africa
Dipak Mazumdar and Ata Mazaheri

33 Trade Policy, Growth and Poverty in Asian Developing Countries
Edited by Kishor Sharma

34 International Competitiveness, Investment and Finance
A case study of India
Edited by A. Ganesh Kumar, Kunal Sen and Rajendra R. Vaidya

35 The Pattern of Aid Giving
The impact of good governance on development assistance
Eric Neumayer

36 New International Poverty Reduction Strategies
Edited by Jean-Pierre Cling, Mireille Razafindrakoto and François Roubaud

37 Targeting Development
Critical perspectives on the millennium development goals
Edited by Richard Black and Howard White

38 Essays on Balance of Payments Constrained Growth
Theory and evidence
Edited by J.S.L. McCombie and A.P. Thirlwall

39 The Private Sector after Communism
New entrepreneurial firms in transition economies
Jan Winiecki, Vladimir Benacek and Mihaly Laki

40 Information Technology and Development
A new paradigm for delivering the internet to rural areas in developing countries
Jeffrey James

41 The Economics of Palestine
Economic policy and institutional reform for a viable Palestine state
Edited by David Cobham and Nu'man Kanafani

42 **Development Dilemmas**
The methods and political ethics of growth policy
Melvin Ayogu and Don Ross

43 **Rural Livelihoods and Poverty Reduction Policies**
Edited by Frank Ellis and H. Ade Freeman

44 **Beyond Market-driven Development**
Drawing on the experience of Asia and Latin America
Edited by Makoto Noguchi and Costas Lapavitsas

45 **The Political Economy of Reform Failure**
Edited by Mats Lundahl and Michael L. Wyzan

46 **Overcoming Inequality in Latin America**
Issues and challenges for the twenty-first century
Edited by Ricardo Gottschalk and Patricia Justino

47 **Trade, Growth and Inequality in the Era of Globalization**
Edited by Kishor Sharma and Oliver Morrissey

48 **Microfinance**
Perils and prospects
Edited by Jude L. Fernando

49 **The IMF, World Bank and Policy Reform**
Edited by Alberto Paloni and Maurizio Zanardi

50 **Managing Development**
Globalization, economic restructuring and social policy
Edited by Junji Nakagawa

51 **Who Gains from Free Trade?**
Export-led growth, inequality and poverty in Latin America
Edited by Rob Vos, Enrique Ganuza, Samuel Morley and Sherman Robinson

52 **Evolution of Markets and Institutions**
A study of an emerging economy
Murali Patibandla

53 **The New Famines**
Why famines exist in an era of globalization
Edited by Stephen Devereux

54 **Development Ethics at work**
Explorations – 1960–2002
Denis Goulet

55 **Law Reform in Developing and Transitional States**
Edited by Tim Lindsey

56 **The Assymetries of Globalization**
Edited by Pan A. Yotopoulos and Donato Romano

57 **Ideas, Policies and Economic Development in the Americas**
Edited by Esteban Pérez-Caldentey and Matias Vernengo

58 **European Union Trade Politics and Development**
'Everything but arms' unravelled
Edited by Gerrit Faber and Jan Orbie

59 Membership Based Organizations of the Poor
Edited by Martha Chen, Renana Jhabvala, Ravi Kanbur and Carol Richards

60 The Politics of Aid Selectivity
Good governance criteria in World Bank, U.S. and Dutch development assistance
Wil Hout

61 Economic Development, Education and Transnational Corporations
Mark Hanson

62 Achieving Economic Development in the Era of Globalization
Shalendra Sharma

63 Sustainable Development and Free Trade
Institutional approaches
Shawkat Alam

Sustainable Development and Free Trade

Institutional approaches

Shawkat Alam

Routledge
Taylor & Francis Group
LONDON AND NEW YORK

First published 2008
by Routledge
2 Park Square, Milton Park, Abingdon, Oxon OX14 4RN

Simultaneously published in the USA and Canada
by Routledge
270 Madison Ave, New York, NY 10016

Routledge is an imprint of the Taylor & Francis Group, an informa business

Typeset in Times by Wearset Ltd, Boldon, Tyne and Wear
Printed and bound in Great Britain by TJI Digital, Padstow, Cornwall

British Library Cataloguing in Publication Data
A catalogue record for this book is available from the British Library

Library of Congress Cataloging in Publication Data
A catalog record for this book has been requested

ISBN10: 0-415-41294-3 (hbk)
ISBN10: 0-203-93606-X (ebk)

ISBN13: 978-0-415-41294-0 (hbk)
ISBN13: 978-0-203-93606-1 (ebk)

To my wife Rosan and my son Sami
for their unbounded support and encouragement

Contents

Preface xiv
Acknowledgements xvii
Table of cases xviii
Table of international instruments xx

1 Establishing the linkage: the trade–environment interface 1

Trade as a means of economic growth 1
Environmental impacts of free trade 3
Addressing the relationship between trade and the environment 4
The emergence of sustainable development 4
Sustainable development: equity and responsibility 6
Understanding the problems of the trade–environment interface in developing countries: confronting their economic realities 8
Organization of the book 21

2 The United Nations' approach to trade, the environment and sustainable development 24

Relevant principles and concepts employed in the context of trade and environment interactions 25
The environment in the United Nations 28
The United Nations Conference on Environment and Development 35
The Millennium Summit 46
The World Summit on Sustainable Development 49
The United Nations Commission on Sustainable Development 53
North–South aspects of the United Nations approach to trade and the environment 55
Conclusion 59

3 GATT/WTO approaches to trade, the environment and sustainable development 60

Genesis of GATT/WTO 60
Trade theory and the WTO 62
GATT's core principles affecting trade–environment issues 64
Environmentalism in GATT 68
Environmentalism in the WTO 74
The concerns of developing countries 99
Conclusion 101

4 The trade–environment linkage in the post-Uruguay Round context 103

Development of trade–environment linkage in the WTO Ministerial Conferences 103
The way forward 118
Conclusion 118

5 Regional approaches to free trade and sustainable development: the European Union 120

Development of the concept of sustainable development in the European Community 121
The trade–environment interface in the European Community 125
The harmonization of environmental standards and the implications 133
Developed and developing countries within the European Union 135
The situations of developing countries (not within the EU) in the trade–environment interface of the European Union 137
Conclusion 143

6 Regional approaches to free trade and sustainable development: the North American Free Trade Agreement 145

Protecting the environment under NAFTA free trading: its scope of operation 147
Dispute resolution 156
The situations of developing countries at the trade–environment interface under NAFTA 159
Conclusion 164

7 Regional approaches to free trade and sustainable development: the Asia-Pacific economic cooperation 166

The environment, and North–South dynamics in APEC's institutional structure 167
The emergence of sustainable development in APEC 169
Recent developments 172
The achievements of APEC in the trade–environment context 174
Continuing trade and environmental issues in APEC and recommendations for reform 174
Conclusion 180

8 Trade restrictions pursuant to multilateral environmental agreements 182

MEA trade measures and developing countries 183
Specific MEA trade measures and developing countries 185
The uneasy relationship between MEAs and the WTO free trade regime 199
Conclusion 202

9 Free trade and sustainable development: challenges ahead 205

Interlinkages between trade, the environment and sustainable development 206
Why do developing countries need an open and equitable international trading system? 207
The current state of play 208
The trade–environment nexus and sustainable development: challenges ahead 213

Notes 215
Bibliography 263
Index 282

Preface

Since the dawning of the era of colonialism, the voices of the world's poorest nations have been all but muted in the most important spheres of international governance and decision-making. Such a trend has been naturally reflected through a severe shortage of scholarly discourse presented exclusively from the perspective of the least developed and developing South. *Sustainable Development and Free Trade* seeks to counter these disturbing trends through a detailed dissection of the interlinkages between two of the most pressing items on the current international agenda: the regulation of world trade and the protection of the global environment.

Sustainable Development and Free Trade begins by openly acknowledging that rhetorical recognition of the plight of the world's poor has been one of the most prominent features of global governance forums since the early 1990s. Having been drafted and refined at various landmark world summits from Rio in 1992 and Johannesburg a decade later, keystone concepts such as 'sustainable development', 'inter- and intra-generational equity' and 'common but differentiated responsibilities' have now been established as integral parts of the vernacular for international discussion of trade and environment issues. However, while the insertion of such terms into a diverse array of international law instruments has indeed become commonplace, the book argues that their extensive practical manifestation has been anything but.

Sustainable Development and Free Trade proposes that in lieu of the vast and widening chasm between the economic and technological resources of developing countries and those of their Northern counterparts, the notion of 'common but differentiated responsibilities' should form a particularly vital ideological basis in striving for a truly sustainable global future. The book scrutinizes this concept and the related trade principle of 'special and differential treatment' and concludes that the merit of such principles has become an increasingly persuasive justification for the instigation of radical changes to the global regulation of trade and environment issues. One need only look to the findings of recent major studies published by bodies such as the International Panel on Climate Change to realize that while it is the actions and wants-based lifestyles of the world's rich that have, and continue to be, the predominant cause of pending and actual environmental crises, it is the world's poorest nations (Small Island Developing

States and Least Developed countries in Africa and Asia) that will suffer most from both present and future calamities.

Sustainable Development and Free Trade examines the impact of two of the most important developments in contemporary international trade regulation, namely, the establishment of the *General Agreement on Tariffs and Trade* ('GATT') and the subsequent emergence of the World Trade Organization ('WTO'). With the aim of identifying and analysing the most pressing issues for developing countries in relation to multilateral trade liberalization and the environment, the book focuses on fundamental concepts (such as the Most Favoured Nation principle) of the GATT/WTO regime and explores their impact on the trade–environment nexus. Case studies form a particularly prominent feature of this aspect of the book, including an exploration of the landmark decisions of the various dispute settlement bodies of the GATT/WTO framework. In undertaking these studies, the book seeks to decipher what issues appear to have been treated as genuinely legitimate policy goals in relation to the trade and environment in contrast to those purported 'policies' that, upon being subjected to the adjudication of a quasi-judicial body, have been exposed as little more than unenforceable rhetoric.

Another crucial aspect of the GATT/WTO regime that is examined in depth is the emergence and controversial increased prevalence of trade-related environmental measures (such as eco-labelling and the imposition of strict product standards). It is through these measures that the damaging effects of so-called 'green protectionism' is often most readily identifiable. *Sustainable Development and Free Trade* also asserts that the current operation of WTO instruments, including the Technological Barriers to Trade Agreement, Application of Sanitary and Phytosanitary Measures Agreement and the Agreements on Agriculture, Textiles and Clothing, remain of tremendous concern from a developing country perspective, despite the concerted and ongoing efforts of various rounds of negotiation. A common thread between all of these instruments is that beneath the thin veil of global partnership and cooperation lie systems that are based inherently on Northern agendas and interests and that operate in a manner that often inflicts great economic and social detriment upon their Southern signatories.

The emergence of regional trade blocs is a dominant feature of modern international economics. The European Union ('EU'), the North American Free Trade Agreement ('NAFTA') and the Asia-Pacific Economic Cooperation ('APEC') are evidence of the increasing importance of the trend towards regionalization. Such regional agreements have emerged to address the perceived shortcomings of the GATT/WTO regime and to hasten the removal of trade barriers. Harmonization of environmental standards has emerged as a major concern of regionalism, as disparate national environmental standards are perceived as restraints to free trade. *Sustainable Development and Free Trade* examines the approaches of these regional trade blocs in addressing the trade–environment interface. The book exposes the pressures that upward harmonization can place on the developing parties to such agreements. In order to reap the benefits of a free trade agreement, developing countries are at risk of setting unrealistic goals for themselves in relation to environmental standards. The book argues against regional measures that punish developing countries for being unable to fulfil stringent environmental standards and urges instead a focus on cooperation, capacity building and an integrative approach to trade, ecology and development. *Sustainable Development and Free Trade* also exposes the risks to developing countries that are not parties to these regional free trade agreements, as stringent environmental standards may act as protectionist barriers against their products. The focus of regional agreements should be the opening of trade barriers, they should not provide a forum for 'green protectionism' writ large.

With the aim of providing a holistic overview of the current trade and environment framework, *Sustainable Development and Free Trade* also presents a detailed analysis of the species of international law instrument most commonly known as Multilateral Environmental Agreements ('MEAs'). The book suggests that despite their proliferation in recent years, an all too common feature of some of the most significant MEAs currently in operation is the stark juxtaposition between provisions concerning *discretionary* contributions to be made by Northern parties to multilateral assistance funds versus the inclusion of *mandatory* enforcement clauses. It is this latter aspect of various MEAs that is most commonly imposed on developing countries for their failure to adhere strictly to certain treaty provisions and, in particular, environmental standards. What is rendered invisible by this often punitive process is that such a failure is not typically attributable to lack of commitment to the objectives of a particular MEA by its Southern parties but is instead due to a desperate lack of economic or technological capacity to properly implement its provisions.

Despite the seemingly insurmountable problems with the global status quo that are presented throughout its chapters, *Sustainable Development and Free Trade* maintains a sense of optimism that the necessary changes can still be made within existing trade and environment paradigms. Proceeding beyond in-principle adherence to the key tenets of sustainable development, a significantly expanded role for the United Nations and its various trade and environment bodies, the immediate abandonment of North/South protectionist trade measures that are currently disguised by a thin veil of purported environmentalism and a truly open rules-based multilateral trading system are all identified as key steps on the pathway to sustainable development.

Acknowledgements

The book derives its origin from my doctoral research in the emerging areas of international law, international trade and finance and environmental law. I have substantially added, adjusted, amended, changed and re-written most of the chapters to deal with the recent developments and changing the PhD dissertation into a proper style and voice of a book for an international audience. It was a daunting task which I could not pursue enthusiastically without the ongoing support, encouragement and assistance from many people. Professor Rafiqul Islam as my doctoral supervisor has earlier reviewed all the drafts of the work and guided me with important ideas, constructive criticism and ongoing encouragement. I owe special thanks and gratitude to all of my friends and colleagues of the Division of Law, Macquarie University, for their suggestions, sustained interest and moral support throughout the project.

I am particularly thankful to David Randle for outstanding research assistance, ideas and support for the book. David diligently reviewed most of the chapters and provided help with insightful comments, ideas and criticism at earlier stages of the project. I would also like to acknowledge the invaluable editorial assistance and crucial support of Shireen Daft at the final stage of the work in helping me put the manuscript together.

I would like to thank my parents and family members for their constant support and encouragement. Particularly, I cannot express how much I owe to my wife Rosan for her unbounded support and understanding during the preparation of the book. This project would not have been possible without her help. Thanks are also owed to my adorable son Sami, who inspired me with love to keep my dream alive all the time.

Finally my thanks are due to the scholarly journals in whose pages some of the content of the book has already appeared for permission to include it: the *Macquarie Journal of International and Comparative Environmental Law*, Macquarie University, Sydney NSW (Chapter 1); *ILSA Journal of International and Comparative Law*, Fort Lauderdale FL (Chapter 2); the *New Zealand Yearbook of International Law*, University of Canterbury, Christchurch NZ, and *Bond Law Review*, Bond University, Gold Coast QLD (Chapter 3); the *James Cook University Law Review*, James Cook University, Townsville QLD (Chapter 4); and the *Journal of World Trade*, Wolters Kluwer Law and Business, New York (Chapter 8). Bibliographical details are cited at the head of the notes on the chapters concerned.

Table of cases

Canada – Measures Affecting Exports of Unprocessed Herring and Salmon, GATT Doc. L/6268, BISD 35S/98.
Case 7/68, *Commission v. Italy* [1968] ECR 423.
Case 8/74 *Dassonville*, [1974] ECR 837.
Case 13/68, *Salgoil* [1968] ECR 453.
Case 95/81, *Commission v. Italy* [1982] ECR 2.
Case 104/75, *De Peiper* [1976] ECR 613.
Case 113/80, *Commission v. Ireland* [1981] ECR 1.
Case 120/78, *Cassis de Dijon* [1979] ECR 649.
Case 788/79 *Gilli and Andres* [1980] ECR 2071.
Case C-2/90, *Commission v. Belgium* [1992] ECR I-4433.
Cases C-401/92 and C-402/92, *Criminal Proceedings Against Tankstation 't Heuske vof and J.B.E. Boermans*, 1994 ECR I-2199.
Dutch Red Grouse Case, Case 169/89, [1990] ECR I-2143.
EC Commission v. Council, Case 155/91, [1993] ECR I-939.
EC Commission v. Council, Case 300/89, [1991] ECR I-2867.
EC Commission v. Denmark, Case 302/86, [1989] 1 CMLR 619.
EC Measures Concerning Meat and Meat Products (Hormones), 1996, WTO Doc. WT/DS26/R/USA.
Ethyl Corporation v. Canada, 38 ILM 708 (1999).
European Communities – Measures Affecting Asbestos and Asbestos-containing Products, 2001, WTO Doc. WT/DS135/AB/R.
Fromancais v. Forma [1983] ECR 395.
Metalclad Corporation v. United Mexican States ('*Metaclad*'), Case No. ARB(AF)/97/1 (30 August 2000).
Thailand – Restrictions on Importation of, and Internal Taxes on, Cigarettes, GATT Doc. DS10/R, BISD 37S/200.
United States – Restrictions on Imports of Tuna ('Tuna–Dolphin I'), GATT Doc. DS21/R, reprinted in 30 ILM 1594 (1991).
United States – Restrictions on Imports of Tuna ('Tuna–Dolphin II'), GATT Doc. DS29/R, 16 June 1994.
United States – Section 337 of the Tariff Act of 1930, GATT Doc. L/6439, BISD. 36S/345 (adopted 7 November 1989).

United States – Standards for Reformulated and Conventional Gasoline, WTO Doc. WT/DS2/R, reprinted in 35 ILM 274 (1996).
United States – Taxes on Automobiles. Reprinted in 33 ILM 1397 (1994).
United States – Taxes on Petroleum and Certain Imported Substances, BISD 34.5/136; GATT Doc L/6175, 17 June 1987.
United States – Prohibition of Shrimps and Certain Shrimp Products, WTO Doc. WT/DS58/AB/R (98–000) (12 October 1998).
Waste Management v. United Mexican States, 2000, Case No. ARB (AF)/98/2 (2 June 2000).

Table of international instruments

Non-binding multilateral environmental instruments

Stockholm Declaration of the United Nations Conference on the Human Environment, 16 June 1972, UN Doc. A/Conf.48/14/Rev. (1973).

Agenda 21, UN Conference on Environment and Development, Annex II, UN Doc. A/Conf. 151/26/Rev. 1 (1992).

Rio Declaration on Environment and Development, UN Doc. A/Conf. 151/5/Rev.1, 14 June 1992.

United Nations Millennium Declaration, UN General Assembly Resolution 55/2, 2000, UN Doc. A/Res/55/2 (2000).

Johannesburg Declaration on Sustainable Development, 4 September 2002, UN Doc. A/Conf. 199/L6/Rev. 2 (2002).

Multilateral environmental agreements

Convention on International Trade in Endangered Species of Wild Flora and Fauna (CITES) 993 UNTS 243. Opened for signature 3 March 1973, entered into force 1 July 1975.

Montreal Protocol on Substances that Deplete the Ozone Layer ('*Montreal Protocol*'). Adopted and opened for signature 16 September 1987, entered into force 1 January 1989. Amended and adjusted, reprinted in 30 ILM 537 (1991) and amended and adjusted, reprinted in 32 ILM 874 (1992).

Basel Convention on the Control of the Transboundary Movements of Hazardous Wastes and their Disposal (*'Basel Convention'*). Adopted and opened for signature 22 March 1986, entered into force 5 May 1992.

United Nations Framework Convention on Climate Change ('*Climate Change Convention*'), New York, 1992.

United Nations Convention on Biological Diversity ('*Biodiversity Convention*'), Rio de Janeiro, 5 June 1992.

Vienna Convention on the Protection of the Ozone Layer, 22 March 1985. UN Doc. IG.53/5.

Multilateral trading agreements

The *General Agreement on Tariffs and Trade* ('GATT'), Geneva, 30 October 1947, as amended, 61 Stat. (pt. 5) 55–61 UNTS 188.

Treaty Establishing the European Community (*'Treaty of Rome'*), Rome, 25 March 1957, 298 UNTS 3.

Single European Act, Luxembourg, 17 February 1986, and The Hague, 28 February 1986. Reprinted in 25 ILM 506 (1986).

Canada–US Free Trade Agreement, 22–3 December 1987 and 2 January 1988, 27 ILM 28 (1988).

Treaty on European Union (*'Maastricht Treaty'*), Maastricht, 17 February 1992.

North American Free Trade Agreement, Canada–Mexico–United States, 32 ILM 605 (1993).

North American Agreement on Environmental Cooperation ('Environment Side Agreement'), Canada–Mexico–United States, 32 ILM 1480 (1993).

Final Act Embodying the Results of the Uruguay Round of Multilateral Trade Negotiations, GATT Doc. MTN/FA (15 December 1993), 33 ILM 9 (1994).

Agreement Establishing the World Trade Organization, GATT Doc. MTN/FA II (15 December 1993).

General Agreement on Tariffs and Trade, GATT Doc. MTN/FA II-A1A-2 (15 December 1993).

Agreement on the Application of Sanitary and Phytosanitary Measures ('SPS'), GATT Doc. MTN/FA II-A1A-4 (15 December 1993).

Agreement on Trade-related Aspects of Intellectual Property Rights ('TRIPs'), GATT Doc. MTN/FA II-A1C (15 December 1993).

Agreement on Technical Barriers to Trade ('TBT'), GATT Doc. MTN/FA II-A1A-6 (15 December 1993).

Agreement on Subsidies and Countervailing Measures, GATT Doc. MTN/FA II-A1A-13 (15 December 1993).

General Agreement on Trade in Services ('GATS'), GATT Doc. MTN/FA II-A1B (15 December 1993).

Agreement on Textiles and Clothing, see World Trade Organization, *The Legal Texts: The Results of the Uruguay Round of Multilateral Trade Negotiations* ('WTO Legal Texts'), New York: Cambridge University Press, 1999, p. 73.

Agreement on Agriculture, see *WTO Legal Texts*, p. 33.

1 Establishing the linkage

The trade–environment interface

Traditionally, economic growth and its ecological consequences have been treated as totally separate concepts within the broader paradigm of development. Economic growth through trade, investment, transferring finance and capital is one of the major vehicles for development, particularly at the international level and within the affluent nations. However, rising world poverty, economic inequalities, and the depletion of finite natural resources have challenged the traditional development paradigm that limitless economic growth is the universal solution to all of humanity's most pressing problems. Instead, recent decades have been punctuated by a shift in focus and an increasingly widespread recognition of the need for the integration of economy and ecology. It has also become widely acknowledged that the existing process of development, based on present technologies, production, distribution and consumption patterns, is not sustainable for either the natural or the human environment. The most notable feature of this ideological shift is the widespread emergence of the concept of sustainable development.

Trade as a means of economic growth

International trade as a source of wealth and welfare gains has always been considered one of the major vehicles of economic growth. In fact, the final two decades of the twentieth century were marked by significant emphasis being placed on the development of world trade as an engine for economic growth and a key aspect of international economic development.

There are numerous commonly cited benefits that are often perceived to flow from the so-called free trade regime. First and foremost, it is argued that free trade and industrialization bring liberalization of the movement of goods, services, persons, capital and payments, and prohibitions of restrictions on competition by the market participants. The liberalization of trade by voluntary exchange of goods facilitates a country's specialization in favourable proportions. According to the principle of comparative production advantage,[1] a country can produce more of the goods in which it is relatively more efficient and export them in return for goods in which its comparative advantage is less. The *Leutwiler Report* describes the concept of comparative advantage in the following words:

> Trade allows countries to concentrate on what they can do best. No two countries are exactly alike in natural resources, climate or work force. Those differences give each country a 'comparative advantage' over the others in some products. Trade translates the individual advantages of many countries into maximum productivity for all. This is the classic theory of international trade. It is still valid today.[2]

Trade liberalization benefits all trading partners by increasing global output and economic growth. The whole world gains from trade and both sides of a trading partnership are at least as well off with some trade as with no trade. Liberal trade contributes to economic growth. Using comparative advantage trade brings about the highest possible welfare in the participating countries by facilitating specialization of production across national boundaries. Thus, an outcome of the free trade regime is the promotion of a mutually profitable division of labour, which in turn greatly improves the potential real national product of all nations. Ultimately, therefore, the free trade regime has the capacity to result in higher standards of living and a worldwide reduction of poverty.[3]

Gross National Product ('GNP') traditionally has been accepted as the primary method of measuring economic growth and indeed, a nation's overall level of development. However, it is now recognized that GNP fails to adequately take into account some social and environmental considerations such as social equity, quality of life and other environmental issues. The *Brundtland Report*, among the most influential development studies written in the late 1970s and early 1980s, has explicitly shown the vital links between the state of our natural environment and economic growth, especially given the accelerating nature of economic and ecological interdependence between countries.[4]

There are a number of well identified reasons as to why, in this present era of globalization, the ecological interdependence of nations has become particularly apparent. Without doubt the most publicized international environmental phenomenon in recent times has been the occurrence of global warming due to human-induced carbon emissions. In light of the total disconnection between the source of the vast majority of carbon emissions (namely the Organization for Economic Cooperation and Development ('OECD') nations) and those least developed and small island developing states that are fully expected to be most adversely affected, it is evident that no issue more poignantly highlights the increasing ecological interdependence among nations than climate change. While, as a group, Small Island Developing States ('SIDS') contribute 95 per cent less *per capita* in carbon dioxide emissions than OECD countries, some SIDS are already suffering the negative effects of global warming. For example, parts of Papua New Guinea are presently experiencing 20 cm per annum loss of land area due to sea level rise.[5]

Other transboundary environmental issues such as international river management, desertification and the over-harvesting of global fisheries on the high seas are also demonstrative of the need for a holistic appraisal of the ecological impact of international economic, social and political systems.

It is argued that putting restrictions on trade through environmental regulation may offset the possibility of receiving international specialization and its contribution, which is necessary for protecting the environment. Sustainable development requires the efficient use of resources, which is fostered, among other factors, by free trade and international competition.[6] This book contends that, despite current trends to the contrary, the establishment of a free trade regime does indeed have tremendous potential in serving as a catalyst for promoting ecological health and safeguarding the environment.

By contributing to economic growth, free trade has the potential to improve environmental quality. Such improvements are likely to occur as individuals, organizations and governments are more likely to raise funds and spend more money on environmental protection. By bringing about income growth, free trade is sometimes believed to have the potential to eradicate poverty.[7] The simple and direct link between the eradication of poverty and decreased environmental degradation in developing countries has long been acknowledged, particularly in relation to issues such as impoverished farmers being forced to overexploit marginal lands thus resulting in the acceleration of desertification.[8]

By stimulating competition, free trade facilitates economies of scale and contributes to product and process innovation, further reducing manufacturing costs and expanding consumer choices. International trade, through a series of multilateral trade negotiations, has reduced import tariffs and other governmental distortions to trade and has increased the value of merchandise trade from one-fifth to one-third of global Gross Domestic Product ('GDP') during the post-war period.[9]

Environmental impacts of free trade

The positive view of liberal trade has been changing because of worsening regional and global environmental problems and the resulting conflicts of trade and environmental interests. With the rapid increase of international trade and investment in the post-war era, the degree of environmental degradation that can be directly attributed to various aspects of the international trading order has become acute. As a result, environmentalists and those who are concerned with development have challenged the free trade positions. Consequently, rather than realizing its potential as a promoter of environmental quality, an exponential increase in international trade over the last several decades has undeniably worsened environmental problems. Nonetheless, from the outset it is important to appreciate that the major problems to date at the trade and environment interface have not been free trade *per se* but rather the specific parameters in which the trade regime has operated and for the protection of certain developed nations interests.

Free trade is seen as substantially damaging to the environment as it does not include the total economic and environmental values of the natural resources in market transactions. The prices charged for non-renewable resources generally do not reflect the true scarcity and the need to replenish those resources, causing continuous and irreversible environmental degradation ranging from climate change and biological impoverishment to species extinction. This failure to encompass social costs may reflect:

> the existence of spillover effects, unpriced resources, absent or thin markets, excessively high transaction costs that discourage otherwise beneficial exchanges, lack of information, technical uncertainty, the public good nature of many environmental resources or a lack of property rights.[10]

Another particularly concerning aspect of this market failure is that it prevents future generations from participating in economic processes and bidding for environmental values, which violates the principle of intergenerational equity. Hence the prerequisite of sustainable development, that it must take account of the interests of both present and future generations, is absent from market transactions.

Addressing the relationship between trade and the environment

This book is an examination of the complex relationship between the environment and free trade. It considers different aspects of the impact of international trade on the environment and the effects of environmental regulations on international trade from national, regional and global perspectives. This impact is studied primarily from the perspective of the marginalized trading plight of developing countries. The different perspective of free-traders, environmentalists, developed and developing countries are highlighted and commented upon. This book examines whether and/or how economic activity can be reconciled with concerns about the environment in order to promote sustainable development particularly in developing countries. In view of the concerns of developing countries regarding the interaction between trade and the environment, it is argued that the objectives of sustainable development can be achieved only by taking into account the broader context of social, economic, historical and ecological factors in trade–environment interactions.

Trade–environment discourse needs to be viewed within the broader framework of sustainable development, poverty alleviation, intergenerational equity and socio-environmental justice. Trade–environment issues have to be addressed in a pragmatic manner by considering the special needs and economic status of developing countries, the issue of global economic conditions and the common but differentiated responsibility principle.

The emergence of sustainable development

While a huge number of derivations are now in existence, the definition of sustainable development that has come to enjoy virtually universal acceptance is the persisting declaration of *Our Common Future*, a report published in 1987 and chaired by the former Prime Minister of Norway, Gro Harlem Brundtland. The *Brundtland Report* established that:

> Sustainable development is development that meets the needs of the present without compromising the ability of future generations to meet their own needs.[11]

The Brundtland definition of sustainable development has subsequently been adopted both domestically and internationally in relation to an incredibly broad area of social and economic policy. Of particular relevance to this book is the fact that the Charter of the WTO establishes sustainable development as its fundamental goal and purpose.[12]

Over the last twenty years, there is a strong lineage of important international events that have affirmed the need to subordinate global trading regimes to the overarching ideology of sustainable development. The *Brundtland Report* emphasized the need for a new development path, pointing out that many present developmental trends are leaving an increasing number of people poor and vulnerable as a result of environmental degradation.[13] The assistance of the world's poorest via economic growth fuelled by the exploitation of natural resources encounters conflict if a high-quality environment is also desirable. In maintaining the acceleration of economic growth, rising pressures on natural resources mean that development is achieved increasingly at the expense of the environment.

Following the landmark 1992 United Nations Conference on Environment and Development ('UNCED') in Rio de Janeiro, Brazil, the *Rio Declaration* recommended that '[s]tates should promote a supportive and open international economic system', which would contribute to economic growth and sustainable development.[14] Chapter 2 of *Agenda 21* recommends a similar approach in regards to the relationship between trade and the environment. It states that the 'development process will not gain momentum ... if barriers restrict access to markets and if commodity prices and the terms of trade of developing countries remain depressed'.[15] These important international declarations unequivocally affirmed that trade liberalization and the environment should be mutually supportive. As both trade and the protection of the natural environment are equally important for sustainable development, there must be a process of integration between the two spheres.

More recently, as a key outcome of the 2002 World Summit on Sustainable Development, the *Johannesburg Declaration on Sustainable Development* affirmed:

> Globalization has added a new dimension to these challenges. The rapid integration of markets, mobility of capital and significant increases in investment flows around the world have opened new challenges and opportunities for the pursuit of sustainable development. But the benefits and costs of globalization are unevenly distributed, with developing countries facing special difficulties in meeting this challenge.[16]

However, perhaps the most crucial and coordinated sustainable development initiative of the twenty-first century to date has been the United Nations Millennium Development Goals ('MDGs'). The eight individual goals that constitute the MDGs were derived directly from the *United Nations Millennium Declaration*, which received support from *every* member state of the United Nations by resolution of the General Assembly on 8 September 2000.[17] Goal 8 of the MDGs is entitled 'Develop a global partnership for development' and asserts that there is an urgent need to further develop an open trading and financial system, address the special needs of developing countries and to work with the private sector, especially in relation to technology transfer.

All of these international initiatives form an important contextual background in seeking to discover the most appropriate institutional approach for facing the challenges posed by the trade and environment nexus as it stands in the new millennium.

Sustainable development: equity and responsibility

The key components of the anthropocentric Brundtland definition of sustainable development refer to the concepts of intra- and inter-generational equity, two distinct yet complementary norms. The former principle establishes that there should be equitable distribution of resources and opportunities *between* the various peoples who presently inhabit Earth. The latter demands that current rates or methods of resource utilization should not inhibit the development prospects of humanity into the indefinite future. In considering the impact of the international trading order on the world's poorest nations it is noteworthy that the phrase 'future generations' in the Brundtland definition is completely non-specific. Therefore, it is reasonable to infer that the sustainable paradigm demands that no human activity should inhibit the capacity of future generations of *any* nation to meet their needs. Furthermore, beyond the explicit recognition of the importance of both inter- and intra-generational equity, a further key feature of sustainable development is its holistic and integrative nature. Social justice and human rights, environmental, economic and cultural factors are all integral considerations in the sustainable development paradigm and are not readily separable.

The equity-based objectives of sustainable development are also intrinsically linked to the principle of common but differentiated responsibility. The notion of common but differentiated responsibilities is succinctly defined by Guruswamy's statement that:

> any obligations to protect the common heritage of humankind need not fall disproportionately on the poor and the deprived. Given the enormous disparities of wealth among nations, equity, fairness and efficiency require that discharging the burden of protection should fall differentially and more heavily on richer nations.[18]

This principle recognizes that while all countries have a responsibility to protect the environment and prevent further environmental harm, these responsibilities vary according to the socio-economic situation of a country. The developed North and developing South have common but differentiated responsibilities in dealing with global environmental concerns. The responsibility of developed countries is greater than that of developing countries because of their strong economic conditions and their contribution to environmental degradation.

Quite clearly, the principle of common but differentiated responsibilities represents a substantial departure from the notion of sovereign equality of states, which has been at the absolute epicentre of modern international law since its inception. Nonetheless, the 1992 *Rio Declaration* affirmed the place of the common but differentiated responsibilities doctrine in international environmental law discourse stating that, 'developed countries acknowledge the responsibility that they bear in the international pursuit to sustainable development in view of the pressures their societies place on the global environment'.[19] It is also particularly significant to note that far before the explicit statement of common but differentiated responsibilities in Principle 7 of the *Rio Declaration*, the possibility of developing countries receiving 'special and differential treatment', was recognized in 1966 via the provisions outlined in Part IV of the GATT.

As a damning illustration of the monumental chasm between the rhetorical commitment to the common but differentiated responsibility principle and the extent of practical implementation it is evident that in the so-called decade of sustainable development beginning with the Rio Earth Summit in 1992, Official Overseas Development Assistance ('ODA') from the North *declined* from an annual figure of US$80 billion to between US$30–40 billion. This massive decline in North–South financial transfer occurred despite rhetorical commitments to *increase* ODA over the same period up to around US$200 billion per annum.[20]

It is vital to appreciate from the outset that while effective implementation of the common but differentiated responsibilities doctrine involves a dramatic increase in North–South financial transfers in the form of ODA, the provision of economic assistance is by no means the complete picture. Khosla describes the situation as follows:

> Making development more sustainable certainly needs more money. But it also needs much more than simply money. It needs fundamental changes in the global economy, as well as in the domestic economies of nations. The agenda, unfortunately, is set by the rich and powerful.[21]

It is these systemic problems with the current global economic order and the overtly North-slanted international trading agenda that will form the primary focus of this book.

Understanding the problems of the trade–environment interface in developing countries: confronting their economic realities

Global economic policy making and developing countries

Developing countries[22] are the most vulnerable, powerless, economically and socially marginalized in trade–environment interactions. Lavanya Rajamani has outlined a series of enduring perceptions at the root of the dissonance between the North and South on trade–environment issues.[23] Developing countries have been, and remain, deeply wary of the legitimacy of the movement on global trade and environmental policies pursued in isolation from the concerns of developing countries and originating from the priorities of developed countries.[24] An understanding of the broader political and economic context of trade–environment issues is necessary in order to properly appreciate the concerns of developing countries.

The development approach that has traditionally been pursued and applied through institutions like the International Monetary Fund ('IMF'), the World Bank and the WTO has worsened the real problems of developing countries. It has widened the existing gap and inequality between rich and poor countries. Developing countries, because of their marginalized position in the world economy, are perceived as vulnerable to external factors which are beyond their control and so economic decisions are made without their active participation.[25] Although the idea of free trade was originally designed to benefit both developed and developing countries, the global architecture of the free trade regime did not accommodate the interests and concerns of developing countries in the various rounds of multilateral trade negotiations.[26] Significantly, one of the key objectives of the Uruguay Round of trade negotiations was to:

> bring about further liberalisation and expansion of world trade to the benefit of all countries, especially less developed contracting parties, including the improvement of access to markets by the reduction and elimination of tariffs, quantitative restrictions and other non-tariff measures and obstacles . . .[27]

Unfortunately, the benefits of the international trading system shared by developing countries are not on parity with those enjoyed by developed countries. The majority of the populations in developing countries continue to live in conditions of poverty and hardship. There are also inequalities in the distribution of income. One of the most commonly cited indicators of this global predicament, as indicated by its explicit recognition in the United Nations' Millennium Development Goals, is the fact that in excess of 3 billion people, or half the world's population, survive on less than US$2 per day. Within this figure, more than 1 billion of these individuals are currently struggling to exist on less than US$1 per day.[28] At the other end of the spectrum, it is an equally unsettling reality that the world's most affluent 100 people have a net wealth that exceeds the individual GNP of dozens of least developed countries.[29]

The world community has a shared challenge and responsibility to facilitate the integration of developing countries into the world economy. The ongoing trade expansion has the potential to be a vehicle of economic growth for developing countries provided that its current and historically detrimental impact on the global environment, particularly in developing countries, is addressed as a matter of urgency. Trade can be an important means of achieving sustainable and equitable development; however, such development is possible only when the needs and concerns of developing countries are recognized and translated into an operational programme for implementation.

Unbalanced distribution of economic benefits from trade

At the rhetorical level, it is interesting to note that consideration of both the global environment and the predicament of the world's poorest nations are two factors that have long been explicitly acknowledged by the dominant global trade institution. As noted by Halle:

> the General Agreement on Tariffs and Trade that emerged from the Havana Conference in 1948 recognised that trade should not harm natural resources nor endanger vulnerable species, and accepted that governments could make exceptions to the normal disciplines of open trade in cases where the risk of environmental damage appeared probable.[30]

Furthermore, Part IV of GATT and the decision of 28 November 1979 of the Contracting Parties established the principle of special and differential treatment to be accorded to developing and least developed countries.[31] While outlining the general principles governing negotiations, the *GATT Punta Del Este Ministerial Declaration* of 20 September 1986 stated that:

> the developed countries do not expect reciprocity for commitments made by them in trade negotiations to reduce or remove tariffs and other barriers to the trade of developing countries ... Developed contracting parties shall therefore not seek, neither shall less developed contracting parties be required to make, concessions that are inconsistent with the latter's development, financial and trade needs.[32]

However, the above concessions granted to developing and least developed countries were subsequently diluted by the Uruguay Round Agreements. Most of the concessions provided to developing countries as a result of these Agreements were designed either to provide a grace period for developing countries to comply with the requirements of the Agreements or to take protective measures to safeguard their interests.[33] It was argued that free trade would lead to the most efficient and profitable use of national production factors, increase national income and foreign exchange earnings, attract foreign private capital and thus stimulate development in the South.[34] This rationale did not translate into action for developing countries. Such countries had high expectations and were prepared to take on fully fledged commitments in exchange for the commitment of developed countries in the Uruguay Round. However, with a few exceptions, developing countries did not benefit as much as expected. The GATT agreement was limited to trade involving manufactured goods but the Uruguay Round added agriculture, trade in services and intellectual property rights.

An analysis of the Uruguay Round negotiations reveals that the overall objective and purpose of the negotiations was not in developing countries' favour. Developing countries stress that the Uruguay Round and its implementation process did little to improve market access for their exports of goods and services, particularly to the markets of developed countries.[35] Indeed, there is persuasive empirical evidence to support such an assertion, a World Bank and OECD study performed in the mid-1990s evaluating the WTO agreements estimated that of the US$213 billion overall expected gain, US$142 billion would accrue to the North, US$37 billion to China and US$21 billion to 'upper-income Asia'. Africa alone was predicted to suffer a loss of US$2.6 billion.[36] According to the former chair of the Group of 77, Ambassador Luis Jaramillo of Colombia, the industrialized countries, which make up only 20 per cent of GATT membership, will disproportionately appropriate 70 per cent of the additional income.[37]

Many developing countries feel that the new WTO rules have been unbalanced in several important development related areas such as the protection of intellectual property rights and the use of industrial subsidies. They also feel that the special and differential treatment accorded to them by the WTO agreements has been inadequate and needs revision.[38] In light of the exclusivity of the final negotiations, many concerns remain about the effects of the Final Act upon some developing countries and the uneven distribution of economic benefits between the North and the South.

Some developing countries view the trade and environment debate as yet another route by which the North might achieve economic domination through protectionism.[39] Against this backdrop, developing countries distrust the agenda of developed countries with regard to the trade and environment linkage. They consider the link as a disguise for protectionist motives designed to keep out imports from countries which have a better competitive edge and a greater comparative advantage.[40] The Uruguay Round made provision for technical and financial assistance to be made available to developing countries and provided Generalized System of Preferences ('GSP') facilities to some developing countries.[41] But these attempts have been flouted for their failure to help or alleviate the trade problems of developing countries, given that, as noted above, most of the benefits of the Uruguay Round are accrued mostly by developed countries.

Limited market access

Developing countries argue that improved access to the Northern market would help them to move toward sustainable development. In the Uruguay Round negotiations, developed countries struck a deal with developing countries in which the North would open up their markets in areas of particular export interest to developing countries. This essentially meant a reduction of import restrictions, reduction of export subsidies and the provision of production subsidies. Developing countries were also accorded a GSP benefit. To date, commitments made by the North in the areas of agriculture and textiles (where developing countries have the comparative advantage) and the provisions on special and differential treatment have turned out to be largely empty promises.

The *United Nations Millennium Development Goals Report 2006* presents a well balanced perspective on the current state of affairs with relation to free market access for the South:

> Developing countries have gained greater access to markets over the past decade. Three quarters of their exports entered developed country markets duty-free in 2004, with the figure rising to 79 per cent for the least developed countries. However, goods that are strategically important to developing economies, such as clothing and farm products, are still heavily taxed ... A major objective of ongoing negotiations in the World Trade Organization is to further reduce such trade barriers. Developed countries have committed themselves in principle to duty-free and quota-free imports from least developed countries. However, further meaningful reductions will require considerable political determination.[42]

It is worth noting that further meaningful compliance with the various WTO open-market provisions (such as the principle of special and differentiated treatment) by developed countries would allay some of the fears of developing countries about the use of environmental measures as protectionist devices.[43] Developed countries have been and are consistently maintaining exceptionally high trade barriers (both tariff and non-tariff) in areas of special interest to developing countries. Each year these barriers cost developing countries approximately US$100 billion – twice the amount they receive in aid.[44] For manufactured goods, the tariffs facing exports from developing countries to high-income countries are on average four times higher than those facing exports from industrialized countries.[45] Perhaps an even more concerning illustration of the institutional challenges predominant under the status quo it is noteworthy that the United States and the European Union (EU) have launched a total of 234 anti dumping cases against developing countries since the end of the Uruguay Round talks in 1994.[46]

Thus, although developed countries recognized the special conditions and needs of developing countries, they have still not removed the restrictions agreed upon during the Uruguay Round especially in agriculture and textiles where many developing countries have a major stake.

Similarly, the Uruguay Round negotiations on the Agreement on Agriculture committed industrialized countries to cutting subsidies to agriculture by 36 per cent and tariffs by a similar amount.[47] In practice little progress has been made. Agriculture remains heavily protected by developed countries with high tariffs and heavy subsidies. The average tariff imposed by industrialized countries on agricultural goods from developing countries is close to 20 per cent, almost five times higher than the average tariff on all goods.[48]

In the case of textiles, developed countries agreed to progressively phase out the discriminatory regime of Multi-Fibre Agreement ('MFA') in three stages by 2005. These commitments did not materialize. For example, the EU and the US should already have phased out around half of their MFA restrictions, but by 2004 developing countries were still subject to quota restrictions on 80 per cent of their exports.[49] The average industrial-country tariff on textiles and clothing imports from developing countries is 11 per cent – three times higher than the average industrial tariff for all goods.[50] Bangladesh, one of 21 least developed countries, faces tariffs as high as 20 per cent on its key exports to the US and Canada.[51] These restrictions are undermining the efforts of developing countries to access the markets of developed countries, which is a prerequisite if they are to address sustainable development.

The provisions for technical and financial assistance were made to enable developing countries to comply with WTO agreements like the *Agreement on Trade-related Aspects of Intellectual Property Rights* ('TRIPs'). The TRIPs Agreement has been seriously criticized as an attempt to protect the interests of developed countries that has far-reaching consequences for the trading plight of developing countries.[52]

Another area of concern for developing countries is agriculture. Developing countries, being primarily producers and exporters of agricultural products, expected a lowering of tariffs on their goods to help them compete in the markets of developed countries. However, while the average tariffs on industrial goods have been reduced from 40 per cent to 4 per cent over the past fifty years, tariffs on agricultural goods have remained at around 40 per cent.[53] Agricultural production and exports are heavily subsidized and protected by certain developed countries, which severely impedes the market access of the products of developing countries that have a comparative advantage in agriculture. At present some US$300 billion a year is spent on providing subsidies to farmers in the developed world and mainly in the EU, US and Japan.[54]

Agricultural subsidies, anti-dumping rules, unilateral trade measures and other tariff and non-tariff barriers used by developed countries reflect their unfair protectionist policies. These protectionist policies are detrimental to the needs and interests of developing countries. The frustration and tension of these countries are succinctly outlined by the joint declaration of the Group of 77 and China prior to the Doha Conference in November 2001:

> We note that the Uruguay Round Agreements have not resulted, as promised, in greater market access to the developed countries' markets for the exports of developing and least-developed countries. The continued existence in developed countries of tariff peaks, tariff escalations, and other non-tariff barriers … has had a serious negative impact on the trade and development prospects of the developing and least-developed coun-

> tries and has prevented these countries from reaping the benefits of trade liberalisation.[55]

The interests and gains of developing countries have further been nullified through 'back door' excuses for renewed protectionism in the name of protection of the environment.[56] For developing countries, the protection of the environment is intrinsically related to their sub-standard level of economic development. They view environmental protection/sustainable development issues as the self-interest-laden creation of the Northern countries and as a manifestation of the unequal trading relationship between the North and South. Alvaro Soto outlines the perception of developing countries in the following words:

> global environmental crisis and the socio-economic decline in the South are the interconnected result of an inequitable world order, unsustainable systems of consumption and production in the North and inappropriate development models in the South.[57]

Indeed, one of the primary justifications for vigorous application of the principle of common but differentiated responsibilities introduced earlier in the chapter is the enormity of global environmental degradation that is directly attributable to the unsustainable rate of resource consumption essential to maintaining the 'wants-based'[58] lifestyles of affluent states. Khosla poses the inescapable question when contemplating development pathways based exclusively on current prevailing conceptions of human advancement:

> if the whole population of the world does start participating in this economy in a manner that resembles the industrialized economies of today, how will our life support systems be maintained?[59]

Furthermore, as a telling indication of the extent to which the North is apparently in control of international forums regarding the achievement of sustainable development, it is noteworthy that despite the urgent need to address current patterns, issues relating to the unsustainable lifestyles and consumption of the world's most affluent nations barely rated a mention at the landmark 1992 Rio Earth Summit.[60]

Declining terms of trade

Current patterns of trade and trade policies have been exerting an unsustainable pressure on the environment particularly in the impoverished resource sector of developing countries. As a result of colonial trade patterns, the primary commodities exported by developing countries for the goods and services of industrialized countries are constantly declining in value, resulting in tremendous income losses. Between 1980 and 1984, developing countries lost about US$55 billion in export earnings because of the fall in commodity prices, a blow felt most keenly in Latin America and Africa.[61] This disparity between the situations of developed and developing countries is forcing developing countries to export their natural resources to keep the balance of payments even. As a result, developing countries are ruining their non-renewable resources through overexploitation. The substantial decline in commodity prices is contributing to debt crisis and the balance of payments deficit. Declining terms of trade are depriving developing countries of the finance necessary for sustainable development.

The income losses from commodity prices are also believed to pave the way for the transfer of real economic resources from the South to the North. Under the present system, many developing countries are converting their lands to the production of export crops. As a result, they are no longer self-reliant as they are no longer able to produce their own foods. This situation has resulted in instability of price and demand. For example, in West Africa cotton farming, an industry first established during the colonial period, is a major export earner for many countries in the region, such as Chad, Burkina Faso and Mali. While West Africa's contribution to global cotton production is quite marginal, the impact of the industry on the region is not. During a period of increase in cotton farming in the region during the 1990s, food production dropped by one-third.[62] It is also worthwhile to note here that export crops can also create environmental problems for the developing countries that produce them. In the case of cotton farming these problems include (but are not limited to) chemical use, water shortages and pollution, soil degradation and desertification.[63]

Developing countries believe that greater trading opportunities and the correction of past imbalances and gaps between North–South trade will help them to address their environmental concerns. The *GATT Secretariat Trade and Environment Report 1992* has confirmed that economic growth enhanced by free trade would help protect the environment. Increases in *per capita* incomes, which are boosted by increased market access and expanding trade, provide more resources with which to mitigate against environmental damage, provide finance for pollution control and support remedial clean up.[64]

It is vital to appreciate that developing countries are not in a position to take environmental issues into account unless their own agenda of economic development is addressed. Such development requires additional financial resources, market access, technology transfer, international cooperation and capacity building to help developing countries mitigate their environmental problems. These countries argue that linkages between trade and environment should be examined in the broader context of sustainable development, which takes into account both the environment as well as the development aspects of human needs.[65]

Consumption pattern standards

For many developing countries, meeting the higher environmental standards set by the North will still fail completely to achieve sustainable development until the North changes its consumption patterns. At present, according to the United

Nations Development Programme ('UNDP') statistics, the 20 per cent of the world's population who live in the North account for 86 per cent of total private consumption expenditures and have been responsible for well over half the increase in resource use since 1950.[66] The concerns of developing countries in this regard are echoed by a statement made by Rajeev Kher, the joint secretary to India's Ministry of Environment, who comments that over-consumption in the North is due to 'environmentally unaffordable lifestyles', and that the present conspicuous consumption patterns of the North threaten the very survival of the planet.[67]

For the South, an equitable trade–environment policy should take into account the cost of this over-consumption which is one of the major causes of environmental damage. The Northern countries should then take the burden of the necessary adjustments for unsustainable production and consumption patterns. It should not be the other way round.

Trade-related environmental measures ('TREMS')

The practice of using trade measures as environmental tools has created controversy among both trade supporters and developing countries who often condemn this measure as protectionist, extra-jurisdictional, eco-imperial and unilateral. TREMS may be used as a ban on trade, as a tool pursuant to multilateral environmental agreements or unilaterally by a developed country. Various GATT and WTO panels' rulings on disputes employing trade sanctions for environmental purposes have fuelled this controversy (see Chapter 3).

Pro-trade and developing countries fear that trade restrictions for environmental purposes have further opened the door to green protectionism. This fear derives its justification from the narrow borderline between genuine, justifiable environmental protection measures and protectionist measures that are, in reality, based on non-environmental vested interests of certain Northern stakeholders. As noted by Rauscher:

> Green arguments can easily be abused to justify trade restrictions that are in reality only protectionist measures and it is often difficult to discriminate between true and pretended environmentalism.[68]

The difficulties associated with drawing a borderline between environmental protection and environmental protectionism are also apparent in the case of process and product standards. The present trading system does not take into account process and production methods ('PPM') in order to determine product standards.[69] Environmentalists are concerned not only with the product but also with the method by which it is produced, used and disposed of. In a situation where consumption of imported goods causes environmental damage, environmentalists support the importing country's authority to enforce its process standards on imported goods. In other words, the importing country is allowed to employ unilateral trade measures for environmental purposes even beyond its jurisdiction.[70] The motivation for environmentalists may be that they know that it is easier to garner support for trade restrictions, which are misleadingly seen as penalizing merely foreigners, than for other kinds of domestically oriented environmental policies that may have a more direct negative effect on internal economic development and are thus more likely to be opposed.[71]

Developing countries criticize these measures as Green protectionism, which is discriminatory and which can give strong trading partners the leverage to impose their own environmental and social standards on others, thus impeding multilateral cooperation. To developing countries, trade measures without assistance in capacity building, technology transfer and finances will impede their move towards improved qualities of life and ultimately, sustainable development. Consequently, they resist such environmental protection initiatives out of fear of having the environmental standards of strong countries unilaterally imposed upon them.

In its 1992 report on trade and the environment, the GATT Secretariat concluded that 'where pollution has only local effects, environmental policies are a matter of preference ... even when pollution crosses national boundaries, unilateral action is rarely justified'.[72] Despite this caution, the use of trade sanctions on the basis of PPM is gaining momentum. The 1999 *Trade and Development Report* of the United Nations Conference on Trade and Development ('UNCTAD'), while criticizing the protectionist tendencies of developed countries, indicated that if the North lifted its protectionism, including those measures under the guise of 'environmental protection' an extra US$700 billion of annual export earnings could be achieved in a relatively short time in a number of low technology and resource-based countries.[73] Developing countries thus reach the conclusion that the emergence of a trend of protectionism, under the guise of environmentalism, is part of a 'disturbing retreat to a mercantilist Fortress America and Fortress Europe'.[74]

Product standards and eco-labelling

Eco-labelling is the well established practice of marking certain consumer goods with some form of logo or symbol to indicate that the product has been manufactured using environmentally acceptable methods. Perhaps the most commonly recognized form of eco-labelling is the emergence of tuna fish tins marked 'dolphin-safe'. From a conceptual and trade policy point of view, eco-labelling involves many complex issues, such as PPMs, the definition of international standards and equivalence. There have been attempts to determine international standards of products based on PPM. PPM-based labels may effectively provide consumers with information regarding whether a product is environmentally friendly. As long as eco-labelling remains voluntary it does not cause a problem under the WTO. However, in para. 32 of the *Doha Declaration*, the Committee on Trade and Environment was instructed to address labelling requirements for environmental purposes.[75] Invoking eco-labelling schemes and approval of industrial benchmark, the International Organization for Standardization ('ISO') is believed to be designed as setting common standards for products. Although such labelling is not compulsory, it can have a significant impact upon the consumer's selection of environmentally friendly products.

Developing countries are concerned that an increasing use of eco-labelling schemes will restrict their products from the markets of developed countries. Consumers of developed countries will base their choices on these eco-labels. At the same time, companies and governments might change their procurement policies based on the environmental requirements of PPM. Developing countries will predictably lack the clean technologies, financial resources and infrastructure to comply with the eco-labelling requirements of the importing country. Eco-labels have been effective in North America, shifting consumer preferences towards 'dolphin-safe' tuna fish, CFC-free air conditioners and the increasing use of recycled products.[76] Some more established schemes are Germany's 'Blue Angel', Canada's 'Environmental Choice' and Scandinavia's 'White Swan'.[77]

There has also been a proposal to extend the coverage of the Technical Barriers to Trade ('TBT') and Sanitary and Phytosanitary Measures ('SPS') Agreements to include eco-labelling schemes with a view to harmonizing the product standards. The criteria in eco-labelling schemes are determined by a national body rather than internationally and vary from product to product. As a result, it is difficult for exporters in developing countries to have sufficient information about and advance knowledge of the standards in order to comply with them. Thus product standards can be used as non-tariff barriers to the trade interests of developing countries.

Developing countries lack the infrastructure, environmentally sound technology, finance and good governance to improve and enforce environmental standards and measures for the integration of trade and environment. Developing countries argue that the distribution of environmentally sound technologies would help them to comply with environmentally friendly PPMs. However, it is absolutely imperative that the social and economic adjustment costs of integration and the capacity of developing countries to bear that burden be properly considered when formulating policies with a view to achieving higher international standards.

Under the status quo, developing countries cannot participate effectively in the process of international standards setting. They cannot afford to send personnel to attend all of the consultative meetings. Nor do they have the technical knowledge or expertise required to participate actively.

The fallacy of the environmental effectiveness of trade measures was that they did not pay heed to the concerns of developing countries and their inability to meet the stricter environmental norms set by the affluent North. Developing countries have been arguing for the necessary financial support and the transfer of environmentally friendly technology to enable them to develop their capacity to tackle environmental issues, but the commitments and promises of the North in this regard have not materialized.

Developing countries perceive the 'harmonization of environmental standards' debate as an effort by developed countries to ignore the commitments they made at UNCED in 1992 to respect the development needs of individual countries.[78] While trade-related measures are gaining momentum in the policy considerations of different forums including the WTO Committee on Trade and Environment, the issues faced by developing countries are still not receiving adequate attention. Issues such as safeguarding and further improving market access, controlling the export of domestically prohibited goods and promoting technology transfer appear to be receiving even less attention than previously.[79] Consequently the gap between rhetoric and reality is becoming wider day by day without any significant improvements in the capacity of developing countries to address environmental concerns.

Subsidies

The WTO *Agreement on Subsidies and Countervailing Measures*[80] made provisions for non-actionable environmental subsidies as an incentive to environmental adaptation. However, there are claims of imbalance in the treatment of subsidies. These claims to imbalance are discussed in Chapter 3.

Trade in services

The *General Agreement on Trade in Services*[81] ('GATS') has substantial implications for the environment around the world. Key issues and concerns of developing countries, which resulted from the operation of GATS, will be considered in Chapter 3.

Intellectual property rights in trade

The *WTO Agreement on Trade-related Aspects of Intellectual Property Rights*[82] ('TRIPS') has increased the context of dichotomy and tension currently exists between developed and developing countries. Some of the environmental aspects of the TRIPs Agreement will be examined in Chapter 3.

Additional financial resources and technology transfer for capacity building

Recent assessment of progress in the implementation of Millennium Development Goals by the United Nations showed that in certain important areas, frighteningly little progress has been made.[83] Imbalances in the trade and environment agenda can only be addressed if sufficient attention is given to the development and implementation of such measures. Measures to achieve the objective of sustainable development – as established and recognized by international stakeholders in various UN agencies such as UNCTAD and the United Nations Environmental Programme ('UNEP'), and as outlined in *Agenda 21* – should be implemented, taking into account the vulnerability of developing countries at the intersection of trade and environment.

The mainstreaming of the environment in WTO agreements

Developing countries have expressed grave concerns over WTO negotiations based on environmental considerations. Inclusion and/or incorporation of environmental policies into the WTO will have a debilitating impact on the trade prospects of developing countries. For example, the use of PPM has the potential to be used against developing countries for the protection of a developed country's own market. This is an area that can be hijacked by the protectionist national interests of certain developed countries.

The agenda for trade negotiations reflects the attitude and inherent motives of developed countries with little or no input from developing countries. The almost exclusively reactive role that has been thrust upon developing countries in the arena of international trade negotiations has been widely condemned. As noted by Khosla, 'the role of the South has been mainly limited to reacting and responding to initiatives taken by others'.[84] In the main, developing countries are trying to resist or oppose the many measures that go against their trade interests, but in large part they are continually being forced by the North either to accept or accommodate the trade measures. Developing countries argue that the trade and environment agenda requires them to have a far more meaningful participatory role if progress is to be made.[85] The Group of 77 has noted that if developing countries want to succeed in promoting their views and interests, 'it is ... essential for them to join forces and pursue group action in most domains on the development agenda'.[86]

The trade–environment debate is inextricably linked to the various perspectives of free traders, environmentalists, developed and developing countries. However, from empirical evidence it may be concluded that trade can have both positive and negative impacts on the environment depending on the particular policy employed and the situation. By increasing the economies of scale trade can improve environmental quality through allocating funds, which can also heighten ecological problems. Similarly, trade enhances the diffusion of products, services and technology that are environmentally friendly but it also increases environmentally harmful PPM.

However, trade may contribute to sustainable development if environmental costs are internalized or environmental resources are properly priced. In practice the current global trading paradigm is far from such a situation. As both trade and environment are equally important for sustainable development, there must be integration between the two spheres. Paragraph 14 of the *Johannesburg Declaration* has recommended that states should promote an open international economic system, which would contribute to economic growth and sustainable development. This is possible when an open international system is formed in conjunction with its ecological resource base, and when economic growth is based on this interaction environmental damage can be avoided and management of the ecosystem can proceed in a constructive and sustainable manner.[87]

The WTO Agreement Preamble also commits the international trade system to promote the optimal use of the world's resources in accordance with the objectives of sustainable development, seeking to protect and preserve the environment and to enhance the means for doing this.[88] However, to make trade and environment mutually supportive the global community needs to deal with the negative impact of trade on the environment. This may be done by giving due attention to environmental as well as developmental principles, and would advance the position of fairness and equity in North–South relations.

In the trade–environment context, principles and policies which have been formulated and recommended by UNCED and other UN agencies such as UNCTAD and UNEP should be given due importance. Strengthening the capacity of developing countries to deal with trade-related environmental and environment-related trade issues must be considered in order to integrate trade and environment. Multi-stakeholder approaches to determine the problems faced by developing countries in integrating trade and environment policies need to be considered. The North needs to assist developing countries with adequate finance, the transfer of environmentally friendly technology and the building of these countries' capacity to address the complex problems of integration.

Trade policy measures for environmental purposes should not constitute a means of arbitrary or unjustifiable discrimination or a disguised restriction on international trade. Special regard must be given by developed countries to the situation of developing countries when considering the imposition of trade-related environmental measures. The trade-related environmental problems of developing countries are closely linked to their development-related problems. The trade–environment issues need to be viewed in terms of their broader socio-economic context. Using trade restrictions to force developing countries to comply with Northern environmental standards is not a panacea for the achievement of sustainable development. Positive and effective alternatives to trade sanctions should be considered. These might include market access, financial and technical cooperation. Differences in environmental standards should be considered in the context of the historical process of production and the present inequities between developed and developing countries.

Trade is a powerful engine for the economic growth which is vital to the creation of conditions which favour advancing environmental protection, improving social conditions and sustaining ethical values.[89] By opening markets, particularly to exports from developing countries, and by keeping markets open through clear and enforceable rules, the global trading system has the potential to become a natural ally of sustainable development.[90] Empirical research on the relationship between trade and the environment supports this view and affirms that trade and growth together can increase the stock of human capital and can lower pollution.[91] The global challenge of sustainable development calls for a shared approach to the elimination of trade restrictions and distortions in the form of import prohibitions, export restraints, taxes and subsidies, unilateral and extraterritorial actions and eco-labelling schemes that include non-product related PPMs. Such an approach will assist developing countries to strengthen their capacity to move towards sustainable development.

Organization of the book

Chapter 1 discussed the complex relationship between trade and the environment and developing countries' interest in this interaction. It critically examined the extent to which free trade and environmental protection are in conflict or have the potential to achieve sustainable development. Consideration has been given to the present inequalities between North–South trade, global economic injustices and their inescapable connectedness to free trade, the environment and development in the context of developing countries.

Chapter 2 examines the contribution of the United Nations to sustainable development. Trade issues came into consideration during the negotiation of a variety of agreements under the auspices of the United Nations. This chapter discusses the treatment of trade policy matters in these agreements as they pertain to the specific concerns of developing countries. This chapter also reviews the *Rio Declaration*, *Agenda 21*, the *Johannesburg Declaration* and the Millennium Development Goals. These four international law instruments are not only amongst the most significant global resolutions of the last fifteen years but are of particular importance considering that they reflect some of the concerns of developing countries and suggest how future trade negotiations should proceed in order to protect the interests of such traditionally disenfranchised nations.

Chapter 3 discusses the trade–environment interface within a legal and institutional context. This chapter also discusses the policies of the *General Agreements on Tariffs and Trade* ('GATT') and World Trade Organization ('WTO') regarding the environment and its impact on the trading plights of developing countries. GATT as a multilateral treaty has been the source of rules governing world trade since 1947. It is criticized for its lack of concern for environmental matters. The objectives and structure of GATT/WTO have had a severe economic and environmental impact upon the trade–environment interests of developing countries. The effects stemming from these objectives and negotiating structures are complex and involve much political and economic magnitude. With their negative impact on environmental measures, the present GATT rules in many cases conflict with principles of sustainable development. Moreover, the GATT Panel's rulings on a number of disputes concerning trade-related environmental measures have fuelled the debate over the trade–environment controversy.

The WTO is the new forum for implementing trade agreements, negotiating new agreements and resolving trade-related disputes. The WTO was formed as a legal and institutional framework for the international trading system following the Uruguay Round of trade negotiations in 1995. Chapter 3 reveals the WTO's environmental priorities by discussing WTO agreements and their implications for trade–environment interactions. This chapter also critically analyses the dispute resolution system of the WTO.

Chapter 4 discusses issues of trade–environment linkage and the development of those issues from the negotiating history of the WTO in the post-Uruguay

Round context. These developments are important in that they highlight the complex nature of the trade–environment debate. This chapter briefly outlines the implications of this debate and the inevitability of addressing the contemporary issues involved in this debate if the goal of sustainable development is to be realistically pursued.

Chapter 5 examines the trade–environment linkage in the EU. This chapter examines the principles and policies used by the EU in integrating trade and environment and their impact on the trading plight of developing countries. The experience of the EU in integrating trade and the environment could be invaluable for both global and regional institutions striving to achieve the objective of sustainable development.

Chapter 6 examines the trade–environment policies and regulations of the North American Free Trade Agreement ('NAFTA') and their effects on developing countries. This chapter examines how NAFTA has attempted to reconcile apparently conflicting trade–environment issues and its success at reconciling these issues under a free trade agreement which conjoins both developed and developing countries.

Chapter 7 examines the initiatives of the Asia-Pacific Economic Cooperation ('APEC') in the integration of economy and sustainable development. Since its inception, APEC has been trying to develop common principles to deal with environmental issues. APEC has displayed a greater awareness than other trade blocs of the trade–environment interface, particularly in relation to its impact on the developmental pathways of poor nations. This chapter will consider the policy and principles of APEC, which aim to harmonize environmental concerns with economic integration.

A number of international treaties already use trade measures to enforce environmental goals. There are currently 180 Multilateral Environmental Agreements ('MEAs'), twenty of which contain provisions authorizing the use of trade measures as enforcement mechanisms. Chapter 8 deals with the relevant trade–environment provisions of the *Convention on International Trade in Endangered Species of Flora and Fauna 1973* ('CITES'),[92] the *Montreal Protocol on Substances that deplete the Ozone Layer 1987*[93] and the *Basel Convention on the Control of Transboundary Movements of Hazardous Wastes and their Disposal 1989.*[94] This chapter outlines the interactions between trade and environment within these three MEAs. It also outlines concerns regarding the use of trade measures in these Agreements, with particular emphasis on their impacts on developing countries.

Chapter 9 summarizes the recommendations made and conclusions drawn from the overall findings of this book. The interaction between and/or integration of trade and the environment has to be considered in the context of sustainable development. This warrants viable and positive interactions between the multilateral trading system and the environment. Sustainable development can be achieved only through proper cooperation and coordination among national and international stakeholders based on common but differentiated responsibilities. Both developed and developing countries must confront their mutual distrust.

The purpose of trade–environment interactions is to achieve sustainable development. To achieve the goal of sustainable development, the integration of developing countries into the process is crucial. Unless their capacity to deal with trade and environment issues is strengthened, particularly as suggested by *Agenda 21*, any pressure from developed countries to negotiate further on these issues will be of no assistance in solving the real problems associated with the trade–environment interface. The consideration of multi-stakeholder approaches to solving the problems faced by developing countries in integrating into global trade and environment policies is indispensable. Yet developing countries must also be provided with adequate finance and environmentally friendly technology to enable them to undertake effective capacity building if they are to address the complex problems of integration.

2 The United Nations' approach to trade, the environment and sustainable development

The complex and transboundary nature of current environmental problems are now truly global issues that involve highly intermingled issues of ecology, economics and politics. The sectoral, fragmented and predominantly *ad hoc* development of institutions to address these global problems has proved inadequate and has done little to address their deeply entrenched causes and often even their symptoms. While the problems are indisputably global in nature, contrastingly, their solutions have so far been predominantly sought in the limited and traditional framework of a geopolitical system founded upon the individual sovereignty of states.[1]

Global environmental problems warrant global solutions on a multilateral basis. Thus, any national effort to address these issues without the support of a network of international institutional instruments and principles is likely to be ineffective or inequitable to the interests of certain international stakeholders. The global nature of environmental problems demands a solution which requires that countries follow a comprehensive and effective set of norms, rules and methodologies in carrying out their commitment to environmental protection. Any individual organization or actor is further prevented from responding to environmental needs because of the North–South dynamics of the problem.

The United Nations ('UN') is exceptionally well positioned for addressing these problems. The UN is the only multilateral organization that is almost universal in its membership and truly global in its scope. It can help governments enhance their environmental protection initiatives because of its multidisciplinary capabilities and broad experiences involving all actors in the full spectrum of trade and environment regimes. The UN continually strives to achieve international cooperation and support for capacity building in trade, environment and development in the South. The UN, through its many specialized agencies, also carries out work and reporting on the development of a framework to integrate trade and environmental policies by taking into account the special needs of developing countries. It is also charged with the responsibility of carrying forward the monitoring of national compliance to develop an integrated approach to sustainable development, most obviously through the work of the UN Commission on Sustainable Development ('CSD').[2]

In addition, the UN process has offered developing countries, despite their weaker bargaining power, an opportunity to participate effectively in a negotiating play in which the industrialized nations had to make considerable concessions.[3] The UN, through the CSD, United Nations Environment Programme ('UNEP'), United Nations Conference on Trade and Development ('UNCTAD'), United Nations Development Programme ('UNDP') and other agencies, has contributed and continues to contribute to the integration of trade and environment in order to achieve the objective of sustainable development. It is therefore relevant to consider how the UN has responded to the imperatives of the global trade and environment relationship. Consequently, this chapter examines the role played by the UN and its institutions in the integration of trade and environment and their inadequacies in achieving the goals of sustainable development.

Developing countries are very important stakeholders in the integration process. In some areas they are vulnerable and have been marginalized by the trade–environment nexus. They have their own views on this nexus and the resolution of this crisis. The UN and its specialist agencies play an active role in the resolution of this crisis, and take into account the special situation of developing countries. In the process of resolution, the UN has suggested various principles, has made recommendations and developed action plans with a view to developing a framework for trade–environment integration on a multilateral basis. It is relevant to assess the formula prescribed by the UN and its implementation problems as well as how and to what extent the formula has been put into practice by the relevant stakeholders. This chapter focuses primarily on the prospects and problems of developing countries in the context of the trade–environment linkage.

Relevant principles and concepts employed in the context of trade and environment interactions

The common but differentiated responsibility principle

This principle, as briefly discussed in Chapter 1, recognizes that while all countries have a responsibility to protect the environment and to prevent further environmental harm, this responsibility varies according to the socio-economic situation of each country. The principle implies that while both rich and poor countries have a responsibility to sustainable development, the contribution of the rich countries to the destruction of the environment and the utilization of natural resources has been greater so far, and so they should take the lead in taking remedial action.

Developed countries also have bigger responsibilities than developing countries because of their superior economic situation. Principle 7 of the *Rio Declaration* puts the principle neatly into words:

> States shall cooperate in a spirit of global partnership to conserve, protect and restore the health and integrity of the Earth's ecosystem. In view of the

> different contributions to global environmental degradation, States have common but differentiated responsibilities. The developed countries acknowledge the responsibility that they bear in the international pursuit of sustainable development in view of the pressures their societies place on the global environment and of the technologies and financial resources they command.[4]

This principle encapsulates the view of the South on taking responsibility for environmental protection. The proposed differential responsibility was subsequently adopted by many international environmental agreements.[5] However, the implementation of this principle has been barely satisfactory. The principle should be translated into an operational principle throughout the UN system, the range of Multilateral Environmental Agreements ('MEAs') and in global financial and economic relations.

The precautionary principle

The precautionary principle[6] states that a lack of full scientific evidence regarding the potential effects of human activity should not operate as an excuse for inactivity to prevent environmental degradation. This principle has developed from the belief that scientific proof often arrives too late to allow an effective response to potential environmental threats. This principle has been used or referred to in the context of preventing pollution, protecting endangered species and preserving biodiversity.

Principle 15 of the *Rio Declaration* outlines the precautionary principle in the following words:

> Where there are threats of serious or irreversible damage, lack of full scientific certainty shall not be used as a reason for postponing cost-effective measures to prevent environmental degradation.[7]

Although apparently reasonable, this explanation is debatable. In particular, 'serious' is clearly subjective and contextual. What developed countries consider serious, developing countries might consider insignificant. Developing countries lack the scientific knowledge, financial resources and the technological base to adequately assess risks which may be necessary for the adoption of precautionary measures. Developing countries find it difficult to comply with the requirements of developed countries in relation to the acceptable risk of a particular product. Developing countries' difficulties in implementing the precautionary principle have been recognized in many international instruments[8] and provisions have been made to assist developing countries to address their implementation problems. Despite this, the situations of developing countries have not improved.

There is also some concern that in the absence of scientific proof, the precautionary actions may be used as protectionist measures to exclude goods from domestic markets.

The intergenerational equity principle

The principle of intergenerational equity has become fundamental to the promotion of sustainable development. The principle outlines the responsibility of each generation to be fair to future generations in the use they make of their natural and cultural resource base. This principle is linked to another, known as the principle of intra-generational equity, which refers to fair dealing in the consumption and exploitation of resources among and between members of the present generation.

The *Rio Declaration* stressed the need for this concept in its Principle 3, which reads as follows:

> The right to development must be fulfilled so as to equitably meet developmental and environmental needs of present and future generations.[9]

The current exploitation, growth and consumption patterns of developed countries are putting extra pressures on global resources. Their consumption patterns are unsustainable and are responsible for much of the existent environmental degradation and resource depletion.

Developing countries are also partly responsible for the unsustainable exploitation of natural resources. However, their unsustainable consumption patterns are the result of a lack of infrastructure and an inability to fulfil even their basic needs. 'A world in which poverty and inequity are endemic will always be prone to ecological and other crises.'[10] Thus the environmental problems in the developing countries are closely linked to their socio-economic situations, underdevelopment and poverty.

Thus while it is the responsibility of all states to protect and preserve the environment for the future generations, responsibilities regarding environmental protection between developing and industrialized countries are not similar. Adil Najam argues:

> The costs to be borne by different parties, the ability to bear these costs, and the responsibility for causing the problem in the first place, are differentiated.[11]

The notion of common but differentiated responsibilities is therefore closely related to intergenerational equity.

Despite the recognition of the common but differentiated responsibility principle and the principle of intergenerational equity by the legal instruments dealing with sustainable development of natural resources, the international community has done little to assist in the realization of these principles 'beyond mere pronouncements in the preambles of treaties and other documents'.[12]

The polluter pays or the cost internalization principle

This principle means that a polluter should pay for the damage caused by their pollution as well as bearing the cost of pollution prevention measures. Instituting the polluter pays principle ensures that the price of goods reflects the costs of producing those goods, including the costs associated with pollution, resource degradation and environmental harm. The costs associated with environmental damage would thus be internalized in the market price. The goods which were not environmentally sustainable would therefore cost a great deal and so be less competitive. This would then act as an incentive for producers and consumers to choose more environmentally friendly products.

This principle was originally recommended by the Organization for Economic Cooperation and Development ('OECD') in 1972, and has already been accepted by many bilateral and multilateral resolutions and declarations, and has been confirmed by the *Rio Declaration*:

> National authorities should endeavour to promote the internalization of environmental costs and the use of economic instruments, taking into account the approach that the polluter should bear the cost of pollution, with due regard to the public interest and without distorting international trade and investment.[13]

However, it should be noted that there is as yet no binding international obligation that enforces this principle.[14]

The Polluter Pays principle often imposes disproportionate burdens on developing countries which lack the pollution control infrastructure, financial resources and environmentally friendly technology necessary to develop and implement new strategies to reduce their pollution. Thus they find it difficult to bring their pollution levels down to or below those required by national and international pollution standards.

Another reason for environmental pollution in developing countries is that they follow the traditional development path of developed countries which is unsustainable. They are dependent on the use of obsolete and/or unsustainable technologies which are barriers to producing environmentally friendly products. In order to make the current practices of developing countries sustainable, realistic initiatives and measures to make those changes should be set in place. These measures must include the provision of technological assistance and financial resources for the implementation of the Polluter Pays principle. Developing countries should be given preferential treatment with respect to access to financial resources and their implementation obligations must be based on the principle of common but differentiated responsibility.

The environment in the United Nations

Environmental protection was not an issue on the UN agenda when it was established over 50 years ago and consequently the UN was not originally formed with a specific mandate to address issues concerning the environment. However, as the organization has developed and global environmental awareness has become acute, the UN has carved out a role for itself in this area by widely interpreting its preamble and other articles which promote economic and social well being and are concerned with the related problems of health, development and education. Examples of these widely interpreted elements include Articles 1(4) and 3 of the preamble to the *Charter of the United Nations*, as well as Article 55, which requires the UN to promote first, higher standards of living, full employment and conditions of economic and social progress and development, and second, solutions to international economic, social, health, and related problems and international cultural and educational cooperation.[15]

The United Nations Conference on the Human Environment

The year 1972 marked a turning point in the UN's role in the protection of the world environment. The United Nations Conference on the Human Environment ('UNCHE'), held in Stockholm in that year, was the first all-encompassing international conference on the environment, and it led to the creation of the first subsidiary body of the UN whose focus was the protection of the environment. As the Stockholm Conference is significant in assessing the role of the UN in relation to the environment, it will provide the starting point for this chapter. It is to be noted that while the environment is a broad topic and the UN can be seen to have played an important role in most aspects of that topic, this chapter will focus exclusively on the role of the UN in relation to issues directly involving both trade and environment.

Three main topics constituted the primary agenda of the Stockholm conference: the planning and management of human settlements; natural resources and aspects of development which could be seen to include developing countries; and the identification and control of pollutants. The most important instruments that emerged from the UNCHE are the action plans and the *Stockholm Declaration* which consists of twenty-six principles. The Stockholm Conference also resulted in the creation of the first international body within the UN system specifically designed to focus on the environment – the United Nations Environment Programme ('UNEP').

Trade–environment issues emerged as a result of the UNCHE recognizing the competitiveness concerns associated with the trade and environment interactions. One of the main concerns at the time was that if one country moved vigorously to establish strong environmental protection through pollution taxes, effluent and emission standards or otherwise, its competitive position within the international community would suffer.[16]

Expressing concern about the identification and control of pollutants, the UNCHE drew attention to environmental protection as an international concern and accordingly put the environment on the international agenda. Pollution was considered the root cause of the environmental problem. As pollution is the result of industrialization, in the early 1970s at the time of Stockholm it did not really represent an immediate concern for the vast majority of developing countries. However, developing countries were aware that 'pollution does not respect borders', and so they insisted that the environmental problems facing them had to be defined in a manner that is mindful of the overriding need for economic development to achieve poverty alleviation and social improvement.

The following section outlines some of the specific ways in which trade and environment issues were addressed by the *Stockholm Declaration*.

Right to development

Principle 4 of the *Stockholm Declaration* recognized that 'developing countries must direct their efforts to development bearing in mind their priorities and the need to safeguard and improve the environment'. It also stated that developed countries should 'make efforts to reduce the gap between developing countries and themselves'. It would seem, therefore, that the declaration recognizes that the protection of the environment is a common responsibility, and also that developed countries have an obligation to both improve their own environmental practices, as well as provide assistance to developing countries so they can improve theirs. It noted that, 'in industrialized countries, environmental problems are generally related to industrialization and technological development'.[17]

Principle 11 of the *Stockholm Declaration* warned against the negative effect of any environmental measures on the development prospects of developing countries. It specifically stated that 'environmental policies of all States should enhance and not adversely affect the present or future development potential of developing countries'.[18] It also states that an agreement should be reached on meeting the possible national and international consequences resulting from the application of environmental measures.

Finance and technological assistance

The *Stockholm Declaration* was also the first international instrument of a truly global magnitude to stress the need for the provision of financial and technological assistance to developing countries to enable them to address their environmental problems:

> Environmental deficiencies, generated by the conditions of underdevelopment and natural disasters, pose grave problems and can best be remedied by accelerated development through the transfer of substantial quantities of financial and technological assistance as a supplement to the domestic effort of the developing countries...[19]

At a time before international law on intellectual property evolved into its current form of overt Northern protectionism, the *Stockholm Declaration* further established that environmental technologies should be made available to developing countries on terms which encourage their wide dissemination and which do not constitute an economic burden to those countries.[20]

Commodity prices

The *Stockholm Declaration* acknowledged the link between the environment and commodity trade and the reality that developing countries are heavily dependent on commodity exports, particularly of raw materials for their trade-based revenue.[21] Specifically, it was recognized that declining terms of trade and price instability greatly affect the capacity of developing countries to address issues of sustainable development as too little economic gain may come at too great an ecological cost.

The special situation of developing countries

The special situation and needs of developing countries, in addition to international technical and financial assistance, were recognized in Principle 12 of the *Stockholm Declaration* that declared resources should be made available for the purposes of environmental improvement. Further, Principle 12 acknowledged that it is essential to ensure that such provision of resources takes into account the specific circumstances and particular requirements of individual developing countries. Any costs that are likely to arise as a result of developing countries incorporating environmental safeguards into their development planning must receive due consideration at the highest levels of international discourse.

However, by way of context it should be appreciated that trade-related environmental measures and environment-related trade measures were largely non-existent at the time the *Stockholm Declaration* was drafted.

The Stockholm Conference: a general assessment

UNCHE was the first comprehensive attempt to address environmental issues on a global scale. Although the Declaration is not binding upon states, it was unanimously adopted by the 113 nations constituting the United Nations General Assembly.[22] The General Assembly's adoption of the Stockholm principles was viewed as a reflection of the political aspirations of governments with regard to the preservation and improvement of the human environment.[23] Indeed, the *Stockholm Declaration* has 'received broad-based recognition and acceptance in the International Community as a result of the fundamental nature of the values expressed'.[24]

Although the *Stockholm Declaration* showed a general recognition of the need for international environmental action and also outlined a scheme designed to ensure effective environmental management, many argue that the conference merely 'represented a compromise rather than a consensus ... since universal agreement between developing and developed countries was difficult to achieve in most areas'.[25] While the *Stockholm Declaration* was confined to the human environment, developing countries attempted to link it to developmental problems and questions of distributive justice. The ideological differences between developed and developing nations in terms of environmental protection continued and were subsequently confronted by the General Assembly and the UNEP.

The output from Stockholm has tended to be heavily rhetorical and the often overtly conflicting ideologies of the various parties to the conference have subsequently resulted in a strong lineage of complaints and disagreements by developing countries with respect to their Northern counterparts.[26] For example, in what many argue was a landmark move away from the traditionally immovable international law norm of state sovereignty, Principle 21 of the *Stockholm Declaration* explicitly mentioned the responsibility of individual states to avoid or prevent any damage to the environment in any other state or area beyond its national jurisdiction. However, despite any rhetorical significance, it is vital to note that no enforcement mechanism for those states that were a party to the Declaration and were subsequently non-compliant was set in place. Also noteworthy is the unlimited sovereign right each state was given to exploit their own resources in accordance with their own environmental policies. Such a 'soft' approach to the developmental commitments made by the parties at Stockholm has largely set the tone for all subsequent global forums.

During the arrangement of the conference agenda, it is believed that the most pressing issues, including the dynamics of the human population, the mismanagement of economic development programmes and the indirect threat of militant ideologies to the global environment, were deliberately avoided.[27] Furthermore, on the issue of liability and compensation for transboundary environmental harm, although it took shape at Stockholm via the general terms of Principle 22, the international community made no firm commitment to the application of a particular standard.[28] Indeed, to this day, meaningful treatment of the issue of liability and compensation has remained stagnant and can realistically be classified as little more than a point of controversy.

Post-Stockholm, the principle of compensation was later formalized by the UN General Assembly in the *Declaration on a New International Economic Order*.[29] While the recommendation was debated at length, it did not result in action because of widespread opposition from developed countries. Conventions dealing with environmental incidents have deliberately skirted the liability issue, often taking the form of a commitment by states to articulate standards of liability without actually prescribing any such standards.[30] Although the Stockholm Conference and those that followed did raise international awareness and concern about environmental deterioration there has been an utter failure to practically implement formulated promises.[31]

The United Nations Environment Programme

Without question the most significant outcome of the Stockholm Conference was the establishment of the United Nations Environment Programme ('UNEP'). UNEP was the first UN agency designed to coordinate the goals of global environmental assessment and management. UNEP has been responsible for supporting numerous 'soft law' instruments and has particularly focused on the inadequacies of existing legal instruments and has thus sought to further develop a more effective international law regime.[32]

However, UNEP has been given the responsibility for global environmental governance without being given any real authority to ensure its effective operation. Although the scope and severity of the threats to the global environment are openly acknowledged as being greater than ever before, both the authority of UNEP and its capacity to address these threats remains extremely limited.[33] A modest and declining budget has made it extremely difficult for UNEP to carry out the functions for which it was established.

With UNEP's headquarters being located in Nairobi, Kenya, one could even make the argument that its Third World geographical location has only served as a further impediment to the organization being considered on equal footing to other UN portfolios. Soon after its establishment, it was realized that UNEP's geographical position placed it in virtual isolation from international diplomacy and even from the UN system. This geographical isolation has further complicated UNEP's communication and coordination with other UN organizations, states, and its contact with the scientific community and environmental movements.

Financing issues in UNEP

UNEP is financed entirely by voluntary contributions of the member states of the General Assembly and the regular UN budget. Until the end of the 1990s, both the direct voluntary contributions to the Environment Fund and the support from the UN budget had been gradually shrinking. In 2004, the Governing Council of UNEP made the humbling admission that 'the UNEP budget is simply too low to meet the needs of dealing with the increasingly complex and growing list of environmental challenges'.[34]

Throughout its history UNEP has suffered severe financial crises on a regular basis. The US, for example, gave US$21 million in 1993 and 1994 but only US$7 million in 1996.[35] Over 90 per cent of the total voluntary contributions to the UNEP fund comes from only fifteen countries, and so any reduction in their contributions can have and has had devastating effects on the implementation of the approved programme, the planning of the work to be carried out by the UNEP and ultimately on the viability of the agency.[36] At the same time, the UN reduced its support for the UNEP due to budgetary shortfalls throughout the UN system. Financial support for the UNEP from the UN legal budget was reduced substantially from US$7 million in 1993 to less than US$5 million in 1995.[37] Similarly, the share of the regular Environment Fund budget being contributed to the UNEP declined from 26.7 per cent in 1973 to 88.4 percent in 1995. Further, the total voluntary contribution to the Environment Fund dropped from US$63.7 million in 1992 to US$47.7 million in 1996.[38]

In 1992, the year in which governments committed themselves to the global partnership of *Agenda 21*, only seventy-five out of 179 UN member states made contributions to the UNEP voluntary Environment Fund. The amount contributed that year totalled only US$62 million and led to suggestions that core programmes and activities would have to be cut back to something in the vicinity of US$120 million for the 1994–95 budget.[39] The UNEP financial crisis demonstrates the general lack of confidence of its members, particularly its developed members, in its operations. Contributions to the voluntary funds have been parlous making and have made a mockery of the mandate that was given to the UNEP in 1972.[40]

Interestingly, in most recent times UNEP has maintained a renewed sense of optimism about its financial woes, declaring:

> UNEP's funding is improving. The number of donor countries and the amount of their contribution are increasing and the funding has become more stable and predictable than it was in the 1990s.[41]

UNEP has indeed reported a 74 per cent increase in the overall number of donor countries that have pledged or contributed to the Environment Fund in 2003 when compared to the average number of countries contributing annually over the previous three decades.[42] The increase was in large part due to the introduction in 2003 of the Voluntary Indicative Scale of Contributions ('VISC'). The aims of the VISC are to increase the amount of donors' contributions to US$72 million annually in this biennium, broaden the donor base and make contributions more adequate and predictable. There was also a rise in UN budgetary support, with the UNEP receiving US$10.5 million.[43] However, whether this actually translates into a long-term increase in the overall quantum of annual contributions to the Environment Fund remains to be seen.

It would also seem that long-debated North–South issues have contributed to the portrayal of the UNEP as a captive of developing countries, in the context of which developed countries have no real control. As mentioned earlier, this perception may well be exacerbated by the unique location of UNEP's headquarters in Africa. Further, according to some commentators, the tactical victory of developing nations on setting priorities for UNEP has threatened to jeopardize the financial and political support of developed countries.[44]

The member states of the UN must address the financial crisis faced by UNEP if they want to see the organization act as a catalyst for a widening sphere of activities for the promotion and protection of the global environment. Although UNEP was established to further international environmental diplomacy and the future development of international environmental law, it was not created with a positive, action-based mandate nor was it given any real enforceability to carry out its objectives. Political factors have caused uncertainty about its authority and power. Developed countries did not wholeheartedly want an organization of this kind, which would inevitably necessitate their financial support while arguably supporting the interests of developing countries. On the other hand, developing countries were reluctant to accept an institution whose decisions might place restrictions on their economic development. Finally, UN agencies were intent on jealously guarding their existing environment-related prerogatives.[45] Consequently, UNEP is often perceived by specialized UN agencies as the representative of a special sectoral interest to which appropriate attention should be paid, rather than as a coordinating body intended to ensure the presence of environmental sensitivity throughout the UN system as a whole.[46]

UNEP's legitimacy within the broader UN framework and beyond

UNEP was established not as a specialized agency but as a programme within the UN system that was designed to further international environmental diplomacy and the future development of international environmental law. Consequently, UNEP has no power or authority to enforce an environment-related programme as its mandate is limited to monitoring, coordinating and instigating various environmental programmes. This lack of political authority is an inherent limitation in the UNEP mandate. It has made it almost impossible for the UNEP to function as a unilateral entity with the authority to impose mandatory rules. UNEP does not even seem to have any influence over the UN agencies. Organizations such as UNDP and the World Bank have shown little interest in examining the environmental consequences of their projects or setting up projects following UNEP guidelines. However, in 2003, the World Bank adopted the Equator Principles with a view to determining, assessing and managing projects in a socially acceptable and environmentally sustainable manner.

UNEP and its relationship with Multilateral Environmental Agreements ('MEAs') and the Commission on Sustainable Development need to be strengthened and clearly defined in order to avoid jurisdictional conflicts and inconsistencies. Nonetheless, the potential for UNEP to be a dominant force in the trade–environment interface still remains largely unrealized. This potential is described by Ling and Khor as follows:

> A strengthened UNEP ... can discuss and throw light on cross-cutting issues such as the relationship between trade and environment (and even wider, the relationship between economics, development and environment) and the results of the discussion can influence the discussions in other fora such as the WTO and the Bretton Woods institutions.[47]

The United Nations Conference on Environment and Development

In 1992, the United Nations Conference on Environment and Development ('UNCED') was held in Rio de Janeiro. UNCED provided a significant forum for the debate about trade and environmental issues and their interrelationship with each other and with sustainable development. This conference was the outcome of the UN General Assembly Resolution of 22 December 1989, which insisted on a global meeting that would 'devise strategies to halt and reverse the effects of environmental degradation in the context of increased national and international efforts to promote sustainable and environmentally sound development in all countries'.[48]

At UNCED, the world community sought to strike a balance in the areas where trade and environment interests were seemingly in conflict. As noted by Halle, '[b]oth the Principles adopted by the UN Conference on Environment and Development and its action plan [*Agenda 21*] focus on trade and trade-led economic growth as a key tool in meeting environmental challenges.'[49] Developed countries wanted to have the environment on the agenda while developing countries were primarily concerned with their development and economic growth through improved trading conditions and other important concessions. Developed and developing countries struck a bargain at Rio in which developing countries agreed to support MEAs[50] and to adopt and enforce the appropriate environmental legislation domestically. At the same time, developed countries promised to help developing countries in their efforts through capacity building, increased financial resources, the transfer of technology, the reduction of trade protectionism and by looking into the trade problems of developing countries.

UNCED solidified the place of sustainable development in the international sphere via the *Rio Declaration on Environment and Development*; *Agenda 21*, a plan of action for sustainable development for the twenty-first century and beyond; and through the creation of the Commission on Sustainable Development. These three key outcomes of UNCED will be explored in the following sections.

The Rio Declaration on environment and development ('The Earth Charter')

The *Rio Declaration* was one of the major documentary outcomes of the Earth Summit. The *Rio Declaration* determined the rights and responsibilities of states necessary to facilitate the process of achieving sustainable development. It reflected the international community's recognition of the fact that long-term economic development cannot be isolated from the need for environmental protection. It set out a new formula which recognized that economic development must be sustainable in order to be equitable and to protect the natural resource base. The *Rio Declaration* integrated, at least in its principles, the aspirations of both developed and developing countries. It provided a balance between the North and the South by addressing their key concerns. It recognized that the eradication of poverty is an indispensable requirement of sustainable development. The special needs of developing countries and the promotion of a supportive and open international economic system are also concerns held by developing countries which were enshrined in the *Rio Declaration*.

Principle 3 of the Declaration, like the *Stockholm Declaration* some two decades prior, affirmed the 'right to development', and noted that this right must be fulfilled in a way that meets the developmental and environmental needs of present and future generations. Developing countries have long insisted that their right to development cannot be sacrificed for the protection of the environment. The special situation and needs of developing countries were considered to be a high priority.[51]

In Principle 7 of the *Rio Declaration*, developed countries acknowledged the responsibility that they bear in the international pursuit of sustainable development in view of the pressures their societies place on the global environment and the technologies and financial resources they command.[52] This common but differentiated responsibility principle imposes an obligation upon the North to provide resources to the South in order that they might achieve sustainable development. The South has argued that it could contribute to sustainable development if the North would give it the necessary resources to do so. The *Rio Declaration* reiterated the responsibility all states have to cooperate to strengthen capacity building for sustainable development through the exchange of scientific and technological knowledge and the transfer of new and innovative technologies.[53]

Principle 12 of the *Rio Declaration* emphasized the necessity of the reciprocal coexistence of trade and environment in the promotion of sustainable development. It stated specifically that 'trade policy measures for environmental purposes should not constitute a means ... [of] disguised restriction on international trade'. It also asserted that 'unilateral actions to deal with environmental challenges outside the jurisdiction of an importing country should be avoided'. As a result, the only time when environment-related trade measures would be justifiable is where the environmental issue in question is transboundary or global in nature. Even when this is the case, the decision to apply trade measures should only occur upon an 'international consensus'.[54]

This principle reflects the sentiments of developing countries regarding trade-related environmental measures which have the potential to be used as protectionist measures – a fear which is not without foundation. On many occasions, developed countries have unilaterally imposed trade sanctions on goods from developing countries in the name of environmental protection.[55]

The Rio Declaration: a general assessment

The *Rio Declaration* was declaratory in nature and was never intended to be binding upon states. Consequently, the language used in the declaration suggested courses of action as opposed to describing what should constitute appropriate behaviour. The Declaration lacked specificity in terms of binding obligations on member states, which was evident from the use of the less assertive word 'should' rather than the more assertive 'shall'.

The *Rio Declaration*, without an accompanying broad framework of action, improved very little on the *Stockholm Declaration* of 1972. The *Rio Declaration* has been characterized by Malanczuk as a 'cumbersome compromise between North and the South which avoids addressing the real North–South controversies'.[55a]

However, the mere process of drafting and agreeing on the *Rio Declaration*, while internationally significant, should in no way be considered an acceptable end in itself. Its success depends on the commitment of governments and other actors to make the Rio principles operational at global, regional, national and local levels. Although linkage between the environment and development was recognized in the *Rio Declaration* and in Stockholm, little progress was made towards real integration of the environment and the development process. While evaluating the outcome of Rio, Ashok Khosla provides the accurate analogy that 'the operation was a success but the patient's health has not improved'.[56]

Agenda 21

Agenda 21 was adopted by the 178 parties of the UNCED.[57] It was designed to provide a comprehensive plan of action in every area of humanity's interaction with the natural environment. Chapter 2 of *Agenda 21*, entitled 'International Cooperation to Accelerate Sustainable Development in Developing Countries and Related Domestic Policies', manifested trade, environment and sustainable development linkage in its four programme areas:

1 The promotion of sustainable development through trade liberalization.
2 Making trade and the environment mutually supportive.
3 The provision of adequate financial resources to developing countries and dealing with international trade.
4 The encouragement of macroeconomic policies conducive to environment and development.

Chapter 2 recognized that the development process would not gain momentum in the South if developing countries were weighed down by external indebtedness, if development finance was inadequate, if barriers restricted access to markets and if commodity prices and terms of trade in developing countries remained depressed.[58]

Programme Area 1: promoting sustainable development through trade

In its basis for action, Programme Area A of Chapter 2 recognized that the trading system of greatest benefit to all trading partners is one that is open, equitable, secure, non-discriminatory, predictable, multilateral, consistent with the goals of sustainable development and leads to the optimal distribution of global production in accordance with comparative advantage. It also acknowledged that improved market access for the exports of developing countries – in conjunction with sound macroeconomic and environmental policies – would ultimately have a positive environmental impact and would therefore make an important contribution to the achievement of sustainable development.[59]

Regarding commodity markets, Programme Area A of Chapter 2 precisely identified the prevalence of very low and declining real prices for most commodities in international markets and the resulting substantial contraction in commodity export earnings for many producing countries in the South.[60] It pointed out that the ability of developing countries to mobilize resources for sustainable development may be impaired by low commodity prices and by tariff and non-tariff impediments, including tariff escalation, which would limit their access to export markets.[61] It urged the removal of the existing distortions in international trade which require substantial and progressive reduction in the support and protection to agriculture covering internal regimes, market access and export subsidies as well as industry and other sectors, in order to avoid inflicting large losses on the more efficient producers, especially in developing countries. It has pointed out that trade liberalization must be pursued on a global scale across economic sectors if it is to contribute to sustainable development.[62]

Agenda 21 provided a succinct and accurate outline of the key problems associated with the prevailing trade paradigm noting that:

> [The] expansion of world trade has been unevenly spread, and only a limited number of developing countries have been capable of achieving appreciable growth in their exports. Protectionist pressures and unilateral policy actions continue to endanger the functioning of an open multilateral trading system, affecting particularly the export interests of developing countries.
>
> An early, balanced, comprehensive and successful outcome of the Uruguay Round of multilateral trade negotiations would bring about further liberalization and expansion of world trade, enhance the trade and development possibilities of developing countries and provide greater security and predictability to the international trading system.[63]

After accurate recognition of the problem, *Agenda 21* set the following objectives for governments, taking into account the results of the Uruguay Round of multilateral trade negotiations:

1. To promote an open, non-discriminatory and equitable multilateral trading system that will enable all countries – in particular the developing countries – to improve their economic structures and improve the standard of living of their populations through sustained economic development.
2. To improve access to markets for exports of developing countries.
3. To improve the functioning of commodity markets and achieve sound, compatible and consistent commodity policies at national and international levels with a view to optimizing the contribution of the commodity sector to sustainable development, taking into account environmental considerations.
4. To promote and support policies, domestic and international, that make economic growth and environmental protection mutually supportive.[64]

In an attempt to make sustainable development a more realistic goal, *Agenda 21* has tried to promote an international trading system that takes account of the needs of developing countries. It has suggested that the following actions be undertaken by the international community:

1 Halt and reverse protectionism in order to bring about further liberalization and expansion of world trade, to benefit all countries, in particular the developing countries.
2 Provide for an equitable, secure, non-discriminatory and predictable international trading system.
3 Facilitate, in a timely way, the integration of all countries into the world economy and the international trading system.
4 Ensure that environment and trade policies are mutually supportive, with a view to achieving sustainable development.
5 Strengthen the international trade policies system by achieving an early, balanced, comprehensive and successful outcome of the Uruguay Round of multilateral trade negotiations.[65]

Programme Area 2: making trade and environment mutually supportive

Agenda 21 recognized that environment and trade policies should be mutually supportive and suggested a number of principles which would encourage the achievement of this goal. *Agenda 21* declared that only an open, multilateral trading system, supported by the adoption of sound environmental policies, would have a positive impact on the environment and would contribute to sustainable development.[66] *Agenda 21*'s principles refer, among other things, to the need for:

1 Adequate studies to improve the understanding of the relationship between trade and the environment for the promotion of sustainable development.
2 Dealing with the root causes of environment and development problems in a manner that avoids the adoption of environmental measures which would result in unjustified restrictions on trade.
3 Ensuring that environment-related regulations or standards do not constitute a means of arbitrary or unjustifiable discrimination or a disguised restriction on trade.
4 Ensuring that special factors affecting the environment and trade policies in developing countries are borne in mind in the application of environmental standards, as well as in the use of any trade measures.
5 Avoiding the use of unilateral actions when dealing with environmental challenges outside the jurisdiction of importing countries. Trade policy measures, when used to enforce environmental policies, should be non-discriminatory, least trade restrictive, transparent, should provide adequate notification of national regulations and should consider the special conditions and developmental requirements of developing countries.[67]

Programme Area 3: providing adequate financial resources to developing countries

Agenda 21 has aptly described the need for financial resources in developing countries if they are to pursue sustainable development noting that much of the South has experienced a sustained period of negative net transfer of financial resources. During this period the financial receipts of the developing countries were exceeded by payments they had to make, primarily for the servicing of external debt. Consequently, it is necessary for these struggling domestic economies to transfer their domestically mobilized resources abroad instead of investing them locally in a manner that could potentially promote sustainable development.[68]*Agenda 21* was appropriately realistic and reserved in its appraisal that for much of the South the movement towards a positive development pathway will not take place until the provision of an early and durable solution to the problems of external indebtedness.

Programme Area 4: encouraging economic policies conducive to environment and development

Agenda 21 repeatedly stressed the importance of sound economic policies by ensuring policy coordination that takes into account the interests and concerns of developing countries and the need to promote positive action that supports the efforts of least developed countries to halt their marginalization in the world economy.[69] It also called upon developed countries to provide developing countries with increased technical assistance for building the capacity of those nations to design and implement economic policies, to increase the efficiency of their tax systems and to promote entrepreneurship.[70]

An Assessment of *Agenda 21*: rhetoric and reality

Progress on most of the issues linking trade and sustainability in *Agenda 21* has been disproportionately insignificant in comparison to the consensus that was reached during the Earth Summit. *Agenda 21* established a programme of action by which the international community might achieve sustainable development. Although it contains the detailed agreement of over 170 countries to pursue the goal of sustainable development, it is largely exhortatory and recommendatory in nature. Also in an analogous manner to the *Rio Declaration* it does not purport to bind UNCED participants to particular actions.[71] The real significance of *Agenda 21* lies in the implementation of its principles and programmes according to the specific commitments of the parties. However, when a total and unflinching review was conducted ten years after the adoption of this noble document, it was openly conceded that there were areas where the performance of developed countries has lagged far behind their promises. Indeed, the general consensus appears to be that the gap between rhetoric and reality in promoting sustainable development has in fact widened. The implementation of *Agenda 21* is more urgent than ever. The following sections outline some of the specific gaps that exist in the implementation of *Agenda 21*.

Consumption patterns (Agenda 21, 4.1–4.27; Rio Principle 8)

Both the *Rio Declaration* and *Agenda 21* recognized the link between unsustainable consumption patterns in industrialized countries and environmental deterioration, yet *Agenda 21* in no way compelled the North to assume greater responsibility for their consumption patterns. Developing countries argue that over-consumption in the North is putting extra pressure on the capacity of the earth and is depriving future generations of their ability to use the environment in a manner that meets their basic needs. They argue that such environmental damage is the result of using environmentally unsustainable technologies, bad fiscal policies and distorted prices which do not reflect the real environmental or social costs of the resources used.[72] The rich are blamed for their overuse of non-renewable resources while the poor destroy their environment for the sake of basic needs and survival. Contrary to the glaring omission of the issue in *Agenda 21*, the reality is that it is hard to achieve the goal of sustainable development without addressing the concerns of overuse or waste of natural resources urgently.

Commodity markets (Agenda 21, 2.9 (c), 2.11, 2.12, 2.16)

Under the colonial patterns[73] of trade which were forged between developed and developing countries, the primary commodities exported by developing countries in exchange for the goods and services of industrialized countries are constantly declining in value, resulting in tremendous Southern income losses. It is estimated that if the ten most important (in terms of export value) export commodities of developing countries had risen in line with inflation since 1980, these exporting countries would have received approximately US$112 billion more in 2002 than they did.[74] This is more than double the total amount of aid distributed globally.[75]The disparity of the situation is forcing developing countries to export their natural resources to maintain the balance of payments. The result is that they ruin their non-renewable resources through over-exploitation. These declines in commodity prices contribute to debt crisis and the balance of payments deficit and deprive developing countries of the finance necessary for sustainable development. A UNDP policy statement has expressed deep concern about the crisis in commodities, given the enormous impact it can have on human development, such as lower wages and incomes and less access to basic social services.[76]

Until recently this was an area which had showed no progress since Rio. However, recently there has been a (relative) commodity price boom, especially since 2002.[77] The effect of this boom is reflected in the recent robust economic growth of developing countries generally, including the least developed countries, reported for 2006.[78] However, while this strong growth is expected to continue, in 2007 a slowdown of the global economy is predicted, and developing countries are the most vulnerable to such changes in the world economy.[79] As long as the economies of developing countries are forced to rely substantially on the export of commodities, these countries will remain defenceless and susceptible to the fluctuating nature of the market.

Also the commodity boom has not been universal. The 2005 *Human Development Report* uses the example of the protracted crisis in relation to coffee production, a key export for developing countries such as Ethiopia and Nicaragua.[80] Likewise prices for cotton, a major export for many developing countries, and especially those in West Africa, have sunk below production cost.[81] This is in large part due to the ability of Northern countries, particularly the United States, to produce cotton at under production cost while still making a profit, as a result of the substantial subsidies that are in place in these countries for cotton producers.[82]

Financial resources (Agenda 21, Chapter 33)

It has been estimated that developing countries will need approximately US$600 billion per annum for the implementation of *Agenda 21*, of which US$125 billion will come from donor countries. This US$125 billion funding commitment is in addition to the existing flow of Official Development Assistance ('ODA') which has been estimated at about US$80 billion. Thus a total of US$200 billion per year has been committed to help developing countries achieve sustainable development. Developed countries were committed to contribute ODA targeted at 0.7 per cent of GNP with no deadlines. Not only have the financial commitments of developed countries failed to materialize, but ODA has fallen drastically since 1992.[83] Although a target of US$200 billion per annum was set for the implementation of *Agenda 21*, the amount of money which has in fact gone into it is closer to zero. Instead of ODA continually increasing from the initial US$80 billion, as it normally used to at the rate of a few per cent a year, to an estimated US$200 billion, it has decreased to between US$30 and US$40 billion, less than half the original amount.[84] The CSD has also noted the lack of resources available for the implementation of *Agenda 21*. It has pointed out the severe problems caused by debt servicing and has requested increased political commitment to bringing ODA flows into line with the target of 0.7 per cent as stated in *Agenda 21*.[85] Thus, with no binding obligation to act on the lofty promises made in *Agenda 21*, the actual financial contributions of developed countries has, with the exception of states in the Nordic region, been nothing short of dismal.

Although Chapter 33 of *Agenda 21* was designed to identify ways and means of providing financial resources to developing countries, it was inherently limited to the so-called 'best efforts' of developed countries. While equitable burden sharing among developed countries is recognized, there has been nothing to show for this rhetorical recognition. Chapter 33 could not bind developed countries to providing the funding required for developing countries to implement *Agenda 21*. Consequently, such funding has not been forthcoming.

Transfer of technology (Agenda 21, Chapter 34)

The demand of developing countries for the transfer of technology on non-commercial terms has not yet been satisfied. Although *Agenda 21* included a chapter on the transfer of environmentally sound technology, cooperation and capacity building, no specific or firm commitments were made by developed countries. *Agenda 21* mentioned that access to technology should be promoted, facilitated and financed appropriately – that is, with an emphasis on technology cooperation and capacity building rather than outright transfer. However, technology transfer is a central element of sustainable development. Developing countries remain concerned about the current dominance of multinational corporations in the area of technology. Transnational corporations are the primary holders of technologies and are not bound by any agreement to provide them on special and/or preferential terms to developing countries. The TRIPs Agreement has also severely impacted developing countries' ability to gain access to environmentally sound technology.[86]

Action on debt (Agenda 21, Chapter 2, Section C)

Debt problems are a serious hindrance to the pursuit of sustainable development in developing countries. Unless this most pressing crisis is addressed urgently, the capacity building of developing countries will be severely affected and their efforts to achieve sustainable development will be virtually futile. Recent efforts to lessen the debt crisis are not enough to have had any real impact on the global debt crisis. According to the *Millennium Development Goals Report 2006* future debt payments for twenty-nine least developed countries have fallen by US$59 billion since 1998, but generally even this reduced level is too high.[87] In 2005 the leaders of the group of eight industrialized countries pledged a cancellation of the debt of heavily indebted poor countries ('HIPC') that meet certain criteria. The World Bank, International Monetary Fund and the African Development Fund will cancel debts to nineteen countries that have met the requirements of the enhanced HIPC Initiative.[88] However these debt relief programmes only target a small percentage of the debt incurred by developing countries. According to the Jubilee Debt Campaign, the total external debt owed by all developing countries stood at US$2.8 trillion at the end of 2005.[89] Over the course of 2005 developing countries paid US$511 billion servicing this debt.[90]

Help build capacity in developing countries to foster sustainable development (Rio Principle 12; Agenda 21, 2.38 (a–c))

The assessment of progress in the implementation of *Agenda 21* by the United Nations General Assembly showed that little progress has been made on what Agenda 21 calls 'implementation issues' such as finance, access to environmentally sound technologies and, perhaps to a lesser extent, capacity-building.[91] Imbalances in the trade and environment agenda can be addressed only if sufficient attention is given to the development and implementation of such measures, taking into account the vulnerability of developing countries at the intersection of trade and environment.

Trade-related Environmental Measures ('TREMs') (Rio Principle 12; Agenda 21, 2.22(i), 39.3(d))

As will be explored in depth in Chapters 3 and 8, the practice of using trade measures as environmental tools has created controversy among both trade supporters and developing countries who often condemn this measure as protectionist, extra-jurisdictional, eco-imperial and unilateral. TREMs may take the shape of bans on trade, which can be used as a tool pursuant to multilateral environmental agreements or unilaterally by a developed country. Various GATT and WTO panels' rulings on disputes involving trade sanctions for environmental purposes have only fuelled this controversy (see Chapter 3).

TREMs based on Process and Production Methods ('PPM') (Rio Principles 2, 11, 16; Agenda 21, 2.22(e), 2.22(g), 20.13(k))

The use of trade sanctions in the context of PPM is on the increase. The 1999 *Trade and Development Report* of UNCTAD, while criticizing the protectionist tendencies of developed countries, indicated that if the North reduced/eliminated its protectionism, an extra US$700 billion in annual export earnings could be achieved in a relatively short time by a number of low technology and resource-based countries.[92]

Green protectionism (Rio Principle 12; Agenda 21, 2.22(c), 2.22(d), 2.22(f))

Pro-trade and developing countries fear that trade restrictions for environmental purposes could open the door to green protectionism. Although cautioned by *Agenda 21* against the use of unilateral trade measures for environmental purposes, several trade–environment disputes[93] which have involved such unilateral trade measures show that this trend is increasing. This trend undermines the spirit of both *Agenda 21* and Principle 12 of the *Rio Declaration*.

Food security (Agenda 21, 3.8(l))

States committed to undertaking activities aimed at the promotion of food security place food self-sufficiency within the context of sustainable agriculture. Policies aimed at food self-sufficiency generally include trade policies such as subsidies and trade restrictions which need to be recognized by the WTO as they risk being in conflict with GATT rules.[94] Such policies have not in fact been implemented, nor has there been an examination of the circumstances under which such policies might be deemed 'appropriate'.[95]

Traditional methods and knowledge (Intellectual Property Rights) (Agenda 21, 15.4(g))

States have made a commitment to recognize and foster the traditional methods and knowledge of indigenous people and their communities which are relevant to the conservation of biological diversity. They have also committed to ensure that those groups have the opportunity to participate in the economic and commercial benefits which are derived from such traditional methods and knowledge. The TRIPs Agreement covers some of these areas, but it has been controversial with respect to its perceived inability to protect the rights and traditional knowledge of indigenous peoples. According to the TRIPs Agreement, plant varieties must be protected either by patents or by a custom-made (*sui generis*) system at the national level. A *sui generis* system, which grants rights to indigenous people and their communities, might constitute fulfilment of the *Agenda 21* commitments regarding the sharing of benefits.[96] However, such *sui generis* systems have been the exception rather than the rule and the international dominance of formal, westernized patent systems is unquestionable.

Conclusions on Agenda 21

Agenda 21 is a comprehensive programme of action which has categorically and systematically addressed the concerns of developing countries in relation to trade and the environment with promises and commitments from the international community. However, the progress that has been made on the implementation of those commitments is inadequate. This is in large part because of a lack of political will in addressing the fundamental cross-sectoral concerns – issues of funding and technology transfer, trade, debt, poverty and inequities in wealth, the nature of international environmental institutions and the role of actors such as multinational corporations and NGOs.[97] Many of these issues were on the agenda at Stockholm in 1972.[98] They were addressed by the World Commission on Environment and Development in 1987 and were on the agenda again in Rio in 1992, yet it is doubtful whether we can claim to have moved in any significant way towards a resolution of these issues in the years since, despite the many conferences, declarations and commitments.[99] The most notable of these subsequent conferences were the Millennium Summit and the 2002 Johannesburg World Summit on Sustainable Development ('WSSD').

The Millennium Summit

The Millennium Summit was held in September 2000 at the UN headquarters in New York. The expressed goal of the summit was to examine 'the role of the UN in the twenty-first century'.[100] At the time it was the largest-ever gathering of world leaders, and among the issues addressed were the impact of globalization; development and poverty eradication; and sustainable development, with a new ethic of global stewardship.[101] The key outcome of the summit was the adoption of the *Millennium Declaration*.[102] The Declaration received support from *every* member state of the UN by Resolution of the General Assembly on 18 September 2000. This Declaration was essentially an affirmation of the values, principles and objectives for the UN and the international community in the twenty-first century. It expressed that the 'central challenge we face today is to ensure that globalization becomes a positive force for all the world's people'.[103] The true importance of the *Millennium Declaration*, however, was its role in the inception of the Millennium Development Goals.

Millennium Development Goals

The Millennium Development Goals ('MDGs') are the most dominant, coordinated and visible sustainable development initiative to date. The eight individual goals that constitute the MDGs were derived directly from the targets contained within the *Millennium Declaration*. They are goals to be achieved by 2015, and are responses to what are seen as the world's main development challenges. Most of the targets contained in the MDG are not new. They are commitments that have been made at various international conferences and summits (including Stockholm and Rio). What makes the MDGs important is that they synthesize these various commitments into a single programme, with concrete goals. This is crucial to sustainable development which can only be achieved with a recognition of the interdependence of social, economic and ecological factors.

The eight Millennium Development Goals aim to:

1 Eradicate extreme poverty and hunger.
2 Achieve universal primary education.
3 Promote gender equality and empower women.
4 Reduce child mortality.
5 Improve maternal health.
6 Combat HIV/AIDS, malaria and other diseases.
7 Ensure environmental sustainability.
8 Develop a global partnership for development.[104]

Of particular importance to the subject matter of this book is goal 8. Goal 8 of the MDGs, 'Develop a global partnership for development', asserts that there is an urgent need to:

1 Develop further an open trading and financial system that is rule-based, predictable and non-discriminatory, includes a commitment to good governance, development and poverty reduction – nationally and internationally.
2 Address the least developed countries' special needs. This includes tariff- and quota-free access for their exports; enhanced debt relief for heavily indebted poor countries; cancellation of official bilateral debt; and more generous official development assistance for countries committed to poverty reduction.

3 In cooperation with the private sector, make available the benefits of new technologies – especially information and communications technologies.[105]

Assessment of the Millennium Development Goals

Like the *Rio Declaration*, the *Millennium Declaration* is declaratory in nature, and so not binding on states. However, unlike Rio, the MDGs have been placed firmly at the heart of the global agenda, and have captured global attention. As Kemal Dervis describes, the MDGs:

> have caught the imagination of the development community and civil society, including non-governmental organizations, young people, and others across the world. Today there is unprecedented global support for achieving the MDGs, the eight goals agreed to by all UN Member States in the year 2000.[106]

The fact that the MDGs are concrete, time bound and deliberately designed to be measurable (which lends to a sense of accountability) makes the MDGs feel more tangible than the often lofty but detached objectives of some other international commitments. As Dervis states the MDGs are of such a nature that people everywhere can immediately relate to them; they speak to the immediate concerns and basic needs of everyone globally.[107]

Progress as a result of the MDGs has been made, and the measurability of the MDGs means that this progress is quantifiable. According to the 2005 *Human Development Report*, '[o]n average, people born in a developing country today can anticipate being wealthier, healthier and better educated than their parents' generation'.[108] It also states that in a little over a decade average life expectancy in developing countries has increased by two years, there are 2 million fewer child deaths, more than 130 million people have escaped extreme poverty, and that 1.2 billion people have gained access to clean water.[109]

However, while progress has been, and continues to be, made, it seems that the efforts as they stand to meet the MDGs will not be sufficient to reach the targets by 2015.[110] To reach the MDGs' targets developing countries must be assisted to benefit more from trade, thereby enabling them to generate the resources needed for development.[111] The 2005 *Human Development Report* acknowledged the importance of trade: 'Under the right conditions international trade could generate a powerful impetus for accelerated progress toward the MDGs'.[112] As Sok Siphana provides:

> The World Bank's *Global Economic Prospects, 2002*, estimates that abolishing all trade barriers could boost global income over a ten year period by US$2.8 trillion. Of this, developing countries stand to reap more than half of these gains and additional reduction in global poverty of 320 million people by 2015.[113]

However, while changes to the nature of international trade are important in assisting developing countries achieve sustainable development and meet the MDGs, as George and Kirkpatrick point out, consideration has to be given to the potentially adverse social and environmental effects that may emerge from economic growth.[114] It should also be kept in mind that '[f]rom a human development perspective trade is a means to development, not an end in itself'.[115]

Another key concern in relation to the MDGs is that while the *Millennium Declaration* was the recognition of the interdependence of social, economic and environmental development, in practice integration of these factors into a holistic approach has been lacking. As George and Kirkpatrick state:

> better integration of economic, social, environmental and development goals will facilitate the implementation of sustainable development and the achievement of the Millennium Development Goals by 2015.[116]

Integration and effective implementation were central issues of the subsequent World Summit on Sustainable Development.

The World Summit on Sustainable Development

The World Summit on Sustainable Development ('WSSD') was held in Johannesburg in 2002. Over 100 heads of state and around 25,000 governmental, business and activist organizations attended the summit.[117] The summit was held as a follow-up ten years on from Rio. The introductory statement on the Summit website summarizes neatly the need for the summit and what it hoped to achieve:

> When the United Nations General Assembly authorized holding the World Summit on Sustainable Development, it was hardly a secret – or even a point in dispute – that progress in implementing sustainable development has been extremely disappointing since the 1992 Earth Summit, with poverty deepening and environmental degradation worsening. What the world wanted, the General Assembly said, was not a new philosophical or political debate but rather, a summit of actions and results.[118]

While *Agenda 21* had offered a plan of action for sustainable development, implementation had been lacking. Two key documents came out of the WSSD, the *Johannesburg Declaration on Sustainable Development*[119] and the *Johannesburg Plan of Implementation.*[120] These documents represent the commitment to strengthening the UN approach to sustainable development. They also reflect an increasing recognition of the importance of a holistic approach to international crises through the UN framework. As Strachan and Roberts attest, the Declaration and JPOI 'deepen the integration of poverty, economic and social issues in to the international framework on sustainable development elaborated through the United Nations'.[121]

The Johannesburg Declaration on Sustainable Development

The *Johannesburg Declaration on Sustainable Development* was intended primarily to reaffirm commitment to sustainable development, and the principles asserted at Rio. It also explicitly recognizes the mutual concerns of trade and environment for the achievement of sustainable development. Paragraph 11 asserts:

> We recognize that poverty eradication, changing consumption and production patterns and protecting and managing the natural resource base for economic and social development are overarching objectives of and essential requirements for sustainable development.[122]

The Declaration also affirmed that:

> Globalization has added a new dimension to these challenges. The rapid integration of markets, mobility of capital and significant increases in investment flows around the world have opened new challenges and opportunities for the pursuit of sustainable development. But the benefits and costs of globalization are unevenly distributed, with developing countries facing special difficulties in meeting this challenge.[123]

Johannesburg Plan of Implementation ('JPOI')

The *Johannesburg Plan of Implementation* ('JPOI') opens with an affirmation of the various commitments the UN had made previously:

> We strongly reaffirm our commitment to the Rio principles, the full implementation of Agenda 21 and the Programme for the Further Implementation of Agenda 21. We also commit ourselves to achieving the internationally agreed development goals, including those contained in the United Nation Millennium Declaration and in the outcomes of the major United Nations conferences and international agreements since 1992.[124]

The JPOI also makes the important step of trying to incorporate not only the various UN commitments made to sustainable development, but also those of other organizations such as the WTO. To this effect, paras 48 and 90 seek to implement the outcomes of the Doha Ministerial Conference (discussed in detail in Chapter 4) organized by the WTO in order to strengthen capacity building and developing countries' ability to effectively and more fully participate in multilateral trade negotiations. Paragraph 92 also encourages implementation of the Doha Ministerial Declaration in relation to market access.

Paragraph 4 of the JPOI recognizes that, as a result of globalization, 'external factors have become critical in determining the success or failure of developing countries in their national efforts'. Paragraph 47 of the JPOI offers an approach to deal with the challenges and opportunities of globalization. According to the JPOI globalization should be fully inclusive and equitable. To achieve this, the JPOI urges immediate action at all levels to:

1 Continue to promote open, equitable, rules-based, predictable and non-discriminatory multilateral trading and financial systems that benefit all countries in the pursuit of sustainable development.
2 Encourage ongoing efforts by international financial and trade institutions to ensure that decision-making processes and institutional structures are open and transparent.
3 Enhance the capacities of developing countries, including the least developed countries, landlocked developing countries and small island developing states, to benefit from liberalized trade opportunities through international cooperation and measures aimed at improving productivity, commodity diversification and competitiveness, community-based entrepreneurial capacity and transport and communications infrastructure development.
4 Enhance the delivery of coordinated, effective and targeted trade–related technical assistance and capacity-building programmes, including taking advantage of existing and future market access opportunities, and examining the relationship between trade, environment and development.[125]

The most important statement of the JPOI however is contained in para. 101, which states:

> States should cooperate to promote a supportive and open international economic system that would lead to economic growth and sustainable development in all countries to better address the problems of environmental degradation. Trade policy measures for environmental purposes should not constitute a means of arbitrary or unjustifiable discrimination or a disguised restriction on international trade. Unilateral actions to deal with environmental challenges outside the jurisdiction of the importing country should be avoided. Environmental measures addressing transboundary or global environmental problems should, as far as possible, be based on an international consensus.

The JPOI offers various ways in which trade should be altered to benefit developing countries. Paragraph 93 calls upon developed countries that have not yet done so to work towards duty- and quote-free access for all least developed countries' exports. Paragraph 95 seeks to build the capacity of commodity-dependent countries to diversify their exports and offers suggestions of how this might be achieved. Paragraph 96 is concerned with enhancing the benefits for developing countries of trade liberalization, through financial support for technical assistance, the development of technology and capacity building. Doing so would:

1 Enhance trade infrastructure and strengthen institutions.
2 Increase developing country capacity to diversify and increase exports to cope with the instability of commodity prices and declining terms of trade.
3 Increase the value added of developing country exports.[126]

Also significant in the JPOI is the recognition of corporate social responsibility ('CSR'). Paragraph 49 asserts the intention to:

> Actively promote corporate responsibility and accountability, based on the Rio principles, including through the full development and effective implementation of intergovernmental agreements and measures, international initiatives and public–private partnerships and appropriate national regulations, and support continuous improvement in corporate practices in all countries.[127]

Assessment of the outcomes of the WSSD

> If Rio was a coming-out party for environmental issues on the global stage, Johannesburg was more like a mid-life birthday party, where the optimism and youth has been tempered by the realities of hard-won experience.[128]

As stated above the WSSD reflected a continuation and reaffirmation of the themes and principles that had come before it, especially at Rio. Important was the summit's attention to a number of issues, including:

1 Deeper integration of the pillars of sustainable development (social, economic and environmental).
2 A strong focus on peace, human rights and governance as all essential to the pursuit of sustainable development.
3 The acknowledgement of the need for demonstrable progress on implementation, and in particular the need for increased flow of resources and the building of strategic partnerships.[129]

As Larry A. Swatuk states, '[w]hereas Rio focused on the state of the planet, Johannesburg focused on the state of human development, more specifically sustainable social and economic development within the context of environmental stewardship'.[130] This is reflected by the far greater emphasis on international trade found in the JPOI compared to *Agenda 2*. However, as Swatuk also notes, while the objectives of the WSSD, like *Agenda 21*, are extensive, there is no certainty that the finance and political will needed for the realization of these objectives will be provided.[131]

The WSSD's value also lies in its recognition of the role the private sector and civil society must take, in particular through the emergent principles of smart partnership and corporate social responsibility.

Johannesburg ushered in an era of 'smart partnership' which acknowledges the need for civil society and business to form a partnership with governments and international organizations to achieve sustainable development.[132] 'If Rio may be thought of as one of the last great inter-state meetings, Johannesburg may be regarded as "states plus".' [133] This move towards smart partnership is a vital recognition of the role civil society must play in the implementation of the objectives outlined in the JPOI.[134] These partnerships are particularly relevant to the trade–environment interface, especially in relation to issues such as intellectual property rights, the transfer of technology and adequate financing and capacity building (be it from government or non-government sources).

Likewise, the principle of corporate social responsibility as encapsulated in para. 49 of the JPOI must also play a role in the trade–environment interface if sustainable development it to be effectively achieved. CSR does not mean accountability in terms of enforcement (which would have been difficult to receive business' support of), but rather answerability.[135] It is an acknowledgement that action from the private sector is necessary if sustainable development is to be feasible. It was a weakness of the Rio Summit that 'the role of business in sustainable development was poorly understood'.[136] At Johannesburg however the role of civil society was not only acknowledged but, through the concepts of smart partnership and CSR, now an essential element of approaches to sustainable development.

The United Nations Commission on Sustainable Development

Following UNCED, in December 1992, the UN General Assembly created the Commission on Sustainable Development ('CSD') as a functional commission of the UN Economic and Social Council. The original role of the CSD was limited to monitoring the implementation of *Agenda 21* and the *Rio Declaration*. More recently however, the CSD has also been charged with the responsibility of providing policy guidance for the ongoing efforts in relation to the *Johannesburg Plan of Implementation* ('JPOI'). Despite widespread criticism of the CSD's effectiveness since almost the date of its inception, para. 145 of the JPOI re-affirmed that the CSD 'should continue to be the high-level commission on sustainable development within the United Nations system'.

The CSD seeks to integrate the roles of different actors in the linking of environment and development. The CSD derives its authority from the *Rio Declaration* and was established in accordance with Article 68 of the *UN Charter*. The CSD reports to the Economic and Social Council in the context of the Council's role under the *United Nations Charter vis-à-vis* the General Assembly.[137] The creation of the Commission was a key recommendation at UNCED,[138] and was designed to ensure effective follow-up, to enhance international cooperation, to rationalize intergovernmental decision-making capacity and to oversee the implementation of *Agenda 21* at national, regional and international levels.[139]

The CSD's mandate states that the organization is to:

> Monitor progress in promoting, facilitating and financing, as appropriate, the access to and transfer of environmentally sound technologies and corresponding know-how, in particular to developing countries, on favourable terms, including on concessional and preferential terms, as mutually agreed, taking into account the need to protect intellectual property rights as well as the special needs of developing countries for the implementation of Agenda 21.[140]

CSD is designed to be a structured forum where governments and other organizations can debate and share information about the implementation of *Agenda 21* and the JPOI at the international, regional, national and local levels. While the CSD was originally created with a scope and jurisdiction that was incredibly broad, the tremendous responsibilities assigned to the CSD have far exceeded the modest resources it has at its disposal for implementing them.[141] This limitation was implicitly recognized by the JPOI through its reference to the need for the CSD to 'be strengthened'[142] and 'limit the number of themes addressed in each session'.[143]

As a result of the acknowledgement of the Commission's significant shortcomings following its ten-year review at Johannesburg, the operational approach of the CSD has undergone major reform in the post-JPOI era with a shift in emphasis towards thematic work programme areas with specific global environmental issues being addressed on a rotational basis. At its eleventh session in 2003 the CSD decided that its future multi-year programme of work would be organized on the initial basis of seven two-year cycles, with each cycle focusing on selected global environmental issues.[144]

In addition to the above broad sustainable development themes, the CSD has devised a list of 'cross-cutting issues' that are to be considered during each and every cycle so as to provide a holistic appraisal of the problems.[145] The identified cross-cutting issues are:

1 Poverty eradication.
2 Changing unsustainable patterns of consumption and production.
3 Protecting and managing the natural resource base of economic and social development.
4 Sustainable development in a globalizing world.
5 Health and sustainable development.
6 Sustainable development of SIDS.
7 Sustainable development for Africa.
8 Other regional initiatives.
9 Means of implementation.
10 Institutional framework for sustainable development.
11 Gender equality.
12 Education.[146]

The CSD's mandate remains incredibly broad and thus its task remains incredibly daunting. Indeed, it is highly questionable whether such a redirection of the Commission's approach will increase the quality of its implementation-related outcomes considering that its resource base remains incredibly limited. It is also interesting to note that, despite the generality of the themes, international trade receives no specific mention. Nonetheless, issues such as 'Sustainable development in a globalizing world', 'Protecting and managing the natural resource base of economic and social development' and 'Changing unsustainable patterns of consumption and production' are of such a nature that detailed consideration of the trade–environment interface will be absolutely vital if effective outcomes are to be achieved.

The CSD has no power or authority with which to discipline member states who failed to comply with *Agenda 21* and it has little influence over the governing bodies of international organizations such as the World Bank groups and the WTO. In order to monitor the implementation of *Agenda 21*, the CSD requires the submission of reports analysing and evaluating progress by national governments and international organizations. These reports are submitted on a voluntary basis, and so whether and how such a report is to be submitted is left to the absolute discretion of the relevant government or organization to decide. Governments and organizations are not seriously committed to the regular submission of such reports; those that do comply with the requirement tend to deliver documents that are long on self-congratulation and short on substantive analysis of remaining challenges.[147]

In its various sessions, CSD has attempted to address the problems facing developing countries in the implementation of *Agenda 21*. It has repeatedly noted the insufficiency of resources and funds for the effective implementation of *Agenda 21*. While CSD is able to initiate more open discussions about the implementation of *Agenda 21*, ultimately the 'success of CSD would depend on the political weight given to its deliberations by governments'.[148]

North–South aspects of the United Nations approach to trade and the environment

Both Stockholm and Rio have been significant steps towards increasing global awareness of the intricate and essential relationship between environment and development. The after-effects of UNCED in particular continue to encourage a major global paradigm shift in the way that environmental and economic concerns are viewed by both industrialized and developing countries.[149] The real issues lurking behind the public debate on trade and environment at UNCED were the North–South relationship and economic development, the transfer of technology, declining terms of trade, intellectual property rights and equitable access to global resources. Tensions arose not only over the principles which should address the relationship between rich and poor countries but also over how those principles should be put into practice.[150] Developed countries insisted that environmental protection should take priority over development while developing countries argued that environment should be an integral part of development.

Throughout the UNCED negotiations, the South asserted that its right to development must be an integral part of environmental protection measures. It views the present environmental degradation as the cause and effect of unsustainable development models and lifestyles on the part of the North. Environmental problems are not isolated from the development process and an integrated approach is needed to address the issue of environmental protection. Developing countries argue that their right to development should be granted priority and that environmental protection measures should not be in conflict with their economic growth and development. The special situation and needs of developing countries warrant special attention from the international community. Their capacity to comply with international standards needs to be considered. They need financial support from the North in order to be able to address environmental issues. For them, poverty is the biggest threat to the environment. Indian Prime Minister Indira Ghandi expressed this concern during the 1972 UN Conference on Human Environment in Stockholm, when she asked '[a]re not poverty and need the greatest polluters?'[151]

The development process of developing countries has been undermined and finally halted due to the unfairness of the global financial system. The inequities of current international economic relations, especially with regard to debt, financing, trade and the transfer of technology have had serious consequences including a reverse flow of financial resources, brain drain and increasing backwardness in the scientific and technological capabilities of the South.[152] It is therefore imperative for a new and equitable international economic order to be established. Such an order must be conducive to the sustained and sustainable development of all countries, particularly developing countries, thereby creating the conditions necessary for global cooperation to protect the environment.[153] Solutions to international environmental problems depend largely on the reform of the inequitable trading relationship between the North and the South.

The global institutions dealing with international trade and finance are believed to protect the interests of developed countries, resulting in economic disparities between developed and developing countries. Developing countries have not been integrated into the global economy and are prevented from effectively participating in it either as consumers or producers because of their lack of purchasing power, skills and resources. International trade could play an important role in helping developing countries to improve their situations. Developing countries in many forums have consistently argued for fundamental changes in the international economic system to make them more open, equitable and supportive. Long term sustainable growth will require far-reaching changes in the system to produce trade, capital and technology flows which are more equitable and better synchronized with environmental imperatives.[154] This has been overlooked in the past and was overlooked at UNCED, though more attention was given to the issue by WSSD, as outlined in the JPOI.

Despite the unprecedented focus on preserving the environment without sacrificing development, the Earth Summit bypassed an opportunity to discuss the reform of the international trading system and its impact on sustainable development.[155] Instead, the participants in UNCED largely accepted the current state of the international trading system and placed the onus for reform on environment policy. It is vital to assess whether the present structures of global trade and finance are major roadblocks for developing countries in their efforts to fully realize the UNCED spirit of sustainable development.

International cooperation in environmental protection should be based on the sovereign equality of each state. States with superior economic clout should not impose their own environmental standards on debt ridden developing countries who lack the necessary resources, technology and infrastructure to adhere to standards equal to those of developed countries. Environmental considerations should not be used as a disguised barrier to international trade. Similarly, trade barriers on environmental grounds jeopardize the exports of developing countries and the access of their products to the markets of developed countries. Environmental considerations should not influence the finance provided for development nor should they impose restrictions or conditionality on foreign aid.

As has been recognized by the various UN-driven international environmental initiatives, environmental protection initiatives should be based on the principle of common but differentiated responsibility. The contribution of developed countries to both past and present global environmental degradation makes it equitable and fair that they should take responsibility for cleaning up the resulting mess. Their economic and technological superiority justify a position as the leaders in setting standards for environmental protection. At the same time they have a dominant position in the international economic order. If they really want environmental protection they should come with clean hands. The South has expressed concern that the North might put the blame for the deterioration of the environment on them, thus making environmental protection another instrument with which the North might further dictate economic and social policies to developing countries.[156] The South has taken the position that it would be unacceptable if, out of concern for the environment, the North were to impose new conditionalities on the debt-ridden and resource-starved economies of the South while Northern countries continued their present, environmentally unsound, patterns of living. The South warned against the danger of the North's consumption patterns which they argued might lead to the extinction of global resources, compromising the needs of the South as well as future generations. Developed countries use a considerable portion of the world's natural resources to meet their high levels of consumption but they often fail to recognize the impact of these consumption patterns on the environment.[157] The South also argued that the North should help developing countries by providing adequate and additional financial resources and the preferential and non-commercial transfer of environmentally friendly technology to enable developing countries to effectively deal with their environmental and developmental problems. This pressing need for resources has been reiterated in a Declaration on Environment and Development, adopted at the Ministerial Conference on Developing Countries in Beijing on 18–19 June 1991.[158]

The North, although agreed about its responsibility for global environmental problems, has not committed additional funding or resources to assist and enable the South to address those problems.

It was argued by the South that environmental priorities such as forest conservation and biodiversity were designed by the North to serve its own interests and that the conditionality attached to those considerations might even be used by the North against the South to ensure that its dominant economic power remained unchallenged in the future. Concern was expressed about the way in which the resources of the developing world, such as tropical forests or species and biodiversity, have been deemed the 'common heritage of mankind', resources which developing countries are now supposed to manage for the good of all.[159] The South repeatedly made it clear that it could contribute to sustainable development only if it had adequate resources transferred from the North and conditions for vastly improved economic growth and development. Thus any solution to the environmental problem will have to begin by bridging the current terms of trade between the South and the North. These issues of environmental space and economic development have become the foundation for the legal position of the South.[160]

Where to go from here?

There is a need to take account of what has been achieved since UNCED and WSSD. It is imperative to refocus attention on the commitments made by developed countries to assist developing countries in their efforts to achieve sustainable development. Developed countries should be cautious in initiating new areas of work, signing new conventions or negotiating further without first implementing their commitments which have already been made to sustainable development. Failure to do so would further undermine the capacity of developing countries to implement the agreed upon framework for sustainable development. Over-commitment would be as problematic (if not more so) as under-commitment for developing countries committed to sustainable development.

Developing countries should not bear the economic burden of environmental protection at the cost of their right to development. Sustainable development requires that stark and difficult choices be made by developed and developing countries. Developing countries entered into the deal made at the Earth Summit by agreeing to the environmental commitments sought by the North in return for increased flows of new and additional financial resources and technical assistance – but developed countries failed to keep their promises. As a result, many issues remained unresolved and North–South relations soured. The current gap between implementation and accountability deeply threatens the process of international negotiation to which we are all so strongly committed.[161] While UNCED established a process for achieving sustainable development, some fifteen years later, its level of practical success remains at the mercy of the political will of certain developed countries and thus remains highly limited.

Conclusion

The role of the UN is unique and indispensable in providing the global framework, context and forms required to enable other actors to contribute effectively and cooperatively to addressing common global concerns.[162] Unfortunately, the UN has been marginalized from the main thrust of policy making in areas such as international trade, development, finance and monetary issues, which are now seen more as the purview of organizations such as WTO and the IMF.[163]

Developing countries seem to be better at representing their needs and demands in the UN than in Bretton Woods institutions which have been accused of being undemocratic in so far as the participation of states and their decision-making are concerned. The UN and its declarations and principles are commendable in their intent and are based on the equitable and developmental needs of developing countries. The UN has provided guidelines on sustainable development which address the trade–environment issues confronting developing countries. The principles and recommendations which have arisen under the UN, particularly at Stockholm, Rio and more recently Johannesburg may be used as a *magna carta* for the resolution of the present crisis with regard to the interrelationship between trade and environment.

To make the UN system more effective and to make it a credible forum for resolving the trade–environment dichotomy, member states need to provide the UN with financial and political support it needs to govern trade and environment related problems. There is a need to make the UN commitments and programmes (such as environmental agreements, social development initiatives, and financing for development) operational and to ensure that WTO agreements and Bretton Woods institutions are supportive of sustainable development.[164] There should be cooperation and coordination among UN entities, Bretton Woods Institutions and the WTO. The roles of UNEP and CSD need to be evaluated and strengthened if they are to police the implementation of the principle of common but differentiated responsibility, and address the needs for additional financial resources and the transfer of environmentally sound technology. With the UN governing at the pinnacle of international law, looking forward there should be a balanced and integrated approach to trade and sustainable development, based on a combination of equitable trade liberalization, needs-based economic development and properly financed environmental protection.[165]

Developing countries should also not have to bear the economic burden of environmental protection at the cost of their right to development. In fact, developing countries, in the Earth Summit, agreed to address the environmental commitments sought by the North in return for increased flows of new and additional financial resources and technical assistance. Developed countries, however, have failed to keep their promises. The current gap between rhetoric and reality deeply threatens the process of international negotiation to which we are all so strongly committed.[166] While UNCED, and later WSSD, established a process for achieving sustainable development, much of its success will depend upon the political will of the developed countries in particular.

3 GATT/WTO approaches to trade, the environment and sustainable development

This chapter considers the approaches of the *General Agreement on Tariffs and Trade* ('GATT') and the World Trade Organization ('WTO') in relation to issues concerning trade, the environment and the struggle to attain sustainable development worldwide. It examines the main principles and rules of GATT/WTO which are relevant for the examination of the trade–environment issues and the dilemmas they pose for trade and development prospects of developing countries. The main objective of this chapter is to identify and illustrate the pressing issues for developing countries in relation to multilateral trade liberalization and intersecting environmental issues.

In view of the concerns of developing countries regarding the interaction between trade and the environment, the chapter argues that the objectives of sustainable development can be achieved only by properly taking into account the developmental needs, limited resources and highly reduced level of economic development of developing countries. As noted by Halle in his recent critique of the World Trade Organization's progress in relation to trade and environment issues:

> it is incumbent on the environmental community to recognise that environmental regulations, norms and standards present developing countries with, at best, a bewildering obstacle course must be run before they can gain access to developed country markets, and at worst a green wall of protectionism.[1]

With such understanding as a conceptual framework and through a detailed examination of the GATT/WTO framework, this chapter argues that developing countries' concerns need to be addressed as a priority in order to make any progress in achieving the global objectives of environmental protection and sustainable development.

Genesis of GATT/WTO

GATT was adopted as an *ad hoc* agreement in 1947 in an attempt to liberalize tariffs and trade in the post-war period.[2] It was designed as a temporary solution to trade-related issues which lasted until the *Havana Charter* and the International Trade Organization came into being. GATT was originally intended to be a component of a larger agreement establishing an International Trade Organization.[3] Driven by the philosophy of market economy, GATT's main objective was economic growth that was to be achieved by providing trade rules and a framework for trade liberalization.

By virtue of the era in which it was drafted, the original GATT agreement was negotiated without any reference to the need for sustainability of economic growth. It did not consider the environmental effects of its trade rules on the production of goods. Rather, environmental protectionism was treated as an unacceptable non-tariff trade barrier. This inattention to environmental matters was most likely due to the fact that environmentalism was a relatively new concern in national and international policy areas, while the concept of sustainable development had not yet been elucidated. However, widespread concern and increasing demand for environmental protection prompted GATT to form a Group on Environmental Measures and International Trade ('EMIT') in 1971. This group recognized the relationship between trade and environment at the inter-governmental level and published a report recognizing the need to make trade and environment policies more supportive of each other.[4]

GATT continued to pursue its objective of regulating trade between national governments until it was incorporated into and strengthened by the 1993 Uruguay Round Agreement. Despite the findings of the EMIT report the relationship between economic growth and environmental protection was not recognized by the successive GATT negotiations until the Uruguay Round, which finally recognized the need for a complementary regime that supported either environmental objectives or something to that effect.

Following the 1994 Uruguay Round of trade negotiations, the World Trade Organization was established by the WTO Agreement.[5] Under this agreement, the WTO became the legal and institutional framework for the international trading system. It provided a forum for implementing trade agreements, negotiating new agreements and resolving trade-related disputes. The WTO Agreement incorporated the original GATT which continues to apply to issues not covered by more specific agreements negotiated during the Uruguay Round.[6] It also includes specific agreements that cover many trade-related environmental issues such as the *Agreement on Technical Barriers to Trade* ('TBT'),[7] the *Agreement on Sanitary and Phytosanitary Measures* ('SPS')[8] and the *Agreement on Trade-related Intellectual Property Rights*[9] ('TRIPs').

The WTO has formally established the Committee on Trade and Environment ('CTE') to identify the relationship between trade and environmental measures and to make recommendations for modifications of the rules of the multilateral trading system. WTO is an improvement over GATT in that the WTO acknowledges that trade liberalization has implications for the environment and recognizes the need to preserve the environment, something the old GATT did not.[10] The mandate of the CTE, its shaky past and the widespread criticisms in relation to its practical impact will be discussed later in the chapter.

Trade theory and the WTO

Before proceeding further in discussion of some of the GATT/WTO challenges in relation to the trade and environment interface, it is worth while to briefly introduce the theoretical and ideological framework upon which it is commonly alleged that the GATT/WTO regime of trade liberalization is founded.

The Agreements establishing the World Trade Organization, as well as the Agreements on Agriculture, Textiles, TBT and SPS, all emphasize the need for trade liberalization. The underlying theory supporting trade liberalization is the Ricardian model of comparative advantage.[11] Developed by the British economist David Ricardo in the early nineteenth century, the theory asserts that international trade liberalization will facilitate economy-wide specialization in production, leading to improvements in productivity and national income.[12]

The Ricardian theory is built upon several assumptions and abstractions. First, it abstracts the world into two trading states that trade only two goods, and use only one type of material to produce those two goods. An example of such a world may be the United States and Bangladesh that only trade computers and calculators between themselves, and there is no difference in the quality of the computers and calculators produced by the two countries.[13] Second, it assumes that there are no costs associated with international trade. For example it assumes that the costs of transport and the creation of legally binding contracts and so on are zero. Finally, it assumes that there will be no deleterious consequences of specializing production into a particular good. An important implication of this assumption is that, under the Ricardian model, there is seemingly no ground for consideration of factors such as environmental deterioration caused by over-exploitation. While these assumptions may seem unrealistic, the purpose is not to draw a definitive conclusion on all matters relating to international trade, but rather to abstract from reality into a simpler world that is easier to model. In effect, this model acknowledges that the real world would be impossible to model accurately in this manner.

Once this process of abstraction is complete, the Ricardian model is able to provide a theoretical justification for the process of trade liberalization. Put simply, if Bangladesh is comparatively more efficient (that is, more productive) than the United States in producing calculators, it will be able to sell them at a lower price compared with the United States. Similarly, if the United States is more productive in producing computers, it will be able to sell them at a lower price than a producer in Bangladesh. Thus, if trade is allowed between these two countries, taking into account the assumptions articulated above, the consumers of both states will benefit. United States consumers will purchase computers from local producers and calculators from Bangladesh, and Bangladesh consumers will purchase calculators from local producers and computers from the United States. In essence, the effect of free trade in this example is to reduce the prices of goods both in the United States and Bangladesh. According to the theory, the reduction in prices will leave the consumers of both states 'better off'.

However, the above analysis applies only where one state is more productive in one good, and the other state is more productive in another. An alternative scenario is where one state is more productive in producing both goods. *Prima facie*, assuming that the United States owing to its superior technological position is able to produce both computers and calculators more efficiently than Bangladesh, there would be no point in opening trade with Bangladesh. This is because if calculators and computers were more expensive to produce in Bangladesh, then importing such devices from Bangladesh would result in higher prices being faced by US consumers of these calculators and computers.

However, the Ricardian model delves further into this issue, and argues that even if the United States is more productive at producing both calculators and computers than Bangladesh, the United States still can benefit from trading with Bangladesh.[14] Adopting the example above, say the United States is three times more productive than Bangladesh in producing computers, but only twice as productive in producing calculators. The theory of comparative advantage shows that if the United States allows trade with Bangladesh, the total number of calculators and computers available for consumption will be higher compared with the situation where no trade with Bangladesh is allowed. The reason for this is that the United States under free trade could specialize in the production of computers, and not produce any calculators at all. Any excess supply of computers to the US market could be sold to Bangladesh in exchange for calculators. In this sense, the United States is able to indirectly produce calculators by manufacturing computers and trading them for calculators. Thus, the United States is able to increase the amount of items available for consumption in its domestic market. Before free trade, it had to produce calculators itself. After free trade, the United States is able to produce a greater number of computers, and sell the excess in order to obtain calculators. The net effect, according to the Ricardian theory, is to increase the items available for consumption in both the US and Bangladesh markets.

Generalizing this example, the overarching proposition of liberal trade theory is that free and open trade will benefit all states, regardless of their comparative levels of productivity. Also, another positive effect of liberalized trade may be that competition between suppliers of products across many states is encouraged, resulting in a reduction in prices, and improvements in the quality of the product.

However, not all of the assumptions of the Ricardian model will hold in reality. Extreme caution should be taken in seeking to generalize the above strictly specified model into overarching propositions. To suggest that the Ricardian model provides a theoretical basis for the WTO's activities seems to be problematic. Throughout this chapter, the consistency between the Ricardian model and the reality of the WTO will be tested via an examination of the Agreements on Textiles, Agriculture, SPS and TBT.

GATT's core principles affecting trade–environment issues

Three core principles form the basis of GATT regime, at least in so far as it affects the trade–environment interface. They are the Most Favoured Nation obligation ('MFN') found in Article I, the national treatment obligation found in Article III and obligations relating to the elimination of quantitative restrictions found in Article XI.

The Most Favoured Nation obligation ('MFN'), Article I

According to the MFN obligation, any advantage, favour, privilege or immunity granted by any contracting party to any product of any other country applies equally to like products of all contracting parties. No country should discriminate against any other. This obligation ensures equal treatment of trading partners and the rapid reduction of trade barriers.[15]

National Treatment, Article III

The National Treatment obligation prohibits trade restrictions which discriminate between foreign products and like domestic products. Foreign products cannot be accorded any less favourable treatment than like domestic products where the goal is the protection of the latter. Article III is framed in very broad terms and refers to

> internal taxes and other internal charges and laws, regulations and requirements affecting the internal sale, offering for sale, purchase, transportation, distribution or use of products and internal quantitative regulations requiring the mixture, processing or use of products in specified amounts or proportions.[16]

General elimination of quantitative restrictions, Article XI

No prohibitions or restrictions other than duties, taxes or other charges, whether made effective through quotas, import or export licences or other measures, shall be instituted or maintained by any contracting party on the importation of any product of the territory of any other contracting party or on the exportation or sale for export of any product destined for the territory of any other contracting party.[17]

GATT rules prohibit the use of quantitative restrictions such as quotas or import and export licences. Article XI provides for exceptions to these restrictions. Under Article XI, countries are allowed to impose trade restrictions if they experience shortages of essential products or where it is necessary for trade in commodities or agricultural or fisheries products.

However, it is doubtful whether parties can use this exception on environmental grounds. Governments may take measures for export restrictions for the following reasons:

1 Protection of natural resources and endangered species.
2 Promotion of higher-value-added downstream industries.

3 Upgrading the quality of export products.
4 Ensuring adequate supply of 'essential products'.[18]

Measures taken by countries for the attainment of environmental objectives may violate the GATT Article XI. A case in point is *Canada – Measures Affecting Exports of Unprocessed Herring and Salmon.*[19] In this case, the United States alleged that Canada's prohibition on the export of unprocessed pink and sockeye salmon and herring contravened Article XI and was intended to protect domestic fish processors by preventing foreign competitors from gaining access to Canadian fish. Canada claimed that the measures were an integral and long-standing component of its fisheries conservation and management regime, and were thus justified under Article XI para. 2(b) and Article XX(g). It was significant that the export prohibitions did not limit access to herring or salmon supplies in general and that the purchase of unprocessed fish was limited in the cases of foreign purchasers only – not in the cases of domestic processors and consumers. It was on the basis of this information that the Panel found that, since the prohibition applied to all unprocessed salmon and herring, the Canadian argument that the prohibition was necessary to prevent the export of unprocessed salmon and herring not meeting its quality standards did not stand. Thus the export prohibitions could not be considered 'necessary to the application of standards' within the meaning of Article XI 2(b), nor could they be considered to consist of 'regulations for the marketing' of the goods in international trade within the meaning of Article XI 2(b).

Countries which impose export restrictions while tackling the uncontrolled exploitation of natural resources may violate their GATT obligations under Article XI. In developing countries, governments might want to use such restrictions to ensure the availability of domestic resources, or to stop the uncontrolled exploitation of those resources. This situation is illustrated by the Indonesian measures which were imposed in 1986 to restrict the export of unprocessed rattan and proposed for imposition on semi-processed rattan from 1 January 1989.[20] These measures were imposed in an attempt to impact the uncontrolled exploitation of forest resources and to address shortages in the availability of rattan. The European Union (EU) raised the matter in GATT, expressing its concern that the Indonesian prohibition on exports did not conform to GATT Article XI. Indonesia argued that the measures were justified under the provisions of Part IV of GATT and Article XI 2(a). During the bilateral discussions, the EU persuaded Indonesia to replace the prohibition with taxes on exports which were more consistent with GATT rules than export restrictions. This example shows that developing countries, while taking measures to protect their natural resources, may come under GATT scrutiny for violations of their obligations under Article XI.

Implications of GATT core principles for the environment

The Most Favoured Nation (Article I) and National Treatment (Article III) principles

As stated above, the Most Favoured Nation clause requires a party to treat like products alike and not to discriminate between trading partners of like products. In line with this principle, countries should not discriminate between domestic and foreign producers by introducing trade restrictions.

The prerequisites for the parties to qualify for equal treatment under Articles I and III hinge on the satisfaction of the criteria for a 'like product'. An examination of the meaning of this phrase is essential to an understanding of the MFN and national treatment principles and their impact upon the environment. The phrase, 'like product', has been the subject of considerable debate in the area of environmental protection because national health and safety standards often restrict the use of polluting or environmentally harmful goods, such as non-recyclable items, products that emit ozone-depleting gases or harmful chemicals.[21] The debate centres around the question of how the likeness of a product may be determined.

Traditionally, the term, 'like products' refers to products with similar physical characteristics. According to the WTO a 'like product' is a product which is alike in all respects to the product under consideration. In the absence of such a product, a 'like product' is one which has characteristics closely resembling those of the product under consideration.[22]

Whether a product is like another is typically determined on a case-by-case basis and any concrete principles based on past precedent is largely non-existent. Nonetheless, the interpretive process of WTO dispute resolution has established that the term 'like product' refers to the nature of the product itself and not its process and production methods ('PPMs').[23] Similarly, like products may not be distinguished on the basis of the manufacturing process so long as the physical characteristics are same. As a result, a product cannot be treated differently because it is produced using an environmentally damaging production process rather than an environmentally friendly one.[24]

In 1971 a GATT industrial pollution study concluded that the low price of goods produced in a state that lacks environmental regulations is simply part of that country's competitive advantage, and may not be viewed as unfair.[25] This interpretation remains popular in its support by developing countries whose lower environmental standards may provide them with much-needed cost advantages and export market access.[26] Developing countries fear that a shift away from this approach towards the definition of like products on the basis of PPMs is likely to be used as a protectionist measure by developed countries.

GATT Article III restricts taxes that afford protection to domestic production. Consequently a nation cannot provide subsidies for a product which is made according to a strict environmental process to make that product more competitive, nor can it favour imports from countries with sound environmental regulation. Environmentalists argue that distinguishing products based on PPMs will help internalize environmental costs. However, the challenge is to find an interpretation of like products that ensures developing countries have continued access to export markets whilst allowing industrialized countries to address their own unsustainable consumption patterns and provide the South with necessary financial, technological and capacity-building assistance to do the same.[27]

The limited, PPM-exclusive interpretation of 'like product' first appeared in the Tuna–Dolphin dispute in 1991. In this case Mexico challenged US restrictions on the import of tuna acquired using methods that had the likely capacity to harm dolphins. Mexico argued that the Mexican tuna and the tuna available in US markets were like products and that US restrictions were discriminating against the Mexican product. The significance of this dispute in relation to the subsequent evolution of the trade–environment debate in the global trading regime is reflected by those commentators who are of the opinion that 'if there is one thing that kick-started the Trade and Environment debate, it is the decisions of the GATT dispute settlement panels in the Tuna–Dolphin cases'.[28]

The GATT Panel ruled that Article III, in so far as it dealt with the national treatment principle, covered only those measures that are applied to products as such. Thus, where the physical characteristics of a product were the same, differential treatment on the basis of any other factor was held to be inconsistent with the national treatment principle.[29] As a result the US *Marine Mammal Protection Act* 1972 regulations were held to be in violation of Article III because they treated the Mexican products less favourably than the domestic US products despite the fact that incidental capture rates in no way affected tuna as a final product. The GATT Panel concluded that 'a contracting party may not restrict imports of a product merely because they originate in a country with environmental policies different from its own'.[30] The Panel went on to declare that:

> Article III:4 calls for a comparison of the treatment of imported tuna as a product with that of domestic tuna as a product. Regulations governing the taking of dolphin's incidental to the taking of tuna could not possibly affect tuna as a product. Article III:4 therefore obliges the United States to accord treatment to Mexican tuna no less favourable than that accorded to United States tuna, whether or not the incidental taking of dolphins by Mexican vessels corresponds to that of United States vessels.[31]

In keeping with the *Tuna–Dolphin case*, the *Thai Cigarettes case*,[32] the *Canadian Fisheries case*,[33] the *Danish Beer Bottle case*[34] and the *Reformulated Gasoline case*[35] have all indicated that discriminatory trade practices will not be tolerated under GATT, even if there is some justification for them on environmental, health or conservation grounds.[36] The non-discrimination principle, with its narrow scope, does not permit parties to impose import or export restrictions for the sake of environmental protection without violating GATT obligations. This situation leads parties to rely on the exceptions to their obligations when adopting trade-related environmental measures.

Environmentalism in GATT

Environmental exceptions to GATT: Article XX

Despite the fact that GATT predates the modern era of environmentalism and ecological sustainability, the Agreement contains a number of provisions that, on superficial examination, appear to support an approach to trade that is quite conservation-based. Most notably, the GATT exceptions contained in Article XX permit a party to restrict or prohibit imports through employing trade measures in a manner that departs from a party's GATT obligations under certain conditions. To qualify as exempt pursuant to Article XX, trade measures must be:

1 Necessary to protect human, animal or plant life or health (Article XX.b); or
2 Related to the conservation of exhaustible natural resources if such measures are made effective in conjunction with restrictions on domestic production or consumption (Article XXg).

A party must also satisfy the following requirements in the application of the above measures:

1 The measure/s cannot be applied to discriminate arbitrarily or unjustifiably between countries where the same conditions prevail.
2 They must be necessary i.e. exhausting all less trade restrictive alternatives.
3 They must not be a disguised restriction on international trade.

Article XX(b), protection of human, animal and plant life or health

Article XX(b) allows trade-related environmental measures where they are necessary to protect human, animal or plant life or health. However, the operation and interpretation of Article XX(b) have created debates among trade and environment interest groups. Concerns arising out of the operation of Article XX(b) are discussed below with special reference to GATT Panel reports.

Necessary test under Article XX.1(b)

Article XX.1(b) permits a party to invoke the exceptions if they are 'necessary to protect human, animal or plant life or health' but two conditions must be met for that purpose:

1 They may not discriminate between parties arbitrarily or unjustifiably.
2 They may not be disguised trade restrictions.

The necessity requirement for the measure for which the exception is being invoked has created controversy. In order to pass the necessity test, a party is required to demonstrate that they have exhausted the alternative, GATT-consistent or less inconsistent options and that the measure in question involves the least degree of inconsistency with GATT provisions. In other words, as long as reasonably alternative measures, or measures that are not inconsistent with GATT, are available these measures are expected to be employed and consequently a party cannot adopt another measure of a different nature and then justify its adoption as 'necessary'.

In the 1991 *Tuna–Dolphin case*,[37] the Panel examined the US prohibition on imports of certain tuna and tuna products from Mexico. The United States argued that the measures were necessary to protect dolphin life and health and no measure other than trade sanctions was reasonably available to them to achieve this objective. However, the Panel found that US trade measures were not necessary because the average incidental capture rate for foreign fisherman was tied only arbitrarily to the US average incidental capture rate and thus it could not be definitively stated that the regulations were necessary to protect dolphins.[38] The Panel found no evidence that the US had exhausted all options, particularly the option of negotiating international cooperative arrangements that would have been consistent with GATT, before resorting to restrictive trade measures. This was especially true given that international cooperative arrangements would seem to be desirable in view of the fact that dolphins roam the waters of many states and the high seas.[39]

The Panel considered that the United States' measures, even if Article XX(b) were interpreted to permit extra jurisdictional protection of life and health, would not meet the requirement of necessity set out in that provision. The United States had not demonstrated to the Panel – as required of the party invoking an Article XX exception – that it had exhausted all options reasonably available to it to pursue its dolphin protection objectives through measures consistent with the General Agreement.

The term 'necessary' was interpreted to mean that no alternative to trade measures was available. In *Tuna–Dolphin II*, the US ban on tuna imports from intermediate countries was challenged by the EU. The EU contended that the US ban violated Articles III and XI of GATT. The United States imposed a ban in accordance with the US *Marine Mammal Protection Act* to prevent intermediary third countries from selling tuna to the US market. The US once again argued that the ban was necessary to protect dolphins and justified this action under Article XX(b). The Panel, in examining the application of Article XX(b), considered the meaning of the term 'necessary' to determine whether US actions were necessary to protect dolphins. However, the Panel noted that, in the ordinary meaning of the term, 'necessary' meant that no alternative existed. This explanation had its origin in the Article XX(d) interpretation of the Panel in the *United States – Section 337 of the Tariff Act of 1930 case*.[40] In that case, the Panel examined the use of the term 'necessary' in Article XX(d) and decided that:

> a contracting party cannot justify a measure inconsistent with another GATT provision as 'necessary' in terms of Article XX(d) if an alternative

> measure which it could reasonably be expected to employ and which is not inconsistent with other GATT measures is available to it. By the same token, in cases where a measure consistent with other GATT provisions is not reasonably available, a contracting party is bound to use, among the measures reasonably available to it, that which entails the least degree of inconsistency with other GATT provisions.[41]

The term 'necessary' was interpreted similarly in the *Thai Cigarette case*.[42] In this case the Panel was established to examine a complaint by the United States about certain import licensing restrictions and internal taxes on cigarettes which it believed were inconsistent with Articles III and XI of GATT. Thailand argued that the import ban fell within the scope of Article XX(b) as the measures were necessary to protect human life and health. The Panel found that Thailand's practice of permitting the sale of domestic cigarettes while not permitting the importation of foreign cigarettes was not necessary within the meaning of Article XX(b). The Panel agreed that smoking constituted a serious risk to human health and that measures designed to reduce the consumption of cigarettes fell within the scope of XX(b). But it followed the interpretation of the term 'necessary' in the *US Section 337* case and concluded that:

> the import ban imposed by Thailand could be considered to be necessary only if there were no alternative measures consistent with GATT or less inconsistent with it which Thailand could reasonably be expected to employ to achieve its health policy objective.[43]

Since Thailand had other measures reasonably available to it, the Panel decided that the trade measures involving import restrictions and internal discriminatory taxes levied by Thailand were not 'necessary'.

The proportionality test

In order to fulfil the requirement of 'necessity' in invoking Article XX(b), a party must ensure that the measures adopted constitute a reasonable, proportionate relationship to the conservation policy or the public health policy. In 1989 the GATT Council laid down substantive guidelines on the application of Article XX(b) which provide that:

> A measure taken by an importing contracting party should not be any more severe, and should not remain in force any longer than necessary to protect the human, animal or plant life or health involved, as provided in Article XX(b).[44]

It was perhaps this proportionality requirement to which the panel in the *Tuna–Dolphin* case was referring when it held that the method of calculating the maximum incidental dolphin capture rate was too unpredictable for trade measures to be regarded as necessary to protect the health or life of dolphins.[45] This proportionality test was also deployed in the *Danish Beer Bottle* case, in which the Panel stated that trade measures should not be disproportionate to their objective and should be least disruptive to trade.[46]

Clearly, the above case studies indicate that the 'necessary' requirement has been a substantial barrier to the justification of legitimate environmental protection measures. The requirement gives the WTO the authority to determine sensitive relative issues such as proportionality and 'less inconsistent alternative', irrespective of the need and urgency of a situation. As noted by McDonald, the assessment of suitable alternatives is a subjective determination, making the requirement to exhaust all such remedies an onerous stipulation.[47]

Although the 'necessary' requirement demands that a party must use the measure that entails the least degree of inconsistency with GATT, it did not set out any guidelines for the determination of the method involving the least degree of inconsistency with other GATT provisions. The result is a situation with great potential for mischief-makers. Charnovitz gives the novel illustration that bans on importing ivory could be challenged on the ground that a more effective (and more GATT-consistent) way to save African elephants is to privatize them.[48]

The 'least restrictive' interpretation of the necessary requirement in Article XX(b) has also been criticized by both trade and environmental groups. It is argued that the least trade-restrictive interpretation does not correspond with the ordinary meaning of 'necessary' in Article XX(b), which focuses on the need for measures to achieve the goal of environmental protection and not on its effect on international trade.[49] As indicated by the above discussion, to date the attitude of various GATT panels towards the interpretation of the term 'necessary' has resulted in an overwhelmingly restrictive application of the Article XX exceptions. The Panel has on many occasions identified measures as not 'necessary' but has not specifically identified less GATT-inconsistent measures which could have been used to protect the environment. Looking forward, it is suggested that GATT dispute settlement panels should take into account the intent of Article XX and should strike a balance between the policy goals of liberal trade and the more environmentally and socially oriented goals encapsulated by Article XX.

Article XX(g) – Protection of Exhaustible Natural Resources

The Article XX(g) exception allows a party to take action when it is necessary to conserve exhaustible natural resources. GATT Panels' interpretations have established that trade measures must satisfy four requirements in order to qualify as an Article XX(g) exception:

1. The particular trade measure must be 'primarily aimed at' the conservation of exhaustible natural resources. As discussed below, the GATT Panel interpreted 'relating to conservation of natural resources' to mean 'primarily aimed at' the conservation of natural resources.
2. It must be made effective in 'conjunction with restrictions on domestic production or consumption'.

3 It must not be arbitrary or unjustifiable discrimination between countries where the same conditions prevail.
4 It must not be a disguised restriction on international trade.

'Primarily aimed at'

The requirement that a trade measure must be primarily aimed at the related conservation purpose was confirmed in the *Tuna II* Panel report.[50] In this case, the US trade measure was not primarily aimed at conservation, because it was based on unpredictable factors such as the incidental capture rate of US vessels, not to any objective standard of dolphin death.

In the US *Automobile Taxes* case, it was decided that the less favourable treatment of foreign cars did not conserve gasoline and was not primarily aimed at the conservation of natural resources.[51]

In the *Canadian Herring and Salmon* dispute, the United States brought a complaint against a Canadian ban on the export of unprocessed herring and salmon.[52] The Panel decided that in order to rely successfully on an Article XX(g) exception, a trade measure had to be primarily aimed at the conservation of natural resources. Canada's export ban on foreign processors and consumers was not considered to be aimed primarily at conservation due to the fact that domestic production and consumption of unprocessed herring and salmon was permitted. Canada's favour of the domestic processor over foreign ones meant that it also failed the 'in conjunction with' test which required that Canada employ the measure against domestic production and consumption at the same time.

Despite this definitive interpretation of the term 'primarily aimed at', the Panels' interpretations of Article XX(g) have left many questions unanswered. It is not clear whether the term 'exhaustible natural resources' covers only commercially valuable resources or all exhaustible natural resources. There have been suggestions that Article XX(g) was inserted to authorize contracting parties to take measures to conserve commercially valuable resources to ensure their availability for future use in international trade.[53] To date, no party has been able to satisfy all the elements of Article XX(g), so it is impossible to anticipate the circumstances in which these tests will be met. It seems clear that the Article XX(g) exception for the conservation of exhaustible natural resources will continue to be interpreted with the same preference for free trade as has the interpretation of Article XX(b)'s health and safety exception.[54]

The chapeau to Article XX

No arbitrary or unjustifiable discrimination and disguised restriction

The chapeau (otherwise known as the introductory paragraphs) to Article XX states that trade measures must not constitute a means of arbitrary or unjustifiable discrimination between countries where the same conditions prevail, nor may they be disguised restrictions on international trade.

'The same situation' connotation of the chapeau seems to include the use of, not only identical, but similar measures. The inclusion of the word 'similar' could be construed as a recognition and circumvention of the loophole contained in the Article XX preamble.[55] For example, in the *Shrimp-Turtle* dispute, the Appellate Body decided that the US measure served a legitimate environmental objective under Article XX(g) but that its discriminatory application constituted an arbitrary and unjustifiable discrimination and as such it was incompatible with the requirement of the chapeau of Article XX.[56]

In the 1982 Panel Report on the *US Prohibitions of Imports of Tuna and Tuna Products*, the Panel interpreted the phrase 'disguised restriction' and concluded that publication of a trade measure was sufficient to prevent that measure being considered a 'disguised restriction'.[57] This interpretation was criticized in subsequent GATT practice because the function of the prohibition on disguised restrictions is not only to ensure transparency, but to supplement the prohibition on unjustifiable discrimination among GATT Contracting Parties via a prohibition on the indirect protection of domestic producers.[58]

Extraterritoriality

GATT does not permit trade measures which are directed against environmental conditions outside of a country's own territory. In other words, a nation is allowed to set environmental policies within its territorial boundary, but it may not use trade measures to enforce its environmental standards beyond its territorial boundary. Such a provision is in conformity with the longstanding international law pillar of state sovereignty. In its 1992 Study on Trade and Environment, the GATT Secretariat emphasized that:

> when the environmental problem is due to production and consumption activities in another country, the GATT rules are more of a constraint, since they prohibit making market access dependent on changes in the domestic policies or practices of the exporting country ... If the door were opened to trade policies unilaterally ... the trading system would start down a very slippery slope...[59]

The *Tuna–Dolphin I* Panel decided that any measures taken to control the production and consumption of exhaustible natural resources can only be effective to the extent that the production or consumption is under its jurisdiction.[60] This view was based on the drafting history of the article which indicated that the concerns of the drafters of Article XX(b) focused on the use of sanitary measures to safeguard life or health of humans, animals or plants within the jurisdiction of the importing country. It further noted that any broad interpretation of Article XX(b) (as suggested by the United States) would authorize contracting parties to unilaterally determine 'the life or health protection policies' from which other contracting parties could not deviate without jeopardizing their rights under the General Agreement.

The *Tuna Panel II* decided that governments could enforce an Article XX(g) restriction extraterritorially only against their own nationals and vessels.[61]

The drafters of GATT were also concerned about the far-reaching implications of the unilateral use of trade measures. To allow each country to determine unilaterally the environmental conditions beyond its jurisdiction would result in interference with the sovereignty of nation states and invite unrest and possible retaliation. This extra-jurisdictional use of trade measures would give large markets the economic leverage to impose their national socio-economic policies upon smaller countries by forcing them to change their policies and thus reducing international trade to a power-based regime. The limitation of the scope of the extraterritorial provision in Article XX is beneficial in preventing or at least attempting to prevent developed countries taking unilateral measures against developing countries for having lower environmental standards. However, the GATT rules seem to have restricted member powers to the combat of transboundary environmental problems in areas which lie outside the legal jurisdiction of any particular country, even where the effect is global.

Environmental measures addressing transboundary or global environmental problems should, as far as possible, be based on an international consensus. However, in the absence of an effective international institution that mandates sound environmental policies and has the requisite powers of enforcement, the limitation of the extraterritorial scope of Article XX has left nations without an instrument to handle global environmental problems.

Scope of Article XX

A review of Article XX shows that although it was fashioned to cover environmental exceptions, its scope has been narrowed by the inclusion of different conditions and distorted interpretations. In addition, narrow interpretations of the plain meaning of the exceptions may ultimately make them high hurdles to those seeking to implement environmentally protective trade measures. The cases which have to date sought to interpret the Article XX(b) and XX(g) exceptions have shown that an extremely limited variety of trade restrictions which *prima facie* violate various GATT principles will be upheld as legitimate exceptions on the grounds that they were set in place to protect the environment.[62]

Environmentalism in the WTO

The WTO is considered to be an improvement on GATT in the context of environmental protection. The WTO contains two agreements concerning national laws on environment and public health. They are the *Agreement on Technical Barriers to Trade* ('TBT') and the *Agreement on the Application of Sanitary and Phytosanitary Measures* ('SPS').[63] However, there are also other WTO agreements[64] that contain provisions dealing with the environment. The following section outlines the impact of the operation of the WTO Agreements on developing countries and the consequences for sustainable development.

However, this section does not intend to be exhaustive with respect to all the WTO Agreements that have environmental implications. This section deals only with the environmental implications of the TBT and SPS Agreements, the *Agreement on Agriculture*, the *Agreement on Textiles and Clothing*, *GATS*, the *TRIPs Agreement* and the *Agreement on Subsidies and Countervailing Measures*. This section also examines the roles of the WTO Dispute Settlement Body and the Committee on Trade and Environment.

The WTO Agreement on Technical Barriers to Trade

The *Technical Barriers to Trade ('TBT') Agreement* deals with product regulations relating to quality, size and performance. Where these regulations are mandatory, they are referred to as technical regulations, and where they are optional, they are referred to as standards.[65] They are mechanisms that both governments and non-government bodies use to specify the characteristics that products must conform to, for reasons of safety, health, or for environmental purposes.

Overall, the *TBT Agreement* was designed to combat the trade distorting effects of different national regulations on products. It does this by encouraging the adoption of international standards, while at the same time allowing individual members to impose their own standards where appropriate.[66] In this sense, it can be said to be liberalizing trade in accordance with the Ricardian model by decreasing certain non-tariff barriers to trade. By doing this, states with a comparatively higher level of productivity will face less restrictions in exporting their goods to markets with comparatively lower levels of productivity. According to the Ricardian model, this will benefit both the exporting state (by increasing their income) and the importing state (by decreasing the price they have to pay for certain goods).

The *TBT Agreement* defines a technical regulation as a document which lays down 'product characteristics, or their related processes and production methods'.[67] In *EC – Asbestos*, the appellate body suggested that a product characteristic may include 'any objectively definable "features", "qualities", "attributes", or other "distinguishing mark" of a product'.[68]

However, the Agreement only covers technical regulations and standards that constitute '*related* processes and production methods'.[69] This phrase would seem to indicate that only those regulations or standards which affect the final characteristics of a product would be covered by the *TBT Agreement*. The more common non-product-related PPMs, such as pollution emission standards, would not be covered by the Agreement.

As a result, an importing member can impose non-product-related PPMs without contravening the *TBT Agreement*. As Gaines noted, these non-product-related PPMs are often used to regulate the acquisition of primary resources, and have regulated the practices of fisheries, farms, loggers, miners and hunters.[70] Given that developing countries often rely heavily on their primary industries for economic development, there is a strong potential for this aspect of the *TBT Agreement* to disadvantage them.

This would also appear to be contrary to the Ricardian model in so far as these non-product-related PPMs are able to give rise to trade restrictions. This is because the TBT Agreement will make it more difficult for comparatively efficient exporters to gain access to markets with these regulations, and thus competition will be inhibited. In essence, trade is being denied not on the grounds of comparative productivity, but rather on a (potentially) arbitrary ground of not complying with a certain non-product-related PPM.

The Preamble to the *TBT Agreement*, as well as Articles 2.2, 5.1.2, 12.2, 12.7 and Annex 3, read together, emphasize that international and domestic standards, regulations and conformity assessment procedures should not constitute an 'unnecessary obstacle to international trade'. This requirement is interesting in that it appears to delineate the point at which the Ricardian model is displaced for other concerns. Where there is a pressing non-trade concern, such as serious environmental degradation, the desired benefits of the Ricardian model are outweighed by the negative effects of allowing the non-trade concern to continue unaddressed. However, the Ricardian model will remain in place where to address the supposed non-trade concern via trade measures would be an 'unnecessary obstacle to international trade'.

However, there are many ways in which this phrase may be interpreted. It may be interpreted widely, and therefore give preference to the notion that the creation of international standards, *prima facie*, leads to distortions in the international market. This is because consumers are denied choice in regard to the characteristics of goods or services that they wish to purchase. Alternatively, a narrow interpretation would give preference to the concern that a lack of international standards may lead to environmental deterioration, and long-term economic decline.

As discussed in the previous part, GATT Article XX contains certain grounds upon which a barrier to trade may be created in order to pursue environmental objectives. It is not entirely clear whether or not these provisions are a part of the *TBT Agreement*, and therefore it is difficult to determine whether a wide or narrow approach to the phrase 'unnecessary obstacle to international trade' should be adopted.[71]

Article 2 of the *TBT Agreement* states that something may be said to not constitute an unnecessary obstacle to trade if the measure is 'not more trade restrictive than necessary to fulfil a *legitimate objective*'. The Agreement goes on to provide a non-exhaustive list of such legitimate objectives, and includes measures designed to protect human health and safety, as well as animal and plant life, and the environment. However, this definition does not eliminate ambiguity in regards to what will constitute an unnecessary obstacle to international trade. For example, the recent European Community ('EC') labelling requirements in regards to the use of genetically modified organisms in products may or may not fall within the legitimate objectives exception. This is because consumer preferences are not contained in the list of legitimate objectives in the *TBT Agreement*.[72] However, if the EC could establish that the labelling requirements relate to human health and safety, then the regulations would not contravene the Agreement.[73]

The relationship between this principle and the Ricardian model is uneasy. Strictly speaking, allowing a so-called legitimate objective to be used to apply trade restrictions would contravene the Ricardian model. The use of trade barriers to inhibit competition would prevent comparatively more productive firms from exporting their goods. On the other hand, the application of trade measures to pursue a legitimate objective may simply be recognition of the fact that there are non-market costs to the production of certain items. For example, although it is a reality that is rendered invisible by the rigid confines of the Ricardian model, environmental deterioration may be an inevitable consequence of a certain production technique, and the only way to remedy this is to change the technique, and in the process expend resources. This has the effect of reducing productivity. Thus, an environmentally damaging method may often be more productive in the Ricardian sense than the environmentally sound method. The use of trade measures in order to impose a cost on environmentally polluting industries may be consistent with the Ricardian model in that it provides a more holistic view of the true cost (market and environmental) of producing a good, and hence true productivity, rather than relying simply on the producer's production costs as the best indicator of productivity.

The WTO TBT Committee has created a set of principles and procedures that bodies should observe when developing international standards, guidelines or recommendations. Among other things, the principles state that the process should be transparent, and membership to the body must be open to all WTO Committee members. More important, the international standards 'should not distort the global market, have adverse effects on fair competition, or stifle innovation and technological development'.[74]

As with the *TBT Agreement*, the TBT Committee has decided that preference ought not to be given to the characteristics of a good from a particular country or region. That is, the international standard, ideally, should be performance based, and not based on certain design characteristics that are specific to certain countries or regions. This is consistent with the Ricardian model in that it requires that producers compete with each other purely on the grounds of quality and productivity, rather than an arbitrary selection based on geographical location or political preference.

The TBT Committee has also indicated that the difficulties faced by developing countries in participating in the development of international standards, should be 'taken into consideration'.[75] The Committee has encouraged developed members to provide technical assistance in accordance with Article 11 of the *TBT Agreement*, to facilitate developing member's involvement in the international standardization process.

As noted above, Article 2.4 encourages members to adopt international standards where appropriate. However, the article further states that a contracting party is under no obligation to use the relevant international standards if to do so would be 'inappropriate or ineffective' to fulfil a 'legitimate objective'. This list applies only to the appropriateness of a technical regulation or measure, and does not aid in the definition of whether the measure constitutes an unnecessary obstacle to trade.

The preamble to the *TBT Agreement* also emphasizes that the imposition of standards and technical regulations by individual members must not constitute 'unjustifiable discrimination between countries where the same conditions prevail'. This appears to be recognizing that the GATT principles of 'Most Favoured Nation' and 'National Treatment' are indeed incorporated into the *TBT Agreement*.

The *TBT Agreement* has made special provision for developing countries in relation to international standards and regulations. Article 12.4 recognizes that while international standards may exist, developing members may adopt 'certain technical regulations, standards, or conformity assessment procedures aimed at preserving indigenous technology and production methods'. As a result, developing members are not required to use 'international standards as a basis for their technical regulations … which are not appropriate to their development, financial and trade needs'.

Despite these principles, in practice, the legitimate objectives exception can be used as an excuse for members to in fact introduce *more* stringent regulations, even if settled international standards exist. The requirements of the *TBT Agreement* regarding standards should thus be regarded as a floor rather than a ceiling.[76] Once again, these standards will need to be imposing a non-market (for example, environmental) cost on the producer that they would not otherwise face in their cost of production in order to be consistent with the Ricardian model.

The WTO Agreement on the Application of Sanitary and Phytosanitary Measures

The *Sanitary and Phytosanitary ('SPS') Agreement* is concerned with the application of food safety, animal and plant health regulations. The Agreement applies to 'all sanitary and phytosanitary measures which may, directly or indirectly, affect international trade'.[77]

The Preamble and Article 3.1 encourage WTO member countries to use international standards, guidelines and recommendations where they exist. However, both Article 5.5 and the Preamble require that members should avoid arbitrary or unjustifiable discrimination between countries where the same conditions prevail. In this sense, the SPS measures must be consistent with GATT's non-discrimination principles of MFN and national treatment, and they may not be used as a disguised restriction on international trade.[78] Similarly, the SPS measures may not be used if another, less restrictive measure is reasonably available which will achieve the appropriate level of protection.[79]

Article 2.1 recognizes the right of individual governments to take SPS measures. However, Article 2.1 states that the measures must be 'necessary for the protection of human, animal, or plant life or health'. Furthermore, Article 2.3 states that the risk to human, animals or plants must be based on 'scientific principles, and not maintained without sufficient scientific evidence'.

The requirement of 'sufficient scientific evidence' introduces a certain level of ambiguity into the *SPS Agreement*, because scientists are often not unanimous on all issues. The ambiguity of this concept may in turn provide developed countries with the opportunity to apply non-tariff barriers in the guise of advanced SPS technologies. The agreement also does not deal with import restrictions aimed at protecting the global commons of a foreign environment.

In the absence of sufficient scientific evidence, a government may provisionally adopt a precautionary restriction[80] under Article 5.7. However, the government imposing the precautionary measure must seek further information within a reasonable period of time.

The precautionary principle is not unique to the SPS Agreement, and has its expression in the *Rio Declaration on Environment and Development*.[81] Under Article 15 of the *Rio Declaration*, where there is a lack of scientific certainty in regard to the effect a good or practice may have on the environment, states have the discretion to engage cost effective measures to prevent environmental degradation. The test for the exercise of this discretion is where there is a 'threat of serious or irreversible' environmental damage.

However, what constitutes a threat of serious or irreversible damage is open to interpretation. Specifically, the seriousness of a threat to the environment is highly subjective and inextricably linked to the context in which it is being considered. This is because the environmental standards partly depend on the level of economic development of the country in question. As a result, a particular measure undertaken in response to a perceived threat of serious environmental damage may be financially viable and justifiable in a developed country, but on the other hand impose disproportionate economic costs on an impoverished developing country. The *SPS Agreement*, however, does not recognize the fact that often there will be asymmetric economic impacts of particular environmental measures.

On a wide reading of the Ricardian model, the threat of environmental damage could be factored into the comparative cost of production/productivity by viewing it as a potential future cost that would be discounted to the present. That said, quantifying the cost of 'serious environmental damage' is highly problematic by virtue of its subjectivity and thus the uncertainty it creates. Thus, there is the potential for states to apply massive trade sanctions to guard against a threat of environmental damage that they perceive to be high, but developing countries believe to be either low or at least overshadowed by the desperate needs to achieve greater degrees of poverty alleviation through economic development. This demonstrates one of the serious limitations of the Ricardian model, that is, the assumption that all costs are perfectly known, including costs of production, opportunity costs and environmental costs and that they can be factored into the international market is completely unrealistic. This is where the generalization that liberalized trade will always leave countries better-off because higher levels of trade will lead to higher levels of productivity begins to unravel. The effect of entirely free trade here would be to provoke a 'race to the bottom' in terms of environmental standards. When one firm employs a cheaper, more polluting method, another firm will employ an even cheaper and even more polluting method, and so on. Consequently, the final effect of strict adherence to the Ricardian model may be to not only destroy the environment, but also in the long term undermine international trade due to the over-exploitation of natural resources.

Also, while the *SPS Agreement* emphasizes the need for risk and scientific assessment, developing countries often lack the capacity to adequately access and assess the scientific evidence upon which a measure is based. Without access to scientific expertise, developing countries may have difficulty in properly assessing these concepts of scientific risk and serious environmental damage.[82] This problem has been borne out in the WTO dispute settlement mechanism, where developing countries rarely bring complaints regarding SPS and TBT measures because of the related costs including a lack of resources to carry out the scientific tests required.[83]

In order to see the benefits of the *SPS Agreement*, developing countries need to be willing and able to participate fully in the institutions and practices established by it. In order to do this, they require membership of the WTO and the opportunity and expertise to actively participate in the setting of international standards, to ensure that such standards take adequate account of their needs and special circumstances. It is significant that only 64 per cent of least developed countries are members of the WTO,[84] especially in the light of the 92 per cent membership of high-income countries.[85] It is also significant that only 33 per cent of the low and lower middle income countries who are members of the WTO are also members of the international standards organizations known as OIE and Codex Alimentarius. This is compared with 64 per cent membership of upper middle and high income countries.[86] Such disparities in membership distribution are bound to lead to imbalances in organizational policy and the tendency to favour Northern interests is almost inevitable.

Most critical to the operation of the *SPS Agreement* is transparency. In this regard, the agreement requires members to establish specific contact points for the facilitation of communication regarding SPS members, in a single national 'enquiry point' and a national notification agency.[87] As at June 1999, only 65 per cent of low and lower middle income countries had specified an enquiry point, and only 59 per cent had specified a national notification agency. Given the importance of these requirements to the implementation of the *SPS Agreement*, these numbers suggest a critical weakness in the participation of developing countries.[88]

Similarly, during the period from November 1995 to September 1998, almost 50 per cent of developing countries did not attend any of the ten (of twelve) meetings of the SPS Committee for which participant lists were available. Less than 20 per cent of developing countries attended five or more of these meetings. While these low participation levels may be reasonably explained,[89] they are nonetheless another indicator of low levels of participation by developing countries in the institutions and thus the standard setting of the *SPS Agreement*.[90]

Given this largely non-participatory context, it is unsurprising that some developing countries have expressed concern regarding their ability to be effectively involved in the implementation of the *SPS Agreement.* They have suggested that the key issue is not only whether they are able to attend SPS Committee meetings, but whether they are able to understand and contribute to the discussions that take place at such meetings. In essence, shortcomings in delegates' technical and scientific expertise can be a significant hurdle for developing countries to overcome, and therefore participate actively in the *SPS Agreement*.[91]

Under Article 4.1, importing members are required to accept the SPS standards of other members as being equivalent, if the exporting member 'objectively demonstrates … that its measures achieve the importing Members appropriate level' of SPS protection. Developed countries remain reluctant to accept the equivalence of sanitary and phytosanitary measures in developing countries.[92] Developing countries have reported that in several cases, the inspectors of developed importing countries have sought identical specification rather than equivalency.[93] This had two effects. First, it deprives Article 4 of its function, namely to give countries flexibility regarding the measures they adopt, as long as they achieve the same level of sanitary and phytosanitary protection. Second, given that developed countries' sanitary and phytosanitary requirements are generally created with a view to the structure and *modus operandi* of their own domestic industry, they can be incompatible with the production and marketing methods in developing countries.

Unless developed countries are willing to accept equivalency in these cases, developing countries may be required to undertake large-scale investment over extended periods of time in order to comply.[94] This is well illustrated by one of the most in-depth analyses of the impact of SPS requirements on developing country exports of agricultural and food products undertaken so far. The subject of analysis was the Bangladesh frozen shrimp sector. From August to December 1997, the European Commission banned exports of frozen shrimp from Bangladesh over concerns about hygiene standards in processing facilities and the efficiency of controls undertaken by Bangladesh government inspectors.[95] It has been estimated that the result of this ban was lost revenue in the sum of US$14.6 million.[96] The upgrading of sanitary conditions in Bangladesh's frozen shrimp industry has been estimated at US$17.6 million over the period from 1997 to 1998.[97] Further to this initial cost, the ongoing maintenance of the required standards in Bangladesh shrimp plants is likely to cost the industry US$2.2 million per annum and the government expects to pay US$225,000 per annum to maintain a monitoring programme.[98]

Those who cannot afford to implement the changes necessary to adhere to such standards lose what would otherwise be a key instrument in the enhancement of market access for their products.

Article 4.2, allows members to enter into Mutual Recognition Agreements ('MRAs'),[99] under which two countries reciprocally agree to import products meeting the other country's standards, tests, or technical regulations. However, developing countries have only a limited capacity to carry out the functions required in order to gain the necessary certification and accreditation. The result is that only a very small number of MRAs involve developing countries, which in turn limits their ability to access the markets of developed countries.

Under Article 9 of the *SPS Agreement*, developed members 'agree' to provide technical assistance, particularly to developing country members, in order to assist them in attaining the sanitary and phytosanitary protection required for their export markets.[100] Under Article 9.2, importing members should particularly consider providing such assistance where substantial investment would be required in order for the exporting member to fulfil the SPS standards of the importing member.[101] However, developing countries report that the level and type of technical assistance provided to them to facilitate the implementation of the SPS agreement, and/or to comply with the sanitary and phytosanitary requirements of developed countries, often fails to address the day-to-day problems faced by developing countries. Many of these problems relate to overall levels of economic development.[102]

Article 10 of the Agreement allows for the special and differential treatment of developing and particularly least developed countries in the preparation, application and phased introduction of new sanitary and phytosanitary measures in order to maintain opportunities for these members' exports. However, as with the analogous provision in the *TBT Agreement*, the provisions of Article 10 promises made have not led to any substantial financial or technical assistance. Developed countries often appear to be unwilling to provide additional time for developing countries to respond appropriately.[103] Similarly, procedures for the negotiation and agreement of international standards within Codex Alimentarius, OIE and IPPC fail to take account of the needs and special circumstances of developing countries.[104]

The overall picture is that developing countries have been unable to participate actively in the workings of the *SPS Agreement*, and thus are unlikely to see any benefits from it. Their failure/inability to attend SPS Committee meetings means that such meetings have a higher likelihood of being driven by the priorities and agendas of developed countries. In addition, developing countries face a number of other constraints which prevent their full participation in the *SPS Agreement*, such as the notification of new SPS measures, risk assessment and the implementation of international standards. In a survey of developing countries, the most significant constraint to participation was found to be an insufficient ability to assess the implications of the sanitary and phytosanitary requirements of developed countries following notification. Other major constraints were considered to be insufficient ability to participate effectively in the dispute settlement procedures, and the demonstration of equivalence of domestic SPS measures.[105] In a 1999 survey of low and lower middle income countries, it is significant that the greatest impediment to exports to the EU, Australia and the United States was considered to be SPS requirements.[106]

North–South tensions in the SPS and TBT agreements

Developing countries feel that both the SPS and the TBT agreements are dominated by the interests of developed countries, and also that the various committees and decision-making processes lack their input, and make great use of multilaterally established standards determined by an economically/politically skewed process.[107]

The authenticity of these concerns is illustrated by the fact that, until recently, debate in standard-setting bodies such as the International Organization for Standardization ('ISO') and the Codex Alimentarius Commission was exclusively the domain of rich, technologically advanced nations. This has resulted in a set of international standards which have largely failed to take into account the characteristics/technology/production methods of products typically exported by developing countries,[108] and which often require developing countries to adhere to standards more appropriate for their industrialized counterparts. This process has been labelled 'techno-imperialism' by some observers.[109]

Some developing countries argue that current rules still give developed countries too much discretion when it comes to setting standards. It has been argued that, in the aftermath of the liberalization undertaken during the Uruguay Round, many nations have simply replaced protectionist tariffs with less obvious but equally restrictive non-tariff barriers.[110] These include the use and enforcement of stringent technical standards, which in turn impose substantial financial costs on developing countries which may undermine their trading competitiveness. However, whether such higher standards are a reflection of a community's concerns for their health and environment, or are an attempt to protect domestic industries, is often difficult to tell. Product standards for example, are often determined on moral values to which certain groups attach importance, and which values may not be understood by other countries of different income and poverty levels.[111]

As was significantly remarked in *Agenda 21* of the United Nations Conference on Environment and Development, 'standards that are valid in the most advanced countries may be inappropriate and of unwarranted social cost for developing countries'.[112] For the purposes of the Ricardian model, a trade barrier will have the same negative effects on competition, regardless of whether it is tariff or non-tariff. An impossible question is then raised: when should the goal of free trade be displaced in favour of environmental protection? It would seem, given the above analysis, that developed countries will tend to favour environmental protection, and developing countries will favour free trade.

The Agreement on Agriculture

Agriculture and agricultural trade are economically important for virtually all regions of the world. While highly industrialized economies such as the United States are overwhelmingly dominant as both exporters and importers of agricultural products, the relative importance of agricultural trade to domestic and regional economies in Asia, Latin America and Africa is rising.[113] In these countries, approximately 2 billion small-scale farmers still live a traditional agricultural way of life in which ecological sustainability is the absolute and immediate prerequisite for economic survival.[114] Because of their relatively lower wages and greater land area, developing countries also tend to have a comparative advantage in the production of primary agricultural products.

While agriculture is important from an economic perspective, its environmental consequences can be equally as serious. For example, in many countries, the largest single use of water is irrigation.[115] Also, agricultural run-off and seepage of fertilizers and pesticides are major sources of groundwater pollution.[116] Changing patterns of land use, for example from forest to agriculture, can destroy the habitats of plant and animal species. Intensive livestock operations in many countries have grown so large that they pose major problems of waste management and disposal, and are sources of air and water pollution.[117]

While the *WTO Agreement on Agriculture* does not directly address environment-related issues, it has allowed WTO members, which as noted in discussion of the SPS Agreement are predominantly from the North, to continue to provide subsidies to their farmers. This seems to be entirely contrary to achieving the goals of the Ricardian model. The *Agreement on Agriculture* also allows for the creation of specific agreements by member states in order to improve market access, and reduce trade-distorting subsidies in agriculture with the ultimate goal of trade liberalization.[118] Under this Agreement, domestic support measures whose trade-distorting effects are minimal are excluded from the requirement to reduce protection measures. These measures include expenditure incurred under environmental protection programmes, provided that they meet certain conditions.

It is notable that the Agreement did not provide for the creation of a global trading system which could accommodate the development of environmentally compatible agriculture.[119] The farm subsidies and trade protections employed by developed countries in accordance with the *Agreement on Agriculture* are increasingly forcing developing countries to employ environmentally unsound practices such as deforestation, the intensification of production, monoculture, the overexploitation of soil, the expansion of farming to biodiversity-rich areas and the use of fertilizers and pesticides. The incentives to undertake such overproduction are huge: in 2001, OECD countries provided a total of US$311 billion in subsidies to the agricultural sector.[120] This exceeded the total amount of foreign aid given to all countries by almost 600 per cent, and was actually greater than the total GDP of sub-Saharan Africa, which was US$301 billion in 2001.[121]

Agricultural support is also a key development issue. Many developing countries have an advantage in agricultural products compared with their developed country trading partners, but are unable to harness this potential engine for growth. This is because the subsidized exports of surplus agricultural production from developed countries depresses prices on international markets, resulting in agriculture becoming a less profitable proposition for individuals residing in countries whose governments simply cannot afford to subsidize their industry.[122] The result is a reduced comparative and competitive advantage on the world market, and results in developing countries being forced to put increased pressure on their natural resources which are an alternative source of export earnings.[123]

Agriculture is seen as a priority sector for developing countries. This is because, in free market situations, agriculture is an excellent source of income, which can then be used by developing countries to address pressing social and environmental issues. The chairman's summary of the G15 Ministerial Conference in Bangalore, India, in August 1999 stated that to 'show the mutual supportiveness of trade and environment, trade distortive agricultural export subsidies should be removed by developed countries'.[124] In justifying such a recommendation the chairman's summary cited the close links between government intervention in the market access of products, domestic support policies, export subsidies and environmental degradation.

The commitments made in the Uruguay Round appeared to be a positive step towards addressing these problems. Developed countries were given six years to cut their average agricultural tariffs by 36 per cent, to reduce their aggregate measures of support by 20 per cent and to cut export subsidies by 36 per cent. Developing countries were also obliged to make cuts in these areas, but theirs were not as large (for many, their levels of support were much lower to begin with), and these changes were to be phased in over ten years rather than six. Despite these provisions, to this day the agricultural sector remains more protected than almost any other. The average tariff remains relatively high at around 40 per cent, and some countries continue to employ 'mega-tariffs' of up to 350 per cent to protect certain products.[125]

The G8 in its meeting in 2005 committed itself to reducing agricultural subsidies. In para. 3 of the document entitled 'Trade' the G8 members stated that:

> we are ... committed to eliminating all forms of export subsidies and establishing disciplines on all export measures with equivalent effect by a credible end date.[126]

These types of commitments notwithstanding, the 1995 *Agreement on Agriculture* has generally not effectively decreased subsidies or increased market access.[127] The comparative advantage of developing countries continues to decline as developed countries continue to provide subsidies to their own farmers, and as those in developing countries try to compete, the decrease in traditional farming methods causes degradation of the environment, without producing the substantial increase in market access through which they might acquire the finances to mitigate environmental damage.

The WTO ministerial conference in Hong Kong went some way to providing a final date for the elimination of agricultural subsidies. Under para. 6 of the declaration, '[states] agree to ensure the parallel elimination of all forms of export subsidies and disciplines on all export measures with equivalent effect to be completed by the *end of 2013*'.[128] The declaration goes on to provide that the elimination of subsidies will occur in a progressive manner in accordance with yet to be negotiated 'modalities'.[129]

The Agreement on Textiles and Clothing

The purpose of the *Agreement on Textiles and Clothing* was to promote trade liberalization via the reduction of tariff and non-tariff barriers to trade, the expansion of existing quotas, the eventual integration of textiles and clothing products into the WTO/GATT, and the introduction of safeguards to deal with cases of market disruption during the integration of the sector into the WTO/GATT.[130] From a developing country perspective, the Agreement has been far from a resounding success. As noted by Mr Sok Siphana, Secretary of State for Commerce of Cambodia, in a speech delivered during 2004, tariffs and quotas for textile exports to developed countries were at the time costing developing countries an estimated 27 million jobs.[131]

On 31 December 2004 the *Agreement on Textiles and Clothing* ceased to operate, and with it the quota system for international trade in textiles and clothing. However, the new, quota-free system does not mean that trade is now entirely liberal.[132] While new markets will open up eventually, in the short to mid-term Europe and the United States are expected to remain the most important markets for clothing and textiles. At present, these markets attract two-thirds of the world's imports in this sector. With the quota phase-out, many small countries will lose guaranteed markets and countries like Bangladesh, for example, which has a 75 per cent share of garment exports in total merchandise exports, will have to struggle to maintain their present markets or they will face higher unemployment rates and deeper poverty. If they are not prepared for the expected business and market changes following the phase-out, such countries may lose their existing markets.[133]

On the other hand, countries with modern textile factories such as Bangladesh may actually increase their market share under the new quota-free system. However, it should also be noted that the efficiency of the textile industry in various countries will also depend on various costs of production which cannot be controlled by the producer. Thus, governments of developing countries will need to invest in infrastructure such as roads, utilities and ports in order for a country to retain its competitive edge.[134]

There is no doubt that environmental matters will have a central role in the future development of the international textile and clothing markets, and so developed country rule makers will need to cooperate closely with developing country exporters/producers in this area.[135] This is particularly evident in the context of developing countries' concerns that eco-labelling, which is currently no more than a marketing tool in the textiles industry, will become a barrier to imports in the future.[136]

This is no unfounded concern, as the 1996 ban on AZO dyes in Germany has shown. The effect of this ban was that textile manufacturers in Thailand switched to AZO-free substitutes with additional costs estimated at between 5 per cent and 20 per cent. Textile manufacturers in some other countries in the Asia-Pacific region, like India, encountered difficulties in obtaining substitutes. Small and medium enterprises were slower to adjust to eco-labelling demands and found the costs of adjustment difficult to absorb. Several of these enterprises preferred to divert sales to the domestic market or other overseas markets which did not have any eco-labelling requirements.[137]

Changes in the area of ecologically friendly products, as well as the lack of a uniform, international eco-labelling scheme, already pose problems for developing countries in terms of acquiring eco-friendly certification, but if and when such labelling schemes form a barrier to market access or place developing countries at a disadvantage *vis-à-vis* local manufacturers, difficulties with market access will be compounded.[138] During a June 1995 workshop on eco-labelling held by the International Trade Centre ('ITC') in Geneva, it became apparent that a number of issues were problematic for developing countries in this context, such as a lack of information regarding basic eco-labelling concepts and terminology, transparency and market factors.[139] From this, it is apparent that developing countries, which often depend very heavily on exports of clothing and textiles, need to be properly informed about developments in the field of environmentally sound products so they can prepare for forthcoming market changes, and understand which rules are mandatory, such as the banning of AZO dyes in Germany.[140] The ITC plans to set in place a monitoring system by which producers in this sector will be kept informed about latest trends in changes to the environment, the gradual integration of products into GATT rules as stipulated by the *Agreement on Textiles and Clothing*.[141]

The General Agreement on Trade in Services

The WTO *General Agreement on Trade in Services* ('GATS') sets out multilateral principles and procedures for the regulation of trade in services. Services consist of a diverse range of human activities that include basic and professional services. They include activities such as health care, education, banking, finance and insurance. They also include infrastructure services such as telecommunications, transport, exploration and drilling, and construction. Article XIX of GATS introduced 'appropriate flexibility for developing countries and LDCs in extending market access in line with their development situation'. Developing countries played a meaningful role in negotiations for the Agreement, ensuring that the interests of developing countries were considered at all stages in the proceedings.[142] The major issue in relation to the implementation of GATS provisions is, however, translating potential benefit into positive results for developing nations. GATS poses internal and external challenges for developing countries. Internally, developing countries will need to strengthen their domestic capacity to withstand the pressure from multinational service corporations. Preliminary evaluations of the impact of GATS suggest that the intentions of GATS may be being eroded by pressure on developing nations from such multinational service corporations.[143] In addition, the regulatory capacity of developing countries will have to be increased to address the challenges of sustainable development. Externally, developing countries will face greater competition as a result of opening their markets up to big multinational corporations without having any power to control them. In its objective statement, GATS mentioned its desire to:

> facilitate the increasing participation of developing countries in trade in services and the expansion of their service exports including, *inter alia*, through the strengthening of their domestic services capacity and its efficiency and competitiveness.
>
> (Preambular Paragraph 5)

Developing countries will certainly benefit from the strengthening of their domestic services capacity and from the liberalization of market access in areas in which they have export interests. However, developing countries do not have the necessary institutions or the technological and financial bases to reap the maximum benefit from the strengthening and expansion of their involvement in international trade in services. They have serious shortcomings in preparing for trade negotiations and in formulating domestic policy reform measures.

Developing countries have voiced concern about the inclusion of services in the WTO, which is the result of the initiatives of developed countries. Of further concern is the exclusion of labour-intensive services from GATS, which would be an export market in which developing countries have comparative advantage.[144] However, GATS included provisions for the obligations of developed countries to help developing countries gain access to technology, increase the availability of technology and to undertake the liberalization of market access in sectors of export interest to developing countries. However, this is an area in which developed countries have an absolute monopoly and consequently they have reaped 100 per cent of the benefit of the agreement without honouring their commitments to facilitate meaningful flows of North–South technology transfer. Areas such as the movement of natural persons, financial services sectors, basic telecommunications and maritime transport services, in which developing countries have an interest, saw no improvement. Similarly, the commitments made in Marrakesh by developed countries did not translate into action. It is argued that opening up the services sector in developing countries will benefit the giant multinational corporations ('MNCs') in developed countries at the cost of the trading plight of developing countries. Developing countries need innovative technologies which will facilitate their integration into the global information network without negative effects on their economy. Without such innovation, GATS may simply become another mechanism by which the North–South divide is entrenched and tensions are increased.[145]

The GATS provisions regarding the trade in services are linked to the environment. Paragraph 31(iii) deals with environmental goods and services. There are significant potential benefits of the liberalization of trade in environmental goods and services.[146] There is not, however, any agreed definition of what constitutes environmental goods and services.[147] Economic and social developments rely upon the progressive development of service sectors in developing countries. Thus, the liberalization of trade in services can have both a direct and an indirect impact upon the environment. While some services, such as banking, finance, insurance, education and health have little or no impact upon the environment, other services can have a direct and severe impact. Services of the latter type may involve exploration and drilling, transportation, construction and electricity generation. Opening up the markets of developing countries to foreign multinational service corporations can have a profound impact upon the environment. Unlike the GATT exceptions contained within Article XX, the WTO's GATS does not provide any exceptions from the rules for the protection of exhaustible natural resources. This means governments will have limited ability to protect the environment by regulating or restricting the acts of foreign corporations. Expansion of the scope of GATS is likely to bring about an increase in already substantial environmental damage. For example, oil exploration and drilling are already among the leading causes of forest destruction worldwide. Similarly, garbage incineration and toxic waste dumping release substantial amounts of toxic chemicals into the environment.[148]

Commitments from developed countries in the areas of environmental services could provide developing countries with new market opportunities under GATS. Developing countries would have greater access to environmental services and thus the scope to improve their environmental services industry. In order to benefit from the liberalization of trade in services, the domestic capacity of developing countries needs to be improved. Domestic infrastructure and regulatory regimes need to be developed and enforced to prevent anti-competitive and restrictive practices. Developing countries do not have an adequate regulatory framework with which to control multinational service corporations which are involved in providing services. Developing countries could impose preconditions or qualifications under which foreign private companies can operate. Such restrictions could impose measures to ensure equitable treatment of developing countries and the implementation of capacity building in conformity with GATS Articles IV and XIX.[149]

The Agreement on Trade-related Aspects of Intellectual Property Rights ('TRIPS')

The WTO *TRIPs Agreement* has increased the disparity and tension which currently exists between developed and developing countries. The *TRIPs Agreement* provides legal protection for intellectual property from imitation or copying through patents, copyrights, trademarks, geographical indications, industrial designs and trade secrets.

The *TRIPs Agreement* has proved to be a device designed to encourage monopolization and other anti-competitive practices of the technologically developed Northern countries and MNCs. By protecting the needs and economic supremacy of developed countries, the *TRIPs Agreement* has made them the sole beneficiaries of its provisions. To many developing countries, an intellectual property protection mechanism translates into a blockade on the transfer of technology and a further impediment to economic development.[150] They argue that the transfer of technology and the dissemination of environmentally sound technologies ('ESTs') would help them to move towards more environmentally friendly PPMs and ultimately, sustainable development.

The majority of intellectual property rights are generated and owned by developed countries. As such the latter can reap the overwhelming share of benefits while the heavy burden of implementation lies with developing countries. Developed countries own almost all intellectual property; as a consequence developing countries do not have much to gain and do not enjoy any reciprocal benefit from the protection of intellectual property rights. In fact, they have lost a lot of flexibility in this matter as they cannot be selective in the protection of intellectual property, nor can they discriminate in favour of their domestic intellectual property if they have any.[151] Developing countries will lose as much or more from the *TRIPs Agreement* as they gain from the tariff agreement on manufactured items.[152] A former TRIPs negotiator, Arvind Subramanian, has estimated that the welfare loss for India alone could be US$1.3 billion, the Philippines US$237 million, Indonesia US$133 million and for Thailand up to US$189 million.[153] The United States on the other hand will gain enormously from the *TRIPs Agreement*, reaping seven-and-a-half times as much as from all countries' tariff liberalization on manufactured items, including its own liberalization.[154]

The *TRIPs Agreement* has instituted what is basically a 'one size fits all' system for intellectual property rights, in which the high minimum standards are set for all countries despite differing levels of development.[155]

The protection of intellectual property rights ('IPRs') through the *TRIPs Agreement* places developing countries in a disadvantageous situation in terms of access to technology, and/or the modernization or upgrading of existing technology levels. This is ironic, given that the *TRIPs Agreement* recognizes the special needs of developing countries to create their own technological base.[156] Article 7 of the *TRIPs Agreement* states that the protection of IPRs is not only intended to promote technological innovation but also the 'transfer and dissemination of technology'.

Article 67 of TRIPs obliges developed country members to provide on request and on mutually agreed terms and conditions technical and financial assistance to developing countries. Article 66.2 obliges developed country members to provide incentives to enterprises and institutions in their territories for the purpose of promoting and encouraging technology transfer to least developed countries. However, several developing countries argue that the agreement and more specifically its implementation does not necessarily promote the dissemination of environmentally sound technologies or the protection of biodiversity. Although the economic benefits and supremacy of developed countries have been overly protected and secured by the *TRIPs Agreement*, their obligations in relation to technology transfer and the dissemination of environmentally sound technologies to developing countries are found only in the 'best endeavour' clauses and remain unfulfilled.

In accordance with the *TRIPs Agreement*, an invention must be new, involve an inventive step and be capable of industrial application in order to be patentable. It has been argued that the *TRIPs Agreement* seems to contemplate only the Northern industrialization model of innovation. It fails to address the more informal, communal system of innovation through which farmers in the South produce, select, improve and breed a diversity of crop and livestock varieties.[157] Due to its more informal and communal nature, the intellectual property of Southern farmers is thus denied recognition, and hence protection.[158]

The *TRIPs Agreement*, with its overly strong IPRs, together with extended protection of the scope and duration of these rights, has failed to protect the interests of developing countries. Instead of fostering innovation and the dissemination of environmentally sound technologies in relation to the use of IPRs to least developed countries, it has further increased the industrialized world's grip on technology. As a result, the *TRIPs Agreement* represents a policy of 'technological protectionism'. It has also failed to protect indigenous knowledge and community rights and has been criticized as a 'knowledge blockade' of developing countries.[159] Furthermore, the Agreement encourages Northern companies to enter developing countries, learn about their local knowledge, reproduce it in a laboratory, and patent it as their own idea. The result is that the local and indigenous populations of developing countries cannot use their own knowledge for their own people.

Its negative effect on access to technology, dissemination of environmentally sustainable technology, investment flow, incentives to community innovators, development potentials and implementation of international environmental agreements such as the *Convention on Biological Diversity*[160] will certainly undermine the capacity and efforts of developing countries to achieve the objectives of sustainable development.[161]

The Agreement on Subsidies and Countervailing Measures

The *WTO Agreement on Subsidies and Countervailing Measures* made provision for non-actionable environmental subsidies as an incentive to environmental adaptation.[162] However, there are instances of imbalance in the treatment of subsidies. Subsidies mostly used by developed countries such as those in relation to research and development ('R&D') and environmental adaptation, have been made non-actionable (i.e. immune from counter-action). In stark contrast, subsidies normally used by developing countries, including those for purposes such as industrial upgrading, diversification, technological development, etc., have been categorized as actionable disciplines.[163] Developing countries' subsidies should not be viewed as a tool of trade distortion: rather they must be accepted as a means of enabling development on an unequal playing field. Therefore, these subsidies of particular importance to the South should not be subject to countervailing duties or counter-action, particularly considering that those areas of greatest interest to the North have been afforded such immunity.

The GATT/WTO dispute settlement system and the environment

Over the past few years, GATT dispute settlement procedures have been used to solve trade–environment disputes. Although some of the Panel rulings created doubt about the efficacy of the system, in the absence of effective enforcement mechanisms and dispute settlement procedures in international environmental law, GATT dispute settlement procedures seem to be the only means of settling trade-related environment disputes. It is therefore pertinent to consider whether and to what extent the GATT/WTO dispute settlement system is successful in striking a balance between two competing priorities, trade and the environment.

Many dispute settlement proceedings under GATT Article XXIII led to Panel reports on trade–environment issues. Just as GATT does not explicitly refer to the protection of the environment, neither does it specify the extent to which GATT rights of market access might be restricted by environmental policy measures. As a result, most of the disputes resolved by the Panel have involved an environmental protection claim concerning GATT Article XX exceptions.

In many cases in which it has been called upon to interpret GATT laws for the effective resolution of environmental disputes, the Panel's reports have created controversy. The scope of this section does not allow an examination of all the cases involving trade and the environment. However, the following dispute settlement proceedings clearly demonstrate that very few trade–environment measures which violate GATT may be justified on grounds of environmental protection.

The Reformulated Gasoline dispute[164]

A GATT dispute resolution panel was set up in 1995 to examine a claim brought by Venezuela and Brazil regarding the US Environmental Protection Agency's ruling on gasoline imports. This ruling required foreign refiners to meet a different standard for conventional gasoline than domestic producers. Under the US *Clean Air Act*, US refiners were required to sell gasoline that was as clean as or cleaner than the gasoline it produced in 1990, while foreign refiners were required to ship gasoline that was as clean as or cleaner than the 'average' for US refiners in 1990. The more stringent average statutory baseline forced foreign refiners to either change their refineries so that they could produce gasoline that complied with the statutory baseline or to supply their product at a lower price to an importer who could average it with other gasoline in order to meet the statutory baseline over an annual period.[165]

Venezuela and Brazil challenged the US gasoline rule, claiming that the United States was using its environmental rules to gain an unfair and discriminatory trade advantage. Venezuela estimated that the law would effect the value of Venezuela's exports to the United States by at least US$150 million, as it was significantly affected by the conditions set for imported gasoline.[166] Venezuela and Brazil argued that the statutory baseline requirements for foreign refiners were discriminatory in that they treated imported gasoline less favourably than protected domestic production and therefore violated GATT Article III.

The United States justified its stance by using documentation to show the difficulties associated with offering individual baselines to foreign refiners as well as the significant problems associated with establishing 1990 levels of gasoline quality for foreign refiners. The United States sought to invoke an Article XX exception by claiming that the Gasoline Rule was necessary to protect human health and was related to the conservation of natural resources. The United States supported these claims by arguing that the objectives underlying the reformulated and conventional gasoline programmes fell within the scope of a range of policies aimed at preserving both clean air and other natural resources.

Venezuela rebutted the United States' Article XX argument by pointing out other, less trade-restrictive measures reasonably available to the United States and that were consistent or less inconsistent with GATT. These alternatives included, among others, the feasibility of using a foreign refiner baseline on the basis of the same records and data as US domestic refiners.

The Panel classified domestic and imported gasoline as 'like products' and accordingly ruled that the standards discriminated against foreign producers. It was argued that this variable treatment would create instability and uncertainty in the competition between domestic and imported goods in a manner fundamentally inconsistent with the object and purpose of GATT Article III.[167]

The Panel found the baseline establishment rule to be discriminatory based on the fact that under the rule imported gasoline was given less favourable treatment than domestic gasoline, in violation of GATT Article III. Indicating other, less trade-restrictive alternatives which the United States could reasonably be expected to employ, the panel ruled that 'more stringent quality requirements for imported gasoline were not necessary to improve environmental condition[s].'[168]

The United States appealed against the panel's decision to the Dispute Resolution Appellate Body.

The Appellate Body ignored the Panel's necessity test as a measure in issue and instead decided that the issue was whether the baseline establishment rules were 'primarily aimed at' conservation rather than 'less favourable treatment' criteria. This approach required a factual enquiry into whether the measure was 'primarily aimed at' the conservation of an exhaustible natural resource.[169]

Given the clear relationship between the baseline rules and the Gasoline Rule's policy objectives, the Appellate Body held that the baseline rules could not be regarded as merely incidentally or inadvertently aimed at the conservation of clean air in the United States.[170] Thus, the Appellate Body ultimately found that while the baseline establishment rules were not entitled to protection under Article XX as they failed to meet the requirements of the chapeau of the article and constituted 'unjustifiable discrimination' and 'a disguised restriction on international trade.'[171]

The Beef Hormone dispute[172]

The *Beef Hormone* dispute was the result of an import ban on American beef treated with growth hormones from the EU on 1 January 1989. The EU had banned the import of US beef because of fears that the hormones used in the production of US beef were dangerous to health protection and the safety of food. The United States estimated that it would suffer a heavy loss as a result of the ban. It challenged it in 1996, claiming that it violated a number of provisions under SPS, TBT and GATT. The United States argued that the ban discriminated against its beef producers because they used hormones in the production of more than half the cattle they sent to market each year. The EU, on the other hand, pointed to the fact that its own producers had ceased using hormones in cattle production several years previously.

The United States based its argument on the *SPS Agreement*, which requires its members to use harmonized sanitary and phytosanitary measures based on relevant international standards. The current internationally agreed food standards were those adopted by the Codex Alimentarius Commission, according to which the five hormones used by United States farmers were approved as safe for human consumption. Thus, the US argued, the EU import ban was not based on appropriate scientific evidence and was therefore in violation of its obligations under the *SPS Agreement*.

The EU justified the ban as non-discriminatory since it applied equally to all beef producers. Nonetheless, the Panel found that the EU ban was inconsistent with the *SPS Agreement* as it was not based on risk assessment and represented arbitrary discrimination.

Both the EU and the US appealed to the Appellate Body against the Panel's findings. The Appellate Body rejected the original Panel's legal interpretation of the SPS but upheld the ban as inconsistent with the SPS Agreement as it was not backed by sufficient scientific evidence. The Appellate Body found that the ban was not based on an adequate risk assessment, but overturned the Panel's interpretation of the EU's different levels of tolerance for growth hormones as discriminatory.

The Appellate Body recognized the right of the EU to adopt higher standards of food safety provided such standards were supported by scientific evidence and were not inconsistent with other EU policies. The EU argued that, by taking the safety measures it did, consumers were given the benefit of the doubt over the scientific uncertainty of certain health hazards which became apparent only long after substances were assumed to be safe. But the Appellate Body upheld the view of the Panel and ruled that the precautionary principle was already incorporated into Article 5.7 of the SPS Agreement. Under this article, members are allowed to introduce measures that are not supported by 'sufficient scientific' evidence on a provisional basis. Beyond its incorporation into Article 5.7, the precautionary principle could not override the explicit wording of Article 5, under which the specific wording of Articles 5.1 and 5.2 prevail over the precautionary principle.

Regarding the risk assessment requirements, the Appellate Body upheld the conclusion of the Panel which stated that the EU measure was contrary to the requirements of Article 5.1 and found that Articles 2.2 and 5.1 must be read together. In other words, the risk assessment must result in a basis of scientific principles and should establish sufficient scientific evidence to justify the measure in question.

The Appellate Body overturned the Panel's interpretation of Article 5.2, which states, in essence, that a risk assessment should not take into account non-scientific factors. In reaching its conclusion, the Appellate Body referred to Article 5.2, which clearly considers 'relevant inspection, sampling and testing methods' as part of the risk assessment process. The Appellate Body agreed with the Panel's conclusion that the EU had not shown that it had considered the problems of policing and control as part of its risk assessment.[173]

Although it had modified and reversed a number of key findings by the original panel, the Appellate Body ultimately ruled the EU ban to be inconsistent with the *SPS Agreement*.

The Shrimp Turtle dispute[174]

The *Shrimp Turtle* dispute arose from a challenge by Malaysia, Thailand, India and Pakistan to the US import ban on wild-caught shrimp from countries which either do not require Turtle Excluder Devices ('TED') on shrimp trawlers or which lack the knowledge and/or technology to set in place measures to protect marine turtles. The US ban was based on section 609 of the US *Endangered Species Act* of 1973 which states that all shrimp imported into the United States must be caught using methods which protect marine turtles from incidental drowning in shrimp trawling nets. According to the United States, TEDs are simple and have been shown to protect turtles effectively, reducing the number of turtles caught in shrimp nets by some 90 per cent. Initially the enforcement of section 609 was limited to the Atlantic coasts of fourteen Caribbean and Western Atlantic countries but in December 1995 the US Court of International Trade widened the trade measure to cover shrimp imports from other countries and requiring the US government to certify that all shrimp imported to the country were caught with vessels equipped with TEDs. The application of the embargo to other countries came into effect in May 1996; however, it had been mandatory for all US shrimp trawlers to be equipped with TEDs since 1994.

A panel was set up in February 1997 as requested by Malaysia, Thailand, India and Pakistan. The complainants claimed that the US embargo constituted a violation of GATT Articles XI (prohibition of quantitative restriction), I (Most Favoured Nation clause) and XIII (the non-discrimination principle). The complainants were particularly concerned about the unilateral nature of the trade measure which involved the extension of domestic laws and standards beyond the national borders of the United States.

The United States defended its measure under GATT Article XX, paras (b) and (g). The United States argued that its measures were necessary because turtles were threatened with extinction as a result of human-induced sea turtle mortality. Other measures not involving the use of TEDs were claimed to be insufficient to protect sea turtles against extinction. It was also argued that sea turtles were an exhaustible natural resource and that section 609 measures were related to the conservation of sea turtles. The US further contended that the TED requirement was designed to protect an internationally recognized endangered species and as such was not a disguised restriction on international trade. Neither were the measures arbitrary discrimination, as they applied the measures between nations only where different environmental and technical conditions prevail.

The Panel, having examined the claims of the parties, 6 April 1998 controversially held that the US import ban on shrimp and shrimp products was clearly a threat to the multilateral trading system and not within the measures permitted under the chapeau of Article XX. The Panel found that the import ban was a quantitative trade restriction and was therefore not required to consider the ban's consistency with Articles I and XIII.

Having considered whether the US measure constituted an arbitrary or unjustifiable discrimination, the Panel focused on the 'chapeau' of Article XX and found that it could be interpreted in a way which would allow importing countries to restrict market access according to the exporters' adoption of certain policies, including conservation policies. Such an interpretation would mean that GATT and the WTO could no longer serve as a multilateral framework for liberalized trade among members.

The Panel therefore held that the chapeau of Article XX allows members to derogate from GATT provisions only as long as they do not undermine the multilateral system. As the US measure constituted a unilateral restriction on trade and was a threat to the multilateral trading system, it was not justified under Article XX.

The United States filed an appeal against the Panel report with the WTO Appellate Body, which overruled the initial panel report in its reasoning but not in its result on 12 October 1998.

The Appellate Body decided that although the US measure served a legitimate environmental objective under GATT Article XX(g), its discriminatory application constituted arbitrary and unjustifiable discrimination between members of the WTO and as such it was not compatible with nor justified under the requirements of the chapeau of GATT Article XX.

The Appellate Body gave the following reasons for holding that the application of the US measure was discriminatory:

1 Section 609 provided for differential treatment among WTO members by determining different 'phase in' periods. While countries in the Caribbean/Western Atlantic region were permitted a three year phase-in period, countries not in that region, including the complainants, had only four months to comply with the mandatory requirement for TEDs.
2 The difference in the level of effort made by the United States in transfer-

ring the required TED technology to specific countries was also a testimony to its discriminatory application of section 609.

3 The US requirement that all countries applying for certification must adopt essentially the same comprehensive regulatory programme as applied in the United States was discriminatory as the United States failed to take into account the conditions prevailing in the exporting countries when determining the appropriateness of that programme. The certification process was not based on due process and fairness and so violated Article X which requires that members grant foreign traders and countries 'due process rights'.
4 The United States could have sought an alternative, multilateral course of action to achieve its policy goal rather than resorting to the unilateral and non-consensual procedures of the import prohibition imposed by a piece of domestic legislation.[175]

For the above reasons, the appellate body found that the application of the US import ban on shrimp or shrimp products constituted arbitrary discrimination which was contrary to the chapeau of Article XX. In arriving at such a conclusion, the reasoning in *Shrimp Turtle* demonstrated the Appellate Body's total willingness to refer to the full spectrum of relevant international law in making the determination as to what parties intended to achieve through the adoption of contentious trade measures.[176]

How green is the WTO dispute settlement body?

It is evident from the preceding discussion of the decisions of the Panel and the Appellate Body that environmental concerns are not considered a legitimate policy goal. In trade–environment disputes, Article XX environmental exceptions have generally been interpreted in a strict manner, thus reducing the scope of the exceptions. A close observation of the decisions of the dispute settlement body confirms that they have adopted a relatively negative approach to environmental matters.

Trade–environment problems are complex and their solution requires that the competing interests of both trade and environment groups be balanced. The complexity of the trade and environment areas require a panel composed of individuals with expertise in both areas of law as well as the participation of interest groups who are impartial and unbiased in the interpretation and application of rules. However, members of the panels are generally drawn from the trade community who are often criticized for their systematic bias towards trade concerns and their lack of concern for environmental matters. The panellists often lack experience with the complexities of the environmental issues implicated in their decisions and consequently often fail to give environmental factors sufficient weight.[177] Members of the environmental community argue that the core of the proportionality of measure (advantage for environment versus damage to trade, or vice versa) cannot be assessed by trade experts alone.[178] However, the trade community refute this view. They argue that trade and environment disputes should be considered in the context of the trading system, as the trading rights of contracting parties are impaired by environmental measures, which results in adverse effects on their trading interests. Environmental considerations are not factors in free trade principles. Environmental arguments have the potential to be used for protectionist purposes. If environmental exceptions were admitted, this would upset the delicate balance of advantages and concessions which were exchanged between the parties as the very essence of the international trading system.[179] By referring to environmental considerations a party could undermine or even withdraw its earlier concessions; concessions that had not been conditioned by any reference to the protection of the environment.[180]

Against this backdrop, the WTO dispute settlement body needs to balance the tension between these two different perspectives. The WTO should consider options for changing the current status quo of the dispute settlement body to create more room for the opinion of experts in connection with the environmental problem at hand. The possibility of seeking an advisory opinion from the International Court of Justice on the environmental aspects and the applicable international environmental law of a case needs to be considered further.[181] More open conversation between the parties concerned and greater transparency of environmental measures would also help to diffuse the tension that gave rise to the dispute.

The Committee on Trade and Environment

The GATT/WTO Committee on Trade and Environment ('CTE') was established to identify the relationship between trade measures and environmental measures and to make recommendations for the reform of the trade regime. Since its inception, the CTE has attempted and often struggled to bring trade-related environmental issues into the mainstream of WTO work. It is important to appreciate that the CTE has been given a broad range of responsibilities encompassing all areas of the multilateral trading system. Its work programme includes the examination of:

1 The relationship between the trade system and the use of trade measures for environmental purposes, including those in multilateral environmental agreements.
2 The relationship between the trade system, environmental charges and taxes, and environmental standards for packaging, labelling and recycling.
3 The effect of environmental measures on the market access of developing countries and the environmental benefits of removing trade restrictions and distortions.
4 Appropriate relations between the WTO and inter-governmental and non-governmental organizations.[182]

In addition to these responsibilities, pursuant to para. 51 of the Doha mandate, the CTE has also been assigned partial responsibility in evaluating the outcomes of the Doha negotiations against the accepted principles of sustainable development.[183]

The CTE has been criticized on numerous levels. First and foremost, the Committee has been criticized as toothless in that it has very little or no power to influence meaningful change within the powerhouse of the GATT/WTO as a whole. It has been noted that both the agenda and the outcomes of the CTE changed very little throughout the passage of time between its reporting to the Ministerial conferences of Singapore, Geneva and Seattle in 1996, 1998 and 1999 respectively. Halle provides the following dispassionate appraisal of the CTE's international reputation:

> the CTE has, cruelly and sometimes unfairly, been described as a sandbox, to which those concerned with environment in trade may be sent to play while the trade delegates get on with the serious work of dismantling trade barriers.[184]

Second, the Committee has been accused of focusing mainly on environmental problems of concern to rich, industrialized countries in return for looking at increased market access for the poor.[185] As a result, environmental issues have wrongly come to be seen as a purely 'Northern' issue, instead of a common global problem.[186] Many developing countries are concerned that the Committee will not adequately represent the South but will merely provide another mechanism for Northern economic dominance within world trade.[187]

In light of its somewhat chequered past, it is apparent that future progress in the Committee will largely depend on its action in areas of special interest to developing countries and its accordance of equal weight to issues of importance to them. The special problems faced by developing countries in the implementation of the agreements need to be taken into account by the Committee. The Committee also needs to find ways and means of compensating for the losses developing countries have suffered as a result of barriers and constraints to market access.

The concerns of developing countries

The major concern of developing countries with the current intersection between international trade and environmental measures is the trend of trade-related measures being adopted allegedly for the enforcement of environmental standards that are suspected to in fact be a means of covert protectionism. As has been duly noted in recent scholarship on trends in international trade:

> With the environmental conditionality on market access growing at a phenomenal pace, developing countries were keen to ensure that at least some disciplines are in place to reduce the scope for green market protectionism.[188]

The use of trade-related environmental measures to achieve environmental objectives has the danger of being discriminatory. Developing countries argue that the environmental standards of developed countries cannot be imposed upon them without considering their socio-economic plight and their depressed level of economic development. They fear that high-income countries will impose lofty environmental standards on low-income countries, without the requisite assistance, and thus deprive them of one aspect of their natural comparative advantage and subject them to trade barriers if they fail to perform up to the standards of developed countries.[189] Developing countries also argue that the North's attempts to dictate their domestic environmental policies by wielding its economic strength through trade sanctions are a form of eco-imperialism.[190] Unilateral sanctions, if unregulated, would fundamentally shift the trading system from a rules-based system towards one based on the raw political and economic power of individual states and regions. Therefore, the use of trade-related environmental measures for achieving the objective of sustainable development is largely undesirable for developing countries.

The fallacy of the environmental effectiveness of trade measures does not pay heed to the concerns of developing countries or their inability to meet the stricter environmental norms set by the affluent North. Developing countries have been asking for the necessary financial support and the transfer of environmentally friendly technology to enable them to tackle environmental issues but the promises of the North in this regard have not materialized. At present, the acquisition of such technology by developing countries from the North comes with numerous conditions, as environmentally friendly technology is transferred from developed countries via official development assistance or through direct foreign investment. Significantly, however, nearly three-quarters of such technology is obtained by the firms of developing countries on purely commercial terms.[191]

The degree to which environmental issues are required to be addressed should be commensurate with the level of development of each country. Applying universal environmental standards to production processes can be detrimental to the economic interests of developing countries. Allowing countries to distinguish between products on the basis of how they are produced threatens rapid descent down the 'slippery slope' to a level of protectionism that would completely undermine the very foundation of the international trade system.[192] Extending these criteria to PPMs might restrict the access of developing countries to the markets of developed countries. As Anderson and Drake-Brockman have cautioned, 'firms will perceive this as an additional way to justify their demands for protection from import competition'.[193] They further argue that employing trade restrictions instead of more efficient instruments that impact directly on production or consumption rather than on trade, 'will unnecessarily reduce the level and growth of global economic welfare and may even add to rather than reduce, global environmental damage and resource depletion'.[194]

The harmonization of domestic environmental standards is often suggested as an alternative to trade restrictions for addressing environmentally harmful production processes used by exporting nations.[195] Yet, from the viewpoint of developing countries, the harmonization of pollution and other process standards could work against their interests.[196] Any harmonization of environmental quality and performance standards should be gradual and incremental, affording special and differential treatment to developing countries. Developing countries perceive the 'harmonization of environmental standards' debate as an attempt by developed countries to ignore the commitments they made at UNCED to respect the development needs of individual countries.[197]

WTO members must address environmental concerns within a broader sustainable development framework that includes structural concerns such as equity, economic development, increased market access and the alleviation of poverty in developing countries. The international trade regime could respond to the needs of developing countries by providing more market access – particularly for textiles and agricultural products – as well as increased labour mobility and greater flexibility regarding technical and sanitary standards.

Developed countries have made commitments concerning the elimination of export subsidies, substantial reductions in agricultural domestic support, significant market access improvements, removal of trade-distorting subsidies and the integration of development and environment concerns. Unfortunately little progress has been made towards the implementation of these commitments. Developing countries remain subject to perverse subsidies, anti-dumping rules, unilateral trade measures and other tariff and non-tariff barriers used by developed countries. Textile and agricultural products, where developing countries actually have a comparative advantage, are more frequently subject to environmental standards. Little progress has been made in the implementation of enabling mechanisms at the international level to assist developing countries to address environmental issues effectively. Imbalances in the trade and environment agenda can only be worked out if such enabling mechanisms are put in place.

The domineering position of developed countries in GATT/WTO negotiations has been translated into the systematic bias of trading structures in favour of developed countries. Developing countries, with their weak bargaining position, have received the tough end of the deal. GATT/WTO cannot address the goal of sustainable development without the integration of developing countries into the trading system. Imbalances in the negotiating position of developing countries and unfairness in the operation and interpretation of WTO Agreements need to be addressed. Bringing developing countries on to the same level playing field would help them to address the global objectives of environmental protection and sustainable development without endangering their right to development.

Conclusion

Principle 12 of the *Rio Declaration* stressed that the mutual coexistence of trade and environment is a key piece in the sustainable development puzzle.[198] Such sentiments have been forcefully reaffirmed by subsequent international instruments such as the *Johannesburg Plan of Implementation* and the Millennium

Development Goals (see Chapter 2). For such mutual coexistence to become a reality there needs to be an urgent reconciliation of economic comparative advantage and environmental comparative advantage. Resource and environmental costs need to be incorporated into the prices of products. Such prices should then provide clear signals to producers and consumers in order to guide their decisions and to enable an efficient and sustainable allocation.[199] In this process the special factors affecting environment and trade policies in developing countries and their significant economic and developmental differences should constantly be borne in mind.

This chapter has outlined the need for GATT/WTO to clarify and/or modify some of its rules if it is to better accommodate the often conflicting concerns of developing countries and Northern environmentalists. An important step in this regard would be the revision of GATT Article XX so that it provides better support for the achievement of environmental goals, ensures that environment-related trade measures do not çonstitute disguised protectionist measures and more clearly and consistently takes into account the special situations of developing countries.

In the meantime, insufficient attention is given to environmental considerations, as illustrated by the cases brought before the GATT dispute settlement panels. A review of the relevant GATT rules should ensure that a balance is struck between competing commercial and environmental goals and that global and transboundary environmental issues are accommodated. GATT must also address doubts regarding the conformity of the measures set out in Multilateral Environmental Agreements ('MEAs').[200]

Striving for an open international trading system may be an important economic instrument for developing countries to both engage in economic development, and protect the global environment.[201] Sustainable development not only benefits the environment through the responsible use of resources, but also provides countries with the financial and technological capacity to engage in environmental protection measures.

As a general theory, open markets encourage or facilitate the efficient allocation of resources and necessarily result in their application to the most profitable use. Thus efficiency essentially dictates that resources are not wasted or depleted through unsustainable practices. However, this Ricardian theory of free trade has been constructed by the developed trading nations under the auspice of the WTO, and as such has often failed to take into account or accommodate developing nations' interests and concerns, when implementing these policies and programmes of free trade. Namely, that the developing nations' economies are not of sufficient strength to effectively participate in multilateral trade negotiations, due to the inadequacy of their financial resources, the level of market access and technological transfer. Consequently, striving for an open international trading system requires that these issues be addressed under the WTO through international co-operation and capacity building for equitable economic development. In turn, this approach is likely to help mitigate environmental problems through providing the South with an increased capacity to engage in environmental protection of scarce resources.

4 The trade–environment linkage in the post-Uruguay Round context

The issues relating to the trade and environment linkage are very complex and evolve in a dynamic manner involving various states and other actors in the process. The linkage has assumed and will continue to assume paramount significance in international trade negotiations, and is often plagued by arguments that ultimately relate to conflicting interests related to the North–South divide. These issues are even more topical today than in the past.

The pressure on developing countries to further accommodate environmental issues is increasing. The demands from various pressure groups to include trade and environment in a possible new round of multilateral trade negotiations are multiplying. While developing countries resisted the linkage between trade and environment initially, they later accepted the reality that economic development cannot be separated from its environmental consequences.

Nevertheless, developing countries are concerned that the inclusion of trade–environment issues in the WTO generally will work against their economic interests. The inclusion of trade and environment-related issues in the WTO also means that developing countries could be forced to engage in negotiations on trade–environment issues without an explicit inclusion of environment in the negotiating mandate.[1]

This chapter primarily focuses on the development of the trade–environment linkage in the WTO Ministerial Conference in the post-Uruguay Round context. It aims primarily to highlight the difficulties that developing countries are encountering in dealing with these new developments and the future dimensions of this complex trade and environment linkage in the context of multilateral trade negotiations.

Development of trade–environment linkage in the WTO Ministerial Conferences

The Ministerial Conference is the WTO's highest decision-making body.[2] It meets once every two years. The Ministerial Conference has the authority to take decisions on all matters under any of the multilateral trade agreements.[3] While the Ministerial Declaration covers a wide range of issues, this section focuses on the provisions relating to the trade and environment linkage.

The 1996 Singapore Ministerial Conference

The first Ministerial Conference of the WTO was held in Singapore from 9 December to 13 December 1996 with a view to assessing the progress of the implementation of the commitments made by member states, and reviewing the ongoing negotiations and work programmes under the WTO.

The *Ministerial Declaration*, the main outcome of the Ministerial Conference, recognized the objective of the multilateral system as '[the promotion of] sustainable growth and development while contributing to a more stable and secure climate in international relations'.[4]

The Declaration addressed issues relating to the implementation of the WTO Agreements and recognized that full implementation of those Agreements would comprise an important contribution to the achievement of sustainable development (para. 16). The contribution of the Committee on Trade and Environment has been recognized. The Declaration approved the continuation of the work of the Committee under the existing terms of reference with further participation of environmental as well as trade experts in the deliberations of the Committee.

The *Ministerial Declaration* also made reference to the importance of the integration of developing countries in the multilateral trading system. The significant commitments that were undertaken by developing countries were recognized. The difficulties developing countries were facing in complying with their commitments were acknowledged. In line with this recognition, the member states made commitments to improve the availability of technical assistance to developing countries under the agreed guidelines.[5]

The first WTO Ministerial Conference ended amid mixed feelings. The division between the North and the South over many issues was starkly apparent. While developed countries and the politicians welcomed the result of the meeting as an 'outstanding success', others, particularly developing countries' representatives, described the results as 'a shared disappointment'.[6] The meeting resolved very few issues between developed and developing countries and it was predicted that the issues raised would continue to create further debate in future negotiations to be held in Geneva.

Developing countries were concerned that the benefits that they were meant to receive from their commitment to the Uruguay Round Agreements had not materialized. Although the Declaration recognized the difficulties that these countries were facing, it was felt that the Ministerial Conference 'should concentrate on a review of the past two years' progress in "digesting" the results of the Uruguay Round'.[7] Developing countries did not consider that the environment should be an issue for the Ministerial Conference. They believed that economic growth could help them to contribute to environmental protection, and therefore that environmental issues should be treated as incidental to development concerns. In plenary statements, a number of developing countries expressed their concerns about the potential of environmental measures to be used as disguised protectionism. For example:

> Malaysia said the indiscriminate use of labeling schemes undermines developing countries' exports. Nigeria noted that poverty is the most significant cause of environmental degradation and trade liberalisation will yield environmental dividends.[8]

The different perspectives of the North and the South with regard to the linkage between trade and the environment were evident in the first WTO Ministerial Conference. Their divergence of views indicated that multilateral trade negotiations would face a rocky road if these differences were not dealt with. In order for this to happen, the WTO needs to ensure that the commitments and promises made to developing countries in the Uruguay Round Agreements are duly met, and that its developing member states are not deprived of their stakes/dues arising from the liberalization of their markets. Since the trade and environment linkage is linked with the socio-economic development of developing countries, their special situation in addressing these issues needs to be taken into account before environmental protection issues are included on the WTO negotiating agenda. The question of whether the WTO Ministerial Conference would be able to respond to this issue in the future remained open until the next Ministerial Conference which was held in Geneva in 1998.

The 1998 Geneva Ministerial Conference

The Geneva Ministerial Conference was held in Geneva on 20 May 1998. There was no significant development in relation to the trade–environment linkage. This may have been partially due to the perception that the Geneva Ministerial Conference was a token one in the face of the celebration of the fiftieth anniversary of GATT. In the Pre-Ministerial Meeting there were efforts from many environmental groups as well as from the United States to establish the linkage between the goals of world trade with those of improving the environment. President Clinton, while emphasizing the need to harmonize the goals of trade with that of the sustainable development, suggested that 'the trading system of the twenty-first century must never become a race to the bottom in the fields of environmental protection, labour standards and consumer protection.'[9] Japan, Canada, the United States and the European Union (EU) also wanted to have a high-level meeting of the WTO Committee on Trade and Environment ('CTE') in an attempt to speed up the progress of the Committee and to save it from its long-standing deadlock. However, the primary outcome of the Geneva Ministerial Conference, the *Geneva Declaration*, only expressed the commitment of member states to continue to improve their 'efforts towards the objectives of sustained economic growth and sustainable development'.[10]

It is relevant to note that although developing countries were pressing for issues such as their market access concerns and implementation difficulties to be addressed as preconditions before linking trade with the environment, progress in this regard was minimal. Developing countries were perceived as not being ready to deal with issues such as trade and environment linkage, and as a result, the environmental NGOs and developed countries continued to pursue their objectives of linking trade with the environment. For example, US environmental groups requested President Clinton to use the 18–20 May GATT fiftieth anniversary celebration as an opportunity to insist on renewed efforts to bring about the trade–environment linkage.[11]

Developing countries did not accept these developments behind the scenes and reiterated their concerns regarding their implementation difficulties. Several developing countries, including Cuba and Uganda, highlighted the marginalization of developing countries, in particular least developed countries ('LDCs'), in the world trading system and the need to focus on this issue and redress the asymmetry between developed and developing countries while drawing upon the benefits of trade liberalization.

Director General Renato Ruggiero, in his address to the Geneva Ministerial conference, recognized the need for implementation of the WTO Agreements in the following words: 'Full implementation is essential to the credibility of our system – and its potential to carry the weight of future responsibilities.'[12] The *Geneva Ministerial Declaration* made references to the need for the commitment to full and faithful implementation of the WTO Agreements; however, developed members made no specific promises in this regard. As a result developing countries were of the view that there should not be any new issues until the contentious issues of previous negotiations were properly resolved. Developing countries felt that they were forced to make concessions to developed countries without receiving concomitant concessions.

The 1999 Seattle Ministerial Conference

The Seattle Ministerial Conference saw significant disagreements between developed and developing countries. As a result, the Seattle Ministerial Conference was a failure in this regard. The Ministerial Conference was suspended on 3 December 1999 when delegates failed to reach a consensus on the text of the Ministerial Declaration. Consequently, the Seattle Ministerial Conference could not resolve the distrust, tensions and conflicts of interests which existed between developed and developing countries in addressing the trade and environment linkages.[13]

Failure to reach any consensus in the third WTO Ministerial Conference in Seattle reflects the frustration and anger felt by developing countries and environmentalists over the issues of development and environment. In fact, 'developing country resentment ha[d] been growing for years – and it came to a head in Seattle'.[14] The environmental community was also disappointed at the very slow progress in the Committee on Trade and Environment's agenda which they criticized as 'nothing more than a distraction from the real agenda'.[15]

Since former EU Trade Commissioner Sir Leon Brittan first put forward the idea of a Millennium Round of trade talks, developing countries have resolutely resisted the placing of new issues on the negotiating agenda until prior Uruguay Round commitments are duly implemented.[16] They felt that they were exploited and excluded from their fair share of the benefits. This sense of injustice and unfairness has united them against new issues which are not concerned with their interests in international trade negotiations.

Before and during the Ministerial Conference, developing countries categorically pointed out the imbalances and inequities in WTO Agreements which deprived them of their expected benefits from trade liberalization. They pointed especially to the review of several WTO Agreements such as the Agreements on agriculture, textiles, trade-related investment measures, trade-related intellectual property rights, subsidies and anti-dumping. Central to this are the concerns of developing countries regarding the WTO Agreements on Textiles and Agriculture in which areas developing countries have a clear competitive and comparative advantage, but were unable to realize the benefits the Agreements offered because of problems with implementation.[17] Regarding textiles, developing countries argue that the limited or little implementation of developed countries' commitment in this area under the Uruguay Round Agreement have 'resulted only in a minimal increase in market opening while reinforcing imbalances in competition between developed and developing countries'.[18]

Martin Khor from the Third World Network argues that:

> it would be dishonest to speak of a 'development round' if further liberalisation were undertaken before these implementation concerns were addressed.[19]

Developing countries firmly reject renewed attempts to introduce trade and environment issues into future trade negotiations which they believe would further deteriorate the negotiating prospects on other pertinent issues which are particularly linked to their products and services. The imposition of the environmental agenda of developed countries would also create deep divisions and distrust between rich and poor countries which would not bode well for the development of a future consensus on the formation of a work programme. This might also further exacerbate the use of trade measures on environmental grounds.

In the Seattle Ministerial Conference, a number of developing countries presented proposals which highlighted their concerns regarding their approaches to the issue of trade and the environment. The countries which presented such proposals included Kenya,[20] Bangladesh,[21] Pakistan,[22] Dominican Republic–Honduras–Pakistan,[23] Cuba–Dominican Republic–Honduras–Pakistan[24] and Cuba.[25] Adil Najam states that their concerns were based in the assumption that the environment is largely the concern of the developed countries and that if provisions in multilateral environmental agreements ('MEAs') are allowed to 'trump' WTO rules, this could create new trade barriers for developing country exports.[26]

Despite resistance from developing countries, the EU and the United States pushed hard for various mechanisms to link trade and environmental protection in the Seattle Ministerial Conference. The US proposal expressed the need for institutional reform to pursue trade liberalization 'in a way that is supportive of high public health and environmental standards'.[27] Meanwhile, the EU pushed for environmental references throughout the whole text of the Ministerial Declaration. Robert Madelin of the EU delegation outlined the position of the EU on the environment in the following words:

> We do not want to put all our environmental demands in just one paragraph, as the nature of the drafting process is such that entire paragraphs get deleted all the time, and we wouldn't want to lose all our demands in this area in one fell swoop.[28]

Consequently, in the draft Ministerial Seattle Text, the link between trade and environment was recognized in the text governing the principles of sustainable development in the following manner:

Principles governing the negotiations (para. 21)

> *Sustainable development:* Negotiations shall promote sustainable development and aim to make trade liberalisation, economic development and environmental protection mutually supportive.[29]

Structure, organization and participation

> *Role of the Committee on Trade and Environment and the Committee on Trade and Development:* The Committee on Trade and Environment and the Committee on Trade and Development, within their respective mandate, will each provide a forum to identify and debate the developmental and environmental aspects of the negotiations in order to help achieve the objective that sustainable development is appropriately reflected throughout the negotiations. The two committees will report regularly to the Trade Negotiations Committee.[30]

Since there was no agreement, the draft Ministerial text was dropped in the end. But it appears that environmental considerations were mainstreamed in the working draft which may be resurrected in future negotiations.

In essence, demonstrations from all environmental groups in Seattle and also the pressure from developed countries to include the environment in the negotiating agenda changed the negotiating reality for developing countries in that they had to make room for environmental considerations apparently for their own sake. This result reflects the current political situation of the North, wherein 'it is hard to imagine any future trade agreement … which does not seriously address environmental concerns.[31]

The power and strength of the Seattle street protests by environmental and labour groups are a reminder that labour and environmental issues are gaining intensity and importance. These protests have implications for both the WTO and developing countries. For developing countries it means that explicit inclusion of environmental issues in trade negotiations is only a matter of time. The increasing pressures to include environmental concerns in trade negotiations from developed countries and from labour and environmental groups have one thing in common: they both have little concern for the interest of the developing countries in promoting their cause. They have no prescriptions for the concerns of the developing countries. Rather, to some extent, developing countries were 'portrayed as generally "anti-environmental" and certainly as the main hurdle to the incorporation of environmental linkages into trade regimes'.[32] Developing countries need to work against this misconception and should highlight their environmental priorities which are different from those of developed countries. They should come up with their own environmental agenda, one which focuses more on sustainable development and their developmental priorities based on the principle of common but differentiated responsibility.[33]

Failure to form a consensus on the Ministerial text was a serious blow for the WTO. As Malini Mehra, Director of the People's Decade for Human Rights Education, argues, Seattle showed the need for the WTO to 'fundamentally reform itself and reassert the centrality of its social mission to bring benefits to its entire membership and the environment'.[34] Martin Khor of the Third World Network argues that the failure of the Seattle Ministerial meeting was a reflection of the undemocratic and non-transparent nature of the WTO system generally, and the refusal of developing countries to continue being subject to the manipulation of that system by the North.[35]

The trade–environment debates in Seattle are intricately linked with the North–South debate in the WTO. This 'reordered North–South interplay was indeed the critical relationship for the failure at Seattle'.[36] Therefore the WTO needs to reorganize its priorities to take into account the concerns of developing countries in the negotiating process. Disappointments and the disagreement of developing countries with regard to the negotiating process must be dealt with in a manner which secures transparency and greater participation of developing countries in the process. The concerns expressed by developing countries in relation to issues with the implementation of the WTO Agreements (especially on agriculture, textiles and anti-dumping) must be addressed before the inclusion of any 'new issues' on the built-in agenda. Unless the situation is improved, the present undemocratic, non-inclusive and highhanded 'green room' approach to the production of a ministerial text at any cost will result in anger and frustration on the part of developing countries that have sufficient numbers to foil any such attempt in the future.

The 2001 Doha Ministerial Conference

After many failed attempts, developed countries and environmental groups finally succeeded in placing trade and environment issues on the negotiating agenda of the Doha Ministerial Conference held in 2001. Developing countries had no choice but to hesitantly accept this mandate. Accepting the trade and environment provisions in the *Doha Declaration*,[37] developing countries realized that it would not be appropriate to resist the agenda, but better instead to act proactively with their own agenda to link the environmental protection issue with the broader framework of sustainable development.

As a result, there is further scope for interpretation and debate regarding the implications of the agenda regarding the achievement of sustainable development in developing countries. While developing countries accepted the agenda they remained sceptical about its implications and the use of its provisions by their developed counterparts. While the *Doha Declaration* recognized the issues that were the subject of developing countries' concerns, the recognition and inclusion of those issues in the Declaration does not guarantee the elimination of those concerns. The extent and breadth of environmental issues are likely to keep the tension between developed and developing countries alive over coming trade negotiations.

The *Doha Ministerial Declaration* provided a platform for the commencement of new negotiations and the continuation of ongoing multilateral trade negotiations.[38] The *Doha Declaration* was a breakthrough which set the stage for trade and environment debate within the WTO. For the first time it put the environment on a negotiating agenda agreed to by WTO members at the multilateral level. It addressed many pressing issues including the relationship between WTO rules and Multilateral Environmental Agreements (MEAs), the elimination of trade barriers, eco-labelling and the effect of environmental measures on market access and the relationship between the TRIPs Agreement and the Biodiversity Convention. The *Doha Declaration* brought the trade and environment debate into the forefront of trade negotiations.

Trade and environment provisions of the Doha Ministerial Declaration

The Preamble to the *Doha Declaration* reaffirmed the commitment of the parties to the objective of sustainable development as stated in the Preamble of the *Agreement Establishing the WTO* (*'Marrakesh Agreement'*).[39] It further elaborated the rights of parties to:

> tak[e] measures for the protection of human, animal or plant life or health, or of the environment at the levels it considers appropriate, subject to the requirement that they are not applied in a manner which would constitute a means of arbitrary or unjustifiable discrimination between countries where the same conditions prevail, or a disguised restriction on international trade, and are otherwise in accordance with the provisions of the WTO Agreements.[40]

The Preamble strongly expressed the belief that the objectives of the multilateral trading system and the 'protection of the environment and the promotion of sustainable development can and must be mutually supportive'.[41]

Negotiations on trade and the environment (Article 31)

To increase the mutual supportiveness of trade and the environment, the *Doha Declaration* made the first move regarding negotiations on:

1 The relationship between existing WTO rules and specific trade obligations set out in multilateral environmental agreements para. 31(i)).
2 Procedures for regular information exchange between MEA Secretariats and the relevant WTO committees, and the criteria for granting observer status (para. 31(ii)).
3 The reduction or, as appropriate, elimination of tariff and non-tariff barriers to environmental goods and services (para. 31(iii)).
4 Subsidies which aim to clarify and improve WTO disciplines on fisheries subsidies (paras 28 and 31).

It is relevant to note that negotiations on the above items form part of the 'single undertaking' package, which were supposed to be completed by 1 January 2005.

Instruction to the Committee on Trade and Environment

The *Doha Declaration* instructs the Committee on Trade and Environment ('CTE') to pursue work within its current terms of reference and specifically to give particular attention to:

1 The effect of environmental measures on market access, especially in relation to developing countries, in particular the least developed among them, and those situations in which the elimination or reduction of trade restrictions and distortions would benefit trade, the environment and development (para. 32(i)).
2 The relevant provisions of the *Agreement on Trade-Related Aspects of Intellectual Property Rights* ('TRIPS Agreement') (para. 32(ii)).
3 Labelling requirements for environmental purposes (para. 32(iii)).

The CTE will identify whether or not there is any need to clarify relevant WTO rules on the above issues and will report to the fifth session of the Ministerial Conference, to be held in Cancun. The CTE will also recommend what future action can be taken on these issues and whether they can be placed on the negotiating table.

Recognition of technical assistance and capacity building for trade and the environment

The capacity of developing countries to address environmental concerns depends upon the transfer of environmentally sustainable technologies from developed to developing countries. Both the world trading regime and the international environmental law regime have recognized this position of developing countries. *Agenda 21*[42] and the *Rio Declaration on Environment and Development*[43] have made provisions for the transfer of technology. However, little progress has been made in regarding the implementation of those provisions (see Chapter 1).

The *Doha Declaration* recognized the need for and importance of technical assistance and capacity building to help developing countries address issues relating to environmental protection. It also states that 'enhanced market access, balanced rules, and well targeted, sustainably financed technical assistance and capacity-building programmes have important roles to play' in ensuring 'developing countries … secure a share in the growth of world trade commensurate with the needs of their economic development'.[44] References to technical assistance and capacity building in the *Ministerial Declaration* are made in the following words:

> We recognize the importance of technical assistance and capacity building in the field of trade and environment to developing countries, in particular to the least developed among them.[45]

Following this recognition, the *Doha Declaration* also:

> establishes a Working Group under the auspices of the General Council to examine the relationship between trade and transfer of technology, and of any possible recommendations on steps that may be taken within the mandate of the WTO to increase flows of technology to developing countries.[46]

The Declaration further affirms that:

> The delivery of WTO technical assistance shall be designed to assist developing and least-developed countries and low-income countries in transition to adjust to WTO rules and disciplines, implement obligations and exercise the rights of membership, including drawing on the benefits of an open, rules-based multilateral trading system.[47]

The Declaration instructed the Director General of the WTO to report to the fifth session of the Ministerial Conference in Cancun with regard to the implementation and adequacy of these commitments in the identified paragraphs.

Other provisions relevant to trade and the environment

The *Doha Declaration* also:

1 Considers the non-trade concerns reflected in the negotiating proposals submitted by Members in the context of negotiations on Agriculture, and confirms that non-trade concerns (non trade concerns include protection of the

environment) will be taken into account in the negotiations as provided for in the *Agreement on Agriculture* (para. 13).

2 Instructs the Committee on Trade and Development and the Committee on Trade and Environment, within their respective mandates, to each act as a forum to identify and debate developmental and environmental aspects of the negotiations, in order to help achieve the objective of having sustainable development appropriately reflected (para. 51).

Relationship between the Agreement on Trade Related Intellectual Property Rights ('TRIPs') and biodiversity

The relationship between biodiversity and intellectual property is complex, with the 'potential both for synergy and tension'.[48] The *Convention on Biological Diversity* ('CBD')[49] aims to conserve biological diversity, the sustainable use of its components and the fair and equitable sharing of the benefits arising out of the utilization of genetic resources.[50] Many of the provisions of the Convention are affected directly or indirectly by intellectual property rights ('IPRs').

As a result, there are potential conflicts between the objectives of the *TRIPs Agreement* and those of the CBD. These conflicts centre on the need to ensure fair and equitable benefit sharing between members. Such conflicts highlight and exacerbate the unequal positions of developed and developing nations in international trade relations. Developing nations are generally richer in biodiversity than the developed nations and seek to restrict access to their biological resources, whereas developed nations and transnational corporations would prefer greater freedom.[51] Issues which illustrate this division are the extension of patents to substances discovered in nature, the improper application of the 'novelty' and 'innovative step' criteria in the granting of patents[52] and the use of traditional knowledge by businesses and researchers.[53] While some proclaim that the IPRs regime is a form of recolonization of the South,[54] the position of 'no patents on life' such as that taken by the African Group in its 1990 WTO submission is not likely to be successful in the near future.[55] It is clear, however, that the current system is not operating fairly to share the benefits of biodiversity, but rather to entrench the wide schism between developed and developing nations.

This is an area which will be highly contentious in the next round of trade negotiations. This conflicting situation may further deteriorate the already bitter relations between developed and developing countries. The *Doha Declaration* made clear the importance of examining the relationship between the *TRIPs Agreement* and the CBD. The Declaration calls for examination of the relationship between the *TRIPS Agreement* and the *Convention on Biological Diversity*, traditional knowledge and folklore (para. 19), and calls for future negotiations on relevant provisions of the *TRIPS Agreement* if recommended by CTE (para. 32).

However, despite this recognition, many feel that the need is not for further study but for definite negotiations on practical means to include the objectives and principles of the CBD into the WTO.[56] A multitude of reforms have been suggested such as greater intervention by international institutions,[57] improving the quality of patent grants to ensure they are genuine and of a high standard,[58] and devising a system of intellectual property rights which recognizes the value of traditional knowledge.[59]

Doha development agenda: rhetoric and reality

The *Doha Declaration* included many contemporary trade and environment issues in the future negotiating agenda. Apparently, this agenda reflects significant issues of concern to both developing and developed countries. It was in fact the result of a carefully designed compromise package between developed and developing countries on trade and environment issues. Doha recognized the concerns of developing countries relating to implementation, agriculture, market access for non agricultural products, special and differential treatment for developing countries. However, concessions on the issues relating to developing countries' interests were not free from conditions. In fact, these concessions were made 'in exchange for stronger language on the environment, investment and competition policy'.[60]

Developing countries have yet to taste the benefits of the *Doha Declaration*. In most instances, issues relating to the interests of developing countries have been passed on to the relevant WTO bodies for further study. The *Doha Declaration* recognized the importance of most of the issues, but did not provide any specific commitments for their resolution. Developing countries want some sort of binding commitment from developed countries on duty-free and quota-free market access for their products. Most of the issues seem to involve no more than a 'best endeavour' attempt to resolve them, rather than legally binding commitments.[61]

The *Doha Ministerial Declaration* calls for negotiations to reduce tariff and non-tariff barriers to trade in non-agricultural products.[62] This might include environmental measures based on process and production methods ('PPMs'). These negotiations will have a definite impact upon environment-related measures which impact on trade. From a trade policy and developing country perspective, the issue is ensuring that like product criteria and factors do not create an open-ended basis for unrestricted differentiation of products based on PPMs. This would raise serious and legitimate concerns about market access, for developing countries in particular. This challenge remains a live one.[63]

The Declaration put the clarification of the relationship between MEAs and WTO provisions on the agenda.[64] It did not specifically mention which MEAs this referred to. In the absence of the clear definition of MEAs, developing countries apprehend that ambiguity in this area might broaden the scope and scale of the topic. Dealing with all MEAs which have trade-related provisions will broaden the negotiating agenda and challenge the limited negotiation capacity of developing countries. It is a well known fact that developing countries have very limited technical expertise and few resources with which to tackle new and emerging issues like the environment. The sheer number of MEAs (if they all are included in the negotiating agenda for the purpose of para. 31(i)), and the complexity of the areas they deal with, will certainly place a greater demand on developing countries to keep up with the resources and technical expertise needed to better understand the issues and contribute accordingly.

Developing countries also have concerns with regard to the status of the WTO rules against MEAs. They are concerned that, under the heavy influence of developed countries, MEAs may eventually take precedence over WTO rules. If this happens, it could give developed countries a powerful weapon with which to protect their markets against the exports of developing countries – which has already been demonstrated in the case of food safety standards.[65]

Developing countries also have concerns about how environmental goods and services will be defined for the purpose of para. 31(iii). At present, negotiations on environmental goods and services centre on goods of interest to developed countries. Developing countries are also concerned about the definition of 'environmental measure' for the purpose of para. 32(i). Developing countries apprehend that developed countries are likely to broaden the scope of the above areas to achieve their protectionist goals. They believe that in the absence of clarity, agenda items could be captured by interest groups who might use them to expand the agenda in future rounds at the cost of the interests of developing countries.

The *Doha Declaration* specifically addressed the concerns of developing countries regarding market access and problems associated with the use of environmental measures to deter the products of developing countries from accessing the markets of developed countries on grounds of environmental and technical standards.[66] However, developing countries are still concerned that inclusion of the trade and environment agenda might at some point include the precautionary principle in the negotiated text which may then be used as an arbitrary barrier to and disguised restriction on trade. In the past, developed countries, especially the EU, have on several occasions used precautionary reasoning to impose bans on technologies in spite of an absence of evidence of harm.[67] This substantiates the fear of developing countries that although not included in the *Doha Declaration*, in the future developed countries, particularly the EU, will try to include the precautionary principle in the negotiating text. If included, developing countries are concerned that the principle may be used for disguised trade measures to restrict the products of the developing countries from the markets of developed countries.

From the negotiating history it is evident that the EU was the main proponent of the inclusion of trade and the environment on the negotiating agenda despite strong opposition from developing countries. The EU has successfully included items such as the relationship between MEAs and WTO provisions and the reduction or elimination of tariffs and non-tariff barriers to environmental goods and services in the negotiating text. Of all the items that are included in the negotiating text, developing countries only requested the issues relating to market access and TRIPs.[68] This indicates that developed countries will expand the agenda on trade and environment if they have the opportunity to do so.

The Doha Round was launched to regenerate confidence in the multilateral trading system. The primary focus of the Doha Round was to bring development and growth to developing countries and so it was also known as the Doha Development Agenda. Despite the recognition of the problems faced by developing countries by the broader WTO membership, 'there were no shared perceptions on how to solve that problem, nor on what the precise "development" dimension of the Doha development agenda would be'.[69]

Although Doha cannot be regarded as fulfilling all the aspirations and demands of developing countries, it was 'in many ways more favourable to their interests than the accomplishments of all previous WTO Ministerials'.[70] Developing countries' concerns and interests are recognized in many areas such as intellectual property rights and public health, market access in agriculture, anti-dumping and the implementation of Uruguay Round commitments on textiles, technological assistance and capacity building. At the same time new issues such as trade and environment have been included despite the resistance of developing countries. The ultimate success of the Doha Round depends on the implementation of the commitments that were made by developed countries to their developing counterparts. Progress in the next round will show the political willingness of developed countries to making the promise of the 'development' round a reality.

The 2003 Cancun Ministerial Conference

The Cancun Ministerial Conference was held in Mexico on 10–14 September 2003. It was intended to review the progress on the Doha Agenda. The meeting ended unsuccessfully after failure to reach a consensus amongst the members. After the Doha Round there had been optimism about the Cancun Ministerial Conference. In Doha, all member states pledged to take into account the needs and interests of developing countries and to place them at the centre of the work programme of the WTO. The Cancun Ministerial Conference failed to take into account the concerns of developing countries. The centre of the fatal disagreement was the failure to make any progress on agriculture. Developing countries resisted proposals from the EU and the United States in relation to negotiations on agriculture and put forward their own alternative draft text as a basis for negotiation. Differences over the issues could not be solved because of lack of willingness on the part of developed countries to put concessions on the negotiation table.

The Cancun Round was launched with acrimonious disagreements between developed and developing countries. The differences between developed and developing countries were further widened by the reckless pursuit of the issues raised in the Singapore meeting by developed countries despite strong opposition from developing countries. The EU in particular argued that the Singapore issues were part of the single undertaking, and consequently needed to be addressed 'as part and parcel of the package that needs to be taken to Cancun'.[71] Some argue that the 'apparent and proximate cause of the Ministerial's collapse was a failure to agree on launching formal negotiations on the so-called Singapore issues'.[72]

Developing countries pointed out their grievances over the Uruguay Round and emphasized the need for the implementation of the commitments of developed countries. They felt that the new round of trade negotiations would not bring any positive result unless the existing discrepancies and imbalances in the negotiating items were removed.

Developing countries united over the disagreement with the North. They formed many alliances and groups with common interests. Among them Brazil, India and China made an effective alliance among more than twenty developing states. They organized themselves even before the Cancun meeting, reaching a firm decision not to support the launch of negotiations on the four Singapore issues. They succeeded in their attempt and the goal of the Cancun negotiation did not come to fruition. Overall, 'intransigence of the industrial economies on agriculture and of that of the developing economies on the Singapore finally led to the failure of the fifth Ministerial conference in Cancun'.[73]

The 2005 Hong Kong Ministerial Conference

The 2005 Hong Kong ministerial conference was held on 13–18 December 2005, and is generally considered to have been a marginally more successful conference than Cancun, but at the same time much more progress needs to be made to bring the Doha round to a close.[74]

Broadly speaking, the declaration coming out of the conference reaffirmed the outcomes of the Doha round, and committed members to completing negotiations on the Doha round by the end of 2006.[75] Paragraph 2 of the same document acknowledged the development dimension to all aspects of the Doha work programme.

Paragraph 31 of the *Doha Declaration* which discussed the interaction between trade and environmental issues (see above) was reaffirmed, and members were 'instructed' to 'intensify negotiations' on all parts of the paragraph to fulfil the mandates in that paragraph. The work of the Committee on Trade and Environment was acknowledged, and members were asked to complete the work of the Committee 'expeditiously'.[76]

However, since the Hong Kong round there has been little progress in the implementation of even the objective to conclude negotiations. Negotiations were suspended by the Director General in July when it became clear that trade ministers from the G6 (United States, India, Brazil, Australia, Japan and the EU) were going to be unable to agree on the magnitude of reductions in subsidies and tariffs for farms.

The net result is that the same position persists for developing countries after the Hong Kong ministerial conference. While positive statements were made, they were deliberately non-committal and as a result any progress on the issues has been slow or non-existent.

There were attempts by some developing countries such as India to garner support for specific trade and environment issues such as the conflict between the *TRIPs Agreement* and the *Convention on Biological Diversity*. However the end result was that the declaration simply took note of the work done in investigating the apparent conflict.

The way forward

Developing countries are really at a crossroads after the failure of the Cancun round and the lack of progress at the Hong Kong round. The *Doha Declaration* recognized their issues and concerns partially and provided them with an opportunity to realize the benefits promised to them in the Uruguay Round Agreements by removing imbalances and inequities in the existing agreements. However, the implementation of the commitments made in the *Doha Declaration* remains uncertain. The *Doha Declaration* recognized the need for the integration of the LDCs into the global trading system. This integration requires the development of solutions to the problems that developing countries are facing in relation to the market access of their products, technical assistance and capacity building. Since the failure of Cancun and Hong Kong, the progress on the above issues remains uncertain. While the commitment of developing countries to open their markets is binding, the concomitant commitment from developed countries to provide assistance for technology and capacity building remains a rather indeterminate 'best endeavour' requirement.

Between 2002 and early 2007, many interlinked and self-imposed deadlines established in the Doha agenda were missed. The chances of reaching an overall agreement in the near future in a manner that satisfies the text of both the Hong Kong and Doha ministerial declarations is far from likely. Deadlines for resolving issues in relation to market access, agriculture and trade-related intellectual property rights have been missed and have set the stage for further frustration and anger in developing countries.

The organized, united and coordinated stand of developing countries and their resulting success in Cancun and Hong Kong, will mean that in future developing countries will make an unprecedented effort to ensure that any future multilateral trade negotiations make allowances for their interests. Developing countries seem to have become major stakeholders in the world trade regime and have the power to refuse to negotiate on issues that do not reflect their interest and concerns. This development will undoubtedly challenge and influence the mandate of future ministerial conferences.

Conclusion

After the Hong Kong Ministerial Conference the stark division and distrust between developed and developing countries at the negotiating table continue to be sharp. If these differences between developed and developing countries continue without any long-term solution, the future of the world trading system will be at stake. The interests and concerns of developing countries warrant searching reappraisal for the continuity of the world trading system. The world trading system must consider how it can make trade free and fair for developing countries. Developing countries in the past agreed to negotiate in a number of areas with the hope that one day they would have the opportunity to achieve liberalization of trade in agriculture, textiles and clothing and other areas where they have a special interest and comparative advantage. But in exchange they had 'taken front loaded obligations in TRIPs, TRIMs and in Services, but had not received any benefits in textiles and clothing trade or agriculture'.[77] Now developed countries are adamantly pushing their agenda on trade and the environment – which is particularly evident from post-Seattle and Doha experiences.

In the past, developed countries have influenced or managed developing countries into accepting their unfair deal using a variety of tactics. If developed countries continue to employ such tactics to push their agenda on to the negotiating table and to compel developing countries to accept it, this

> will increase the contradictions within the WTO, as well as erode – quite possibly beyond repair – its legitimacy. As the number of people disenfranchised by this crudely unequal globalisation project increases, global civil society resistance can only be expected to increase, and move on to a larger stage.[78]

Overall, Cancun and Hong Kong could be a lesson to reassess the Doha mandate. Developed countries must fulfil their commitments and focus on the concerns of developing countries. Fulfilling the promises made at Doha could be the first step toward gaining the trust of developing countries. Developing countries should also come up with a positive and constructive agenda. Resisting agendas with their numerical strength is unlikely to create opportunities or secure their interests in the world trading system. It is in the interests of both developed and developing countries to make the world trading system operational. The complex nature of the interactions between trade and the environment calls for multilateral cooperation. Multilateral cooperation in this respect must be based on the principle of common but differentiated responsibility.

There is a need to review the progress of the Doha Development agenda and to thoroughly reassess the development implications of the WTO Agreements. Removing the inequities and imbalances in the WTO Agreements and fulfilling the promises made in Doha could help developing countries to tackle the trade–environment linkage without sacrificing their development priorities. Hollow development emphasis with empty promises will further deteriorate the already bitter relationship between developed and developing countries with the possibility of another backlash regarding the North–South agenda at the intersection of trade and the environment.

5 Regional approaches to free trade and sustainable development

The European Union

Economic regionalism has become the dominant trend in the international trading system. This trend has paralleled the movement towards globalization since the early 1990s. Regionalism is likely to evolve as a spontaneous phenomenon to further progress in the multilateral world trading system. It accelerates the removal of restrictions in trade and investment.

The formation of regional economic blocs has received the implicit support of the *General Agreement on Trade and Tariffs* ('GATT'), which has incorporated the possibility of regional trading arrangements into Article XXIV. This article provides, under certain conditions, for exceptions to other GATT provisions for the establishment of customs unions and free trade areas, dropping barriers among themselves. This exception was included because it was thought that free trade area groupings would facilitate trade between regional parties without harming free trade between other contracting parties.[1] This rationale was incorporated into Article XXIV in the form of a condition precedent to the operation of the article.

Uncertainties about the successful conclusion of the Uruguay Round accelerated the emergence of new trade groupings committed to regional and bilateral trade liberalization. While the Uruguay Round accord was finally concluded in 1994, some gaps in its provisions – such as failure to reach agreements on agriculture, services and trade-related investment measures as well as ambiguities and loopholes in GATT, have, in part, led to increasing reliance on new forms of regional arrangement.[2] The creation of the European Union ('EU'), the *North American Free Trade Agreement* ('NAFTA') and Asia-Pacific Economic Cooperation ('APEC') are testimony to this trend.

However, the pace of regionalization, accompanied by increasing investment and production ties for creating the economies of scale, has had negative impacts on the global environment. National measures for the protection of the environment are often in direct conflict with the trading interests of regional trading blocs. Disparate national environmental standards have been considered a barrier to free trade. As a result, the pressure to harmonize national policies such as common environmental policies, monetary and fiscal policies and common labour standards is increasing within free trade areas in an attempt to further the competitive advantage of the member states in trade and investment.

For this reason, harmonization of the environmental standards of member states has been a priority for regional trade agreements.

This chapter examines trade and environment linkage in the EU. The EU's environmental and trade policy is very complex and comprehensive. Full consideration of the European trade and environmental policy is beyond the scope of this chapter, which only examines the development of the trade–environment nexus and the treatment of this development by the EU. The trade–environment relationship in the EU is also examined from the perspective of developing countries.

Development of the concept of sustainable development in the European Community

The EU was officially known as the European Economic Community until 1987. The *Single European Act* of 1986 introduced the term European Community ('EC') which remained in popular use until the 1993 *Treaty of the European Union ('Maastricht Treaty')* created the EU with its structure of European Commission, Council of Ministers and European Parliament. The European Economic Community was established in 1957 by the *Treaty of Rome* with the aim of creating economic growth and stability among the member states. The *Treaty of Rome* was designed to form a common market for the free movement of goods, services, labour and capital by eliminating tariffs, import quota restrictions, export subsidies and all non-tariff barriers. An equivalent and undistorted competitive position for EC member states was the Community's priority during its early stages. As the environment as a policy consideration did not emerge until later, the 1957 *Treaty of Rome* did not specifically refer to the need for an environmental policy and contained no provision regarding environmental protection.

However, rapid economic growth, with its resulting effect on the environment and the shifting of public values toward greater environmental protection compelled the European Community to integrate economy and ecology. Environmental protection became a political issue. In the aftermath of the 1972 UN Conference on the Human Environment, the European Community recognized the pressing need for Community policy to protect the environment. Of particular concern was the transboundary nature of pollution which can cause problems for any state which shares its borders with others and the distorting effects on competition and trade arising out of the differences in national environmental policies. These concerns prompted the European Community to develop policies for the harmonization of environmental standards. In 1972 the Paris Summit openly acknowledged that environmental protection was a legitimate Community goal and decided to take action accordingly.[3] In 1973 the EC adopted its first Environmental Action Programme which stated that 'effects on the environment should be taken into account at the earliest possible stage in all technical and decision making processes.'[4] The Second Environmental Action Programme was concerned with clean-up measures to reduce pollution and to improve certain aspects of the environment. However, the concept of environmental protection remained underdeveloped until the Third Environmental Action Programme.

The Third Environmental Action Programme

The Third Environmental Action Programme was indicative of a major shift of European Community policy towards environmental protection. It expressed the objective of economy and ecology integration, noting that:

> concern for the environment [would be incorporated] into the policy and development of certain economic activities ... [which would] thus promote the creation of an overall strategy making environmental policy a part of economic and social development.[5]

This initiative paved the way for the concept of sustainable development in the Community. Thus the Community explicitly recognizes the importance of environmental protection to competitiveness in the longer term and to a continuation in the improvement of quality of life and standards of living.

The Community environmental policy at this stage evolved independently of the *Treaty of Rome*. As a consequence, the legitimacy of Community environmental policy was often questioned. Without an explicit legal basis, it was not mandatory for member states to follow the policy. Yet despite their 'soft status', the Environmental Action Programmes have provided the guidelines and directions for Community environmental policy making.

The **Single European Act** *1986: a new move towards legitimizing environmental policy*

The *Single European Act* of 1986 amended the *Treaty of Rome* and provided a legal basis for the Environmental Action Programmes by incorporating specific environmental provisions into the Treaty. The increasing importance of the environment prompted the European Community to add a new Title VII to Part III of the *Treaty of Rome*, dealing with the environment. Title VII gave legal foundation to all the Environmental Action Programmes which had been developing since 1972. The new provision upgraded the integration principle expressed in the Third Environmental Action Programme into a legally binding obligation for the Community. The new framework clarified the principles of the European Community's environmental policy (such as the preventive action, rectification of environmental damage at source and polluter should pay principles) and provided that 'environmental protection requirements shall be a component part of the Community's other policies'.[6] The provision also gives the European Commission the authority to consider the environmental implications of proposed Community legislation.

Another legislative process intended to upgrade the integration of environment principle was the introduction of qualified majority voting ('QMV') by the *Single European Act*. This meant that measures related to the completion and functioning of the 'Internal Market' would be adopted by a qualified rather than 'absolute' majority. Under QMV each member state is allocated a certain number of votes in the Council of the European Union, weighted according to the size of the population of the state (though adjusted for small countries, which are thus relatively over-represented). To achieve a qualified majority, there must then be agreement from a majority of states, and a set number of votes (currently 258 out of 345). The European Commission took advantage of this qualified majority voting, frequently seeking to introduce environmental legislation under Article 100A (now Article 95)[7] of the *Treaty of Rome*, which provided that 'harmonization measures could be adopted by a qualified rather than absolute majority'. In other words, decisions relating to the harmonization of environmental standards may be passed into EU/EC law despite the objection of a member state.[8]

In replacing the traditional absolute voting system with a system of qualified majority voting, Article 100A (1) has considerably simplified the decision-making process. In addition, qualified majority voting helped the European Community to adopt more stringent environmental standards.

A basis for environmental regulation: Article 130S or 100A?

The *Treaty of Rome* does not make any clear division between Article 100A (now Article 95) and Article 130S (now Article 175). This has created some ambiguity and uncertainty as to their application. Article 130S allows the Community to regulate the environment independently of its connection with the internal market. On the other hand, Article 100A gives the Community the authority to harmonize policies for the creation or operation of the internal market. While most proposed measures could fall equally well under Article 100A or 130S, the procedures for adopting environmental regulations differ depending on which article is chosen.[9] Article 100A permits qualified majority voting. By contrast Article 130S requires unanimous voting to form Community norms on the environment. As the harmonization of environmental standards is relevant to the functioning of the internal market, the Commission has justified its past use of Article 100A by referring to the need to create an internal market, although member states' national environmental standards could have been better dealt with under Article 130S. Under Article 130S, member states, subject to certain conditions, can keep or adopt stronger environmental protection measures than those contained in EC law, even when they interfere with the operation of the internal market. This division between the two articles has led to serious institutional conflict within the Community, with the European Community Commission and Parliament favouring Article 100A, and the Council (i.e. member states) preferring Article 130S.[10]

The Maastricht Treaty *and the Fifth Environmental Action Programme: towards sustainable development*

The *Treaty of the European Union* 1992 (the *'Maastricht Treaty'*) transformed the European Community into the European Union in 1994. The Treaty's objective was to provide the European Community with a single currency, a single central bank and common foreign and defence policies. However, this treaty has brought about significant changes in Community environmental policy through its Articles 2 and 3 which describe clearly the environmental goals of the EU. Article 2 made sustainable development with one of the Community's fundamental objectives by making it obligatory for the Community to 'promote throughout the Community a harmonious and balanced development of economic activities, sustainable and non-inflationary growth respecting the environment'.[11] To give effect to, or reinforce, Article 2, Article 6 (now Article 12) provides for the integration of environmental requirements into other policies.

In addition to existing Community environmental policy, the *Maastricht Treaty* added two new principles to Article 130R(2) (now Article 174(2)):

1 Community policy on the environment shall aim at a high level of protection, taking into account the diversity of situations in the various regions of the Community.
2 Community policy on the environment shall be based on the precautionary principle.

The first of these two new principles, with its stress on a high level of protection of the Community environment, reflects the increased importance of the Community environmental policy which was previously found in Article 100A(3) (now Article 95(3)) of the *Treaty of Rome*.[12] More innovative is the precautionary principle which now precedes the principle that preventive action should be taken.[13] Article 130R(2), among others, has provided for the integration of environmental protection into the definition and implementation of other Community policies. Integrating provisions for environmental protection into other Community policies is a bold innovation which builds upon the earlier commitment in Title VII (now Title IX) of the *Single European Act* which simply required environmental protection to be a component of the Community's other policies.[14]

The EU has made the promotion of 'sustainable growth respecting the environment' an overriding objective. It has clearly given a substantial boost to the reconciliation of the nexus between trade and the environment. By including Article 3(k) in the *Maastricht Treaty* the EU expressly includes environmental policy in the sphere of Community activity. In making sustainable development the objective of Community policy, the EU has placed environmental protection on an equal footing with the original economic concerns of the *Treaty of Rome*.

In 1999 The European Commission integrated a programme of sustainable development into the EU's trade policies, through the development of a *Trade*

Sustainability Impact Assessment ('TSIA'). The TSIA was designed as a new assessment tool for trade negotiators, NGO's and other relevant stakeholders to identify the social and environmental impact of trade agreements, and to stimulate initiatives that would yield the most beneficial outcome in terms of trade, economic growth and the environment.

The TSIA is composed of a sophisticated and comprehensive assessment criterion that uses indicators which include social, environmental and economic components, and variables which include: equity and poverty, environmental air quality, biological diversity and natural resource stocks to determine appropriate development outcomes. Since its inception in 1999, the TSIA has been carried out for all major EU trade negotiations, including negotiated agreements with African, Caribbean and Pacific ('ACP') countries. This broad commitment to sustainability was given greater credence with endorsement of the TSIA by the European Council at Gothenburg in 2001. In 2002 this commitment to sustainable development was enshrined by the European Commission in its *Communication on Impact Assessment*,[15] which introduced a comprehensive regulatory and assessment framework for all policy areas, including trade.[16] In 2002 the integration of environmental requirements into European Standards was also explicitly stated in the Sixth Environment Action Programme[17] adopted by the Council and European Parliament in 2002. In 2006, the TSIA was used by the EU as an assessment tool in WTO and Mercosur negotiations.

The trade–environment interface in the European Community

The interface between trade and the environment in the European Community has been marked by frequent clashes of policy. The European Community was designed to be a customs union, with the free movement of goods within a common border being one of the fundamental freedoms enshrined in the *Treaty of Rome*. Article 30 (now Article 28) of that treaty states that:

> Quantitative restrictions on imports and all measures having equivalent effect shall without prejudice to the following provisions, be prohibited between member states.[18]

In the *Dassonville Case*, the ECJ has interpreted 'measures having equivalent effect' as 'all trading rules enacted by member states which are capable of hindering, directly or indirectly, actually or potentially, intra-Community trade'.[19] It is clear from this statement that one must look to the effects of a measure and not to its aim in deciding whether it falls under Article 30.[20] As a result, any environmental measures resulting in import bans, import licensing systems, and/or packaging and labelling obligations which treat imported goods differently from those produced domestically may fall under Article 30. The *Dassonville* formula in relation to the ambit of Article 30 has been criticized as being too broad. Many authors have suggested that limiting the scope of the application of this article may be necessary to avoid future trade environment conflicts.[21]

Article 34 (now Article 29) of the *Treaty of Rome* also prohibits quantitative restrictions on exports and all measures having equivalent effect. In the *Inter-Huiles Case* the ECJ held that Article 34's prohibition included:

1 All national measures whose specific object or effect is to restrict patterns of exports.
2 [The] establishment of differing treatment between the domestic trade of a member state and its export trade so as to provide a special advantage for domestic products.[22]

The scope of Articles 30 and 34 is examined further in the following section in light of the environmental exceptions provided by Article 36 (now Article 30).

Exceptions for environmental justifications under Article 36

Article 36 (now Article 30) of the *Treaty of Rome* sets out exceptions to the fundamental prohibition on quantitative restrictions on trade between member states, stating that:

> [T]he provisions of Articles 30 to 34 shall not preclude prohibitions or restrictions on imports, exports or goods in transit justified on grounds of public morality, public policy or public security; the protection of health and life of humans, animals or plants; the protection of national treasures possessing artistic, historic or archaeological value; or the protection of industrial and commercial property. Such prohibitions or restrictions shall not, however, constitute a means of arbitrary discrimination or a disguised restriction on trade between member states.[23]

Article 36 does not mention the word 'environment', and only touches upon environmental protection incidentally through the clause 'the protection of health, and life of human animal or plant'. As a consequence, member states can justify environmental protection measures only for the purpose of protecting non-economic values such as public morality, public policy, public security and the protection of human health, animals and plants.

In a consistent line of precedents,[24] the ECJ has made it clear that Article 36 must be strictly interpreted and that it does not extend to justifications not mentioned in the article. In the famous *Cassis de Dijon* case, the ECJ established an important principle known as the 'rule of reason' which describes some measures that may be justified as limiting the application of Article 30 (now Article 28), the free trade principle. In the absence of clear guidelines, the 'rule of reason' determines the circumstances under which Article 36 environmental exceptions can be resorted to restrict the free movement of goods and services. The rule allows member states to adopt non-discriminatory trade-restrictive measures to protect the environment in certain situations, and has established this principle in the following words:

> Obstacles to movement within the Community resulting from disparities between the national laws relating to the marketing of the products in question must be accepted in so far as those provisions may be recognized as being necessary in order to satisfy mandatory requirements relating in particular to the effectiveness of fiscal supervision, the protection of health, the fairness of commercial transactions and the defence of the consumer.[25]

The *Cassis de Dijon* is a very significant case in that it has established the principle by reason of which the Article 36 environmental exception could legitimately restrict the free movement of goods and services. In this case, West Germany banned the French liqueur Cassis de Dijon, claiming that it had a low alcohol content and was likely to be hazardous to some sections of the population as it could be abused by certain groups of people. They also claimed that the banned imports had a comparative advantage over domestic beverages because tax rates for liqueurs were tied to the percentage of alcohol they possessed. The ban was challenged before the ECJ.

The Court examined the interrelationship between Articles 30 and 36 and concluded that the relationship between the environment and human, animal and plant health was sufficient to merit the use of Article 36 exceptions for environmental purposes. In this context the Court adopted a balancing or proportionality test to weigh the means and ends of an environmental measure against its impact on trade. They employed this test in finding that the German ban was illegal. According to the ECJ, Cassis de Dijon was not proved to be a real health danger to consumers. Moreover, if the German objective was to protect the public health, a less intrusive measure such as a labelling requirement could have been adopted. The balancing test established that disparities in national laws for the sake of the public good could be legitimate and were to be expected until full harmonization of standards could be accomplished within the common market.[26] However, while this case specifically addressed health measures, subsequent decisions have extended the 'rule of reason' and the proportionality analysis as bases for the adjudication of cases involving environmental regulations with trade effects.[27]

In its judgement the ECJ established that any measure which directly or indirectly restricted intra-Community trade did not breach Article 30 if the measure was necessary to satisfy 'mandatory requirements'. In the *Waste Oil* case,[28] the ECJ confirmed that environmental protection constituted one of the 'mandatory requirements' recognized in *Cassis de Dijon*. In adding environmental protection to the list, the decision represented a significant extension of *Cassis de Dijon* jurisprudence.[29]

The *Waste Oil* case arose over the validity of Directive 75/439/EEC which was aimed at protecting the environment by creating a system of safe disposal for waste oils. The Court insisted that:

> the principle of freedom of trade is not to be viewed in absolute terms but is subject to certain limits justified by the objectives of general interest pursued by the Community provided that the rights in question are not substantially impaired ... There is no reason to conclude that the Directive has exceeded those limits. The Directive must be used in the perspective of environmental protection, which is one of the Community's essential objectives.
>
> (Procurer de la République V Association de défense des bruleurs d'huiles usagées (ADBHU) Judgement March 23, 1983, Case 240/83 [1985] ECR 531, point 12)

It is evident from the decisions of both the *Cassis de Dijon* and the *Waste Oil* cases that trade-related environmental measures in non-harmonized areas of European Community integration can be justified only if they meet the following conditions:

1 The measures are necessary to protect the environment.
2 They are proportionate to their aim.
3 They do not constitute an arbitrary discrimination or a disguised restriction on trade between member states.

The principle of proportionality and necessity

In the European Community, a considerable body of case law relying on the proportionality principle has been established.[30] A succinct definition of what the principle entails was provided by the ECJ in *Fromançais v. Forma*:

> [I]n order to establish whether a provision of Community law is consonant with the principle of proportionality, it is necessary to establish, in the first place, whether the means it employs to achieve the aim correspond[s] to the importance of the aim and in the second place, whether they are necessary for its achievement.[31]

Member states derogating from their obligations under Article 30 of the *Treaty of Rome* can adopt measures to impose quantitative restrictions on trade but:

1 They must be pertinent, i.e. there must be a causal relationship between the measure adopted and the attainment of the objective pursued.
2 The measures must be the least trade-restrictive method of attaining that purpose.[32]

The proportionality test was first applied to a potential conflict between free trade and environmental protection in the *Danish Bottles* case.[33] In this case the ECJ had to decide on a complaint brought by the European Commission regarding the law in Denmark governing the reuse of beverage bottles and whether this law was in breach of Article 30 of the *Treaty of Rome*. In 1978 Danish legislation empowered the relevant Minister to adopt certain rules restricting, limiting or prohibiting the use of certain materials and types of drink container to prevent pollution. The National Agency for the Protection of the Environment ('NAPE') was given the necessary power to administer the law relating to those rules. Pursuant to this power legislation was adopted in 1981 requiring that:

1 All beer and soft drinks must be sold in reusable containers and all producers wishing to market those drinks on the Danish market must participate in a compulsory deposit and return system.
2 All drink containers are to be pre-approved by the NAPE.

Producers of beverages and containers in other member states considered this system a barrier to trade which restricted the import of their products into Denmark. This view was shared by the European Commission, which urged the Danish government to change the law. As a result, in 1984 the Danish government amended the 1981 law in such a way that foreign companies were allowed to import established non-approved containers, not exceeding 3000 hls a year, per producer, into Denmark. However the amendment did not satisfy the Commission and consequently the Commission brought an action under Article 169 (now Article 226) of the *Treaty of Rome*.[34] The Commission argued that the measure adopted by Denmark was designed to protect domestic soft drink and beer industries and was an unnecessary restriction on imports from foreign companies. Proceedings to have both the compulsory deposit and return system and the NAPE bottle approval system declared incompatible with Article 30 (now Article 28) of the *Treaty of Rome* were begun. The Commission claimed that the Danish measure was discriminatory in that it treated foreign companies differently. Moreover, the measure was not proportionate to its environmental gain.

The ECJ considered the two issues separately. Regarding the former, the ECJ referred to a range of case law and stated that in the absence of common rules relating to the marketing of the products in question, obstacles to free movement within the Community resulting from disparities between the national laws must be accepted in so far as such rules, applicable to domestic and imported products without distinction, may be recognized as being necessary in order to satisfy mandatory requirements of Community law.

However, such restrictive rules must be proportionate to the aim in view. The ECJ held that if a member state has a choice between various measures to achieve the same objective, it should choose the means which least restrict the free movement of goods. Therefore, the protection of the environment is a mandatory requirement which may limit the application of Article 30 of the *Treaty of Rome*.[35]

The ECJ considered the obligation to participate in a deposit and return system an essential element of a system aimed at securing the reuse of containers and therefore necessary to attain the objectives of the disputed regulations. In view of this finding, the restrictions which they impose on the free movement of goods should not be considered as disproportionate. The proposed measures were therefore considered necessary to achieve the aim pursued and held proportionate.

On the second issue, the Court found that the requirements for approval of NAPE were disproportionate to the objective pursued and a breach of Article 30. The Court concluded that:

> In [the] existing system of return ... approved containers guarantee a maximum percentage of re-use and therefore gives considerable protection to the environment. However the system for returning non-approved containers is capable of protecting the environment and, so far as imports are concerned, covers only limited quantities of beverages by comparison with the quantity consumed in the country because of the restrictive effect of the compulsory return of containers on imports. Under these conditions, limiting the quantity of products which can be marketed by importers is disproportionate to the objective.[36]

The proportionality principle was also interpreted in *Commission v. Republic of Germany*.[37] In this case, Germany had enacted a law which required all imported livestock to be slaughtered at slaughterhouses approved by the German government. West Germany justified its measures as necessary for sanitary reasons. However, the ECJ adopted the proportionality test and found that German law went much further than was reasonably necessary to achieve the legitimate purpose of ensuring that meat sold to German nationals was safe. As a result, the ECJ struck down the provision, suggesting that other methods were available to achieve the same objective, such methods including regulations requiring slaughterhouses to furnish proof of their sanitary conditions.[38]

In many cases the proportionality test has made it difficult to justify a legitimate health and environmental measure.[39] Even once the need for some form of regulation is recognized, as it was in the *German Meat* and *Danish Bottle* cases, the precise method of implementation must be one that achieves its objective with the least disruption to trade.[40] In this context, free trade seems to have received a far higher priority than environmental protection. Free trade has also been prioritized in the accession treaties for the recent enlargement of the EU, with the inclusion of a 'safeguard clause' in Article 38 which allows the Commission to take 'appropriate measures' against new members that fail to implement their commitments made during accession negotiations.[41] This clause reinforces the primacy of the internal market over other policy areas such as the environment.[42]

The application of the proportionality principle is a matter of judgement. It is becoming increasingly clear that courts are structurally ill equipped for dealing with trade measures for non-trade purposes.[43] This gives rise to profound issues of legitimacy, which, ultimately, have consequences for the acceptance of their decisions and their authority.[44]

The determination of 'least restrictive to trade' criteria by the ECJ raises the question of whether the ECJ should be given the authority, in absence of any guidelines, to make difficult social choices reconciling the conflict between trade and the environment. By striking down national environmental measures which involve unreasonable restrictions on trade on the ground of proportionality, the ECJ is embarking on a programme of negative harmonization.[45] The ECJ's trend towards limiting environmental measures as being necessary to achieve their aims may lead to the 'downward pressure of environmental protection within the Community'.[46]

Negative harmonization could be viewed as dismantling progressive national solutions in favour of less effective solutions. By judicially invalidating progressive environmental laws because of conflict with the goal of economic integration, the ECJ in effect freezes environmental protection standards at a level lower than those possible if states and market forces were left free to act. The accession of twelve new members to the EU increases the risk of such 'freezing', as the status quo will be kept at the lowest common denominator. Newly acceded countries such as Poland, Slovakia and Malta simply do not have the resources or policies in place to match the more developed member nations or raise environmental standards.[47]

The ECJ, in interpreting and applying the proportionality principle in the *Danish Bottle* case, has made an 'uncertain and ambiguous' distinction between, on the one hand, measures which ensure an effective degree of environmental protection (such as the deposit and return system) and, on the other hand, measures which ensure a *very* effective degree of environmental protection (such as the licensing system).[48]

In the process of applying this delicate balancing test, the highest environmental standard measure is likely to be treated as a disguised form of protectionism. As the proportionality and necessity tests are not strictly distinguished in the case law, the ECJ may leave the member state concerned a broad power of factual appraisal and policy discretion as to whether the national measure is 'necessary' and 'proportionate' for achieving the public policy objective.[49]

However, the evolution of environmental rules by judicial bounding has certain limitations. It cannot address the root causes of the problems. Neither can it intervene to set common standards at the Community level. Although the ECJ is criticized for the proportionality principle, it is through this principle that balances between the necessary and least trade-restrictive requirements can be struck. The ECJ, in applying this principle, can make sure that competition is not distorted by variations in environmental rules.

The principle of non-discrimination

The principle of non-discrimination was established by the *Cassis de Dijon* case which clarified that national laws must be non-discriminatory in order to be covered by the 'rule of reason'. However, in the *Wallonian Waste* case,[50] the ECJ had the opportunity to set a new definition of the notion of non-discrimination. The case concerned the validity of a decree of the Walloon Regional Executive which prohibited the importation of all waste into Wallonia. It provided for some exceptions in respect of the other Belgian regions such as

Flanders and Brussels. The European Commission challenged the decree, alleging that the Walloon measures were discriminatory and contrary to the objective of Directive 75/442 on Waste, Directive 84/631 on the Supervision and Control within the Community of the Trans-frontier Shipment of Hazardous Waste, as well as to Article 30 (now Article 28) and 36 (now Article 30) of the *Treaty of Rome*.

Belgium justified the ban on environmental grounds, arguing that it was necessary to protect Wallonia from becoming the target of waste from other member states with strict regulatory regimes. Moreover, as the waste did not have commercial value it could not be considered 'goods' and therefore did not fall within the scope of the provisions on the free movement of goods. The European Commission challenged the Wallon measure as discriminatory because it prohibited only the movement of foreign waste into the Wallon territory, not the storage or disposal of any waste produced in Wallonia. The Commission argued that the measure could not be justified on environmental grounds because it discriminated between national and imported products and as such was not justifiable with reference to mandatory requirements, as discrimination against imported goods precludes reliance on mandatory requirements.

The ECJ examined the case in two stages. First, the ECJ rejected Belgium's claim that waste could not be classified as goods in the absence of commercial value. It confirmed that waste, whether recyclable or not, constitutes goods, the free movement of which is protected by Article 30 of the *Treaty of Rome*.

Second, the ECJ found that Belgium's action was justified as an environmental protection measure. The ECJ realized that the accumulation of waste, even before it reaches levels that present dangers to health, constitutes a danger for the environment, especially when considering the limited capacity of each region or locality to deal with it.[51] The ECJ did not accept the European Commission's argument regarding the discriminatory character of the impugned measure.

According to the ECJ, even though mandatory requirements could be relied on only in the case of measures which applied indiscriminately to national and imported products, it was necessary to take account of the specific nature of waste in order to determine whether or not the nature of the trade restriction was discriminatory.[52] The ECJ then relied on the principle that environmental damage should be rectified at its source, which implied that it was for each region, commune or other locality to take the appropriate measures to ensure the proper treatment and disposal of its own wastes. This, according to the ECJ, meant that waste had to be disposed of as close as possible to the place of its production in order to minimize the transport of waste.

The ECJ referred to the principle of self-sufficiency and proximity set out in the *Basel Convention* of 1989,[53] to which the Community is a signatory. Taking into account the differences between wastes produced in one place and wastes produced in another and considering their connection with the place where they are produced, the ECJ decided that the contested measures could not be regarded as discriminatory.

The harmonization of environmental standards and the implications

The EU provides for the upward harmonization or approximation of member states' environmental measures through both legislation and voluntary standards,[54] which are managed in the EU by international organizations such as the European Committee for Standardization.[55] Whilst legislation and standards are two different measures,[56] each complements the other, and in many circumstances standards are often the precursor to legislation. Standards and conformity assessments are developed in an open and transparent manner between the relevant member state stakeholders on a basis of consensus. European standards may be based on international standards if they are available and meet the needs of the EU.[57] The standards 'may refer to how the product is made, used, maintained and treated at the end of its life cycle.'[58] Imports into the EU of the particular product require permits from a multitude of certification and accreditation bodies[59] determining bilateral equivalency standards and agreements,[60] under the approval of a designated minister of the relevant member state. This harmonization of environmental product standards has been used as a prime instrument to ensure the free movement of products, and has relied more heavily on uniform standards than any other approach.[61] It has been successful in substantially harmonizing environmental standards because of the similarities in the economic systems of member states.

Although harmonization has had many positive effects on trade–environment relationships, it does not come without costs. Upward harmonization can force comparatively weaker parties to accommodate the stringent environmental standards of stronger, greener parties who disregard the special condition of the former. This is reinforced by the fact that although a standard may be developed across the EU, the method of implementation of the relevant regulations is at the discretion of the member states, which makes possible multiple interpretations of the relevant rules, particularly import procedures and requirements[62] that affect exporting countries outside the EU, and in particular developing countries.[63] The nature of the European rules and standards are such that they are relevant to European circumstances, and are often not 'suitable to agro-ecological conditions of exporting countries'.[64] Further, exporters may lack the capacity to comprehend important details of import measures; they may not be in a position to have the import measures translated; or have the capacity to apply certain measures[65] and obtain original certification of conformity and equivalency[66] of products for entry[67] into the EU.

In a positive step, the pre-accession negotiations for the latest enlargement involved a forum for 'structured dialogue' between the central and eastern European countries and the EU members, as well as the provision of significant aid in support of meeting environmental standards.[68] The financial challenge of compliance with high environmental standards has also been recognized in a number of situations where derogations from standards have been allowed. The Large Combustion Plants Directive[69] regarding cuts in EU emissions of sulphur dioxide allowed Greece, Ireland and Portugal to increase their emissions and allowed Spain special derogations. Concessions remained in the revised version of this directive in 2001.[70] Similarly differential treatment was applied with respect to the EC's Kyoto Protocol commitment of 2002 and the Packaging Waste Directive of 1994. A directive on the quality of petrol and diesel fuel[71] allows members to request derogations of time regarding the provisions on lead and sulphur to take into account geographical or climatic conditions or serious socio-economic difficulties.[72] While such measures are encouraging, they are not comprehensive, and reflect the further need for a more sensitive approach to the formulation of environmental policies.

In March 2006 the south-eastern European countries concluded negotiations to consolidate thirty-two bilateral agreements into one central European Free Trade Agreement, and formed a single pact to liberalize trade in more than 90 per cent of industrial goods on 19 December 2006.[73] Being the region's largest external trading partner, the EU was instrumental in providing financial, technical and political support. EU trade with the south-eastern European countries amounted to €75 billion in 2005, and represented an increase of 53 per cent from 2001.[74] This process of increased trade links and economic cooperation will certainly require the harmonization of environmental standards and measures for entry of Southern European goods into the EU.[75]

The requirement to harmonize environmental standards has far-reaching implications for the market access of countries outside the EU. The EU, with its heterogeneous membership, has attained the highest standards in relation to environmental rules, product standards, intellectual property rules and competition policy. The harmonization of technical and product standards, processes and production methods requires the same standards from foreign goods if they are not to be given any kind of special treatment under preferential or Generalized System of Preferences ('GSP') arrangements. These standards have the potential to be used as non-tariff barriers which could be used as a protectionist weapon with which to deny market access to the products of developing countries. Even in the absence of protectionism, the adoption of different product standards may fragment the market, increase transaction costs and generate diseconomies of scale for all producers.[76] In the context of EU law, this problem has been clearly described by Advocate General Van Gerven in his opinion in joined cases C-401/92 and C-402/92:

> Product requirements by nature impede the access to the market of the Member State which laid them down, because they mean that a product lawfully manufactured and marketed in the Member State of origin must be adapted when it is imported into another Member State in order to suit the product requirements in force there, and therefore have the effect of requiring the product to satisfy the requirements of two different sets of legislation … which almost certainly has the effect of impeding the imported product's access to the market or even, when these costs are prohibitive, of making access impossible.[77]

Developed and developing countries within the European Union

There is a North–South split within the EU in relation to trade and environment policy-making, which has become more pronounced with the accession of Cyprus, the Czech Republic, Estonia, Hungary, Latvia, Lithuania, Malta, Poland, Slovakia, Slovenia, Bulgaria and Romania. The split between stronger northern European countries and relatively weaker southern European countries is evident from the setting of environmental standards to the implementation and enforcement of environmental rules. Thus, while Germany, the Netherlands and Denmark have strong and stringent environmental standards and other environment-friendly measures, Greece, Italy, Portugal and Spain, as well as the majority of the newly acceded members, have weaker environmental standards and measures.

The trade and environment agenda of the EU is strongly driven and influenced by powerful states' domestic health and environmental standards. Most of the environmental regulations have had their origin in the national environmental rules and norms of powerful northern states. The power and interests of the greener and richer countries have dominated the trade–environment agenda and have influenced the adoption of those national rules and regulations at the Community level. This was evident in the 1996 Inter-governmental Conference, where Denmark, Sweden and Germany pushed for the 'environmental guarantee' which would allow members to adopt higher environmental standards. Other member states were concerned that such measures would be used to favour domestic producers.[78] Richer states, particularly Germany, have used their power to exert environment-friendly pressure on international environment rules, coercing poorer countries into accepting greener rules, compensating them for doing so or signalling likely coercion or compensation.[79]

Richard H. Steinberg illustrates how Germany has used its market power to dominate trade–environment disputes. For example, when bargaining over auto emissions standards, Germany coerced other member states into raising their standards, with the threat of closing its market to other states' automobiles if they did not comply.[80] Likewise, Germany used its market power during the negotiations over the content of the *Single European Act* and the *Maastricht Treaty* to impel the rest of Europe to raise environmental standards, in return for Germany agreeing to further access to its market. Germany sought to ensure the most stringent standards possible through the language of the *Single European Act* and the *Maastricht Treaty*:

> Germany held fast for language in the Act stating that, in harmonizing national regulations, 'the Commission ... shall take as a base a high level of protection'. And for language in the Maastricht Treaty requiring that Community environmental measures 'shall aim for [a] high level of protection'.[81]

This is part of a pattern in which individual countries try, sometimes successfully, to transpose their domestic policy concerns and approaches on to the

European stage.[82] The northern European countries of Germany, Denmark, the Netherlands, Sweden and Finland have great power over countries such as Greece, Portugal, Spain, Italy, Cyprus, the Czech Republic, Estonia, Hungary, Latvia, Lithuania, Malta, Poland, Slovakia and Slovenia.[83] However, the expansion of the EU may make it more difficult for 'northern' countries to succeed in increasing environmental standards in the EU.[84]

There is also a concern that the environmental policy of the EU is paying too much attention to the post-materialist concerns of northern Europe and insufficient attention to the sustainable development concerns of southern Europe. The EU has been charged with pursuing expensive solutions to achieve marginal improvements in water quality whilst ignoring the damage caused by water abstraction in the more arid regions of Europe.[85] Powerful greener states propose and initiate environmental legislation with a view to upgrading common environmental standards, meanwhile weaker states find it hard to adhere to these standards in their national circumstances. Differences in circumstances call for differences in standards, yet the national circumstances of individual members are being sacrificed for the upward harmonization of environmental standards. Member states are bound by similar or comparable common environmental standards and as a result there is widespread inequality in relation to the implementation and enforcement of those standards among member states.[86] With the increasing diversity of member states there should be an increasingly diversified approach to the development of environmental policy.[87]

There are considerable gaps between the rules and their actual operation. This implementation deficit raises serious concerns about the overall effectiveness of the environmental policy of the EU. If not implemented, EU environmental policy risks becoming a paper exercise with little tangible effect on sustainable development.[88]

The European Commission is entrusted with the responsibility of overseeing the implementation and enforcement of EU environmental policies. The Commission can also initiate, formulate and make recommendations for new environmental policies. Commissioners are appointed by member states and are meant to be free from national affiliation and bias. They are given the sole power to initiate measures, though in practice this has been qualified by the growth of various conventions, which allow the Council and the Parliament to bring to the attention of the Commission items which they want on the agenda.[89] Although the Commission is producing some ambitious legislation in many areas, member states heavily influence the formulation of particular policies by the Commission. Member states tend to push their own priorities and approaches on to the Commission's agenda. A member state is better off in the implementation and enforcement of its own rules if its national standards/rules can be made the EU's rule. In effect, the Commission is heavily dependent upon member states for the development of particular policy measures and general principles. For instance, the directives on eco-audit or integrated pollution control were heavily dependent upon the attempt of the government of the United Kingdom to secure its approach within the EU.[90]

The European Commission has the power to initiate proceedings if a member state has not implemented or enforced the standards of the EU. It can initiate legal proceedings against that member state before the ECJ by claiming that the member state has failed to comply with its obligations under the law of the EU. This process is extremely slow and has proved a weak deterrent to violators. Thus the European Commission's power to implement and enforce the law is inadequate. When it comes to putting the law into effect at the national level, the Commission is on a steep upward slope, possessing neither the political resources nor the legal competence to delve substantially into national affairs.[91] There is a need and a proposal to enhance the capacity and role of the Commission in implementation and enforcement. Yet because the current political context is dominated by the principle of subsidiarity, it is unlikely that the powers of the Commission will be increased.[92]

The situations of developing countries (not within the EU) in the trade–environment interface of the European Union

Developed countries have been pioneers in the protection of the environment as they have incorporated different rules and regulations regarding product standards and set out specific requirements for product quality. The continuous growth of eco-labelling requirements and the multitude of country-specific product standards have become a serious market challenge for developing countries, and are putting them at a competitive disadvantage. Standards often increase the costs of goods beyond what developing countries can bear.

The EU initiative to harmonize product standards is directed towards achieving undistorted competition through uniform economic conditions among members of the EU. EU law is predicated upon the mutual recognition of standards – this implies that a product which complies with the standards of the exporting country should have free access to the markets of its trading partners. The Community's initiative regarding the harmonization of standards for production and processing methods has played a vital role in making this mutual recognition of standards a reality. This principle of mutual recognition has had a positive impact on the market access of the products of member states. Pursuant to mutual recognition, manufacturers no longer need to adapt products to varying standards in each of the countries of destination.[93] The mechanism works only while member states or trading partners have homogeneous standards. However, this principle of mutual recognition can have a negative impact on the market access of products which do not have a domestic standard comparable to the standards of importing countries. This will undoubtedly reduce the export opportunities of non-EU developing countries to the markets of developed countries in the EU. It is impossible for developing countries to meet the environmental requirements developed in EU countries. Thus, in effect, these environmental requirements may discriminate between domestic and imported products.

EU laws permit import bans or restrictions on products with poor environmental standards. EU member states are required to ban imports of goods involving animal parts from other member states and from outside the EU.[94] EU member states, under some directives, are also required to ban imports of goods from outside the EU not produced in accordance with specified EU production and processing methods. At least one ECJ decision suggests that a member state may maintain national environmental rules that are more stringent than EU or international standards and which ban the importation of goods from other member states with the intention of protecting animal life outside its border.[95]

In *Commission v. Denmark*, the ECJ interpreted Article 36 (now Article 30) of the *Treaty of Rome* to mean that each EU member may prohibit the import of goods if it is necessary to meet that country's chosen level of health or environmental standards. Despite the effects on intra-Community trade, measures prohibiting foreign imports were considered justified. These requirements, along with the homogeneous characteristics of the markets, will eventually make the EU a fortress to which the products of developing countries will have limited or no access.

Developing countries have different domestic infrastructure barriers. Many industrial processes cannot cope with the stringent environmental regulations but they are still competitive in the export market because of their low labour costs or their locational advantage. These countries tolerate higher levels of pollution as a trade-off for faster economic growth; to them environmental considerations are secondary given their widespread poverty.[96] However, if their lower environmental standards affect the production of goods, they are likely to become the victims of unilateral trade-related environmental measures.

Under the *Lomé Convention*,[97] developing countries receive some preferential trade arrangements from the EU. Although preferential schemes are designed to give developing countries trade preferences on non-reciprocal basis, a growing number of analyses show that preferences have either been of limited use or have benefited a much narrower set of recipients than intended when the preference scheme was originally designed.[98] A study carried out by the IMF and the World Bank has shown that the preference schemes at large have had limited success in generating significant export growth or improving the trade shares of beneficiaries.[99] Preferential systems are operational under the periodic renewal and the sole intention of the country giving preference. The country giving preference may make a unilateral decision about justification, purpose and content of the preference scheme and its duration. It can also select the countries who will receive the benefit of its non-reciprocal preference.

The preferential scheme under the Lomé Convention

The *Lomé Convention* is the most structured preferential system extended to developing African, Caribbean and Pacific ('ACP') countries by the EU. The system was propelled by compelling political reasons which were further backed by the perceived imperatives of the Cold War. The latter was reflected in the Convention's membership, which was dictated by selective post-colonial ties in a geographical region and the Cold War rather than by any set of coherent and consistent criteria.[100] While Angola, Dominica, Nigeria and Fiji are covered by the Convention's provisions, India, Bangladesh, Vietnam and Nepal are not, although they are fairly similar from a socio-economic point of view. Although the *Lomé Convention* was designed to provide a firm and solid foundation for trade cooperation between the ACP states, developing countries have witnessed a dramatic shift of the EU's preference in favour of the Central and Eastern EU since the fall of communism. This changing status has seriously downgraded the privileged positions of the preference-receiving South in terms of trade and aid. In 1995, for example, 8.6 per cent of the EU's imports and 10.2 per cent of exports were with the Central and Eastern European countries. By contrast, the seventy Lomé states only supplied 3.7 per cent of the EU's imports and took just 3.1 per cent of exports.[101] Despite the reiterated assurances of the EU, ACP access to the EU market has been declining rapidly. In 2003 EU total imports from ACP states accounted for only 3 per cent of total imports, 65 per cent of which was of raw materials.[102]

Rules of origin

To receive non-reciprocated trade preferences, or nil tariff rates (depending on the 'sensitivity' of the products imported into the EU) ACP countries must satisfy the rules of origin[103] of the EU's Generalized System of Preferences ('GSP'). The effect of the GSP is both to promote and restrict trade. To be eligible for preferential tariff treatment a product must wholly originate in a GSP beneficiary country, namely one of the fifty Least Developed Countries.[104] If however the product contains inputs from other countries, they may be considered for preferential treatment only if the product has undergone sufficient processing. Information on the rules of origin must be made available at each stage of processing of the products, by means of labelling, packaging or accompanying commercial documentation.[105] These requirements are creating an unfavourable bargaining position for ACP countries, making it hard for them to gain a market share in the EU.

Under the *Lomé Convention*, Professor S.K.B. Asante has observed, the rules of origin requirement in many cases cancels out the benefit of preferential access to EU markets and discourages the essential expansion of the value and range of manufactured goods from ACP countries.[106]

A restriction as high as 50–60 per cent of the total value added of the goods exported is, indeed, too stringent a qualification for products of ACP countries, nearly all of which are at a very early stage of industrialization.[107] Investigations by the Commonwealth Secretariat suggest that:

> few manufactured mineral products from Commonwealth Africa reach the required 50 percent of value added. Most of their processed and manufactured products do not benefit from the Lomé Convention's access provisions because they have only between 20 and 48 percent of value added as a proportion of their gross value.[108]

Deprivation of market access fostered the asymmetry which required ACP states to concentrate on exporting primary products if they hoped to benefit from the *Lomé Convention*. As the demand for primary products was falling in world markets, it shielded ACP producers from market access. Further, the most favoured nation ('MFN') based liberalization and removal of tariff barriers being undertaken by the EU, particularly in agriculture, is likely to further erode existing preferences to beneficiary countries.[109] The MFN reforms to least developed countries in Africa and in Bangladesh have been estimated to impose a welfare loss of US$460 million and US$100 million respectively.[110] The implementation of the *Agreement on Textiles and Clothing* in 2005 also represents a recent erosion of preferences. The expectant income loss for the preferential erosion has been estimated at US$1.7 billion dollars annually.[111]

ACP countries' dependence on a limited number of primary products was further exacerbated as a market access problem when multiple health and environmental regulations were imposed on their products. As a consequence, ACP markets have become markets captive to the maintenance of the status quo, and so they remain the producers of primary products and importers of EU manufactured goods.

Decades of preferential privilege through *Lomé* seem to have failed to bring any fundamental changes to the crucial problems of the ACP countries.[112] The effectiveness of trade preferences is being increasingly questioned.[113] After seventeen years of cooperation under the *Lomé Convention*, extensive data are now available showing that no significant progress was made by ACP states during this period and that ACP states are worse off now than they were before signing the *Lomé Convention*.[114]

The Cotonou Convention

The *Cotonou Convention*,[115] between the seventy-seven ACP countries and the fifteen EU states, was signed in the economic capital of Benin on 23 June 2000 and marks an important change in EU–ACP cooperation.[116] In 2004 sixteen East and Southern African ('ESA') countries from the ACP group of states officially launched WTO-compliant bilateral trade negotiations towards Economic Partnership Agreements with the EU.[117] The Convention, which replaces the fourth *Lomé Convention*, has been signed for twenty years and is to be revised every five years after that.

The central aims of the *Cotonou Agreement* are the building of a partnership between the EU and the ACP states[118] and the reduction of poverty.[119] While the *Lomé Convention* emphasized a non-political partnership between the EU and the ACP states, the *Cotonou Agreement* places politics at its centre with its emphasis on political dialogue and the effective management of aid.[120] It uses notions of 'dialogue', 'partnership' and ACP states 'owning' their own development strategies to create the impression that the relationship will be consensual and cooperative.[121] Yet the EU's presentation of Economic Partnership Agreements ('EPAs') as the only viable alternative to satisfy the principles and rules of the WTO as well as the implementation of frequent reviews of aid provision that have political conditionalities attached are in fact more coercive than cooperative, and tend to banish any sense of partnership between the EU and the ACP states.[122] This sense of coercion rather than cooperation or partnership is supported by the methods outlined for the achievement of the partnership, which are in fact more likely to hinder than assist the meeting of the goals expressed by the Agreement. This coercive approach to trade by the EU can also be seen in relation to WTO negotiations on cuts to agricultural tariffs, where concessions granted to developing nations are offset by conditions and exceptions which seem to undermine the real impact of any concessions.[123]

The trade pillar of the Cotonou Agreement

In 2007 the non-reciprocal trade preferences which were the cornerstone of previous *Lomé Conventions* will expire, and EPAs compatible with the multilateral trade rules of the WTO will come into force by 2008, and progressively remove barriers to trade between the EU and the ACP countries.[124] In order to solve the issue of WTO compatibility, under this new arrangement, the ACP membership will be divided into two subgroups – LDCs and non-LDCs. The classification of ACP countries into either group is based on WTO criteria except as regards non-WTO member states. Nonetheless, some serious anomalies regarding which states are classified LDCs and which are not have arisen: Samoa, the Solomon Islands, Lesotho and Equatorial Guinea are considered LDCs while they have a higher human development index ('HDI') value[125] than Cameroon, Congo, Kenya and Nigeria, which are not considered LDCs.[126]

Under the new arrangement, LDCs will continue to receive non-reciprocal trade preferences, while non-LDCs will be offered reciprocal EPAs, to be negotiated with the EU at an individual country or regional level. The alternative for non-LDCs is to become members of the EU GSP, which is less advantageous than the non-reciprocal Lomé preferences, as it covers fewer products and has stricter rules of origin.[127] The GSP is unilaterally offered by the EU, is not negotiated, and would thus remove 'even a rhetorical notion of partnership in EU–ACP relations'.[128] In addition, the reciprocity which is to be given to the non-LDCs is only likely to have some of the benefits officially predicted if ACP states are able adapt their economies to absorb the costs of adjustment.[129]

Two problems relating to the implementation of these new trade arrangements have been identified. First, the EU has a clear preference for the negotiation of EPAs on a regional basis. This is problematic, given the weakness common to the various regional groupings of a very underdeveloped institutional design and a 'disappointing history of regional integration efforts'.[130] If EPAs are to be negotiated with the EU, ACP regional groupings will need to make significant progress in their internal regional groupings integration projects, which may prove a substantial barrier to effective representation of the needs and interests of the organization during negotiations with the EU. Second, the impact of EPAs on many ACP states may be damaging, especially for the poorest members of these societies.[131] For example, the implementation of EPAs will substantially reduce the customs revenues of ACP states, which are unlikely to be compensated in the short term.[132]

One positive step in the *Cotonou Agreement* has been the acknowledgement of the relationship between trade and environment in Article 49, affirming the need to develop international trade in a way that ensures sustainable management. Also important is the support for the principle that environmental measures should be designed and implemented with due regard to the specific situations of ACP countries.[133]

The aid pillar of the Cotonou Agreement

Significant aspects of the *Cotonou Agreement* are Articles 96 and 97(3). Article 96 permits the suspension of co-operation when one of the parties considers that essential elements of the agreement have not been fulfilled. The *Cotonou Agreement* allows the suspension of aid if any of the following three essential elements are violated:

1 Respect for human rights as defined at international law.
2 The promotion of universal democratic principles and the independent rule of law.[134]
3 Good governance.[135]

The definition of these elements is crucial to ACP states, yet they are not clearly defined in detail in the *Cotonou Agreement.*[136] Article 97(3) also requires ACP countries identified as having corrupt practices to take steps to eliminate occurrences of corruption. ACP countries that fail to undertake remedial measures under Articles 96 and 97 will be prejudiced by the enforcement trade restrictions. This may pose significant obstacles for ACP countries such as Zimbabwe and the Democratic Republic of the Congo, among others.

Another significant aspect of the aid pillar is 'rolling' programming which allows the EU to regularly monitor aid allocations through political dialogue between the EU and each ACP state. This will allow the EU to reward those ACP states which successfully meet their European Development Fund ('EDF') resource targets.

This approach to aid provision further and seriously undermines any notion of equal partnership between the EU and ACP states.[137] This, in tandem with the provisions of the trade pillar of the *Cotonou Agreement*, suggests a relationship of coercion rather than cooperation or partnership.[138] In addition, the Agreement's requirement of compliance with WTO rules and principles – which just so happen to coincide with EU policy objectives – suggests that the EU is doing what it has done before – using regional and bilateral trade arrangements to achieve its foreign policy objectives rather than acting out of concern for or a desire to assist the developing countries of the ACP region.[139]

Conclusion

The EU has achieved a more developed and unique environmental policy than any other international or regional trade regime. The experience of the EU in integrating trade and the environment can be invaluable for global and other regional institutions striving to achieve the objective of sustainable development. The European institutions dealing with trade and the environment are better developed and perform more functions than those in the GATT/WTO. Most EU environmental legislation is adopted by qualified majority voting, which has helped the EU to adopt more stringent environmental standards. The absence of a unanimity requirement makes it easier to adopt principles and policies for the harmonization of environmental standards.

The EU has succeeded substantially in the harmonization of production and processing standards – a thorny issue in trade and environment relations. The EU approach demonstrates a careful balance between the two competing policy goals of trade and environment. The European Community developed the principle of preventive action, the Polluter Pays principle and the precautionary principle, which govern the EU's action relating to trade and the environment. In applying these principles, the EU should take into account the special situations of developing countries, the applicable legislation in some jurisdictions and scientific methods of risk assessment.

The EU, with its heterogeneous membership, has attained the highest environmental, product, intellectual property and competition policy standards. The harmonization of technical and product standards, processes and production methods requires the same standards from foreign goods if they are not given any kind of special treatment under the preferential or GSP arrangements.[140] These standards have the scope to be used as non-tariff barriers which in turn may be used as protectionist weapons to prevent the market access of developing countries. The ECJ has struck a balance between the objectives of free trade and environmental protection. It has struck a balance between necessary and least trade-restrictive requirements in terms of proportionality. But the ECJ has certain limitations to its ability to solve the real problems in relation to trade and environment. It cannot set environmental standards. It can address only the impediments, not the root causes. Mechanisms must be developed to ensure that unjustified differences in the stringency of environmental process standards do not distort competition. Although the harmonization of environmental standards among EU member states has resolved this problem to some extent, there are still major disparities among member states as regards the implementation and enforcement of environmental standards and rules. The EU maintains well developed and environmentally friendly trade–environment rules because it is the economic organization with the greatest level of integration and power in the world, and this is concentrated in favour of green countries.[141]

Non-EU member states and particularly developing countries, in the absence of the same environmental standards, do not get the same treatment as EU member states. They do not have the power or economic clout necessary to gain the same treatment. As a result, developing countries and non-EU member states have very little to gain from the well developed trade–environment rules of the EU. Rather, deeper integration and stringent environmental regulations have the potential to restrict the European market further for the goods of non-EU members and developing countries. In addition, uniform environmental standards may be used as protectionist barriers to the free movement of goods between states.

6 Regional approaches to free trade and sustainable development

The North American Free Trade Agreement

The *North American Free Trade Agreement*[1] ('NAFTA') was concluded between the United States, Canada and Mexico in 1993 and came into effect on 1 January 1994. It was grounded on the trade principles of the General Agreement on Tariffs and Trade ('GATT') and supersedes the *Canada–US Free Trade Agreement* ('CUSFTA').[2] NAFTA, the largest free trade zone[3] in the world, was created with the objective of phasing out tariff and non-tariff barriers to trade between the United States, Canada and Mexico. It was designed to promote fair competition and investment opportunities by furthering trilateral regional and multilateral cooperation. NAFTA presents a useful case study for the analysis of the situations of developing countries at the interface between trade and the environment. Mexico, as one of the parties to NAFTA, demonstrates the North–South clash in the integration of international trade and environmental priorities. Significantly, Mexico is the only developing country in the world to have entered into a free trade agreement which contains an environmental clause.[4]

NAFTA was designed to set principles and rules to eliminate barriers to trade in goods, services and investment. NAFTA rules are based on GATT governing principles (see Chapter 3). Prior to NAFTA negotiations, the trade–environment linkage was not perceived to be a serious issue. Environmental issues were not part of the original NAFTA negotiating agenda, being intentionally excluded from negotiations and the final text in order that the agreement might be speedily concluded.

Environmental issues emerged in NAFTA in early 1991 during the US Congress's debate over granting the President of the United States the authority to negotiate NAFTA under special 'fast track approval procedures'.[5] The debate gave rise to a sharp clash of cultures as the trade community began to address new environmental issues and the United States' environmental community entered the unfamiliar territory of international trade.[6] As a result of widespread public pressure from citizen groups and environmental organizations, NAFTA eventually provided for the integration of environmental concerns into its trade goal.

Although the Preamble to the NAFTA refers to a commitment to environmental protection, this protection is not afforded a special section within the agreement itself. Rather, the issue was addressed in the subsequently negotiated the *North American Agreement on Environmental Cooperation* ('Environmental Side Agreement') in 1993.[7] Thus any analysis of environmental issues within NAFTA must trace their progress through the negotiating process itself.[8]

NAFTA's attempt to reconcile the two potentially conflicting values raised some concerns for environmentalists as well as free-traders. Environmentalists were concerned that NAFTA as initially drafted did not sufficiently respect environmental values. They were afraid that the North American environment would face increased pressure as a result of an increasingly competitive economic climate, unregulated by a proportional respect for the preservation of that environment.[9] Environmentalists also expressed concern about the possibility that NAFTA's lax environmental standards could open the door of a 'race to the bottom' by compromising high US standards of environmental protection as part of downward 'harmonization' process. Thus NAFTA may eventually place a large amount of pressure on its parties to harmonize their environmental standards down to the lowest common denominator.[10] Mexico's poor environmental regulation enforcement record was another concern for environmentalists, who felt that Mexico might become a refuge for companies unwilling to comply with strict US/Canadian environmental regulations.

It was feared that NAFTA would give rise to a serious threat of economic and social polarization and faster environmental destruction in developing countries. In Mexico, this fear was strongly linked with North–South asymmetry and concerns that NAFTA would entail domination of the Northern culture of materialism and over-consumption over Mexico.[11]

On the other hand, the trade community viewed NAFTA as a pro-environment free trade Agreement which had not been captured by extremist interest groups.[12] The trade community saw in NAFTA the potential for increased *per capita* income. They felt that the agreement would give rise to a higher standard of environmental protection, that it would increase access to cleaner technology, and create a tendency to upgrade standards. The ultimate outcome, they felt, would be that environmental regulations in Mexico would eventually reach a standard equivalent to those in the United States and Canada.

It was apprehended that stricter environmental standards could constitute protectionist and non-tariff barriers to trade. The trade community and particularly Mexico viewed NAFTA as a vehicle for economic growth, which would give these countries the financial resources and advanced technology necessary to better care for the environment. Mexico resisted the inclusion of the environmental chapter in NAFTA because of concerns that the stringent environmental regulations of participating countries, particularly the United States, had the potential to be used against Mexican products as non-tariff barriers.

Without economic growth, a developing country like Mexico cannot achieve the level of environmental protection demanded by environmental advocates. NAFTA has recognized this and has reached a certain degree of balance between trade and environmental concerns.

This chapter examines how NAFTA has addressed and reconciled the apparently conflicting trade–environment issues and the extent to which NAFTA facilitates the reconciliation of trade–environment values under a free trade arrangement, which conjoins both developed and developing countries.

Protecting the environment under NAFTA free trading: its scope of operation

In both its political origin and ultimate formulation, NAFTA was stretched and twisted to include more than trade as a reaction to the intense public scrutiny generated by the media.[13] As a result NAFTA was supplemented by two side agreements which took account of social and environmental concerns. The *Environmental Side Agreement* was the centre of attention as it could determine the fate of NAFTA and was a significant step towards linking environmental standards with trade policy. The *Environmental Side Agreement* was parallel to but separate from NAFTA itself, and the question of whether 'separate but parallel' is equal to 'single and consistent' with the NAFTA Agreement remains a concern.[14] NAFTA made significant improvements regarding environmental protection by incorporating environmental provisions. It is still doubtful whether NAFTA as a trade agreement *par excellence* can strike an equitable balance between trade policy and environmental protection. This section examines NAFTA's trade environment regime and its actual operation.

Preamble

The Preamble of NAFTA has committed to sustainable development. The Preamble states that the agreement is intended to:

> contribute to the harmonious development and expansion of world trade … in a manner consistent with environmental protection and conservation;… promote sustainable development … [and] strengthen the development and enforcement of environmental laws and regulations.[15]

In its preamble, NAFTA recognized the lofty ideal of sustainable development as its legitimate objective. However, NAFTA's preamble declaration promoting sustainable development as a primary goal is not consistent with the operation of the subsequent provisions that follow the preamble. According to the *Vienna Convention on the Law of Treaties* 1969, the preamble's declaration must be applied as a term with special meaning in the interpretation of the NAFTA provisions.[16] The objectives of the preamble to the NAFTA Agreement should be taken into account when interpreting NAFTA. NAFTA's objectives, as contained in Article 102, do not correspond to the environmental goals mentioned in the Preamble. As a result NAFTA has been criticized as an agreement which was designed to be 'green' only in so far as it would reflect the colour of money.[17]

However, an aggrieved party may have recourse under the limited circumstances specified in Article 32 of the *Vienna Convention* to use the negotiating history of the relevant Article of NAFTA in order to resolve the issue of their interpretation. However, the NAFTA tribunal, in *Mondev*, emphasized that 'the application of the customary international law standards does not *per se* permit resort to other treaties of the NAFTA Parties or, indeed, other provisions within NAFTA'.[18]

Environmental protection was clearly stated as a priority in the preamble to the agreement, which typically establishes the principles and themes of an agreement, and the details of relevant specific and binding obligations were given within each section of the agreement. Therefore the provisions of the agreement should then be read in the light of those notions laid out within the Preamble.[19] However, it can also be said that the broad objectives in the Preamble do not have any legal effect, as neither Article 756 nor Article 1114 contains any language to indicate a binding commitment. In addition, Article 1114 only deems 'inappropriate' any attempt by a NAFTA party to lower its 'environmental standards in order to attract or retain foreign investment'. There are also no enforcement mechanisms, and the language used in the environmental provisions suggests compliance is voluntary.

Trade-related environmental measures under NAFTA

NAFTA adopted GATT Article XX to empower the parties to the Agreement to take the necessary action to protect human, animal or plant life or health as well as to employ measures which aim to preserve living or non-living exhaustible natural resources. Such actions are subject to the following requirements:

1 They may not be applied in an arbitrary or unjustifiable manner.
2 They may not constitute a disguised restriction on international trade and investment.[20]

GATT panels have interpreted the above two requirements very narrowly to maintain the existing dominant position of trade over the environment.[21] The GATT panel's interpretation of 'arbitrary' or 'unjustifiable manner' and what constitutes a 'disguised restriction on trade' may leave the door open to interpret them in the same line (as GATT panel did) to protect the trading interest.[22]

NAFTA's standards regimes and their implications for the trade and environment linkage

Many of the most challenging issues within the trade and environment debate arise from the requirements imposed by parties upon their domestic products and those products of international commerce which enter their domestic markets.[23] Countries with stringent environmental regulations impose tough environmental standards on their domestic products. Such standards are very often treated as non-tariff barriers by the trade community which fights to eliminate such barriers to prevent them from being used as protectionist measures.

NAFTA has set out a framework of rules and disciplines to guide the development, adoption and enforcement of standard measures that may directly or indirectly affect trade between the parties to the Agreement.

Chapters 7 and 9 of NAFTA set out its standards related provisions. Chapter 7[24] deals with Sanitary and Phytosanitary Measures ('SPS') and Chapter 9[25] deals with all other Standards-related Measures ('SRM') which are commonly thought of as environmental standards.

NAFTA's sanitary and phytosanitary measures

NAFTA confirms its parties' rights to adopt, maintain or apply sanitary and phytosanitary measures ('SPS') which are necessary for the protection of human, animal or plant life or health in their territories, including the application of measures more stringent than international standards, guidelines or recommendations.[26] Each party is also allowed to set its SPS measures at levels that it considers appropriate.[27] However, SPS measures are to satisfy the following requirements:

1. They must be based on scientific principles (including a risk assessment – Article 712(3)).
2. Such measures may not arbitrarily or unjustifiably discriminate between the goods and like goods of another party or between the goods of another party and like goods of any other country where identical or similar conditions prevail – Article 712(4).
3. Such measures may be applied only to the extent necessary to provide the country's chosen level of protection – Article 712(5).
4. Such measures may not create a disguised restriction on trade – Article 712(6).
5. Such measures must be in accordance with Article 757.

Under NAFTA, international standards, guidelines or recommendations are to form the basis of sanitary and phytosanitary conditions (Article 713(1)). Article 713 establishes that measures conforming to international standards are presumed to be consistent with Article 712, but that measures which differ from such international standards shall not, for that reason alone, be presumed to be inconsistent with Chapter 7. Article 710 also states that Article 301 (which deals with the National Treatment principle) does not apply to any sanitary or phytosanitary measure.[28]

Article 715 sets out the factors which are to be taken into account in conducting risk assessments. These include the relevant techniques and methodologies of international standardizing organizations; relevant scientific evidence; relevant processes and production methods, inspection and testing methods; relevant ecological or other environment conditions; certain specified economic factors and the objective of minimizing negative trade effects and arbitrary or unjustifiable restrictions on trade which discriminate or constitute a disguised restriction on trade.

Assessment of NAFTA standards regime

NAFTA encourages its members to use international standards and permits them, where capable, to adopt more stringent measures than the international standards but imposes several conditions, i.e. the measure adopted would be based on scientific principles and a risk assessment (Article 715).

The parties' rights to set individual, appropriate, levels of protection can be used for protectionist purposes. NAFTA establishes the right of a party to ban imports that in its view do not meet the appropriate level of domestic health and where the risks from a given product are too heavy – as long as the ban is not arbitrary or unjustifiable. Thus, while NAFTA generally requires that scientific evidence support the finding of a potential risk to the environment, health or safety, the social value judgement as to what level of risk is acceptable is left entirely to each party without any requirement for scientific justification.[29] The parties' right to determine the standards they deem appropriate deviates from the notion that international standards should operate as a 'ceiling' for national SPS measures.

NAFTA also requires that parties base their standards on 'scientific principles'. In theory, this means that a party does not need to give a scientific justification for the measures it imposes. Unlike GATT, which requires scientific proof for the imposition of import prohibitions, under NAFTA member countries are at liberty to set their own standards and impose them on imports, even to the point of refusing access.[30] In practice, it means that while science must be used to determine the risks posed by a product, regulators can then set the tolerable risk at any level they like. NAFTA leaves the value-laden process of risk management up to the domestic experts.[31] The privilege of setting technical standards may result in setting technical standards higher than those for the domestic product in question to keep a certain competing product out of the domestic market. This may particularly be the case where the unjust protectionist standard is set by more powerful market players against the interests of smaller and vulnerable trading partners like Mexico.

Under the *Environmental Side Agreement*, parties to NAFTA are able to decide their own levels of environmental protection.[32] This may enable strict environmental standards to be established, that are unchallengeable in the way that challenges on the basis of disguised protectionism have been brought under GATT Article XX. The result is that excessively high standards may be presumed to be acceptable – as proving that such standards constitute disguised restrictions on trade is very difficult.[33]

The *Environmental Side Agreement* merely reinforced the language of NAFTA, under which parties were explicitly granted the right to adopt environmental standards which exceed international requirements.[34] Similarly, under NAFTA Article 714(1), parties are required to raise their SPS measures to a level equivalent to those of other parties. In conjunction with the articles on the environment, it may be implied that this equivalence requirement will result in SPS levels unifying at the highest level of enforcement, consistent with the upward harmonization apparent above.

In other words, the NAFTA paradigm is one which has granted the right to high, even to the point of excess, SPS and TBT environmental standards, which may only with difficulty prove to be protectionist measures.[35] It would appear that NAFTA is going all-out to eliminate the possibility of dilution of these environmental standards.[36]

This point is discussed further in the section below which deals with the situations of developing countries.

Technical barriers to trade

Technical standards used as non-tariff barriers have often been the reason for the arbitrary denial of market access. Technical standards are an essential element of national sovereignty in that they allow governments to take measures to protect consumers through the regulation of product and process standards. NAFTA rules relating to technical standards apply directly to the national governments of each party. NAFTA establishes four basic standards-related obligations:

1 Right to take standards-related measures.
2 Right to establish level of protection.
3 Non-discrimination.
4 Unnecessary obstacles to trade.

Right to take standards-related measures

NAFTA specifically allows each party to adopt, apply and enforce standards-related measures ('SRM') to protect human, animal or plant life or health (Article 904.1). Such measures may well be trade-restrictive, prohibiting the import of a good or service from another party that does not comply with domestic standards.

Right to establish a level of protection

NAFTA grants each party the right to establish the appropriate level of protection to meet its environmental policy objectives and to conduct the assessments of risk to ensure that those levels are achieved (Article 904.2).

Non-discrimination

Each party is required to extend its National Treatment and Most Favoured Nation obligations in its standards-related measures. Parties applying their SRMs cannot discriminate between domestic and foreign goods. However, SRMs that violate the national treatment can be justified under NAFTA's restatement of GATT Article XX(b) or XX(g).

Unnecessary obstacles to trade

Under NAFTA, parties are prohibited from setting SRMs in place if the result is an unnecessary obstacle to trade, unless it can be shown that the purpose of such measures is a legitimate objective, or if such measures do not result in the exclusion of the goods of another party which meet that legitimate objective.[37] Environmentalists feel that this language could be subject to interpretation under GATT jurisprudence, which would require that environmental standards be 'least trade restrictive.' If such a reading were implied, the result could be a serious hindrance to parties' freedom to set and implement their desired level of environmental protection. However, NAFTA parties do not believe that such a reading should be implied.

NAFTA encourages parties to use international standards as bases for its standards-related measures. However, this commitment is softened by the inclusion of the proviso that a party can disregard international standards where such standards would be an ineffective or inappropriate means of fulfilling its legitimate objective. The proviso implies that a party can disregard international standards which contradict the level of protection that the party considers appropriate. A party's discretion to disregard international standards and this freedom to decide about appropriate individual levels of protection has seriously weakened NAFTA's commitment to follow international standards. Article 905 sets out detailed requirements should a party enact standards exceeding the established international standards. These requirements permit the enacting party itself to be the ultimate judge of the validity of those higher standards.[38] If this is a correct reading of Article 905, then none of the other articles in Chapter 9 that call for scientific justification would ever be applicable.[39]

The precautionary principle

Article 715.4 of the SPS text and Article 907.3 of the SRM text allow the NAFTA parties to promulgate environmental, health and safety measures even where the scientific evidence is insufficient to determine the actual risk posed by a given product or service (Article 907.3). A party has an obligation to revise its precautionary regulations once adequate information becomes available and eliminate standards if no scientific basis can be found for them. These provisions allow the domestic authorities of each party to adopt measures aimed at avoiding environmental, health and safety risks before real, and often times irreversible, harm actually occurs.[40] Thus, for example, although some may still question the environmental risks associated with global climate change, even in the absence of perfect science, the NAFTA parties remain free to take measures aimed at addressing the threat from climate change.[41] This provision has potential to serve the interests of protectionist groups who can pursue their vested interest without resorting to the proportionality test. Application of a given measure does not have to be proportionate to the consequences it may cause.

In the *Danish Bottles* case, the European Court of Justice set out a proportionality principle which involved 'a balancing of interests between the free movement of goods and environmental protection'.[42] This principle may prove to be a useful tool for determining whether an SRM constitutes an unnecessary obstacle to trade within the meaning of NAFTA Article 904.4.[43]

Process and production methods ('PPMs')

NAFTA's SRMs, which a party can adopt and enforce, are defined to include standards and technical regulations to be applied not only to goods but also to the characteristics of related process and production methods.[44] The inclusion of the PPMs of a product in the SRM definition raises the issue of whether NAFTA allows its parties to regulate the standards of a product as well as its production and processing methods. Despite the inclusion of PPMs as standards in the definition of SRMs neither Article 907 nor Article 915 explicitly includes PPM-based restrictions as 'legitimate objectives' which might be protected from challenge. It has been suggested that the inclusion of the word 'related' in the phrase 'related process and production methods' indicates an intent to limit the extent to which production and processing methods can be regulated independently of the goods produced.[45] PPMs can be regulated only to the extent that they affect the characteristics of the goods themselves and not on a basis unrelated to the goods.[46]

Any PPM which is not covered by NAFTA is by default covered under GATT's *Technical Barriers to Trade ('TBT') Agreement*. The GATT dispute resolution panel has traditionally interpreted GATT law to prohibit PPM-based standards.[47] Thus, as long as the physical characteristics of the Mexican cans of tuna are identical to those of other, imported, products, its harvesting technique, which kills large numbers of dolphins, is considered irrelevant and unrelated to the goods. From an environmental perspective the production and processing methods of a product are at least as important as the product itself. If NAFTA parties are not able to regulate the environmentally harsh process and production methods, the severe environmental impact of most products at their production stages will continue unabated. NAFTA's inability to resolve the PPM issue simply reflects the incredible difficulties this issue will pose for future trade negotiations.[48] Significantly, failure to resolve this issue may result in a continuation of the trade-related environmental measures imposed upon key Mexican products such as cement, tuna fish, avocados and textiles, if they fail to meet the strict PPM requirements of the United States and Canada.

SRM as unnecessary obstacles to trade

A NAFTA party can apply SRMs for the protection of the environment.[49] Such measures are subject to qualification and limitation by factors such as fundamental climate or other geographical factors, technological or infrastructural factors and scientific justification. Paragraph (a) of Article 904.4 requires that the purpose of the SRM (to achieve the legitimate objective) must be demonstrable.

The purpose of an SRM evidently must not only be an assertion. Determining the legitimate objective is again subject to controversy. In the case of Canada's *Landing Requirement for Pacific Coast Salmon and Herring*[50] it was held that for an SRM to be a legitimate objective it would have to have been adopted for environmental reasons alone.

The process set out in paras (a) and (b) of Article 904.4 for identifying an SRM which does not create an unnecessary obstacle to trade is expressed in deeming language, not in terms of a definitive test of what constitutes an unnecessary obstacle to trade.[51] In the absence of a definitive test, the term necessary is likely to be interpreted along the same lines as the GATT panel. In GATT jurisprudence, a trade-related environmental measure is 'necessary' only if there is no reasonably available alternative measure consistent with GATT and if the measure in question is the least inconsistent of all available alternatives.[52] NAFTA's specific affirmation of GATT rules (NAFTA Article 103.1) confirms concerns that NAFTA's determination of 'legitimate objective' may create a controversy.

A similar controversy as to the legitimate objectives of standard-related measures has occurred under Chapter 11 of NAFTA, which is directed at stimulating and reducing barriers to foreign investment.[53] Chapter 11 sets out the standards of National Treatment[54] and Most Favoured Nation treatment.[55] It also mandates a minimum standard of treatment in accordance with principles of international law.[56] The effect of Chapter 11 is to create private rights in investors to sue NAFTA governments for breach of Chapter 11 provisions.

Under Article 1110 of NAFTA there is a prohibition on the direct or indirect nationalization or expropriation or any 'measure tantamount to nationalization or expropriation' of the investment of an investor of another country unless the expropriation is:

a for a public purpose;
b on a non-discriminatory basis;
c in accordance with due process of law and Article 1105(1); and
d on payment of compensation.

On the basis of these provisions there have been successful claims for compensation (together with interest and costs) in arbitration[57] under Article 1110 brought against a NAFTA party for the losses caused by environmental measures (laws and regulations) that have had the effect of:

1. Denying foreign producers the best treatment: Article 1102.[58]
2. Intending to discriminate against foreign investors and their investments: Article 1105.[59]
3. And where a substantial portion of its investments, including its share of the market, were taken by patently discriminatory measures and handed over to the domestic industries: Article 1110.

Under Article 1110 all four conditions must be satisfied, otherwise the environmental measures[60] will be considered inconsistent with the substantive provisions of Chapter 11, and will require such environmental measures to be repealed and compensation paid to the injured party.

In the case of *Metalclad Corporation v. United Mexican States*,[61] pursuant to federal and state construction permits, Metalclad undertook construction and operation of a hazardous waste landfill in Guadalcazar. Guadalcazar ordered Metalclad to stop construction because Metalclad did not have a construction permit from that city. Metalclad had been operating under the assumption that there was no requirement for a municipal construction permit. Metalclad under arbitration alleged breaches of Articles 1105 and 1110. The tribunal held that Mexico violated Article 1110 through 'indirect expropriation' of Metalclad's investment by allowing Guadalcazar to prevent operation of the landfill.[62] The tribunal stated that:

> [E]xpropriation under NAFTA includes not only open, deliberate and acknowledged takings of property, such as outright seizure or formal or obligatory transfer of title in favour of the host State, but also covert or incidental interference with the use of property which has the effect of depriving the owner, in whole or in significant part, of the use or reasonably-to-be-expected economic benefit of property.[63]

As such Metalclad was thus not given fair and equitable treatment in accordance with international law standards imposed on Mexico under in Chapter 11.

However, in regard to more recent claims brought against NAFTA parties based on the interpretation of 'expropriation' in the decision of *Metalclad*, the tribunal has sought to reinterpret 'expropriation'. In *S.D. Myers* the tribunal stated that expropriation was more concerned with the transfer or deprivation of a person's property ownership by an authority authorized to do the taking,[64] whereas environmental regulation was a lesser economic intervention or interference by the state. And as such:

> regulation screens out most potential cases of complaints concerning economic intervention by a state and reduces the risk that governments will be subject to claims as they go about their business of managing public affairs.[65]

Minimum standards of equitable treatment have also been reinterpreted by later decisions of the tribunal. In *Waste Management v. Mexico*[66] the tribunal stated, with respect to the 'minimum standard of fair and equitable treatment', that 'in applying this standard it is relevant that the treatment is in breach of representations made by the host State which were reasonably relied upon by the claimant'.[67]

In the determination of *Methanex*[68] in 2005, a claim concerning the ban by the United States on the sale and use of the potentially toxic gasoline additive known as 'MTBE' (methyltertiary-butylether). The tribunal determined that:

> as a matter of general international law, a non-discriminatory regulation for a public purpose, which is enacted in accordance with due process and which affects, *inter alia*, a foreign investor or investment is not deemed expropriatory and compensatable unless specific commitments had been given by the regulating government to the then putative foreign investor contemplating investment that the government would refrain from such regulation.[69]

Hence government regulatory action in terms of environmental standards and measures may no longer be considered as a legitimate action to be brought against NAFTA signatories under Article 1110, unless representations are made that environmental standards and measures would not apply. However, tribunal decisions do not establish binding precedents for later tribunal determinations, and further claims under Article 1110 by an aggrieved party may see the determination that environmental regulations shade into expropriation.

Dispute resolution

NAFTA Chapter 20 sets out the general provisions for the resolution of disputes. Disputes arising out of environmental concerns are dealt with by the *Environmental Side Agreement*. The *Environmental Side Agreement* establishes a set of procedures to deal with such environmental disputes. Under Chapter 20, parties can have recourse to a dispute settlement mechanism for all disputes between the parties regarding the interpretation or application of NAFTA. A dispute settlement mechanism may also be employed where a party considers that an actual or proposed measure of another party is or would be inconsistent with the obligations of Agreement or would cause any modification or improvement of the Agreement (Article 2004 of Chapter 20).

Part V of the *Environmental Side Agreement* allows parties to have recourse to dispute resolution mechanisms in the event that another party engages in a 'persistent pattern of failure to effectively enforce its environmental law' (Article 22). NAFTA established the Free Trade Commission, the principal governing body of the agreement, to supervise the implementation of the agreement and to resolve disputes. However, the *Environmental Side Agreement* has established the Commission for Environmental Cooperation, which consists of a Council, a Secretariat and a Joint Public Advisory Committee. The Council has a number of roles. These roles include the effective enforcement of and compliance with each party's environmental laws; participation in the dispute resolution procedures under the *Side Agreement* and a part in the prevention or resolution of environment-related trade disputes.

NAFTA provides a number of options for the settlement of disputes. If a dispute concerns an action which is subject to Article 104 (Relation to Environmental and Conservation Agreements) or if it is about an environmental, health or safety measure (SPS and SRM), the challenged party has the option to choose either NAFTA or GATT for the settlement of its dispute (Article 2005). This freedom to choose is important, as the environment-related NAFTA disciplines and dispute settlement mechanisms appear more environmentally friendly than those of GATT.[70]

Assessment

Certain aspects of the NAFTA dispute resolution process are an improvement on the GATT Dispute Settlement Procedure ('DSP') for the protection of the environment. NAFTA has granted its parties the option of choosing either GATT or NAFTA for the resolution of a dispute involving an environmental issue. Also important is that under Chapter 11 of NAFTA private parties have standing, whereas at the WTO and under NAFTA's trade chapters only member governments have standing.

NAFTA acknowledges the right of its parties to have environmental disputes determined under the substantive and procedural provisions of NAFTA. Article 2005 states that once 'procedures have been initiated' in a particular forum, that forum will be used to the 'exclusion of the other'. This prevents challenging parties from bringing their dispute for resolution under GATT which does not provide such special protection for environmental measures, and where a challenging party might therefore be more likely to succeed in undercutting environmental measures.[71]

It is important to remember that three conditions underlie the principle of *res judicata*; the overlapping proceedings must involve:

1 The same parties.
2 The same subject matter.
3 The same legal claims.[72]

Since the parties of Chapter 11 NAFTA disputes can be private parties, they can be distinguished from WTO disputes between governments. Also in relation to 'legal claims' issues brought before WTO deal with violations of WTO rules, while NAFTA panels examine violations of the terms of NAFTA.[73] Thus cases have arisen in both the jurisdictions of NAFTA and the WTO which, while dealing with the same broader dispute, do not violate the principle of *res judicata*.[74] These cases have raised the complicated, and as yet unanswered, question of what happens when a WTO finding comes out differently from a finding under NAFTA. Whether Article 2005 is broader than the principle of *res judicata* and therefore should be applied is uncertain, as the article has not been raised in the existing case law.[75]

NAFTA also allowed dispute panels to have access to environmental experts in disputes concerning environmental issues. Although trade–environment disputes are traditionally determined by trade experts, NAFTA's attempt to seek environmental experts' opinions certainly carries the prospects that questions regarding environmental cost benefit would be evaluated by environmental experts. NAFTA also explicitly includes burden-shifting provisions under which the challenging party bears the burden of proving that the measure in question is inconsistent with a NAFTA trade obligation. Under GATT the burden of proof is laid on the party defending the environmental programme which is allegedly in conflict with trade obligations but could be justified under Article XX GATT exceptions. Despite the improvements NAFTA has made regarding its dispute resolution provisions, it has been criticized for its failure to address a number of important environmental concerns.

Under NAFTA, when a party believes that another party has shown a persistent pattern of failure to enforce its environmental laws effectively, the parties can have recourse to NAFTA dispute resolution procedures. This persistent failure must relate to a situation concerning the production of goods or which are traded between the parties or which compete in the territory of the party subject to the complaint with goods and services of the complainant (Article 24). After certain procedures have been followed, the dispute resolution panel prepares an initial report in which a determination is made regarding whether or not the party has failed to enforce its environmental laws effectively. However, the *Environmental Side Agreement* contains no environmental injury test and the complaining country does not have to show environmental injury to it.[76] Above all NAFTA has not made it clear how and when a panel can determine when a party fails to effectively enforce its own domestic environmental laws. The panel may seek the advice of expert groups, but only if the parties agree. As long as neither party objects, Article 2015 (1) permits the panel or a disputing party to request a written report from a scientific review board on any factual issue concerning environmental health, safety or other scientific matters raised by a disputing party. If this article is applied to limit scientific input to merely fact reporting, rather than interpretation, then the panel will be left to decide the scientific legitimacy of a health or environmental regulation without a scientific evaluation of its merits.[77] As a result, NAFTA leaves the door wide open for panel members to use their discretion to determine what constitutes non-enforcement, in the absence of any definitive test.

If panel reports eventually lead to an agreement between the disputing parties on a mutually satisfactory action plan, the non-implementation of this action plan may lead to the panel being reconvened and a monetary assessment being imposed. It is unclear what theories of deterrence underlie this novel approach to punishment.[78]

Transparency and public participation have been identified as important components of the various programmes developed to protect the environment under the *Environmental Side Agreement* (Article 1(n)) and related Agreements. The NAFTA dispute settlement procedures have been criticized for lack of public participation and transparency. It is argued by environmental groups that NAFTA maintains the status quo of GATT/WTO dispute resolution mechanisms in relation to maintaining the secrecy that often surrounds the proceedings of the dispute resolution panel.[79] NAFTA Article 2012 requires the Commission to establish the rules of procedure, which assure that 'the panel's hearings, deliberations and initial report and all written submissions to and communications with the panel shall be confidential'. This means that any interested member of the general public and/or non-government organizations cannot participate in or have access to the hearings or consultations conducted during the settlement of a dispute.[80] Nor can these individuals and groups obtain the filings of the parties to a dispute.[81] To make this system more reliable and transparent, records of procedures regarding all meetings and standard setting procedures should be made public.

The situations of developing countries at the trade–environment interface under NAFTA

In NAFTA, Mexico is the sole representative of developing countries. This section outlines the Mexican situation under the NAFTA Agreement.

The way Mexico has adapted its standards and regulations to the Agreement, and its negotiation of environmental issues in the NAFTA, provide useful information and experience for other developing countries. The negotiating agenda of NAFTA did not take into account the existing asymmetries among the Mexican, American and Canadian economies. Economically Mexico lags way behind America and Canada, with a gross national product only one-tenth of that of the United States, while wages in Mexico are only a fraction of those in the United States and Canada.[82] In the similar situation of the European Community, the EU has provided specific compensatory mechanisms for the integration of weaker parties into the Community. In recognition of the disparities that exist among member countries of the EU, a Social Development Fund has been established specifically to assist the economic and social development of weaker economies such as those of Portugal, Greece and Ireland.[83] As the Union expands eastward, encompassing a greater number of developing countries, this fund becomes increasingly important.

The asymmetries between Mexico, the United States and Canada are greater than those between any of the countries in the EU, yet no such compensatory mechanisms were considered during the negotiating process of NAFTA. The debt-burdened Mexican economy was not in a position to accommodate the external pressure applied by the world's biggest market force in relation to environmental, labour and human rights problems. But Mexico had to accept the deal which came with the environmental protection requirements. The environmental standards that were required from Mexico were similar to the standards which existed in the United States. The Mexican situation was totally different from that of the United States, with little or no infrastructure or financial resources for the implementation of the environmental requirements. Requiring Mexico to meet the environmental standards of the United States in order to trade erodes Mexico's comparative advantage and forces Mexico to promote a close political relationship with the United States, rather than devoting its limited resources to environmental priorities more appropriate to its current economic situation.[84]

The Mexican perspective on NAFTA was outlined by the Red Mexicana de Accion Frente al Libre Comercio (Mexican Action Network on Free Trade).

They argued that while the Mexican government insisted that issues such as environmental and human rights issues should not be included in the negotiations; in practice these issues have been negotiated via bilateral agendas without taking account of civil society or the necessary frameworks.[85]

The idea behind NAFTA was that it would increase the *per capita* income of Mexico and in the process assist Mexico to address environmental issues by providing cleaner technology. With economic development there would be increased awareness of the need for environmental protection; this would ease the way to upward harmonization of standards. However, the restructuring of the Mexican economy that preceded Mexico's accession to NAFTA has not prompted the economic recovery promised by its government.

> In 1993 economic growth, at 0.4 per cent, was outstripped by population growth for the first time since 1988. Mexico still had a substantial trade deficit of US$13.6 billion in 1993, and an external debt in excess of US$124 billion.[86]

Mexico was selected as a party to the NAFTA treaty because of its cheap labour, its proximity to the United States and its superior natural resources. With all these advantages, the United States has reaped the maximum benefit from the NAFTA deal, while Mexico has been left with the hard end of the deal. Mexico bears testimony to the assumption that equal treatment is not possible between unequal partners.

NAFTA promotes the upward harmonization of environmental standards, a process which is particularly costly for Mexican entrepreneurs, small businesses and consumers. For example, in 1994, demand for pollution control equipment was approximately US$1.4 billion, and was expected to double during the next few years. This led the Mexican Confederation of Chambers of Industry to call for tax relief to offset the increased spending on pollution control equipment under NAFTA. Similarly, the upward harmonization of vehicle emission standards, engine manufacturing requirements and fuel standards has driven up the operational costs of Mexican motor carriers to levels equivalent to those of the United States. Yet Mexicans appear to have no choice about this less than ideal situation. As one California state official remarked, 'They will have to change to meet our requirements or they will not be allowed in California.'[87]

This process of upward harmonization is undermining regulatory competition between countries and is eroding Mexico's comparative advantage – the whole purpose of free trade. Businesses are prevented from competing effectively by regulations which stifle competition, raise production costs and punish consumers. By acting as a trade barrier, these regulations exacerbate the problem of trade diversion – and, given that the remedy for non-enforcement of environmental laws is trade sanctions, the trade–environmental process is open to exploitation by forces seeking to close markets and undermine free exchange.

The main legal tool for environmental protection in Mexico is the 1988 *Environmental Law*. The *Environmental Law* – like a number of other new

Mexican laws in the areas of hazardous waste, transport, forestry, fisheries and water standards – comprises standards and rules which have been inspired by those of other countries (mainly the United States) but adapted to the Mexican reality.

During the period of negotiation of the Mexican environmental regulatory framework, the significance of the environment was highlighted and public awareness of this significance and the need for environmental protection was raised. The result has been a number of changes regarding the standards and laws relating to the environment – the most uncertain and conflicting aspects of which have related to the need to adapt these rules to new international environmental requirements.

Mexico initially set unrealistically high standards for itself, probably inspired by those of the United States, and was not able to adequately enforce them. It has now turned towards deregulation and to the modernization of its environmental law to consider pollution in a wider sense. It has introduced economic instruments to achieve environmental goals, created the necessary channels for public participation, and has made the rules more easily applicable overall.[88]

Yet the law remains too demanding for a Mexico which lacks the financial and institutional capacity to implement those standards (set mainly by the United States) effectively. There are too many standards and it is almost impossible to ensure their application because of the lack of trained personnel, pollution measurement equipment and funds.[89] As a whole the cost of environmental impacts on air, soil and water was 10 per cent of gross domestic product in 2002.[90] Without organizations capable of achieving results in meeting environmental standards, the environmental problems will not be resolved.[91]

There is, however, the opportunity to meet some of the necessary environmental standards through debt exchanges, in which a government creditor or environmental NGO (which purchases the debt) can cancel a portion of Mexico's foreign debt in exchange for Mexican government expenditure on an environmental infrastructure project.[92] Such a scheme is an excellent, if only partial, solution to Mexico's quandary. Mexico has no formal programme but performs debt exchanges on an *ad hoc* basis, giving priority to debt exchanges promoting social benefits and environmental programmes.[93]

NAFTA allows each party to establish and maintain its own standards-related measures relating to environmental, health, safety or other standards-related measures, including measures to prohibit the importation of products failing to meet those standards or technical regulation.[94] This provision could open the door to unjust protectionist measures which may be used to protect the market interests of big parties such as the United States. Such measures could easily be used against Mexican products, on the basis of 'lower environmental standards'.

In the United States, the setting of technical standards is done by private companies.[95] Each state has autonomy over its standard setting. There is no uniformity about the standards. If a particular product is very competitive, there is the possibility that states/companies could set the technical standards relating to environment/health/safety higher than the product in question could reach. The

Mexican small business may be more vulnerable than ever to this provision. For example, one Mexican cooperative was enjoying a niche market in the United States for its fruit juice exports.[96] The cooperative lost its market because technical standards were raised suddenly.[97] For developing countries, the imposition of the highest level of technical standards has a profound impact on the market access of their products. Market access is essentially linked to their capacity to successfully address environmental protection issues.

A major source of conflict in US–Mexican trade relations has been and will continue to be the increasing tariff and non-tariff entry barriers to the US market, particularly as trade with NAFTA party's accounts for 90 per cent of Mexico's total exports and represents 38 per cent of Mexico's gross domestic product.[98] The strict implementation of anti-dumping and countervailing measures by the US government has become a serious threat to key Mexican export products such as cement, tuna fish, avocados and textiles, which have traditionally been subject to protectionist measures in the US market.[99] This was one of the main reasons for Mexico's agreement to join NAFTA – guaranteed access to the US market. In return for the opening up of the highly protected US market in the textile and steel industries, in which Mexico could exploit its natural competitive advantages, NAFTA established new rules and principles by which preferential access to the US market has become much more regulated.[100] In addition to the 'old' non-tariff barriers, NAFTA has introduced new rules and principles – such as standardization rules, sanitary requirements, emergency mechanisms and labour and environmental regulations – which might function as a novel stock of barriers.[101] In essence, there was no great advance beyond previous GATT negotiations in the NAFTA chapter on subsidies and dumping. Meanwhile, all the retaliatory stock embodied by the United States in its Trade Law of 1988 remained intact and were even legitimized by NAFTA.[102] The result was that a more predictable enforcement mechanism was deemed necessary.[103]

NAFTA has implied that the lenient enforcement of environmental standards is an unfair trade practice, and that 'fair' trade can be guaranteed only through increasing the degree to which Mexico enforces the US Environmental Protection Agency ('EPA') standards and regulations. Some have argued that NAFTA may give rise to a new form of cooperative environmental regulation as the US exports its 'command and control' form of regulation to Mexico. It has also been argued that the enactment of trade sanctions – the likely remedy in the event of an environmental dispute arbitrated by the Commission for Environmental Cooperation ('CEC') – may violate the terms of GATT, and so constitute a setback for free trade.[104]

Under Article 5(1) of the *Environmental Side Agreement*,[105] the effective enforcement of environmental laws requires the appointment and training of inspectors; the monitoring of compliance and investigation of suspected violations; the public release of non-compliance information; the promotion of environmental audits; record keeping and reporting; and the use of licences, permits and authorizations.[106]

Failure to use these enforcement techniques gives rise to the argument that the party is not effectively enforcing its law, thus placing the party in question in violation of the agreement. Thus, if Mexico's non-enforcement continues, it will be held to be in violation of an international treaty. As party to the treaty, the United States would have the right to suspend the benefits it has conferred upon Mexico. It is likely that Mexico will use its resources to ensure enforcement rather than suffer a suspension of its sorely needed benefits.[107]

This linkage of trade benefits to environmental compliance is a powerful tool for coercing parties into compliance, and is the first of its type in history. No other trade agreement has ever levied sanctions against parties for failing to enforce their environmental laws. By establishing its own dispute resolution mechanism, with automatic jurisdiction over environmental disputes, NAFTA has taken an important step towards removing any scepticism about compliance with the Agreement's environmental protection rules.[108]

Prior to NAFTA, Mexico repeatedly failed to enforce its environmental laws. The activation of NAFTA dispute resolution procedures when there is a 'persistent pattern of failure by the Party complained against to effectively enforce its environmental law' clearly aims to eliminate such behaviour.[109] The choice of a 'persistent pattern' standard, and thus the higher threshold than that offered by a non-enforcement standard, was a concession in recognition of the structural and resource deficiencies that Mexico faced in introducing a stringent environmental regime.[110]

The impact of NAFTA's internationalization of domestic environmental policies on the Mexican economy will be severe. The bureaucracies whose responsibility it is to implement trade agreements may be manipulated and/or overtaken by special interests.

Under NAFTA, complex rules have been devised to determine the percentage of domestic content for a wide range of imports, including textiles and apparel, automotive products and consumer electronics. Trade bureaucracies are able to determine the national identity of traded products with some precision – the result is the application of higher tariffs to foreign goods than to domestic goods.[111]

NAFTA has introduced strict rules of origin[112] for limiting the benefits of trade agreements to the products which have originated from the NAFTA region. The rules of origin have a severe impact on the market access of Mexican products. This is especially the case for small and medium sized businesses which import raw materials from outside Mexico and process and/or assemble them in Mexico before selling them to the United States. This is not possible under the rules of origin as processing and/or assembling will not be qualified under the rule.

The overall impact of NAFTA on the trade–environment interface has not been uniform and is therefore difficult to evaluate. There are some examples of economic success, and some of environmental innovation, but it is difficult to make a general judgement. For example, since the introduction of NAFTA more than 30,000 rice producers in Mexico have had to abandon cultivation and almost half the rice processing mills closed, due to the impact of competing with highly subsidized rice production in the United States.[113] Similarly, corn exports from the United States to Mexico have grown by over 240 per cent.[114] In other markets free trade has favoured Mexican produce, with vegetable and fresh fruit production for the US market increasing by 80 per cent and 90 per cent respectively.[115]

Although there is no final word in on the economic success of NAFTA for Mexico, the economic imperatives of free trade do not always sit comfortably with principles of environmental sustainability. The overall impact has been to strain the already threatened natural resources and further damage fragile ecosystems. Rural agriculture has been under particular stress as a result of both reduced government support and the non-viability of some areas of production. As a result there have been isolated attempts to seek environmentally friendly alternatives in order to tap into price premiums available through organic, fair trade, and sustainable production.[116] Projects such as sustainable agriculture, community forest management, non-timber forest products, bio-prospecting and eco-tourism have had varying degrees of success. Organic coffee is now thought to make up approximately 10 per cent of Mexico's national production.[117] In terms of a broader environmental perspective, it is yet to be seen how environmental degradation is dealt with in the context of the NAFTA dispute resolution regime.

Conclusion

Environmental provisions were incorporated into NAFTA hastily to compensate for the environmental effects of free trade. The provisions were not carefully designed to protect the environment or promote sustainable development. Despite this, NAFTA is the first international trade agreement to deal with environmental issues broadly. NAFTA has, to a certain extent, balanced the tension which exists between the *Trade Agreement* and *Multilateral Environmental Agreements*.[118] It is an improvement on the GATT/WTO and offers insights into the paths which future trade agreements might take in regard to environmental issues.[119] NAFTA provides that, where a party has a choice between equally effective and reasonably available means of complying with such obligations, the party must choose the least inconsistent with the other provisions of the Agreement.[120] Where a dispute arises between NAFTA parties regarding an international environmental agreement or an environmental health or safety measure, the party responding to the challenge may elect to have the case heard exclusively under the substantive and procedural provisions of NAFTA (Articles 2005.3, 2005.4). This gives an element of additional protection to each country's environmental measures by preventing the country challenging the measures from bringing the dispute before GATT where no such protections exist and where the measures might therefore be undercut.[121]

However, NAFTA has not resolved the ambiguities which exist in relation to process and production methods. Mexico might be subjected to numerous trade measures because of its lower environmental production standards. Mexico will undoubtedly face extra pressure to adapt to the environmental standards of the United States despite its limited capacity to do so. Mexico itself has set unrealistically high standards, probably inspired by those of the United States, and has not been able to enforce them adequately.[122] The problem Mexico faces in relation to the trade–environment interface is closely linked to the huge social, economic and political disparities that exist between Mexico and the United States. Mexico fears that the environment may be used as a protectionist weapon against its market access efforts. The stringent and restrictive environmental standards of the United States may be used against Mexico as disguised trade barriers. Mexico's asymmetrical position in relation to the trade–environment nexus needs to be taken into account. Mexico needs a level of economic development comparable to that of the United States if it is expected to maintain the same level of environmental standards. In the absence of such commensurate economic development, disparities between the two trading partners may result in sanction rather than cooperation in solving environmental problems.

The *Environmental Side Agreement* gave the NAFTA parties a powerful mechanism through which they might improve Mexico's environmental quality. However, the source of this mechanism's power – the threat of trade sanctions – can be an inappropriate strategy for achieving environmental protection. A further criticism of the NAFTA enforcement mechanism is that it may compel the misallocation of environmental expenditure in Mexico, where limited financial resources mean that cost effectiveness is an essential requirement of environmental protection efforts. Until such basic measures as monitoring, sewage and water treatment, and the environmental education of business managers, are established throughout Mexico, the expenditure of environmental enforcement funds may constitute an inefficient use of scarce budgetary resources.[123]

The development of environmental infrastructure has some important advantages over the existing trade-sanction-based NAFTA enforcement mechanism. Environmental infrastructure development may provide a form of 'insurance' against the degradation of the Mexican environment. 'Debt for [infrastructure] development' exchanges may prove a partial solution to the major obstacle to development of a Mexican environmental infrastructure – lack of capital – if incorporated into the existing *Environmental Side Agreement*. But the greatest advantage of this option is that it would not require the use of protectionist trade sanctions.[124]

7 Regional approaches to free trade and sustainable development

The Asia-Pacific economic cooperation

The Asia-Pacific Economic Cooperation ('APEC') emerged as a regional forum to facilitate trade and economic cooperation in 1989. Its primary aim was to achieve economic benefits for all member states through regional cooperation. Specifically, it was designed to 'reduce barriers to trade in goods, services and investment among members in a manner consistent with GATT/WTO principles, where applicable, and without detriment to other economies'.[1]

The *Bogor Declaration* of 1994[2] outlines the objectives of APEC and the mechanisms by which its objectives should be met. It stated that APEC's overall goal of enhancing trade and investment in the Asia-Pacific would be facilitated by adopting a long term goal of 'free and open trade and investment in the Asia-Pacific'.[3] The Declaration also states that developed members should remove all barriers to trade by 2010. However, it provides a concession to developing members, by allowing them to retain their trade barriers until 2020.

Finally, the declaration makes it clear that APEC will expand its trade and investment facilitation programmes in order to 'promote further the flow of goods, services, and capital among APEC economies'. In the long term, this is aimed at removing 'administrative and other impediments to trade and investment'.[4]

It has been argued that the increasing economic cooperation between APEC member states has resulted in substantial economic growth in the Asia-Pacific region.[5] However, the increasing prosperity of the region has placed alarming pressures on the environment. Unsustainable population growth, high levels of capital mobility, as well as market and policy failures, are all contributing to environmental degradation.[6] Furthermore, the increasing use of raw materials, unsustainable production processes and the pollution resulting from these practices will have negative effects on the environment in the longer term.

There are several aspects of APEC's institutional structure that make it interesting from a trade and environment perspective. Its use of a loose, non-binding, consensus-based approach to decision making has resulted in some very positive statements regarding the linkage between trade and environmental issues. This may be because members feel more free to make such decisions and pronouncements without having to take into account the binding nature of decisions that are made within other multilateral trade-related institutions. In fact, no other multilateral trade-related institution examined in this book has been as progressive as APEC in terms of addressing trade and environment issues within the context of these non-binding decisions.

That said, the reason why there have been such positive statements may reflect a desire of certain members to simply 'appease' developing members by agreeing in principle to certain concepts and ideals such as sustainable development but not actually follow through on any decision that has been made.

As a result, the loose, consensus-based, non-binding nature of decision making at APEC is probably both its greatest strength and its greatest weakness. Overall, this chapter will examine the initiatives of APEC in regards to the integration of the economy and sustainable development.

The environment, and North–South dynamics in APEC's institutional structure

The consensus-building approach and individual action plans

As mentioned above, APEC has adopted a loose, consensus-based, non-institutional approach to policy coordination.[7] Unique in structure and scope, APEC has rejected a legalistic approach to multilateralism in favour of a framework based on reciprocity, flexibility and mutual benefits.[8] The main principle under which APEC operates is known as 'concerted unilateralism'[9] in which APEC members design policy and common goals collectively. Essentially, APEC operates on the basis of the consensus between all its member states. Individual member states design specific provisions for the implementation of common goals nationally, known as the Individual Action Plan ('IAP'). The emphasis on consensus suggests that common initiatives are taken, not primarily through a process of side payments and threats of sanctions, but through the perception of self-interest, as well as more subtle forms of political pressure.[10] Consensus building and concerted unilateralism create real interest among states in the implementation of action programmes, without requiring compulsion by powerful developed members. Therefore, state self-interest plays a vital role in the implementation measures. APEC's focus on the efforts of member states to build their capacity to implement action programmes is an innovative approach.

Trade sanctions and retaliatory measures may be effective to some extent in addressing environmental concerns but these measures do not solve the problem when the playing field is not level. Without some consideration of issues relating to capacity building, comparative levels of economic development, and the environmental priorities of individual states, trade-related environmental measures are likely to complicate the situation further. From this perspective, the APEC experience in capacity building management could be a useful lesson for other institutions.

However, the consensus-building approach also has its down side. The unanimity requirement might make it difficult to move on to new issues where members have differences of opinion. Significantly, even pressing issues sometimes fail to obtain consensus.

APEC's committees and decision-making groups

APEC has several Committees and Working Groups. The Committee on Trade and Investment ('CTI') promotes and coordinates work related to trade and investment facilitation and liberalization.[11] The Budget and Management Committee oversees and allocates APEC's central funds and the Economic Committee is responsible for economic and technical (including environmental) cooperation.[12] However, it should be noted that working groups have tended to be composed of trade-oriented bureaucrats, rather than technical or environmental experts.[13] Inclusion of environmental experts in the working groups is of great importance in making decisions for the integration of trade and the environment. Environmental or technical expertise could offer insights into issues that are crucial to environmentalists.

North–South tensions in APEC

APEC has a multilateral framework with a diverse group of states. It is a very dynamic and complex regional organization which consists of both developed and developing members, as well as the already highly integrated sub-regions of North America and East Asia. It embraces two of the world's largest economies, the United States and Japan, as well as industrialized and industrializing economies such as Singapore and Indonesia. Developing members such as Papua New Guinea also participate in APEC. However, this diversity in membership has the potential to cause conflict. Differences in language, culture, social and political structures and the comparative level of economic development are clearly apparent both between and within nations. As a result, *prima facie* there is potential for a North–South split within APEC based on individual members' level of economic development.

As with other international trading organizations, this split may generate substantial differences in both the approaches to sustainable development, and the level of commitment to it. For example, developed members within APEC tend to be the champions of environmental protection in an effort to secure their economic interests by protecting their own markets with environmental conditionality.[14] Developing members on the other hand have stressed the need for sustainable development to enhance economic and technical cooperation to ensure the building of their capacity to address environmental issues. Significantly, there is no support for the notion that market access should be unilaterally or regionally conditioned on the basis of environmental performance.[15]

North–South tensions manifest in a variety of ways in the APEC context. These include issues with broad approaches to sustainable development, the harmonization of environmental standards, and the need for financial and technical resources.

The emergence of sustainable development in APEC

This part will outline the emergence of the concept of sustainable development in APEC in a chronological form.

The 1993 Economic Leaders' Vision Statement

APEC leaders initially recognized the environmental challenges posed by economic growth in the APEC Economic Leaders' Economic Vision Statement, drafted at Blake Island, Seattle, in November 1993. In approving the inclusion of sustainable development in APEC's work agenda, the leaders stated that:

> [o]ur environment is improved as we protect the quality of our air, water and green spaces and manage our energy resources and renewable resources to ensure sustainable growth and provide a more secure future for our people.[16]

The 1994 Bogor Declaration

The *Bogor Declaration* explicitly linked sustainable development with the economic cooperation of member economies. In Article 8, the Declaration states that:

> Our objective to intensify development cooperation among the community of Asia-Pacific economies will enable us to develop more effectively the human and natural resources of the Asia-Pacific region so as to *attain sustainable growth and equitable development of APEC economies*, while reducing economic disparities among them, and improving the economic and social well-being of our people. Such efforts will also facilitate the growth of trade and investment in the Asia-Pacific region.[17]

The Declaration also provided that member economies should undertake cooperative programmes with the aim of contributing to sustainable development. Examples of these included human resource development, the creation of APEC study centres, cooperation in science and technology, and steps to improve economic infrastructure, including energy, transport, information and telecommunications infrastructure.[18]

The 1994 Environmental Vision Statement

In the APEC Ministerial Meeting held in Vancouver in 1994, the ministers adopted an Environmental Vision Statement.[19] In it, the ministers expressed their commitment to the development of economically and environmentally sound policies, which they felt would be necessary to ensure the continued growth of APEC member's economies and their long-term sustainability.[20] In particular, the ministers stated that 'we have to improve the quality of air, water and manage energy resources to ensure sustainable development and provide a more secure future for our people'.[21] The ministers agreed to develop programmes and strategic initiatives that would encourage member states to integrate environmental considerations into their economic policies, decisions and work programmes.

The Environmental Vision Statement seems to reflect the spirit of the *Rio Declaration of Environment and Development*,[22] which reaffirms the long-term relationship between environmental protection and economic growth. The Vision Statement confirmed that recognition of this relationship is fundamental to building sustainable development in the region, and expressed support for the goals of the United Nations Conference on Environment and Development.

The Environmental Vision Statement also stated that APEC should take the lead in achieving sustainable development.

The 1994 Framework of Principles for Integrating Economy and Environment in APEC

The Framework of Principles provides nine central principles for the implementation of the Environmental Vision Statement. As with the Vision Statement, the Preamble to the Framework emphasizes that the 'challenge of sustainable development requires the integration of economy and environment in all sectors and at all levels'.[23] Member states are asked to take the principles into consideration in order to reconcile the objectives of economic growth with improved environmental outcomes. This will ensure sustainable development in the region. The APEC Framework of Principles has drawn heavily from the principles of the *Rio Declaration on Environment and Development.* Some of the APEC principles are actual reproductions of the Rio Principles. This section will outline some of the APEC Principles relevant for sustainable development.

The first principle states that 'member economies should promote sustainable development and a higher quality of life for all people'. Based on Principle 4 of the *Rio Declaration*, the APEC Principle requires that 'all possible measures should be considered to bring about a society where environmental protection shall constitute an integral part of the development process'. This principle, however, is extremely general and does not delineate the point at which economic concerns should give way to environmental considerations. Furthermore, it ignores the fact that most developed countries built up their economies on the back of unsustainable environmental practices, such as the industrial revolution.[24] Developed members may interpret this principle in a way that would require developing members to bear the cost of certain environmental protection measures that they themselves never undertook. Given that there is also no positive requirement under APEC for developed members to provide compensation to developing members that are undertaking costly environmental protection measures, it would seem that developing countries could potentially be strongly disadvantaged under this principle.

Under the second principle of the Framework, members should adopt an approach based on the notion that the 'polluter should, in principle, bear the cost of pollution'. This approach partially addresses one of the issues raised earlier in this book that market prices do not accurately reflect environmental costs. Under this 'polluter pays' principle, polluters must pay for the environmental damage caused by their activities.[25] By making polluters bear this cost, arguably, they will be forced to raise the prices of goods that are environmentally unsound. The result of this will be a lowering of demand for polluting goods, and an increase in demand for environmentally friendly goods.

The fourth principle of the Framework requires that members should 'cooperate to strengthen capacity building for sustainable development through exchanges of scientific and technical knowledge'. This principle endorses Chapter 34 of *Agenda 21* of the United Nations Conference on Environment and Development,[26] which relates to technological transfer. However, like its UN equivalent, the primary issue with this principle is the fact that it does not place any mandatory obligations on members to transfer technology. As a result, technology is likely to be transferred only when it is in the host country's best interests to do so. This host country is unlikely to transfer technology that will have the effect of reducing its comparative advantage with the country it is transferring the technology to.

The fifth principle suggests that members should apply the 'precautionary approach' as defined in Principle 15 of the *Rio Declaration*. This principle essentially states that a lack of scientific certainty regarding the potential effects of polluting activities should not itself operate as a bar to taking measures to prevent environmental degradation. This principle, however, has the potential to be misused. For example, the precautionary principle could be invoked to exclude the products of developing countries from the markets of developed countries. For example, the European Commission has invoked precautionary style reasoning to impose bans on natural animal growth hormones, despite lack of evidence of any evidence of harm.[27] Furthermore, developing countries often lack adequate technical and financial resources to assess the 'risk' that an activity may pose to the environment.

The sixth principle encourages members to 'support multilateral efforts to make trade and environment policies mutually supportive'. This is a very general statement, and appears to give broad support to movements that attempt to reconcile economic and environmental concerns. *Prima facie*, this principle seems to reject the WTO's tendency to support trade liberalization measures over and above environmental protection.[28]

Finally, the seventh principle outlines the need for financial resources in order to achieve all of the objectives outlined above. It stresses that members should cooperate to meet this goal, taking into account the conditions and priorities of the various APEC members.

It should be noted that, unlike the principles of the *Rio Declaration* which the APEC Framework is based on, it does not contain any reference to the concept of common but differentiated responsibility. Under the *Rio Declaration*, this principle states that while environmental protection is every country's responsibility, the level of responsibility and financial commitment required should vary in accordance with each individual country's socio-economic situation. The lack of recognition by APEC of this principle will be discussed further in the final section of this chapter, 'Recommendations for reform'.

The 1995 Declaration for Action

Environmental issues were further considered in the APEC Economic Leaders' Declaration for Action, issued in Osaka, Japan, in November 1995.[29] This Declaration reiterated the commitment to the integration of environment and sustainable development into APEC activities.

Other APEC leaders' statements and declarations

Many subsequent APEC meetings and declarations have made references to sustainable development. For example, the Economic Leaders' Declaration in Canada in November 1997 mentioned that sustainable development was at the heart of the APEC mandate.[30] This Declaration directed ministers to implement an initial work programme for sustainable development that included the themes of sustainability of the marine environment, clean technology, clean production and sustainable cities. In 1998, the APEC leaders reiterated their commitment to 'advance sustainable development across the entire spectrum of [their] workplan'.[31]

Ministers have repeatedly referred to, for example, a need to 'revitalize APEC's agenda on sustainable development'.[32] However, until recently, leaders have rarely gone beyond these general statements of intention.

Recent developments

Fund for supporting capacity building

APEC has recently approved the establishment of a fund for supporting capacity building in developing countries.[33] This could potentially be used to provide funding to developing countries to acquire and develop environmentally sound technologies. However, the effectiveness of this fund will most likely depend on the level of commitment of developed countries to actually provide financing for it. Given the lack of any formal dispute resolution mechanism in APEC, developing countries will have to rely on the goodwill of developed countries to provide them with adequate funding.

Furthermore, funding should be provided for more innovative financing methods which might include:

> Educating and mobilizing banks and other private sector lenders, perhaps through a regional Banker's Sustainable Development Code … the creation

of an APEC Environmental Trust Fund; and the creation of an environment investment window at the Asian Development Bank.[34]

APEC Climate Centre

In November 2005, APEC launched the APEC Climate Centre. Its stated goals are:

1 Developing a value-added reliable climate prediction system.
2 Acting as a centre for climate data and related information.
3 Developing improved methods of utilizing socio-economic innovation.
4 Coordinating research toward the development of an APEC-integrated climate environment–socio-economic system model.[35]

The general aim of the climate centre therefore seems to be focused on a scientific analysis of the issue of climate change, and using the results of the analysis to build up information on the likely social and economic effects of climate change.

In its report to APEC's Industrial Science and Technology Working Group in September 2006, the Climate Centre set up a team of climate experts from meteorology-related areas from government agencies in member states. The current focus is to arrive at a climate change prediction model, which could be provided to developing countries that currently lack the capacity to undertake their own climate predictions, and therefore the likely effects of climate change on their country, from both a social and economic perspective.[36]

While an investigation of the likely effects of climate change is important, it is also important that the results of the investigation are not used as a 'scare tactic' to force developing countries into accepting certain carbon-based environmental standards without providing them with appropriate compensation, or addressing their need for capacity building to effectively deal with climate-related concerns.

The APEC High Level Meeting on Sustainable Development

In mid-2006, APEC hosted a 'High Level Meeting on Sustainable Development' in Santiago, Chile. The meeting included representative environment ministers from APEC members, as well as the United Nations Commission on Sustainable Development. It was the first formal meeting of APEC ministers since 1997.

In documents provided for the meeting, APEC admits that there has been no cross-sectoral, coordinated approach to sustainable development, although there have been around 400 separate projects that have had sustainable development as an issue.[37]

The recommendations coming out of the meeting mostly related to improving the exchange of information between APEC, its working groups, its member states, outside environmental organizations and the development of a coordinated approach to sustainable development within the APEC organization.[38]

Significantly, there is also a recommendation to 'ask [Senior Officials' Meetings] to consider civil society participation and dialogue in the future work on Sustainable Development'.[39] The inclusion of such groups would be highly advantageous, given that they are able to take an 'all of society' approach to issues, rather than just being on environmental or economic issues, or focused on the self-interest of member states.

The future of sustainable development in APEC

While these developments are undoubtedly positive, without there being a formal enforcement mechanism within APEC, the capacity of the organization to implement these mechanisms will entirely depend on the members reaching a consensus. Therefore, any issues of importance to developing countries may be passed over.

The achievements of APEC in the trade–environment context

APEC has at least in principle recognized the importance of the integration of economy and ecology. It has also prioritized the needs of developing countries at the intersection between trade and environment. APEC has emphasized the need for effective cooperation rather than trade measures to promote sustainable development in the region. It has attempted to strike a balance between economic development and environmental protection. The principles it has suggested for the reconciliation of the conflict between economic growth and environmental protection are noble. Most of the principles are drawn from the *Rio Declaration on Environment and Development*, in which world leaders generally agreed upon the need for and importance of these principles in the integration of world economy and the environment. However, these principles are very broad and only have a 'soft' enforcement status. Nonetheless, these principles have provided the foundations on which action programmes and methodologies will need to be developed for the implementation of the principles.

Continuing trade and environmental issues in APEC and recommendations for reform

North–South tensions

The free trade agenda in APEC has been greatly shaped by the influence of its developed member states, and is predominantly driven by the interests of the United States in opening service industry markets and investment flows.[40] In 1993, developed members pressed hard for 'free and open trade and investment in [the] Asia-Pacific'.[41] In 1994 APEC members accepted the broad vision for the achievement of free and open trade by 2020 for developing country members and 2010 for developed members.[42] The United States, as well as Canada and Australia,[43] have continually pushed hard to have a trade agenda linked with environmental considerations.

However, developing members of APEC are more apprehensive about linking environmental conditionality with their development efforts and economic growth. They instead tend to give priority to economic development, and want to address environmental concerns by increasing capacity-building programmes and technological cooperation.[44] For developing members, economic growth is the precondition for them to address the requirements of sustainable development.[45] Moreover, they are concerned about the potential of disguised protectionism in the link between trade and the environment. The growing number of product standards, packaging requirements and labelling systems may work as disguised trade barriers and hinder their efforts to have access to the markets of developed partners.[46] Eventually, disputes arising from environmental standards may give rise to unilateral trade measures. Such measures could have severe consequences for developing members which lack the institutional framework, sophisticated technology and financial resources to deal with the demand from developed partners to have environmental standards parallel to theirs. In the final analysis, developing members tend to be the victims of the environmental standards game.

This concern was echoed at the First Environment Ministers' Meeting held in Vancouver in March 1994. Article 36 of the Summary Report of the meeting stated that:

> the use of economic instruments and standards should not create unfair competition and trade distortions, and that standards do not need to be mandatory. However, the private sector should be involved in creating new standards to encourage their compliance.[47]

Developing economies are also concerned about the issue of market access, and have sought a strong emphasis on the achievement of development goals in the design of the liberalization process.[48] This objective was described by Lyuba Zarsky and Jason Hunter in the following words:

> For developing countries, incentives for regional environmental cooperation stem from the desire to enhance domestic management capacities, both technological and managerial, maintain market access in developed country markets, and to encourage green foreign investment.[49]

Lack of specific principles and work programmes

Despite the various frameworks, vision statements and declarations that APEC has made over the years for integrating the economy and the environment, sustainable development cannot be pursued without a focused programme addressing these trade and environment issues.[50] The recommendations of the High Level Meeting on Sustainable Development recommend a more coordinated approach to sustainable development issues, but nonetheless these are only 'soft' recommendations, and their implementation will be entirely at the behest of member states.

Experiences from other multilateral and regional trade agreements suggest that:

> to optimize social welfare in the context of economic integration, systematic attention must be given to environmental protection in parallel with trade and investment liberalization.[51]

APEC should focus on specifically addressing the trade–environment issue, and move beyond the broad approaches that it has generally adopted.

APEC's institutional structure and lack of a dispute settlement body

APEC lacks a formal institutional structure for dealing with implementation issues. Member states abide by the rules voluntarily and no formal enforcement mechanisms are in place to compel member states to comply with the rules. While it takes into account the individual member's developmental situations in the implementation process, institutional structures could follow up the progress and special problems contributing to the failure of the implementation by member states. Without an institutional mechanism to enforce the rules, APEC members 'may contribute to the liberalization process to their own ends, by their own rules and at their own pace'.[52] This might make APEC a 'talkshop of many men with many minds' with little or no strategic action regarding the integration of environment in the trade liberalization process.[53]

For example, the *Environmental Vision Statement* emphasizes the need for the integration of economic development and environmental protection initiatives. However, there is no central committee responsible for the coordination of the integration process. Different working groups and committees oversee the integration process but there is such a lack of uniformity and consistency across the APEC committees and sectoral groups that it is difficult to discern any real accomplishments.[54] The effect of this lack has succinctly been explained as follows:

> Although many argue that the allocation of a separate body with responsibility for ecologically sustainable development hinders its integration into all aspects of APEC work, the absence of such a body means that the other APEC Groups and Committees have no real guidance on how to approach their task.[55]

Differences in values, priorities and level of economic development can be considered both as an advantage and a disadvantage for the integration of economy and ecology. However, these differences within the loose nature of the institutional structure may make it difficult to implement the lofty ideals of APEC regarding the mutual supportiveness of economic development and environmental protection. As noted above, state self-interest plays a vital role in the implementation measures. APEC's focus on the capacity-building efforts of member states to ease implementation is an innovative approach. However, individual members may find excuses for their lack of implementation measures. It is recommended that there should be a supervisory organization/institution to review the implementation process and to coordinate the tasks of various working groups and committees. Such an institution could be set up along the lines of the GATT/WTO Trade and Environment Committee or the NAFTA Commission on Environmental Cooperation. This institution would, in turn, review the progress of the integration of trade and environment.

APEC also lacks a formal and legalistic framework for the resolution of disputes between member economies. It has been argued that, because of its diverse member group, APEC does not require a traditional GATT/WTO type dispute settlement mechanism where generally large economic powers have the ability to exert political and financial pressure over weaker parties. As Rafiqul Islam argues, a GATT/WTO-type dispute settlement system in APEC might be used by influential members of the institution, such as the United States, where their national interests are likely to prevail and that such influential members might simply flout the rules when it is otherwise.[56] However, APEC could set up a different type of dispute settlement mechanism separate from GATT. This would be acceptable because the basic principles upon which the APEC agreement is formulated are different from those on which the GATT is based.[57] Nonetheless, any future APEC dispute settlement mechanism should be transparent and equitable. It should also ensure the participation of interest groups and experts.

Incorporation of environmental considerations into individual action plans

APEC has provided the basic guidelines for the formulation of policies and action programmes and has left the implementation of those policies and action plans with individual member states and subject to their respective priorities. Individual Action Plans are the primary instruments by which individual countries implement APEC objectives. However, these action plans are not subject to environmental review and are developed in isolation from sustainable development principles. There is also no requirement for an Individual Action Plan to be reviewed and/or modified on environmental grounds, nor is it required to include specific commitments to improve environment management capacities.[58]

APEC has, however, held a workshop on assessing the environmental impacts of trade liberalization. In the workshop, the members reaffirmed their commitment to undertake environmental reviews of their trade liberalization measures, and recommended a process of multi-stakeholder consultation in the environmental review process.[59] This process would include representatives from government, business, academics, non-governmental organizations, as well as the general public. However, the measures committed to are not mandatory, and the workshop itself was not even attended by all APEC members.[60]

Harmonization of environmental standards

Developed members, particularly the United States and Canada, have suggested that the standardization of environmental regulations in the APEC region should be considered.[61] One motive for this may be that the harmonization of environmental regulations may affect the comparative advantage of the products of a particular country. For example, countries that have higher environmental standards may produce a product with higher cost. This product may be more expensive and less competitive than a product produced in a country that has lower environmental standards. As a result, it would seem that developed members, with their higher environmental standards, are better off competing against the products of developing country members if environmental costs are reflected in market prices. Therefore, the move towards the harmonization of environmental regulation may result in developing countries losing their comparative advantage, and therefore benefiting the economies of developed countries. In addition, developed members will gain the commercial benefit of being able to export environment management products and services, as well as leading-edge, environmentally friendly technology.

Therefore, it would seem that, without any compensatory mechanism, developing countries could be seriously disadvantaged by a movement towards the standardization of environmental regulations. This issue, however, has been addressed in other trade and environment fora. For example, in Europe compensatory mechanisms were put in place to support weaker members in their efforts to achieve upward harmonization. In recognition of the disparities that exist among member countries of the EU, a Social Development Fund has been established specifically to assist the economic and social development of weaker economies such as those of Portugal, Greece and Ireland.[62] In the APEC context, the differences and gaps between developed and developing country members are much greater than that in the EU. In APEC helping weaker members to achieve the same standards as developed members is a huge challenge but must be done in order for the integration process to be fair and equitable for all participating APEC members.

Another issue that needs to be acknowledged in the harmonization debate is the fact that there are significant differences in the environmental concerns facing APEC member states, given the diversity of membership.[63] For example, countries with primarily agrarian economies are primarily concerned with problems of land and/or water degradation, while heavily urbanized areas face different concerns such as pollution and the excessive production of waste.

Despite these issues, the gradual convergence of environmental standards among APEC members was actually recommended by APEC's Eminent Persons Group.[64] However, the APEC governments ultimately did not accept this proposal. At the same time, it was considered that 'significant economic and developmental differences between APEC members implies that harmonization could be unduly costly'.[65]

The special needs and situations of developing country members must be taken into account before introducing a certain level of product or process standards. Developing country members require technological assistance if they are to develop the same advanced level of product standards as developed countries. If developing countries are not provided with resources and technological assistance to assist them in capacity building, any attempt to impose the environmental standards of developed members on them would be counterproductive.

It is true that common environmental standards may help avoid discriminatory trade measures and retaliatory trade sanctions. The harmonization of environmental standards may also achieve economic as well as environmental goals. However, this will only be the case if the playing field is level. Developed members such as the United States, Canada and Australia have stringent environmental regulations and standards while countries like Papua New Guinea have barely got any environmental regulations and standards at all. These differences in standards may create pressure for upward harmonization, without regard for the socio-economic situation of a country and its other priorities. This situation has the potential to create unfair competition and trade distortions. APEC member countries should find common ground for addressing the harmonization of environmental standards. Addressing this issue will require careful navigation between the tendency of powerful, developed members to simply impose their own standards on others, and the tendency of newly industrializing countries to resist environmental constraints on fast-track growth.[66] However, rather than proposing the same standards, APEC could instead aim to standardize information gathering and testing procedures. It could also consider standardizing the actual standards-setting methodologies, such as environmental and health impact studies, as well as risk assessment procedures.[67]

Member states should be allowed to set their own standards on the basis of their appropriate level of standards and abilities. Environmental standards should be transparent. While member states should be cautious about disguised protectionism, they should place greater emphasis on the question of how environmental considerations could be incorporated into trade liberalization. This balanced approach would allow APEC to effectively address the issue of sustainable development.

Inclusion of the common but differentiated principle

APEC should include in its Framework of Principles for Integrating the Economy and the Environment the principle of common but differentiated responsibility. This is because in the past, the major polluters have tended to be developed countries.[68] Even now, most of the environmentally unsustainable practices occur in developed countries. As a result, it would be inequitable to expect developed and developing countries to bear the same financial burdens.

This concept is implicitly referred to in the fourth principle, which covers capacity building, and the seventh principle, which suggests that financial resources should be shared. However, without explicitly incorporating the principle of common but differentiated responsibilities, the Polluter Pays concept found in the second principle, and the precautionary approach adopted under Principle 5, have the potential to be used by developed countries for their own economic advantage without having to provide any compensation to developing countries. In particular, developed countries could use these principles to insist that developing countries bring their environmental standards into line with the standards of developed countries. Without any mechanism for compensation, this behaviour could result in developing countries losing any comparative advantage that they may have. This may in turn lead to a decline in their terms of trade, and ultimately a reduction in their levels of economic growth.

Conclusion

APEC has made environmental considerations an integral part of its regional free trading arrangement. Although APEC's primary objective is to facilitate trade and economic cooperation, it has formally integrated sustainable development principles as a legitimate part of itself. It has rightly emphasized the significance of capacity building in addressing environmental concerns. The approach of APEC to sustainable development is innovative in that it has focused not on the conflicts between trade and environmental rules, but on positive measures. Examples of this include multilateral discussions on the topic, and the design of practical, voluntary initiatives which broadly promote sustainable development in the context of trade liberalization.[69] APEC addresses environmental problems through negotiation and consensus among member economies. This facilitates cooperation in the integration of economy and ecology. Developing country members within APEC are not forced by strong counterparts to follow the latter's ideology, standards and environmental requirements. The self-interest of member states provides the incentive to strive to achieve the vision of sustainable development. Given the high degree of diversity and economic disparity between member economies, its pragmatic and consensus-based approach is noble. From this perspective it is more akin to a UN than a WTO model of international collective action.[70]

Addressing the issue of capacity building and technology transfer as fundamental to sustainable development, APEC has reaffirmed the Rio consensus. It has adopted many of the principles formulated in the *Rio Declaration*, and recognized that without helping developing country members to increase their capacity to deal with environmental concerns, the imposition of the standards of developed members will reduce their level of economic growth.

Although APEC, through its many programmes and action plans, has paved the way for the future integration of sustainable development with the liberalization process, actual progress on the trade and environment linkage has not been remarkable. Despite some environmental steps taken in the name of 'economic and technical cooperation, virtually nothing has been done to integrate trade and environmental policy making in the APEC context'.[71] Trade and the environment have emerged on separate and parallel tracks both within individual APEC economies and in APEC as an institution.[72] Taken as a whole, APEC's initiatives regarding the integration of economy and ecology have fallen short of what is required to make them mutually supportive. There have been many vague statements of intent, but unlike other areas of APEC's activities, there are few clear programmes of work in the areas of trade and environment linkage.[73] The APEC leaders' rhetorical commitments on sustainable development must lead to common frameworks for substantively dealing with the trade and environment interface. This reality has been outlined by Lyuba Zarsky in the following words:

> To truly promote sustainable development, environmental goals must be linked to and integrated with trade and investment rules and norms – not in a neo-liberal framework which blindly asserts the primacy of trade but in a new approach to regional economic governance based on the co equal status of economic development, environmental protection, and social justice.[74]

Therefore, APEC should as a matter of priority begin dealing with trade and environmental issues in a more substantive way. The High Level Meeting on Sustainable Development would be an excellent forum for undertaking this task. There should be an environmental review of trade liberalization policies. This would help to address issues such as market failure and the harmful environmental consequences that might flow from trade liberalization. There should be a dispute settlement body that could handle the conflicts that would naturally arise from any substantive recognition of the trade–environment linkage. It should also begin providing more substantial financial and technical assistance to developing members to enable them to build their capacity to deal with environmental issues.

Finally, it should recognize the central importance of the common but differentiated responsibility principle. Without this principle underlying its work programmes and action plans, the potential will remain for developed countries to exploit the organization and its developing countries to meet their own economic ends.

8 Trade restrictions pursuant to multilateral environmental agreements

Multilateral Environmental Agreements ('MEAs') provide the regulatory framework of principles and policies for the protection of the global environment and for addressing international environmental problems. Many environmental issues, such as air and water pollution, are multinational in character and therefore cannot be effectively addressed through national policies alone. The increasing scope and development of the MEAs' framework underscores the need for international cooperation in such matters.[1]

According to United Nations Environment Programme ('UNEP') and World Trade Organization ('WTO') surveys, of the 238 international treaties and other agreements in the field of the environment[2] that were operational in the 1990s, only 13 per cent contain trade-related measures under which trade provisions have been adopted by parties in furtherance of the objectives of the agreements.[3] While this figure may appear to be relatively low, it includes some of the most important and widely ratified treaties that currently exist within the sphere of international environmental law.

MEAs that use trade measures to achieve their objectives and aim to regulate and control or prohibit environmentally harmful trade include:

1 *Convention on International Trade in Endangered Species of Wild Fauna and Flora* ('CITES').[4]
2 *Montreal Protocol on Substances that Deplete the Stratospheric Ozone Layer.*[5]
3 *Basel Convention on the Control of Transboundary Movements of Hazardous Wastes and their Disposal.*[6]

Other MEAs that contain trade measures with significant implications for the trade–environment linkage include the *Convention on Biological Diversity,*[7] *United Nations Framework Convention on Climate Change,*[8] *Rotterdam Convention on the Prior Informed Consent Procedure for Certain Hazardous Chemicals and Pesticides in International Trade,*[9] *Cartagena Protocol on Biosafety*[10] and the *Stockholm Convention on Persistent Organic Pollutants.*[11] However, only CITES, the *Montreal Protocol* and the *Basel Convention* are within the scope of this chapter, as it is these three MEAs in particular that incorporate a wide range of specific trade measures designed to achieve their stated environmental objectives.

MEAs prescribe different types of trade measures. Some of the more common provisions include outright bans or prohibitions, quotas, prior informed consent procedures, mandatory labelling schemes and certification arrangements that include import and/or export permits. Such trade measures have at times been considered negative, coercive and even punitive[12] because the '[i]mprovements of environmental performance only become sustainable if supported by viable economics'.[13] Clearly, a setting of 'viable economics' remains lacking in the developing world. Despite such criticisms, these coercive trade measures may be applied between parties to an MEA and even between parties against non-parties.[14] As this chapter will reveal, some of the trade measures created under certain MEAs are a source of serious tension between free trade promoters, developing countries and environmentalists.

This chapter examines the interaction of trade and the environment in three MEAs. It does this by analysing various trade measures designed to ensure compliance and argues that such mandatory measures should only be seen as part of a broader package of positive measures, including capacity building, technological transfer and increased finance to meet all incremental costs. A central thesis of this chapter is that to impose trade measures in the absence of a commitment to provide positive measures will simply punish the non-compliant party to a relevant MEA and will fail to achieve the required environmental objectives or promote sustainable development. Furthermore, this chapter argues that these MEA trade measures, without a resolution or consensus on their relationship with GATT and the WTO, may in the future be disputed by a party to an MEA to the extent to which the particular measure is in conflict with global free trade agreements.

MEA trade measures and developing countries

The trade provisions of MEAs are typically designed to realize four major objectives. First, they are designed to control and restrict international trade where such trade is considered an environmental threat, such as trade in endangered species. Second, trade measures aim to increase the coverage of the agreement's provisions by encouraging governments to join and comply with the MEA. Related to this, the third objective of restrictive trade provisions is to seek to control trade with non-parties in order to prevent such non-member states from reaping the benefits of a free trade regime without assuming their equitable share of responsibility for international environmental issues. Finally, MEA trade measures attempt to control the traffic in certain harmful substances, thereby protecting the environment of the importing state.[15]

In theoretical or analytical modeling, trade measures contained in MEAs have received some positive attention in raising the standards of implementation, enforcement and compliance.[16] However, analysis based solely on the theoretical virtues of MEA trade measures can obscure the practical reality of implementation, compliance and enforcement of the Conventions, and their impact on developing countries. The practical effectiveness of trade measures achieving the various environmental goals contained in MEAs has been ill studied so far.[17] Indeed, the lack of credible analysis into the effectiveness of trade measures in promoting sustainable development has prompted some commentators to suggest that '[a]ssessing the effectiveness of trade provisions in environmental agreements is more an art than a science'.[18] Further, while the small number of existing empirical studies may provide some guide to policy makers, such studies are typically based on self-reporting, and correspondingly, they often suffer from a lack of accuracy, particularly in developing countries.[19]

Nonetheless, according to the case studies undertaken by the United Nations University, even MEAs without trade measures impose a substantial burden on the limited capacity and resources of developing nations, often to such an extent that the international demands created by MEAs compete for the limited financial resources that would otherwise be invested in domestic policy aimed at promoting sustainable development.[20] Therefore, rather than illustrating a mechanism for joint decision making[21] with regard to common resources[22] and reflecting the 'common but differentiated responsibility' principle, MEAs have the potential to become little more than mechanisms for unilateral decision making and instruments for unequal gains in trade.[23] Such failures are largely due to systematic factors that prevent the full realization of the aims of the agreement.[24] The specific systematic shortcomings that are most relevant to this chapter include the limited administrative, institutional, technical and financial capacities that are inherent to the predicament of developing countries. As will be explored, such pre-existing factors are often exacerbated if an MEA contains punitive trade measures that mean the economic burden placed on developing countries is only worsened, with little environmental gain.

Further, whether a country is in fact complying with an MEA is usually a matter of largely subjective interpretation, as Conventions are typically vague and ambiguous in terminology.[25] Often the situation is such that, '[p]owerful States, and they alone, use sanctions to enforce those international rules that suit their immediate interests'.[26] The vague and ambiguous terminology in the Conventions is also detrimental to the provision of positive measures with regards to capacity building and financial assistance. Indeed, while many MEAs contain provisions obligating developed member states to provide resources to assist developing parties in meeting the incremental costs of compliance, there is a virtual absence of specific, quantifiable and binding commitments. Unfortunately, while it is often these positive incremental costs measures that induce a developing country to become a signatory to an MEA in the first place,[27] commitments made to developing countries by their developed counterparts with regards to the provision of additional finances to meet the incremental costs of implementing treaty provisions are typically minimalist in substance. In stark contrast, the trade sanctions for non-compliance and enforcement are, by nature, both mandatory and non-discretionary.[28] Hence, due to their inherent institutional, technical and financial incapacities and contrary to established thinking, so-called 'non-compliance' with MEAs by the South is more accurately viewed as expected rather than deviant, and an 'inherent rather than deliberative'[29] aspect of governmental decision making in developing countries.[30]

In stark contrast to the discretionary nature of funding provisions and the compulsory nature of trade measures that characterize the MEAs discussed in this book, effective implementation of Goal 8 of the *Millennium Development Goals*, namely, 'global partnership', calls on the North to increase aid, support debt reduction and open markets to Southern goods.[31] It is contended that this goal represents an important benchmark because it remains vital for the interests of developing countries that the world community finds an effective alternative to trade measures that can provide financial and technological assistance to help build their capacity to address global environmental concerns.[32]

Specific MEA trade measures and developing countries

Convention on International Trade in Endangered Species of Wild Fauna and Flora ('CITES')

Trade measures under CITES

The aim of CITES is to control and regulate trade in endangered species and products made from such species. CITES established an international legal framework for the regulation and restriction of trade in wild plant and animal species in an attempt to reconcile international trade with the conservation of species.[33] CITES contains three appendices which list the species identified as being endangered by the Parties. Appendix I details species threatened with extinction that may be affected by trade, Appendix II lists the species that will be threatened with extinction if harmful trade is not curtailed and Appendix III lists domestic species of which member states commit to prevent the exportation. To protect these species, CITES sets out a number of provisions for the regulation of trade via a system of permits, certification and licensing.

For each appendix different rules apply, depending on the nature of exploitation and the resulting dangers arising from over-exploitation of a particular species. Each state party to CITES is required to designate a Management Authority to issue permits for trade in species listed in the appendices.[34] Each Party to the CITES is also required to designate a Scientific Authority to provide scientific advice on imports and exports.[35] The specific international trade restrictions that are designed to facilitate the enforcement of CITES are discussed in the following section.

Appendix I includes all species threatened with extinction which are, or may be, affected by international trade. Trade in Appendix I species is strictly regulated and authorized only in exceptional circumstances. These exceptional grounds are set out in Article VII and include, *inter alia*, acquisition of a specimen before the Convention's application, species bred in captivity for commercial purposes or any specimen of a plant species that has been artificially propagated. It should also be noted that for international trade to take place under these exceptions, CITES import and export permits, each of which are subject to various conditions, must be granted. The main consideration of the management authority in granting the permit is that trade will not further endanger the survival of Appendix I species.

Appendix II includes all species that, although not necessarily threatened to the point of extinction, may become so unless trade is subject to strict regulation.[36] Appendix II covers a wide range of species. Trade in Appendix II species is subject to export permits or re-export certificates granted by a management authority on the advice of a scientific authority. Granting of the permits is dependant on the management authority's satisfaction that trade is not detrimental to the survival of the species involved. While CITES does not specifically require an import permit for trading in Appendix II species, this is the requirement of most OECD countries under their domestic implementing legislation. For example, EU regulation 3626/82 imposes stricter domestic measures than those imposed in CITES by placing EU members under an obligation to require an import permit or import certificate for *all species* listed in CITES, irrespective of their categorization.[37] Thus, the effect of EU Regulation 3626/82 is to impose CITES Appendix I type protection to species listed in Appendices II and III.

Two further notable CITES restrictions are that trade in Appendix II species is allowed only when it is not detrimental to the survival of the species[38] and exports of a species should be limited in order to maintain that species at a level consistent with its role in the ecosystem.[39] In other words, Appendix II species must be managed in a manner that ensures population sizes remain well above the level at which that species might become eligible for inclusion in Appendix I.

Appendix III includes all species which any Party identifies as being subject to regulation within its jurisdiction for the purpose of preventing or restricting exploitation. Appendix III also includes species for which a Party requests the cooperation of other CITES Parties in controlling an illegal trade.[40] Trade in Appendix III species requires the granting of an export permit when the management authority of the state of export is satisfied that the specimen was legally obtained. In order to import Appendix III species it is compulsory for the management authority of any other Party exporting an Appendix III species to issue certificates of origin.

Article X of CITES provides that while trade with non-Parties is permitted, non-Parties need to provide documentation comparable to CITES permits and certificates. The documentation must conform to the requirements of CITES and be issued by the appropriately qualified authorities in that state. In practice, trade in Appendix I species with non-Parties is strictly limited to special cases.

Parties to CITES are required to adopt national legislation to enforce the Convention.[41] As has been seen in the EU, CITES also allows Parties to adopt stricter domestic measures restricting or prohibiting trade to achieve the objectives of the Convention.[42] In fact, the CITES Standing Committee has on many occasions recommended single or multi-species trade bans against parties for their failure to codify CITES obligations into domestic law.[43] Such trade measures restrict the rights of parties to trade in listed species when such parties are not fulfilling their Convention obligations, irrespective of their socio-economic situation. An excellent illustration of the operation of CITES trade measures is the non-compliance of Thailand. Although Thailand had been a member of CITES since 1983, for many years it had no domestic legislation in place to enforce the CITES. In 1991, after compelling evidence came to light of the blatant domestic and international trade in endangered species through the forgery and laundering of CITES documentation for protected species, the Conference of Parties ('COP') imposed a temporary trade ban on Thailand from 22 April 1991 to 2 April 1992. The CITES COP also threatened further trade sanctions if Thailand did not ensure the strengthening of laws to achieve compliance with the standards of the MEA.[44]

Despite their superficial appeal, stricter domestic measures have the potential to be used and abused by certain interest groups in the name of environmentalism. The purported purpose of restrictive trade measures is to improve compliance with the Convention, and restrict and/or control trade where such trade is considered an environmental threat. However, in the absence of the capacity and the resources to deal with such a crisis, sanctions such as the Thai ban can be used as weapons by protectionist groups who are unafraid to abuse their power in order to protect their share in domestic markets. Further, the threat or use of trade measures against non-complying (particularly developing country) Parties may force such Parties to invest their limited resources in improving their compliance with CITES rather than using these resources to attend to their pressing domestic developmental priorities.

Developmental implications of CITES for developing countries

Developing countries experience severe problems in the implementation of the provisions of CITES, as illustrated by the Thai case study. These difficulties are largely due to the fact that the Convention does not specifically address the issues faced by developing countries,[45] or provide financial assistance mechanisms for compliance.[46] That is, CITES does not consider:

> The diversity of historical and political systems worldwide [which] explains why the effectiveness of CITES varies from country to country, because no single uniform model fits for its implementation in all countries.[47]

Thus, it is evident that the uniform trade measures contained within CITES' provisions do not have uniform effects or impacts on developing countries and their standardized nature significantly affects overall levels of compliance and enforcement.[48] The reality rendered invisible by CITES is that developing countries simply do not have the human and financial resources or the institutional capacity to take appropriate measures to regulate trade according to CITES' provisions which require a system of permits, certificates and licences and responsible public authorities to administer this system.

Thailand's non-compliance with CITES until ten years after its implementation highlights the difficulty of eliminating the often lucrative trade in endangered species, both domestically and internationally.[49] Like all developing countries, Thailand's disobedience is perhaps most attributable to 'the lack of adequate funding and capacity building for the creation and enforcement of domestic legislation pursuant to the Convention'.[50] Thus, it is evident that the international trade ban imposed on Thailand was unlikely to eliminate the domestic trade in lucrative species when the majority of the population is living in poverty. The wild protected species under CITES can be a significant source of income in marginal agricultural areas.[51] Hence CITES cannot be expected to have a significant impact on the preservation of endangered species unless it also provides the necessary financing and capacity mechanisms to address issues of poverty and public environmental awareness.[52] Indeed, imposing trade bans simply increases the price of endangered species on the black market.[53] It is therefore foreseeable that coercive trade measures designed to achieve the objectives of CITEs are actually operating in a manner contrary to the treaty's goal to end the black market trade in endangered species.

This situation of limited administrative, institutional and financial capacity is also faced by Indonesia, a key exporter of wildlife and the second richest country in the world in terms of biodiversity. It has been estimated that Indonesia is home to 15–25 per cent of all the world's species.[54] The size of Indonesia and the massive expanse of sea surrounding its constituent islands makes monitoring and enforcement of CITES virtually impossible, particularly without the provision of substantial outside resources.[55] In addition, like Thailand, trading in endangered species is a source of income for local populations who often live in poverty and rely on subsistence farming. Further, Indonesia is still recovering from the Asian economic crisis of 1997/98, where 60 per cent of Indonesians faced periods of extreme poverty.[56] Indonesia's state of economic development is such that, at the end of July 2001, its national debt exceeded US$135 billion.[57] In light of this somewhat dire financial situation it is evident that any instigation of trade measures against Indonesia for non-compliance with CITES is only likely to further exacerbate the exploitation of natural resources in order to sustain livelihoods.[58] In order to stem the trade in endangered species, a package of positive measures based on international cooperation including the provision of incremental financing of the *real* costs of implementing CITES is desperately needed.

CITES requires the granting of exports by the Management Authority to be supported by the advice of a scientific authority. Developing countries, such as Thailand,[59] Indonesia[60] and Cambodia,[61] lack the research base and technological advancement to fulfil these requirements.[62] Where export permits issued by developing states are not based on the sound findings of a competent scientific authority, most OECD countries require import permits under domestic legislation. This is particularly the case where 'import permits [are required] for Appendix II species, additional to the CITES requirement of export permits'.[63]

The need for capacity building and adequate financing mechanisms was outlined by a 1997 OECD report. The report concluded that several developing countries had no specialized administrative authority in charge of issuing export permits, whereas other Southern states lacked the capability to print the official security CITES permits.[64] The report also confirmed that around 85 per cent of CITES parties do not have adequate legislation for the implementation of the Convention.[65] Without appropriate legislation in place, countries often lack the framework to 'verify the validity of the import, export and re-export permits and certificates essential for regulating trade in CITES-listed species or interdict or seize illegal shipments or prosecute violators',[66] as was the case in Thailand.

CITES has provided very limited financial and technical support to assist developing countries with building their capacity to implement the Convention. The third Conference of Parties in 1997 recognized the need for capacity building in developing countries and the problems these states encounter in their attempt to implement the provisions of CITES. Despite this rhetorical acknowledgement and the ongoing call for increased financial and technical assistance from international aid agencies to developed states to support specific Convention-related activities, to date CITES has not benefited significantly from multilateral financial and technical assistance.[67]

The Global Environment Facility ('GEF') is the international community's single most significant environmental fund[68] and the exclusive financial mechanism for four key MEAs.[69] The GEF was created in 1991 in response to demands from developing countries for financial assistance to ensure protection of their environment. Managed by the World Bank, UNEP and UNDP, the GEF is designed to cover the incremental costs of environmental protection in developing countries with respect to global warming, international waters, biological diversity and the ozone layer. It should be noted that the mandate of the GEF has attracted substantial criticism because of its alleged tendency to favour those environmental issues that are of most concern to developed countries.[70] Historically, the GEF has neglected the developmental priorities of developing countries themselves and has instead funded projects that have had destructive environmental consequences. For example, in the Arun Valley in Nepal, GEF biodiversity money has been used to fund the Arun Hydro-project, thereby indirectly contributing to biodiversity destruction.[71] In essence, the problems inherent in the functioning of the GEF call into question the value of certain financial concessions presently offered by developed countries.[72] In response to an environmental resource management questionnaire, 95 per cent of replies called for more use to be made of the GEF for CITES-related activities.[73] However, the economic criteria[74] set for attracting GEF funding generally 'work to favour ecosystem-oriented projects rather than a species approach, along the lines of which CITES operates'.[75] As a result, compared with numerous other MEAs, CITES appears to be receiving minimal benefit from the provision of GEF funding.[76]

The Montreal Protocol

Trade measures under the Montreal Protocol

The *Montreal Protocol* aims to reduce the production and use of ozone-depleting substances ('ODS') particularly chlorofluorocarbons ('CFCs'). The Protocol regulates the trade of ODS, products containing ODS, and products manufactured using ODS. It lists certain substances as a threat to ozone depletion and bans all trade in these substances between Parties and non-Parties. The Protocol also has scope to allow the creation of import bans on products made with, but not containing, ODS – a ban based on process and production methods.

The *Montreal Protocol* was one of the first MEAs to use trade measures to achieve environmental objectives. The primary objective of measures restricting trade with non-Parties is to encourage broad participation in the Protocol and coerce non-member states to join.[77] The *Montreal Protocol* imposes restrictions on trade through bans on the import[78] and export[79] of controlled substances between Parties and non-Parties. Trade with non-Parties is permitted if Parties have determined that non-Parties are in full compliance with the Protocol's control measures[80] and have submitted data to that effect.[81]

The import of products containing controlled substances from non-Parties is also the subject of trade restrictions. Parties to the Convention must provide a detailed and complete list of all known products that contain the controlled substances.[82] The *Montreal Protocol* also imposes trade restrictions on products made with, but not actually containing, controlled substances. The Protocol requires Parties to determine the feasibility of banning or restricting imports of such products from non-Parties within five years of the Protocol's entry into force.[83]

The *Montreal Protocol* required Parties to license each import and export of controlled substances by 2000 or alternatively within three months of the Protocol's date of entry into force.[84] The treaty also aims to discourage Parties from exporting technology for the purpose of producing and utilizing controlled substances to non-Parties.[85] In addition, Parties are required to refrain from exporting to non-Parties any products, equipment, plants or technology that would facilitate the production of controlled substances.[86]

However, it is important to note that the above-mentioned restrictions do not apply to 'products, equipment, plants or technology that improve the containment, recovery, recycling or destruction of controlled substances, promote the development of alternative substances, or otherwise contribute to the reduction of emissions of controlled substances'.[87] Clearly, this provision was introduced to facilitate the distribution of techniques and technologies that reduce the use of ODS, even if such transfers involves non-Parties to the Protocol.

Developmental implications of the Montreal Protocol *for developing countries*

The *Montreal Protocol* has recognized that developing the capacity of parties to fulfil their obligations 'will depend upon the effective implementation of the financial co-operation as provided by Article 10 and the transfer of technology as provided by Article 10A'.[88] The Protocol takes into account the special situations and difficulties encountered by developing countries in compliance with, and enforcement of, the control measures of the Protocol. It recognizes that non-compliance is frequently the result of 'technical, administrative or economic problems, and so it seeks to work constructively with Parties rather than as a judicial-type process'.[89] This approach is innovative in this manner of dealing with problems relating to non-compliance of developing countries. The *Montreal* Protocol has emphasized positive measures such as technical and economic assistance. This is an exceptional example which needs to be followed by other environmental treaties and institutions if they are to effectively involve and empower developing countries in the process of addressing environmental protection. However, as will be discussed, the extent to which this commendable theoretical framework has been effectively put into practice has been extremely limited.

The *Montreal Protocol* has created a multilateral fund to pay developing countries for the agreed incremental costs of their adherence to the Protocol.[90] The fund aims to provide financial and technical co-operation, including the transfer of technologies, the dissemination of information and training, the facilitation and monitoring of opportunities for bilateral and regional co-operation and the financing of investment projects of Article 5 developing countries.[91] For 1991–93, the Multilateral Fund received US$160 million in funding, followed by a further US$510 million in the period of 1994–96 and a third replenishment of US$540 million for 1997–99.[92] For the period 2006–08 total estimated funding is US$419.4 million.[93] What is immediately evident from these statistics is that, even ignoring inflation, the 2006–08 pledge is 77 per cent less than the 1997–99 pledge, indicating a significant decline in financial contributions in recent years. Nonetheless, the *Montreal Protocol*'s independent financial mechanism has contributed to the attraction of extensive participation of many developing countries. Indeed, after the 1990 London Meeting of the Parties, 'India and China made it clear that their participation was contingent on adequate financial assistance being forthcoming, and the Multilateral Fund was the result'.[94] In essence, the financial mechanism set up by the *Montreal Protocol* has made almost universal participation in the Protocol a reality, illustrating the importance of supportive measures in dealing with non-compliance.

The *Montreal Protocol* has also provided a commendable framework to facilitate the transfer of environmentally safe and related technologies to developing countries under fair and favourable conditions.[95] However, despite promises from developed countries, developing countries have yet to receive technology on the 'preferential and non-commercial terms' they desire.[96] In practice 'technology diffusion and related technical assistance have been delivered through the investment projects approved by the Multilateral Fund, through bilateral assistance programmes, and the OzonAction programme implemented by UNEP'.[97] Technology transfer on non-commercial terms would help developing countries to be less dependent on developed countries due to a reduced economic burden. As the following discussion will illustrate, this issue continues to be the subject of ongoing debate and negotiations.[98]

In the case of India, Korea and China, the inducement to accede to the *Montreal Protocol* was mostly derived from the provisions regarding positive measures in the form of environmentally sound technologies ('ESTs'),[99] including local capacity building to meet indigenous needs.[100] However, the Protocol is vague and imprecise as to how the agreed outcomes are to be achieved.[101] That is, there is very little in the MEA that outlines the specific manner in which the phase-out of OSD methods and their replacement with environmentally sound technology is actually going to occur. Neumeyer has stated that 'with such ambiguity built into the system of treaty making, developed countries could, on the whole, get away without making any specific or substantial commitments'[102] to provide positive measures in support of compliance and enforcement. Despite the fact that the *Montreal Protocol* is an agreement between nation states where ESTs are to be transferred on the terms that are 'fair and most favorable', the relevant technology, including the know-how in the production process,[103] is privately owned and therefore subject to trade secrecy and intellectual property rights.[104] Such private property protection is particularly strong under the *Agreement on Trade Related Aspects of Intellectual Property Rights* ('*TRIPS*'). Therefore, despite the aspirations of the *Montreal Protocol*, the use and transfer of ESTs is typically subject to the payment of substantial royalties, user licensing fees and commercial market terms.[105] Thus, whilst most developing countries want the transfer of EST and its technical 'know-how' for their own local capacity building and development, multinational corporations and owners of intellectual property rights prefer to transfer the capital only if they are able to retain some sort of control and make some form of profit.[106] This overwhelming of the intention of the *Montreal Protocol* by the more corporately popular *TRIPS* Agreement is detrimentally affecting the capacity of developing countries to move towards sustainable development in conformity with the aims of the Protocol. As will be explored in later section, such a conflict between an MEA and a more mainstream trade treaty is unfortunately a common phenomenon.

The incremental costs in the transition from ODS-based technologies to ESTs are subject to conditions such as those terms that are 'mutually agreed' and 'where necessary'.[107] Hence certain actual costs that developing countries may have to pay in the transition process may not be recoverable under the Multilateral Fund.[108] In addition, there is no dedicated funding for technology development under the *Montreal Protocol.*[109] Correspondingly, there is an inadequacy of funds to support switch-over to non-ODS technologies in Article 5 developing countries.[110] Therefore the incremental costs of adjustment from those imposed by the OSD trade restrictions are not wholly or partly compensated for by global environmental financial mechanisms.[111] Thus it is evident that, contrary to the theoretical observation that the Multilateral Fund under the *Montreal Protocol* is an ideal model upon which further MEAs should be based, in reality technology transfer under the Protocol has *not* been advantageous.[112] In recognition of this reality, Blaustein and Shanker assert, 'for the vast majority of Developing countries, technology, as well as the human and institutional capacity necessary to apply technologies, remain scarce resources'.[113] In the cases of India, Korea and China, 'the MEA is in place and the recipient is supportive to it and ready to receive technology but donors are not supportive and not willing to transfer'.[114] Once again, it should be noted that that it is not so much the institutional framework itself but rather than lack of willingness of donors to make positive contributions under that framework that has so far frustrated the effectiveness of the *Montreal Protocol.* India acceded to the *Montreal Protocol* on the basis that it would receive technology on fair and favourable terms to meet the economic burdens of transitioning of ESTs. However, India's efforts to acquire the HFC 134a technology (for the refrigerator sector) were not successful, 'as the owners of these technologies did not want to endanger their production base by rival production capacities in developing countries'.[115] Companies such as Du Pont, ICI and Elf-Atochem feared losing their control over production in these large markets[116] and 'upsetting the delicate balance of supply and demand',[117] especially when such firms seek to recuperate the high cost of research and development early in a new product's life cycle.

Hence, India's efforts to acquire alternative technology have so far been largely unsuccessful due to the often high price quoted for the use of technology protected by intellectual property rights. In one example, producers of ODS in India wanting to purchase the alternative technology were quoted US$25 million, when their original cost estimates were in the vicinity of US$8million.[118] Furthermore, as this technology is held by large multinational corporations, the bargaining power of developing countries is low.

The majority of large firms interviewed in an Indian case study on the *Montreal Protocol*[119] indicated that either financing under the Multilateral Fund had been cut and was inadequate for the phase-out of ODS technologies, or there had been significant delays in receiving funds.[120] Some of the interviewed firms also indicated that they had been waiting almost two years to receive approval for projects, with decisions still pending. The incremental cost guidelines for the transition to the alternative technologies in India were also significantly revised from their preliminary assessments. In one example concerning the conversion of refrigerators and air conditioning compressors, the World Bank's initial assessment was that incremental cost funding would be provided to the Indian company at a rate of US$107 per kilogram. The World Bank revised this assessment of the cost of conversion to US$36 per kilogram. This was further reduced by the technical experts assisting the Executive Committee to US$14 per kilogram.[121] Thus, the recipient stands to receive only 13 per cent of the amount of financial assistance that was originally assessed. In view of this vastly discounted figure, the prevailing opinion among most large Indian firms was that the technical experts were 'not cognisant of the circumstances prevailing in the affected sectors, leading to recommendations which were sometimes not in keeping with the adjustment needs of the firms'.[122]

Korea acceded to the *Montreal Protocol* on the basis that a significant portion of its exports in ODS-related industries went to developed countries. Consequently, if Korea did not sign the Protocol it would have been restrained in its trade with developed country Parties, resulting in a significant loss of market share. Indeed, approximately 42.4 per cent of Korea's total electronics industry exports and a large proportion of its chemical exports were covered under the Protocol. Such exports account for 10 per cent of Korea's total GDP.[123] Like India, however, although Korea has actively sought environmentally sound technologies as an alternative to ODS processes, it has been and continues to be constrained by the unwillingness of developed countries and large multinationals to transfer EST. Korean firms have been faced with the high cost of acquiring patented technology, the exorbitant royalties expected by multinational intellectual property rights holders and the stringent conditions that would apply if such technology were transferred.[124] Some of these conditions included a prohibition on exports, no possibility of dealing in competitive products and non-consignment of the technology to third parties.[125]

As a reclassified developing country, Korea accepted the resolution of the sixth Meeting of the Parties to abstain from relying on the *Montreal Protocol's* Multilateral Fund.[126] This abstention constitutes a substantial economic burden for Korea, as the cost of materials for the production of non-CFC refrigerators was estimated to increase production costs by as much as 30 per cent when the environmentally favourable substances HFC-134a and HCFC-141b were used as alternative refrigerating agents.[127] Further, no efficient alternative to CFC-based cleaning agents in the electronics industry has yet been found and alternatives that have been tested have exhibited a marked deterioration in quality and performance. In light of these factors it is reasonable to suggest that Korea's compliance with the *Montreal Protocol* would significantly reduce its competitive edge in the world market and thus have a negative impact on its development prospects.[128]

It is important to note that Korea's predicament is by no means an isolated exception. China also has experienced similar issues with compliance, namely the high price and low availability of substitutes, especially when factors such as the Multilateral Fund and EST were critical in China's ratification of the *Montreal Protocol*.[129] Officials in China have attributed the low level of domestic OSD substitutes as a result of the failure of the Multilateral Fund to support EST development and acquisition.[130] This lack of funding can be attributed to the fact that the Protocol's funding is primarily aimed at the closure of CFC production facilities, rather than the construction of new facilities that produce environmentally sound substitutes.[131]

The Basel Convention

Trade measures under the Basel Convention

The *Basel Convention* regulates the transboundary movement of hazardous[132] and certain other categories of waste.[133] The Convention originated as an initiative of developing countries based on their concerns regarding the unregulated state of global trade in hazardous waste. UNEP has estimated that the total annual generation of all hazardous wastes is between 300 million tonnes and 500 million tonnes, of which the OECD countries produce about 80–90 per cent.[134]

The *Basel Convention* recognizes in its Preamble the sovereign right of each country to ban the entry or disposal of foreign hazardous wastes and other wastes in its territory.[135] It accepts that hazardous and other wastes should ideally be disposed of in the state in which they were generated. The Convention also acknowledges the limited ability of developing countries to manage hazardous and other wastes.[136] The objectives of the *Basel Convention*'s trade measures are the protection of human health and the environment by controlling transboundary movements of hazardous wastes.[137]

The core mechanism by which the *Basel Convention* originally regulated and controlled trade was through a notification and consent procedure. The *Basel Convention* provides that the exporting state has the responsibility to notify the competent authority of the importing state and the state of transit (if applicable) of all transboundary movements of hazardous waste. The notification must contain detailed information about the contents of the waste and the risks associated with the intended movement. The state of import must consent in writing to the movement and can provide its consent on a conditional or unconditional basis. The receiving state may deny permission for the movement or request the provision of further information. The state of export must also receive confirmation that the waste will be disposed of in an environmentally sound manner.[138]

In response to an outcry from developing countries that the above provisions of the *Basel Convention* were merely providing a framework by which developed countries could legally offload their hazardous waste on the South, in 1994 at the second Conference of Parties, the provisions of the Convention were substantially strengthened. Decision II/12 of the COP states:

> Recognizing that transboundary movements of hazardous wastes from OECD to non-OECD States have a high risk of not constituting an environmentally sound management of hazardous wastes as required by the Basel Convention;
>
> 1 Decides to prohibit immediately all transboundary movements of hazardous wastes which are destined for final disposal from OECD to non-OECD States;
> 2 Decides also to phase out by 31 December 1997, and prohibit as of that date, all transboundary movements of hazardous wastes which are destined for recycling or recovery operations from OECD to non-OECD States.[139]

Despite the ban on OECD to non-OECD transfers implemented by the second COP in 1994, the *Basel Convention* continues to be criticized by developing countries for not effectively curbing the trade in hazardous waste. In 2001, Adeola reported that of the officially acknowledged volume of hazardous waste, more than 50 per cent is still exported to developing nations.[140] In general, developing countries lack the ability to monitor and effectively enforce import restriction policies due to a lack of technical expertise at the customs level, problematic legal regimes and other economic factors.[141] In the absence of a regulatory regime, developing countries have the potential to be used as dumping grounds for the industrial waste of developed countries.[142] The export of toxic waste to developing countries may be regarded as economically efficient and a lucrative source of revenue for impoverished and debt-ridden nations.[143] For example, in countries such as Brazil, Nigeria and South Africa, a total of 274 million tons of toxic waste from the United States has been found.[144] This hazardous waste could not have been disposed of in developed countries because of public protests, health and environment risks.

Under the *Basel Convention*, member states are also obliged to refuse permission for hazardous wastes to be imported to or exported from a non-Party state[145] unless they have a bilateral, multilateral or regional agreement or arrangement that contains provisions no less environmentally sound than those of the *Basel Convention*.[146] The Convention also requires the Parties' hazardous or other wastes to be exported and managed in an environmentally sound manner in the state of import or elsewhere.[147] Parties are also obliged to return the waste to the state of export if it cannot be disposed of in accordance with the guidelines outlined in Article 4.8.[148] The obligation to manage waste in an environmentally sound manner may not under any circumstances be transferred to the state(s) of import or transit.[149] Finally, the *Basel Convention* requires that hazardous or other wastes that are to be the subject of a transboundary movement are packaged, labelled and transported in conformity with generally accepted and recognized international rules and standards in the field of packaging, labelling and transport.[150]

Developmental implications of the Basel Convention *for developing countries*

The *Basel Convention* has granted Parties the right to determine the definition of hazardous waste. Lack of a universal definition of hazardous waste and basic data on the volumes and characteristics of hazardous waste generated and shipped across borders has contributed to uncertainty, particularly as to the scope of the Convention's impact on industries involved in trade in recyclable wastes. Further issues arise due to the fact that industrial states differ in their approach to the classification of mixed wastes and the threshold levels in relation to what is considered 'hazardous'.[151] Despite the outright prohibition on the transfer of hazardous waste between OECD and non-OECD nations imposed by the second COP in 1994, the persistence of significant flaccidity in the definition of what constitutes 'hazardous waste' continues to provide a possible loophole through which the economic desperation of many developing countries can be exploited.

In a manner analogous to the discussion above on the *Montreal Protocol*, technical 'know-how' in the manufacturing and production process and their environmental consequences may be held under patent rights by multinational corporations and are therefore protected under the *TRIPs* Agreement. Often this information is crucial in understanding the total impact of waste in a host country. The reason for this is that when multinational corporations fail to disclose the worst-case scenarios of these production processes in an environmental impact assessment when they export waste to the host country,[152] developing countries can easily fall into the trap of being inappropriately and unknowingly exploited as hazardous waste sinks for industrialized countries.

Industrialized nations often argue that developing countries are economically better off as a result of the waste trade, as it creates jobs, income and technological advancement.[153] However, these are only short-term gains, and in most cases developing countries use any hard currency they receive for debt servicing rather than advancing their sustainable development prospects.[154] Even more fundamentally, the economic realities that compel developing countries to accept hazardous waste that wealthier countries clearly do not want within their own borders must not be forgotten. Cusack has poignantly outlined the difficulties faced by developing countries:

> Fundamental bipolar economic inequities force Third World nations to accept shipments of toxic waste ... because they are poor and have unequal bargaining power. Consequently, the toxic waste trade between industrialised nations and the Third World resembles economic blackmail. Only the Third World's complete ban on toxic waste imports will challenge industrialised nations to confront the uncontrolled generation of hazardous waste.[155]

Beyond issues of North–South equity, the practical effectiveness of the *Basel Convention*'s mechanism to reduce and control the transboundary movement of hazardous and other waste is wholly dependent upon its proper implementation. To run the system effectively requires technological capacity, an adequate scientific resource base, huge financial resources and, above all, properly established infrastructure. Unfortunately, most developing countries do not have sufficient financial, technical or administrative resources to comply with the requirements for the implementation of the Convention's provisions. Such insufficiency also prevents developing countries from making informed judgements about particular shipments of waste or the prevention of illegal movements of waste. In addition, developing countries 'lack the capacity to mitigate the harmful effects of wastes and pollution and are unlikely to build such capacity in the near future'.[156] Those in Management Authorities and customs agencies, particularly in developing countries, often do not have the expertise 'to discern the difference between types of shipments [or] to know what is and what is not covered by the MEAs, and which category they fall in'.[157] Improving the capacity of developing countries to deal with these issues is absolutely essential to the holistic global management of hazardous wastes in an environmentally sustainable and economically viable manner.

Although the pressing resource needs of developing countries have been recognized, as with all MEAs discussed in this chapter, it has been left to Parties to the *Basel Convention* to voluntarily contribute to rectifying the monumental problems of capacity building and technical assistance. Due to inadequate voluntary contributions, gross lack of financial resources has limited the effectiveness of non-trade measures in the promotion of environmentally sound hazardous waste management. Whether voluntary funding for beneficial technology transfers will be more readily available in the future remains to be seen.[158] At present there is very little to indicate that the trend of inadequate resource provision by developed countries is likely to change.

The contrasting approaches of the Basel and Bamako Conventions

The *Bamako Convention*[159] represents a response to continued dumping of toxic waste on the African continent. More specifically, the *Bamako Convention* was instigated by several African nations that were dissatisfied with the fact that, prior to the above-mentioned amendments by the second COP in 1994, the original provisions of the *Basel Convention* merely prescribed regulations for the trade in toxic waste rather than prohibiting it. The *Bamako Convention* is limited to member states of the Organization of African Unity ('OAU'). The African nations' perceptions of the shortcomings of the *Basel Convention* included the lack of mechanisms to control shipments of mixed waste, enforcement against an importing state's failure to adequately dispose of the waste and the prevalence of forgery and bribery throughout the requisite certification process.[160]

The *Bamako Convention* provides an interesting alternative framework to the *Basel Convention* for controlling the transboundary movement of hazardous waste. The *Bamako Convention* requires its members to ensure that there are facilities available for the adequate treatment and disposal of the waste in an environmentally sound manner,[161] and imposes a collective responsibility on the parties to achieve monitoring and compliance. The *Bamako Convention* imposes strict, unlimited liability as well as joint and several liability for hazardous waste generators.[162] The notification requirements also have much stricter control and monitoring procedures.[163] Notification under the *Basel Convention* is subject to a substantial degree of interpretation. The ambiguity of these provisions means they are open to abuse and misuse. In contrast, the prior notice and consultation principle under the *Bamako Convention* requires that importing countries should be fully informed as to the content of the wastes so as to make an informed decision. This includes the exchange of information, the harmonization of technical standards and co-operation in the transfer of technologies for hazardous waste management systems.[164] Hence, the provisions of the *Bamako Convention* create 'an obligation to implement a preventive, precautionary approach to pollution problems [that] is a major improvement on the *Basel Convention*'.[165] Indeed, this book fully supports the assertion that, 'the *Bamako Convention* is one of the most effective and extensively provided international agreements on the trans-boundary movement of hazardous waste'.[166]

The uneasy relationship between MEAs and the WTO free trade regime

As the environment and economy are interlinked, the environmental protection measures set out in MEAs will inevitably overlap with global rules designed to promote free trade.[167] This overlap is particularly evident considering that MEAs and free trade instruments often have the same parties and address the same issues, albeit from different perspectives. This overlapping results in MEA–WTO linkages. Such linkages have the potential to impact upon the scope and amount of global free trade.[168] While such tension is a significant concern for *all* countries it is particularly worrying for the developing world, given their predisposition to being disadvantaged in the sphere of global trade.

In some circumstances, the linkages between MEAs and the WTO–GATT regime may result in contradiction or discordance between the objectives of each regime, especially considering that MEAs allow the imposition of trade barriers whereas the WTO does not.[169] However, the growing interdependence of economy and ecology warrants policy coordination between MEAs and the WTO.[170] At an international level the need for such collaboration requires 'efforts to ensure that the policies, rules and institutional structures of MEAs and the WTO are mutually supportive, to maximize their joint contribution to sustainable development'.[171] These ideals have been incorporated into various international agreements. For example, Chapters 2 and 39 of *Agenda 21* outline the need to 'develop more precision where necessary and clarify the relationship between GATT provisions and some of the multilateral measures adopted in the environment area.'[172] Principle 12 of the *Rio Declaration* also reiterated the danger of MEAs' prescribed unilateral trade measures for environmental protection and warned against the distinct possibility of 'arbitrary or unjustifiable discrimination or a disguised restriction on international trade'.[173] In similar vein, *Agenda 21* stresses the need for trade and environment policies to be consistent and mutually supportive and urges that 'account should be taken of the fact that environmental standards valid for developed countries may have unwarranted social and economic costs in developing countries'.[174]

If the free trade regime and the environmental regime are both mutually supportive they may yield positive results for the promotion and implementation of sustainable development.[175] Developing countries could take advantage of such a mutual coordination of the two regimes, with cooperation helping to avoid uncertainties, tensions and conflicts between these two emerging areas of the international sphere. Currently, developing countries are caught in the middle and paying a huge price for adjusting their social and economic policies to deal with the prescriptions of MEAs to protect the global environment.[176] Such compliance is preventing them from fully and beneficially engaging in the free trade regime and thus further disadvantaging them economically. Trade measures tend to have a more direct and severe impact on the development prospects of developing countries,[177] given their limited capacity to address issues relating to environmental standards[178] and the causal link that exists between poverty and poor environmental standards.[179] Hence, trade measures are not the most effective MEA policy instrument for developing countries, unless trade is directly related to the environmental harm.[180] In all other circumstances, the imposition of trade measures on developing countries is only likely to 'have the effect of punishing the recipient country, but will, in most cases not improve either compliance or enforcement'.[181]

In a situation where two countries are both members of the WTO but only one is a party to the relevant MEA there is potential for conflict between MEA trade measures that are specifically directed at non-parties and the obligations of parties under the GATT/WTO regime. In implementing the obligations of MEAs, a party may violate GATT/WTO principles, including Most Favoured Nation status, National Treatment or obligations to prohibit quantitative restrictions.

To date, there have been no cases of conflict between the obligations set out by MEAs and the WTO. However, there is definite potential for future conflict in a number of areas where the actions of a party pursuant to trade measures in MEAs may be challenged in a WTO dispute settlement system.

MEAs and the core principles of the GATT–WTO regime

According to the Most Favoured Nation principle,[182] any advantage, favour, privilege or immunity granted by any Contracting Party to any product of any other country applies equally to like products of all GATT/WTO Contracting Parties. This provision essentially requires all parties to treat like products alike. This obligation may give rise to problems when trade with non-Parties is restricted and/or prohibited pursuant to the obligations in any of the MEAs examined in this chapter, as they are instruments that explicitly prohibit trade with non-Parties unless non-Parties fulfil certain requirements.[183] Similarly, the approach of MEAs in discriminating between classes of countries (for example the *Basel Convention's* Annex VII and non-Annex VII countries) appears to directly contradict the GATT/WTO non-discrimination principle.

The National Treatment obligation[184] prohibits trade restrictions that discriminate between foreign products and like domestic products. Such a provision presumably includes a prohibition on the introduction of import or export trade restrictions for the sake of environmental protection. The *Montreal Protocol* provides a pertinent illustration of the seemingly direct conflict between MEAs and the GATT principles. Under the *Montreal Protocol* various regulations and taxes have been used by parties to help meet their consumption and production phase-out commitments. If compliance with these measures under the *Montreal Protocol* results in a member according less favourable treatment to foreign products compared with like domestic products, a violation of GATT Article III may occur. Should this happen, parties must rely on Article XX exceptions to justify their trade-related environmental measures (discussed below).

GATT Article XI prohibits the use of quantitative restrictions such as quotas, import and export licences. It also lists the exceptions to these restrictions, the main one being that countries are allowed to impose trade restrictions if they experience shortages of essential products or where it is necessary for trade in commodities, agricultural or fisheries products. However, Parties cannot apply this exception on environmental grounds. Consequently, the consistency of MEA provisions concerning export and import bans with GATT Article XI is debatable. For example, the obligations of GATT Article XI concerning quantitative restrictions may be at odds with CITES measures such as import and export permits and re-export certificates to regulate trade in endangered species including the prohibition or restriction of trade of Appendix I species for 'primarily commercial purposes'.[185]

Similarly, irrespective of whether they are applied to Parties or non-Parties enforcement measures taken pursuant to CITES Article VIII.1 or the 'stricter domestic measures' referred to in CITES Article XIV may violate GATT Article XI.[186] The compatibility of Article XI of GATT with the import and export bans introduced by parties in compliance with the provisions of the *Montreal Protocol* (Article 4) and the trade bans and trade controls instituted by the Parties pursuant to the 'General Obligations' of the *Basel Convention* (Article 4) is also highly questionable.

In the event that a trade measure pursuant to an MEA obligation is regarded as inconsistent with the MFN principle, that trade restrictive measure can be justified only if it falls under one of the GATT Article XX general exceptions. However, for the exception to apply such measures must be made in conjunction with restrictions on domestic production or consumption.[187] Furthermore, for Article XX exceptions to apply, a Party must ensure that the measure(s) cannot be applied in a manner that discriminates arbitrarily or unjustifiably between countries where the same conditions prevail, all less trade restrictive alternatives must have been exhausted and the measures must not constitute a disguised restriction on international trade.[188]

The Article XX(b) exception can be adopted where the regulation of trade is necessary for the protection of human, animal or plant life or health. However, the general consensus appears to be that it would be difficult to justify trade restrictions between Parties and non-Parties on such grounds. As David Hunter, James Salzman and Durwood Zaelke questioned:

> If the primary purpose of the trade restriction is to pressure non-Parties to ratify the Convention, is this "necessary to protect human health"? If the primary purpose is to provide safeguards for hazardous waste trade between Parties and non-Parties, is that 'necessary'?[189]

Ultimately, the ambiguity of Article XX(b) does little to clarify the potential conflict between the trade measures of certain MEAs and the rules of the WTO/GATT regime.

Similarly, it is not yet clear whether trade measures under the *Basel Convention* would be covered by the Article XX(g) exception (conservation of exhaustible natural resources). One could argue that hazardous waste treatment comes under exhaustible natural resources. Nevertheless, this line of argument can be questioned as to whether landfills and treatment facilities are natural at all or, rather, an artificial creation.[190]

The tense relationship between MEAs and the WTO has been the subject of debate in the recent past. Proposals from both developed and developing countries have been put forward in an attempt to clarify the ambiguity in this area without any consensus being reached. However, according to the International Centre for Trade and Sustainable Development ('ICTSD') and the International Institute for Sustainable Development ('IISD') procedural issues have slowed down the negotiation process that has been instigated to clarify the relationship between the WTO and MEAs. This reconciliatory process was initiated by para. 31(i) of the *Doha Declaration*. The ICTSD and IISD also report that discussions on environmental measures, market access, eco-labelling and sustainable development are virtually at a standstill.[191] A consensus on the relationship between MEAs and the WTO under para. 31(i) of the *Doha Declaration* also went unresolved at the WTO Ministerial Conference in Hong Kong in 2005.[192]

Further extensive consideration is required to solve the many issues relating to the use of trade restrictions for environmental purposes in this area. In the absence of consensus, the trade measures pursuant to MEAs have the potential to be used as deeply disguised protectionist measures, giving rise to future trade–environment disputes.[193] As domestic standards become tailored to MEAs and discriminate against imports on the basis of environmental standards, higher environmental standards in importing countries compared with exporting countries are likely to lead to inevitable conflicts with free trade agreements.[194] In the absence of a formal dispute settlement mechanism established by the MEAs regime, WTO dispute settlement mechanisms remain the only viable option for parties to both MEAs and the WTO.

Conclusion

In the absence of consensus on a regulatory regime, MEAs resort to trade measures to ensure compliance. For some of the most globally significant MEAs, trade sanctions are an integral means of achieving environmental objectives. However, while free trade advocates and developing countries generally approve of the overall goals of the various MEAs discussed in this chapter, they are largely unsupportive of the trade measures prescribed by them.[195] Such parties fear that environmental trade measures have the potential to be used as disguised protectionist measures against competition from the developing world.[196] It is also perceived that trade tools created by MEAs have the potential to be used by the environmental regime to force other countries to change their environment policies.[197] Punitive trade measures may also give more powerful actors the authority to restrict trade without having to explain and qualify the restrictions via scientific justifications concerning the protection of health and safety. Indeed, the authority to force other countries to change their environmental policies is a distinct objective of the use of these tools by way of trade leverage.[198]

The general perception in developing countries appears to be that the enforcement of trade measures in MEAs is an attempt by developed countries to impose their own interpretation of the rules of the international environmental regime, rather than aiming to achieve a consensus and dialogue on joint decision making with regard to common resources.[199] Developing countries generally object to the unilateral imposition of the environmental priorities of developed countries through trade-restrictive measures, fearing that the imposition of environmental standards (including process standards) could become a new trade barrier to developing-country exports.[200] On the other hand, the freedom of WTO members to utilize their comparative advantage is forfeited by giving large economies the right to restrict trade in cases where parties do not comply with their preferred non-trade policies. Oxley is accurate in his assertion that, 'the effect of large economies having the right to impose their labour standards on developing economies is obvious. The economic impact of allowing a comparable right with environment policies could be similar.'[201]

Most developing countries are concerned about the cost of compliance with MEAs. The cost of compliance for a particular member state is directly dependant on its level of economic development and the stringency of environmental standards. As outlined in the previous sections, developing countries' lack of human and financial resources, institutional capacity, and technological advancement means that compliance with MEAs is highly problematic.

An UNCTAD study summarized the current problems that exist regarding the commitments of developed countries for financial and technological transfer. While there is little doubt that developed countries are serious about the enforcement of non-compliance measures, including against developing countries,[202] the UNCTAD study concluded that 'the volume and effectiveness of supportive measures in most MEAs are insufficient.'[203]Against this backdrop, developing countries contend that an unhealthy emphasis on the imposition of trade sanctions for non-compliance vastly overshadows a virtual absence of meaningful technology and resource transfer commitments from the North to facilitate capacity building in the South.[204] As Uimonen and Whalley note:

> [d]eveloping countries are increasingly concerned that global environmental resources which industrialized countries come to define as valuable – such as the ozone layer, climate, biodiversity and tropical forests – will dictate to them abatement policies under threat of trade sanctions as [a] substitute for the technology transfers which may be arguably more efficient in achieving the desired end, as well as being more desirable from the standpoint of income distribution.[205]

In Thailand and Malaysia, major obstacles that have prevented the institutional implementation of MEAs such as CITES and *Agenda 21* include a lack of institutional and staff capacity, coupled with low levels of institutional and public awareness.[206] These issues were also reflected in Sri Lanka, where it was identified that the lack of appropriate mechanisms for compliance and enforcement of MEAs was due to the absence of effective information management systems to handle MEA-related data and information.[207] Similarly, in Pakistan the responses to a survey listed the key problems and constraints in setting up and maintaining the institutional framework for MEA management.[208] Some of the problems listed in the survey included limited financial and human resources, lack of a centralized authority and lack of understanding of the legal aspects of various MEAs.[209] The legal implications of MEAs are also not clearly perceived by various stakeholders in developing countries.[210] Further, public awareness concerning MEAs in developing countries is extremely poor, due to low levels of literacy and communication, extremely limited access to information, poverty, and the 'lack of dissemination to lower formations of government functionaries, NGOs and private institutions'.[211]

Overall, global environmental governance may have a positive impact on the interests of the South provided that it is possible for developing countries to meaningfully participate in the forum of global environmental regulation. The extent to which such participation will occur depends on the functioning of key principles of common but differentiated responsibility, technology transfer, capacity building and new and additional financial resources geared to sustainable development. Although global environmental governance appears to be constantly and forcefully reaffirming these core principles, to date, practical manifestation of the rhetorical commitments has been far from satisfactory. Global environmental governance needs to ensure that the above principles and frameworks are implemented in all MEAs and in financial institutions and mechanisms. Without properly resourced implementation strategies, those MEAs containing restrictive trade measures will further deepen the difficulties faced by developing countries in addressing sustainable development.

A recent OECD study reveals that if parties, especially developing countries, have the financial and technical capacity to properly implement and establish measures, they will become more likely to achieve targeted results.[212] Such a finding is indicative of the reality that a state's failure to comply with the requirements of MEAs is 'rarely the result of the deliberate policies of parties, but rather the consequence of deficiencies in administrative, economic or technical infrastructure'.[213] This reality of an inability to comply as opposed to an unwillingness to comply persuasively justifies the position that trade measures should not be viewed as the sole policy instrument for achieving the objectives of MEAs. Instead, trade and positive supportive measures should complement one another and operate as a balanced and integrated package.

Above all, the interests and concerns of developing countries deserve searching reappraisal if the MEA regulatory framework is to ever be truly effective. The sheer number of MEAs and the complexity of the areas they deal with will certainly place greater demands on the resources of developing countries if they are to comply with the relevant requirements. This situation calls for appropriate

9 Free trade and sustainable development

Challenges ahead

The main objective of this book has been to critically examine the most pressing issues for developing countries at the intersection of multilateral trade liberalization and ever-increasing environmental concerns. Presenting the perspective of developing countries in the development of the trade and environment debate has been a primary objective. Through examination of numerous international law issues it is an unequivocal conclusion of this book that the current treatment of trade–environment issues is inseparably entwined with the economic, social and political construction of the current dominant world system and consequently has resulted in major conflicts of interests between many states and other actors.

Developing countries are among the major actors and are a political force in global economic and environmental processes. Yet the South remains strangled by the parochial self-interest of the powerful Northern countries on the one hand, and the egocentricity of international environmental institutions and various actors such as multinational corporations ('MNCs') and non-government organizations ('NGOs') on the other. This is 'due to the continuing emphasis on resource-intensive growth and trade, the maintenance of debt and global inequities and the powerful and central role played by global corporate and business interests'.[1]

This book has argued that trade–environment linkages must be addressed within the broader framework of sustainable development, a framework which, when properly applied, places a *primary* emphasis on the developmental needs and priorities of developing countries. Trade–environment issues have to be addressed in a pragmatic manner by considering the economic and social problems and stages of development of the South on the basis of the principle of common but differentiated responsibility. Proper recognition of the fact that the development needs of developing countries cannot be separated from, let alone sacrificed to, the trade–environment debate is long overdue. Developing countries will be able to take appropriate measures to deal with the proximate causes and effects of environmental degradation only through vastly increased economic development and capacity building measures. For this to happen, the competing North–South interests as manifested in the global economic and environmental governance must be reconciled as a matter of urgency. Recognition of, and providing appropriate implementation strategies for, resolving the concerns of developing countries will go a long way in fostering global collaboration on sustainable development. The inherent inequities in the current international trading system and the inequitable power relationship between the North and the South in virtually every geopolitical sphere must be dealt with in order to build confidence between the North and the South and to advance the global quest for sustainable development.

Drawing upon the observations and submissions made throughout the book, this chapter refers to some major dilemmas encountered by developing countries when attempting to respond to trade and environment issues. This chapter concludes by briefly canvassing some possible strategies for mitigating or reconciling the conflicting positions of developed and developing countries in the international debates on the trade and environment relationship in promoting sustainable development.

Interlinkages between trade, the environment and sustainable development

As noted in Chapter 1, the relationship between trade and the environment has been the subject of intense debate at both national and international policy levels. The trade–environment debate is inextricably linked with the often vastly different perspectives of free traders and environmentalists, developed and developing countries. The *Brundtland Report* has explicitly shown the vital links between the state of the natural environment and economic growth. It also recognized the need for making trade and environment mutually supportive in order to promote sustainable development.

A decade and a half ago, Principle 12 of the *Rio Declaration* recommended that states should 'promote a supportive and open international economic system' which would contribute to economic growth and sustainable development.[2] At the same time, Chapter 2 of *Agenda 21* recommended a similar approach in relation to the relationship between trade and the environment, stating that the 'development process will not gain momentum ... if barriers restrict access to markets and if commodity prices and the terms of trade of developing countries remain depressed'.[3] In essence, trade liberalization and the environment should be mutually supportive. As positive trade growth and environmental protection are both equally important for sustainable development, there must be a process of integration between the two spheres.

However, despite the progress that has arguably been made in the past fifteen years at numerous global forums focused on sustainable development, there remains a stark and significant disparity between developed and developing countries as to what particular strategies should be adopted to achieve the objectives of sustainable development. These differences are manifested in the principles and policies designed to achieve the objectives of sustainable development. At the United Nations Conference on Environment and Development the world community sought to strike a balance between trade and the environment by means of their relationship with development. The UN suggested various principles, made recommendations and developed action plans with a view to developing a framework for trade–environment integration on a multilateral basis. Despite these understandings, the international community has done little to assist in the realization of these principles 'beyond mere pronouncements in the preambles of treaties and other documents'.[4] Developed and developing countries are still divided over the question of how to put existing principles and policies into practice. Developed countries have not accepted the responsibility of paying for the environmental degradation caused by them in the past and also as a result of present unsustainable rates of 'wants-based' consumption. This book has argued that substantial and ongoing resistance to the elevation of the notion of common but differentiated responsibilities to normative status has effectively meant that the primary ideological framework for achieving sustainable development is still uncertain and remains unresolved.

The inequities of current international economic relations have contributed directly or indirectly to environmental degradation and to persisting underdevelopment. The development process of developing countries was initially undermined and in many instances has now virtually halted due to the unfairness of the global financial system. Fundamental development changes need to be implemented in order to transform unsustainable practices into sustainable ones. These changes depend largely on the reform of the inequitable trading relationship between the North and the South. It is therefore imperative for a new and equitable international economic order to be established. Such an order must be conducive to the promotion of sustainable development of all countries, particularly developing countries, thereby creating the conditions necessary for global cooperation and equitable assumption of responsibilities for the protection of the environment.[5]

Why do developing countries need an open and equitable international trading system?

Trade is an important contributor to economic growth, which in turn produces the necessary conditions for the advancement of environmental protection and sustainable development. Empirical research on the relationship between trade and the environment supports this view and affirms that trade growth has the capacity not only to increase the stock of human capital but also to lower pollution.[6]

By opening markets particularly to exports from developing countries, and by keeping markets open through clear and enforceable rules, the global trading system can become a natural ally of sustainable development.[7] Trade liberalization can therefore be an important contributor to sustainable development, especially when implemented in conjunction with complementary environmental policies.[8] Consequently, striving for a genuinely open and fair international trading system is a vitally important economic instrument for developing countries to effect their development and protect the global environment.[9]

The current state of play

The unfairness of fair trade

The economic, classical and neoclassical theories of trade illustrate the benefits of trade liberalization to all trading partners by increasing global outputs and economic growth. By using the principle of comparative production advantage a country can produce more of the goods in which it is relatively more efficient and export them in return for goods in which its relative advantage is less. Consequently, trade brings about the highest possible welfare in participating countries by facilitating the specialization of production across national boundaries. The logical assumption of the theory of free trade that upholds its benefit seems to be inconsistent with the consequences of its operation in recent decades. Beyond the realm of abstract theory, global experience has to date shown that the prevailing species of international trade liberalization has predominantly served the protectionist interests of the world's economically strong.[10] Consequently, the debate over trade and the environment often marks the major split between the North and the South regarding the goals and practical effects of the conventional theory of trade.

Growing environmental concern is linked with the operations of the multilateral trading system in a very complex manner involving many actors and interest groups, often using trade–environment issues as an increasingly powerful bargaining chip to gain a competitive advantage. While developed countries persist for the continuation of the free trade ideals propelled by a largely status quo-based trading system, developing countries question the ability of such a system to satisfy their needs and are concerned about the social and environmental implications of its continuance. Against this backdrop, developed countries' attempts to address environmental problems *within* the current rules-based multilateral trading system are perceived by developing countries to be little more than another protectionist instrument for the expedient pursuit of Northern market interests. These concerns have been confirmed by the arbitrary and discriminatory use of environment-related non-tariff barriers and other technical standards for the restriction of trade for environmental protection.

Despite the adolescence of the era of globalization, developing countries have not yet been properly integrated into the global economy and remain inhibited from participating in it either as consumers or producers. This inability stems from an acute lack of purchasing power, skills and resources. In addition, 'Protectionist pressures and unilateral policy actions continue to endanger the functioning of an open multilateral trading system, affecting particularly the export interests of developing countries.'[11] Continued protectionism, whether in the name of environmentalism or otherwise, raises barriers against manufactured exports from developing countries and limits their opportunities to diversify from commodity-based exports which rely on the unsustainable use of non-renewable resources.[12] The natural resource base that contains the primary commodities exported by developing countries in return for the goods and services of industrialized countries are constantly declining, resulting in tremendous income losses and often catastrophic losses in biodiversity. This situation has restricted their capacity to diversify their production and export base and is depriving them of the finance necessary for sustainable development.

Market access, removal of subsidies and reduction of tariffs

For developing countries, improved market access is a vital step on the pathway to sustainable development. Market access can be secured by eliminating all forms of export subsidies and by substantially reducing trade-distorting domestic supports. Unfortunately rampant tariff peaks and tariff escalation still discriminate against a range of imports from developing countries. In developed countries, agriculture and textiles remain heavily protected by high tariffs and substantial subsidies. Developed countries have long persisted with maintaining exceptionally high trade barriers (both tariff and non-tariff) in areas of special interest to developing countries. Each year these barriers cost developing countries approximately US$100 billion – *twice* the amount they receive in aid.[13] Such restrictions are contrary to free market principles and greatly undermine the efforts of developing countries to make progress towards sustainable development. Protection of the environment has become the new route for the proliferation and legitimization of widespread protectionism by developed countries against developing countries.

Capacity building for sustainable development

The key aspect of the North–South cooperation in achieving the goal of sustainable development is providing developing countries with the necessary assistance to make meaningful advancements towards sustainable development. Despite having reached rhetorical consensus on the above need, there has been no progress towards meeting commitments made regarding financial resources and the transfer of technology. Most of the multilateral commitments that have been made are inherently limited to the non-binding and discretionary 'best efforts' of developed countries. Experience and statistics derived from the minimal contribution of developed countries to the Official Development Assistance ('ODA') and the Global Environmental Facility ('GEF') show the serious gaps between the in-principle commitments made by developed countries and the reality of the situation.

Transfer of and access to environmentally sound technologies on viable non-commercial terms for developing countries is another important area towards the realization of lasting North–South consensus on sustainable development. Once again, the action on the promises made by developed countries appears hollow and lacklustre. The current dominance of multinational corporations in the area of technology and the commercialization of knowledge and intellectual property through the World Trade Organization TRIPS[14] and GATS[15] agreements has largely rendered the initial North–South consensus ineffective. Developing countries have had only limited access to the burgeoning supply of technology, services and knowledge because of their inability to afford such access on purely commercial terms. Instead of fostering innovation and the dissemination of environmentally sound technologies, the *TRIPs Agreement* has further increased the industrialized world's grip on technology via its onerous protection of intellectual property rights. It has also failed to protect indigenous knowledge and community rights and has been accurately criticized as a 'knowledge blockade' of developing countries (see Chapter 3).

The application of the 'special and preferential treatment' and 'common but differentiated responsibilities' principles impose obligations upon the North to provide resources to the South for the sole purpose of achieving sustainable development. The share of developed countries in global environmental degradation and their overwhelming economic superiority are but two of the legitimate justifications for these cornerstone principles. These obligations were elaborated in the *Rio Declaration* as policy premises. Despite their further crystallization through the Millennium Development Goals, in Johannesburg and at countless other international forums over the past fifteen or so years, the obligation to provide financial resources and technology transfer remains largely unfulfilled. Consequently, developing countries' capacity to deal with long identified impediments to sustainable development has failed to improve noticeably. The failure of developed countries to act on their promises has monumentally weakened the ability of the international community to attain the goal of sustainable development. This inaction is also rightly interpreted as a denial of the historical responsibility of the North for their contribution to the global environmental problems and their continuing unsustainable consumption patterns. Instead, the Northern media depicts the poverty of the South as the main cause of environmental degradation. Regrettably, 'wealth, or concentration of wealth, in the North as the source of environmental pressures, or indeed as one of the causes of the global poverty, is mostly overlooked'.[16]

Trade-related environmental measures and protectionism

The practice of using unilateral trade measures as environmental tools has been increasing. This is evident from the 'restrictions on the importation and use of certain commodities, imposition of environmental regulations, standards and other non-tariff barriers on imports as well as increased production costs reflected in higher export prices'.[17] Within an inherently asymmetric GATT/WTO trading system the setting of standards, norms, trade restrictions and enforcement-driven retaliations to secure compliance has become a part of the manipulative protectionist process for maintaining and extending the asymmetry of the system.[18] Unilateral and unrealistic national actions theoretically initiated to achieve environmental protection have in reality turned into the worst form of protectionism and are being invoked arbitrarily by developed countries to keep some of the exports of developing countries out of their own markets. The difficulty and severity of the green protectionism has been demonstrated in the case of process and product standards as evident in an ensemble of disputes employing trade sanctions for environmental purposes.

Developed countries, with their dominant economic power, are the leaders in setting standards and making rules for environmental protection which include technical standards and regulations, product-content requirements (such as provisions limiting the amount of hazardous substances that can be traced in a product), sanitary and phytosanitary ('SPS') measures, mandatory labelling, packaging requirements and voluntary measures such as eco-labelling.

Subsequent to this standard-setting process, the developed countries then take action to give effect to those standards, typically without taking into account the different development levels of the South. Consequently, such trade measures do not heed the concerns of developing countries in relation to their practical inability to meet the strict environmental norms set by the affluent North. For developing countries, differences in environmental standards should be considered in the context of past injustices of developed countries in their production process and present social and economic inequities between developed and developing countries. Developing countries lack the infrastructure, environmentally sound technology, finance and good governance to improve and enforce environmental standards and measures for the integration of trade and the environment. While trade-related measures are gaining momentum in the policy considerations of different forums, including Multilateral Environmental Agreements, the issues faced by developing countries are still not receiving adequate attention.

Using trade restrictions to force developing countries to comply with Northern environmental standards that are beyond the South's extraordinarily limited means is not the way to achieve sustainable development. Solving environmental problems by restricting trade will threaten developing countries' prospects of sustainable development. Unilateral trade measures to pursue what are primarily the self-interests of rich and powerful countries are likely to do little more than undermine the integrity of the multilateral trading system.[19]

Asymmetries and imbalances within the WTO agreements

The imbalances and inequities in various WTO agreements and institutional arrangements are unfair to developing countries and a major barrier to their quest for sustainable development. Significant imbalances between rights and obligations in several WTO agreements such as the agreements on Agriculture, Textiles, Trade-related Intellectual Property Rights, and Subsidies and Countervailing Measures have deprived developing countries of their expected benefits from trade liberalization. Most of the imbalances in these vital international agreements stem from the inadequate or imperfect implementation of the agreements both in letter and spirit by the most powerful parties to the agreements. This situation has reduced the credibility of the multilateral trading system and has 'resulted only in a minimal increase in market opening while reinforcing imbalances in competition between developed and developing countries'.[20]

Despite the enormity of concerns with the status quo, this book maintains that a development-oriented multilateral trading system can still be salvaged as a true instrument for sustainable development. Such a change will be realized when developing countries begin to receive their due shares of economic benefits arising from the liberalization of their markets not merely in the form of words, promises and commitments, but in reality and substance. Tangible progress in this venture warrants a new mind set in the North – a mind set that unflinchingly acknowledges the concerns and interests of developing countries in the context of trade and environment issues. This remains a daunting challenge for the future.

Notes

1 Establishing the linkage: the trade–environment interface

I would like to acknowledge the following source for granting copyright permission to reproduce my earlier work 'The Trade–Environment Interface: Issues Lurking behind the North–South Tensions' with substantial revision: *Macquarie Journal of International and Comparative Environmental Law* 2:1, 2005, 121–44.

1 Comparative advantage is considered to be the philosophy behind liberal trade. David Ricardo developed the theory of comparative advantage in 1817. It is the theoretical justification of the benefits of liberal trade.

2 Leutwiler Report in *Trade Policies for a Better Future: Proposals for Action*, Geneva: GATT, 1985. Cited in Organization for Economic Co-operation and Development ('OECD'), *Trade Principles and Concepts*, OECD Doc., OCDE/GD (95) 141, 1995, p. 18.

3 Paul Samuelson, *Economics*, 11th edn, New York: McGraw-Hill, 1989, cited in OECD, 'Trade Principles and Concepts', p. 18.

4 World Commission on Environment and Development ('WCED'), *Our Common Future*, London: Oxford University Press, 1987, p. 5.

5 F. Ghina, 'Sustainable Development in Small Island Developing States: The Case of the Maldives', *Environment, Development and Sustainability* 5, 2003, 156.

6 P.A.G. van Bergeijk, 'International Trade and the Environmental Challenge', *Journal of World Trade* 25:6, 1991, 106.

7 WTO Press Release, 'Free trade helps reduce poverty, says new WTO secretariat study', 13 June 2000, WTO Doc. Press/181. Online. Available HTTP: <http://www.wto.org/english/news_e/pres00_e/pr181_e.htm> (accessed 30 April 2007).

8 UNCCD Press Release, 'Executive Secretary of UN Convention to Combat Desertification Calls for Enhancement of International Cooperation against Land Degradation', 17 June 1999. Online. Available HTTP: <http://www.unccd.int/publicinfo/pressrel/showpressrel.php?pr=press17_06_99> (accessed 30 April 2007).

9 K. Anderson and J. Drake-Brockman, 'The World Trade Organisation and the Environment' in B. Boer, R. Fowler and N. Gunningham (eds), *Environmental Outlook: Law and Policy*, No. 2, Sydney: Federation Press, 1996, p. 140.

10 K. Miranda and T.R. Muzondo, 'Public Policy and the Environment', *Finance and Development* 28:2, 1991, 25.

11 WCED, *Our Common Future*, p. 19.

12 *WTO Agreement (Marrakesh Agreement Establishing the World Trade Organization)*, 1994, Preamble. See WTO, 'Environment – 1994: The Marrakesh Agreement and the decision'. Online. Available HTTP: <http://www.wto.org/English/tratop_e/envir_e/hist2_e.htm> (accessed 16 February 2007).

13 WCED, *Our Common Future*, p. 4.

14 *Rio Declaration on Environment and Development* (*'Rio Declaration'*), 14 June 1992, Principle 12, UN Doc. A/CONF.151/5/Rev.1 (1992).
15 *Agenda 21: Programme of Action for Sustainable Development*, UN GAOR, 46th Session, Agenda Item 21, Principle 1.2, UN Doc. A/Conf.151/26 (1992).
16 *Johannesburg Declaration on Sustainable Development*, adopted at the 17th plenary meeting of the World Summit on Sustainable Development, 4 September 2002, para. 14, UN Doc. A/Conf.199/L.6/Rev.2 (2002).
17 *United Nations Millennium Declaration*, UN General Assembly Resolution 55/2, UN GAOR, 55th Session, 8th plenary meeting, UN Doc. A/Res/55/2, 2000.
18 L.D. Guruswamy, 'The Convention on Biological Diversity: Exposing the Flawed Foundations', *Environmental Conservation* 26:2, 1999, 81.
19 *Rio Declaration*, Principle 7.
20 A. Khosla, *The Road from Rio to Johannesburg*, The Millennium Papers, Issue 5, UNED Forum, 30 April 2001, p. 7.
21 Ibid., p. 9.
22 The term developing countries refers to both developing and least developed countries. Developing and the least developed countries are also known as the South, non-industrialized countries, underdeveloped countries and emerging nations. They are generally characterized as technologically less advanced than developed countries, with high population growth, widespread poverty and a traditional and rural socio-economic infrastructure. They typically have a colonial past and foreign exploitation has severely affected their economic growth for a long period of time. Their economy has been distorted by exporting primary products to the developed world. They are the market for the finished products of the developed world.
23 L. Rajamani, *Developing Country Resistance to Linking Trade and Environment: The Perceptions of Inequity and the Politics of Autonomy*, Global and Environment Trade Study: North–South Series, No. 1, August 2000. Online. Available HTTP: <http://www.gets.org/library/listcontent.cfm> (accessed 16 February 2007).
24 For details on the perspective of developing countries on this issue, see generally, K. Nath, 'Trade, Environment and Sustainable Development' in V. Jha, G. Hewison and M. Underhill (eds), *Trade, Environment and Sustainable Development: A South Asian Perspective*, London: Macmillan, 1997, pp. 15–20; M. Shahin, 'Developing Country Perspective' in D. Brack (ed.), *Trade and Environment: Conflict or Compatibility?*, London: Earthscan/Royal Institute of International Affairs, 1998, pp. 150–63; A. Najam and N. Robins, 'Seizing the Future: the South, Sustainable Development and International Trade', *International Affairs* 77:1, 2001, 49.
25 C. Thomas, 'Where is the Third World now?' *British International Studies Association*, 1999, p. 226. Online. Available HTTP: <http://journals.cambridge.org/download.php?file=%2FRIS%2FRIS25_05%2FS026021059900225Xa.pdf&code=e32e8bbf267c9182d990e75cf703ee45> (accessed 2 April 2007).
26 Developing countries' positions in this respect will be outlined in Chapters 3 and 4.
27 Paragraph A (i) of the *Uruguay Round Declaration* 1986, 25 ILM 1624 (1986).
28 United Nations Development Programme ('UNDP'), *Human Development Report 2003 – Millennium Development Goals: a compact among nations to end human poverty*, New York: Oxford University Press, 2003, pp. 40–1.
29 Khosla, *The Road from Rio to Johannesburg*, p. 6.
30 M. Halle, 'Trade and Environment: Looking beneath the Sands of Doha?', *Journal for European Environmental and Planning Law* 2006:2, 2006, 107.
31 See para. B (iv) of 1986 *GATT Punta del Este Ministerial Declaration*, 25 ILM 1624 (1986).
32 Paragraph B (v) of the 1986 Declaration, 25 *ILM* 1625 (1986).
33 GATT, Article XVIII. For details see S. P. Subedi, 'The Road from Doha: The Issues

for the Development Round of the WTO and the Future of International Trade', *International and Comparative Law Quarterly* 52:2, 2003, 427.

34 Clair Wilcox, *A Charter for World Trade*, New York: Macmillan, 1949, p. 141.

35 For details see speech of Rubens Ricupero, Secretary-General, UNCTAD, in Jagdish Bhagwati (ed.), *The Next Trade Negotiating Round: Examining the Agenda for Seattle*, proceedings of the Conference held at Columbia University, 23–4 July 1999.

36 M. Khor, 'The South at the End of the Uruguay Round', *Third World Resurgence*, May 1994, 38. Cited in A.C. Durbin, 'Trade and the Environment: the North–South Divide', *Environment* 37:7, 1995, 16.

37 Ibid.

38 Rubens Ricupero, in Bhagwati, *The Next Trade Negotiating Round.*

39 S. Vaughan, 'Trade and Environment: Some North–South Considerations', *Cornell International Law Journal* 27:3, 1994, 600.

40 Statement made by Malaysian Minister of Environment at the GATT Marrakesh Ministerial Conference, cited in Third World Network, 'After the Uruguay Round: Third World Resurgence', *Third World Network Features*, May 1994. Online. Available HTTP: <http://www.twnside.org.sg/> (accessed 16 February 2007).

41 The GSP is an arrangement under which preferential tariff treatment is granted by developed countries to manufactured and semi-manufactured products of developing countries. The aim of this arrangement was to increase the export earnings of developing countries and help them achieve economic growth and industrialization.

42 United Nations, *Millennium Development Goals Report 2006*, New York: United Nations, 2006. Online. Available HTTP: <http://unstats.un.org/unsd/mdg/Resources/Static/Products/Progress2006/MDGReport2006.pdf> (accessed 15 February 2007).

43 V. Jha and R. Vossenaar, *Breaking the Deadlock: A Positive Agenda on Trade, Environment and Development?*, 1999, p. 13. Online. Available HTTP: <http://r0.unctad.org/trade_env/test1/publications/positive.pdf> (accessed 16 February 2007).

44 The World Bank, with P. Collier and D. Dollar (eds), *Globalization, Growth, and Poverty: Building an Inclusive World Economy (A World Bank Policy Research Report*), New York: Co-published by the World Bank and Oxford University Press, 2002, p. 9. See also, K. Watkins, 'Eight Broken Promises: Why the WTO is Not Working For the World's Poor', *Oxfam Briefing Paper 9*, 2001, p. 3. Online. Available HTTP: <http://www.oxfam.org.uk/what_we_do/issues/trade/bp09_8broken.htm> (accessed 16 February 2007).

45 P. Wolfowitz, 'Doha's Last Chance', President of the World Bank Group Special to *The Wall Street Journal*, 1 July 2006. Online. Available HTTP: <http://www.worldbank.org/> (accessed 16 February 2007).

46 Watkins, 'Eight Broken Promises', p. 3.

47 See WTO, 'Understanding the WTO – Agriculture: fairer markets for farmers'. Online. Available HTTP: <http://www.wto.org/english/thewto_e/whatis_e/tif_e/agrm3_e.htm> (accessed 16 February 2007).

48 International Monetary Fund ('IMF'), 'The Truth About Industrial Country Tariffs', *Finance and Development* 39:3, 2002. Online. Available HTTP: <http://www.imf.org/external/pubs/ft/fandd/2002/09/smith.htm> (accessed 16 February 2007). See also Watkins, 'Eight Broken Promises', p. 5.

49 Watkins, 'Eight Broken Promises', p. 6.

50 Ibid. See also, IMF, 'The Truth About Industrial Country Tariffs'.

51 Ibid.

52 See Chapter 3 for details.

53 Special Report, 'Playing Games with Prosperity', *The Economist*, 28 July 2001, p. 26.

54 Subedi, 'The Road from Doha', 430.

55 *Declaration of the Group of 77 and China on the Fourth WTO Ministerial Conference at Doha, Qatar*, WT/L/424 of 24 Oct 2001, [6]. Cited in ibid., 429.
56 Subedi, 'The Road from Doha', 440.
57 A. Soto, 'The Global Environment: A Southern Perspective', *International Journal* 47, 1992, 679.
58 As opposed to the 'needs-based' lifestyle contemplated by the Brundtland definition as, 'development that meets the *needs* of the present without compromising the ability of future generations to meet their own *needs*' (emphasis added): WCED, *Our Common Future*, p. 19.
59 Khosla, *The Road from Rio to Johannesburg*, p. 13.
60 Ibid., p. 12
61 UNCTAD, *Trade and Development Report 1986*, New York: UNCTAD, 1986.
62 G. Kütting, 'Globalisation, Poverty and the Environment in West Africa: Too Poor to Pollute?', *Global Environmental Politics* 3:4, 2003, 49.
63 For more detail on the potential problems see ibid., 49–54.
64 GATT, *GATT Law and the Environment*, GATT Doc. 1529, 13 February 1992.
65 See, e.g., *Rio Declaration.*
66 UNDP, *Human Development Report 1998*, New York: United Nations, 1998, p. 4.
67 Statement by Mr. Rajeev Kher, Joint Secretary, Ministry of Environment and Forests at the Second Preparatory Session of the Commission on Sustainable Development acting as a preparatory meeting for the World Summit on Sustainable Development, 31 January 2002.
68 M. Rauscher, *International Trade, Factor Movements, and the Environment*, Oxford: Clarendon Press, 1997, p. 3.
69 GATT jurisprudence distinguishes a product from its processing methods. For details on the conflict between production and processing methods see generally W.J. Snape III and N.B. Lefkovitz, 'Searching for GATT's Environmental Miranda: Are Process Standards Getting Due Process?', *Cornell International Law Journal* 27, 1994, 777.
70 A unilateral action can be defined as a nation's use of its administrative and enforcement agencies to secure a policy goal set by its domestic political process. See B. Anderson, 'Unilateral Trade Measures and Environmental Protection Policy', *Temple Law Review* 66, 1993, 751.
71 P. Low, 'International Trade and the Environment: An Overview' in P. Low (ed.) *International Trade and the Environment*, World Bank Discussion Paper, No. 159, Washington DC: World Bank, 1992, p. 10 (copy on file with author).
72 GATT, *GATT Law and the Environment*, pp. 2–6.
73 UNCTAD, *Trade and Development Report 1999*, New York: UNCTAD, 1999, p. 10.
74 C. Ruiz, 'Green Protectionism: The North's Latest Trade Weapon', *Third World Network Features*, 5 August 1997. Cited in Rajamani, *Developing Country Resistance to Linking Trade and Environment*, p. 15
75 *Doha WTO Ministerial Declaration*, WTO Doc. WT/MIN(01)/DEC/1 (2001), para. 32.
76 S.S.C. Tay, *International Trade and Environment in Asia: A Survey of the Issues*, Monograph Commissioned for the Asia Conference on Trade and the Environment, Singapore, June 1996, p. 18.
77 Ibid.
78 It was recognized at UNCED that national environmental standards and laws should be allowed to differ and may reflect different stages of economic development.
79 Jha and Vossenaar, *Breaking the Deadlock*, p. 10.
80 *Agreement on Subsidies and Countervailing Measures*, see World Trade Organization, *The Legal Texts: The Results of the Uruguay Round of Multilateral Trade Negotiations* ('*WTO Legal Text*'), New York: Cambridge University Press, 1999, p. 231.
81 *General Agreement on Trade in Services*, see *WTO Legal Text*, p. 284.

82 *Agreement on Trade-related Aspects of Intellectual Property Rights* ('TRIPS'), see *WTO Legal Text*, p. 321.
83 See generally United Nations, *Millennium Development Goals Report 2006.*
84 Khosla, *The Road from Rio to Johannesburg*, p. 10.
85 Jha and Vossenaar, *Breaking the Deadlock*, p. 10.
86 Group of 77, *The Group of 77 at Forty: Championing Multilateralism, A Democratic and Equitable World Order, South–South Cooperation and Development*, Geneva: South Centre, 2004, p. 16.
87 T. Anderson, C. Folke and S. Nystrom, *Trading with the Environment*, London: Earthscan, 1995, p. 113.
88 D. Hunter, J. Salzman and D. Zaelke, *International Environmental Law and Policy*, New York: Foundation Press, 1998, p. 1188.
89 R. Ruggiero, Director General of WTO, in his speech in Bonn on the subject of sustainable development on 9 December 1997. See for details *Bridges* 1:6 (December), 1997, 7.
90 Ibid.
91 T. Panayotou, 'Economic Growth and the Environment', Harvard University Centre for International Development, Working Paper No. 56, July 2000, pp. 76–7.
92 *Convention on International Trade in Endangered Species of Flora and Fauna* ('CITES'), 3 March 1973, 993 UNTS 243, entered into force 1 July 1975.
93 *Montreal Protocol on Substances that deplete the Ozone Layer*, 16 September 1987, 26 ILM 1550 (1987), entered into force 1 January 1989.
94 *Basel Convention on the Control of Transboundary Movements of Hazardous Wastes and their Disposal*, 22 March 1989, 1673 UNTS 126, entered into force 5 May 1992.

2 The United Nations' approach to trade, the environment and sustainable development

I would like to acknowledge the following source for granting permission to reproduce my earlier work 'The United Nations' Approach to Trade, the Environment and Sustainable Development', with substantial revision: *ILSA Journal of International and Comparative Law* 12:3 (summer 2006), Fort Lauderdale FL, and the journal's sponsors, the International Law Students' Association of Chicago.

1 L. Elliot, *The Global Politics of the Environment*, London: Macmillan, 1998, p. 97.
2 M. Imber, 'The Impasse in UN Reform', *Global Environmental Change* 9, 1999, 330.
3 R. Ricupero, 'UNCED and Agenda 21: Chronicle of a Negotiation', *Colorado Journal of International Environmental Law and Policy* 4:1, 1993, 81.
4 *Rio Declaration on Environment and Development ('Rio Declaration')*, 14 June 1992, Principle 7, UN Doc. A/CONF.151/5/Rev.1 (1992).
5 For example, *United Nations Framework Convention on Climate Change*, 9 May 1992, 1771 UNTS 107, entered into force 21 March 1994, Article 3; *Montreal Protocol on Substances that Deplete the Ozone Layer*, 16 September 1987, 26 ILM 1550 (1987), entered into force 1 January 1989, Article 5.
6 For a detailed discussion on the status of this principle see generally A. Trouwborst, *Evolution and Status of the Precautionary Principle in International Law*, Boston MA: Kluwer, 2002. Also see J. Cameron, 'The Precautionary Principle' in G.P. Sampson and B. Chambers (eds), *Trade, Environment and the Millennium*, Tokyo: United Nations University, 1999, p. 239.
7 *Rio Declaration*, Principle 15.
8 *Agreement on the Application of Sanitary and Phytosanitary Measures (SPS Agreement)*, see World Trade Organization, *The Legal Texts: The Results of the Uruguay Round of Multilateral Trade Negotiations ('WTO Legal Text')*, New York: Cambridge University Press, 1999, p. 59. See Chapter 3 for an in-depth discussion of the Agreement.

9 *Rio Declaration*, Principle 3.
10 The World Commission on Environment and Development, *Our Common Future*, Australian edition, Sydney: Oxford University Press, 1990, p. 87.
11 A. Najam, *The Case for a South Secretariat in Environmental Negotiation*, Program on Negotiation Working Paper, Cambridge MA: Program on Negotiation at Harvard Law School, 1994, pp. 94–8. Cited in G.F. Maggio, 'Inter/intra-generational Equity: Current Applications under International Law for Promoting the Sustainable Development of Natural Resources', *Buffalo Environmental Law Journal* 4, 1997, 206.
12 For further discussion see ibid.
13 *Rio Declaration*, Principle 16.
14 Joint Working Party on Trade and Environment, *The Polluter Pays Principle as it Relates to International Trade*, 2001, OECD Doc. COM/ENV/TD (2001) 44/Final, p. 15.
15 See P. Birnie, 'Environmental Protection and Development', *Melbourne University Law Review* 20, 1995, 68.
16 C.S. Pearson, 'The Trade and Environment Nexus: What is new since '72?' in D. Zaelke, P. Orbuch and R.F. Housman (eds), *Trade and the Environment: Law, Economics and Policy*, Washington DC: Island Press, 1993, p. 24.
17 *Stockholm Declaration*, Principle 4.
18 Ibid., Principle 11.
19 Ibid., Principle 9. Pearson, 'The Trade and Environment Nexus', p. 24.
20 *Stockholm Declaration*, Principle 21; Pearson, 'The Trade and Environment Nexus', p. 24.
21 *Stockholm Declaration*, Principle 10.
22 Principle 21 of the *Stockholm Declaration* affirmed an existing international legal obligation which reads as follows:

> [s]tates have, in accordance with the Charter of the United Nations and the Principles of International law, the sovereign right to exploit their own resources and the responsibility to ensure that activities within their jurisdiction or control do not cause damage to the environment of other states or of areas beyond the limits of national jurisdiction.

23 M. Pallamaerts, 'International Environmental Law from Stockholm to Rio: Back to the future?' in P. Sands (ed.), *Greening International Law*, London: Earthscan, 1993, pp. 1–19.
24 T. Simpson and V. Jackson, 'Human Rights and the Environment', *Environment and Planning Law Journal* 14, 1997, 270.
25 V. Nanda, 'Trends in International Environmental Law', *California Western International Law Journal* 20, 1989–90, 190.
26 L.K. Caldwell, *International Environmental Policy: Emergence and Dimensions*, Durham NC: Duke University Press, 1984, p. 54.
27 Ibid., p. 55.
28 W. Lang, 'Environmental Protection: The Challenge for International Law', *Journal of World Trade Law* 20:5, 1986, 490.
29 Caldwell, *International Environmental Policy*, p. 58. Paragraph (b) of Stockholm Recommendation 103 stated the essence of the compensation issue: 'where environmental concerns lead to restrictions on trade, or to stricter environmental standards with negative effects on exports, particularly from developing countries, appropriate measures for compensation should be worked out within the framework of existing contractual and institutional arrangements.'
30 R.E. Levy, 'International Law and the Chernobyl Accident: Reflections on an Important but Imperfect System', *University of Kansas Law Review* 36, 1987–8, 99.
31 R.L. Panjabi, 'From Stockholm to Rio: A Comparison of the Declaratory Principle

of International Environmental Law', *Denver Journal of International Law and Policy* 21, 1993, 233.

32 P. Sands, *Principles of International Environmental Law* I, New York: Manchester University Press, 1995, p. 72.

33 D. Hunter, J. Salzman and D. Zaelke, *International Environmental Law and Policy*, New York: Foundation Press, 1998, p. 396.

34 Governing Council of the UNEP, *North American regional civil society statement to the sixth Global Civil Society Forum and the twenty-third session of the Governing Council/Global Ministerial Environment Forum* (2004) UNEP Doc. UNEP/GC/INF16/Add.5, p. 4.

35 Ibid., p. 392.

36 Ibid.

37 See *The Environment Fund and Administration and other Budgetary Matters*, UNEP Doc. UNEP/GC 19/INF 10 (22 November 1996).

38 Ibid.

39 See Anon, 'UNEP: 17th Governing Council', *Environmental Policy and Law* 23:3–4, 1993, 119, cited in Elliot, *The Global Politics of the Environment*, p. 110.

40 P.S. Thacher, 'Multilateral Cooperation and Global Change', *Journal of International Affairs* 44:2, 1991, 429; cited in Elliot, *The Global Politics of the Environment*, p. 110.

41 UNEP, 'Financing of the UNEP'. Online. Available HTTP: <http://www.unep.org/rmu/en/Financing_of_UNEP/index.asp> (accessed 12 March 2007).

42 Ibid.

43 UNEP, 'Financing the UNEP – Regular Budget'. Online. Available HTTP: <http://www.unep.org/rmu/en/Financing_of_UNEP/Regular_Budget/index.asp> (accessed 9 March 2007).

44 See Caldwell, *International Environmental Policy*, p. 62.

45 See Elliot, *The Global Politics of the Environment*, p. 13.

46 See Caldwell, *International Environmental Policy*, p. 71.

47 C.Y. Ling and M. Khor, 'International Environmental Governance: Some Issues from a Developing Country Perspective', *Third World Network Working Paper*, September 2001. Online. Available HTTP: <http://www.twnside.org.sg/title/ieg.htm> (accessed 26 March 2007).

48 UN GA Resolution 44/228, 22 December 1989, UN Doc. A/Res/44/228.

49 M. Halle, 'Trade and Environment: Looking Beneath the Sands of Doha?', *Journal for European Environmental and Planning Law* 2006:2, 2006, 107–8.

50 For example, *United Nations Convention on Biological Diversity*, Rio de Janeiro, 5 June 1992. Reprinted in 31 ILM 818 (1992); and *United Nations Framework Convention on Climate Change*, New York, 1992. Reprinted in 31 ILM 849 (1992).

51 *Rio Declaration*, Principle 6.

52 Ibid., Principle 7.

53 Ibid., Principle 9.

54 Ibid., Principle 12.

55 For further discussion of this issue refer to Chapter 3.

55a B. Boer, 'The Globalisation of Environmental Law', *Melbourne Law Review*, 20, 1995, p. 105.

56 A. Khosla, *The Road from Rio to Johannesburg*, Millennium Papers, Issue 5, UNED Forum, 30 April 2001, p. 6. Online. Available HTTP: <http://www.stakeholderforum.org/publications/millennium/millpaper5.pdf> (accessed 26 March 2007).

57 *Agenda 21: Programme of Action for Sustainable Development*, UN GAOR, 46th Session, Agenda Item 21, UN Doc. A/Conf.151/26 (1992).

58 Ibid., Chapter 2, para. 2.2.

59 Ibid., para. 2.5.

60 Ibid., para. 2.7.
61 Ibid.
62 Ibid.
63 Ibid., para. 2.8.
64 Ibid., para. 2.9.
65 Ibid., para. 2.10.
66 Ibid., para. 2.22.
67 Ibid.
68 Ibid., para. 2.23.
69 Ibid., para. 2.36 C.
70 Ibid., para. 2.39.
71 J.D. Werksman, 'Greening Bretton Woods' in J. Kirkby, P. O'Keefe and L. Timberlake (eds), *The Earthscan Reader in Sustainable Development*, London: Earthscan, 1995, p. 301.
72 See Khosla, *The Road from Rio to Johannesburg*, p. 11.
73 Throughout the colonial period, outright exploitation by the developed countries severely limited the capacity of developing countries to accumulate capital. Even after decolonization in the 1950s, 1960s and 1970s, the economic growth of the developing countries was slow and growth rates declined sharply. Under this pattern, costs of imports of developing countries rise faster than income from their exports. They are limited to exporting primary products to developed countries' market in return for finished products.
74 Food and Agriculture Organization of the United Nations ('FAO'), *The State of Agricultural Commodity Markets 2004*, Rome: FAO, 2004, p. 23.
75 Ibid.
76 UNDP, 'Policy Statement on Trade Issues', Fifth World Trade Organization Ministerial Meeting held in Cancun, Mexico, 10–14 September 2003, 2 (copy on file with author).
77 See, generally, United Nations, *World Economics Situation and Prospects 2007*, New York: United Nations, 2007. In particular see p. 36 and figure II.2.
78 Ibid., p. iii.
79 Ibid.
80 UNDP, *Human Development Report 2005*, New York: UNDP, 2005, pp. 139–42.
81 G. Kütting, 'Globalisation, Poverty and the Environment in West Africa: Too Poor to Pollute?', *Global Environmental Politics* 3:4, 2003, 47.
82 Ibid.
83 See Ling and Khor, 'International Environmental Governance'.
84 See Khosla, *The Road from Rio to Johannesburg*, p. 7.
85 P. Doran, 'The UN Commission on Sustainable Development', *Environmental Politics* 5:1, 1996, 103.
86 See Chapter 3 for details.
87 United Nations, *Millennium Development Goals Report 2006*, New York: United Nations, 2006, p. 23.
88 Ibid.
89 Jubilee Debt Campaign, 'How big is the debt of poor countries?' Online. Available HTTP: <http://www.jubileedebtcampaign.org.uk/?lid=2647> (accessed 10 March 2007). For detailed information on individual countries' external debt see IMF, *World Economic Outlook Databases*. Online. Available HTTP: <http://www.imf.org/external/ns/cs.aspx?id=28> (accessed 12 March 2007).
90 Ibid.
91 United Nations General Assembly, 'Sustainable development: implementation of Agenda 21, the Programme for the Further Implementation of Agenda 21 and the

outcomes of the World Summit on Sustainable Development', UN Doc. A/61/422/Add.1, 13 December 2006.

92 UNCTAD, *Trade and Development Report 1999*, New York: UNCTAD, 1999, p. 10.

93 Details of these disputes will be discussed in Chapter 3.

94 International Institute for Sustainable Development, *Rio+5 Special Focus Report on Trade and Sustainable Development*, 13–19 March 1997. Online. Available HTTP: <http://iisd1.iisd.ca/trade/tradedoc.htm> (accessed 27 April 2006).

95 Ibid.

96 Ibid.

97 See Elliot, *The Global Politics of the Environment*, p. 256.

98 Ibid.

99 Ibid.

100 See, UN Factsheet, 'The Millennium Assembly and the Millennium Summit', March 2000. Online. Available HTTP: <http://www.un.org/millennium/sg/report/fact.htm> (accessed 12 March 2007).

101 UN Press Release, 'World Leaders Adopt "United Nations Millennium Declaration" at Conclusion of Extraordinary Three-day Summit', UN General Assembly Plenary, 8 September 2000, Press Release GA/9758.

102 *United Nations Millennium Declaration*, UN General Assembly Resolution 55/2, UN GAOR, 55th Session, 8th plenary meeting, Agenda item 60 (b), UN Doc. A/Res/55/2 (2000). Online. Available HTTP: <http://www.un.org/millennium/declaration/ares552e.pdf> (accessed 15 February 2007).

103 Ibid.

104 UN Millennium Development Goals, derived directly from the *United Nations Millennium Declaration*. Online. Available HTTP: <http://www.un.org/millenniumgoals/#> (accessed 15 February 2007).

105 Ibid., 'Goal Eight – Develop a Global Partnership for Development'.

106 K. Dervis, 'Bridging the Gap: How the Millennium Development Goals are Uniting the World in the Fight against Global Poverty', *Sustainable Development Law and Policy* 6, 2005, 2.

107 Ibid.

108 UNDP, *Human Development Report 2005*, p. 19.

109 For these and other figures, see ibid., pp. 18–20.

110 To see the current status of progress and its current shortfalls see, generally, ibid. See also the *Millennium Developments Goals Report 2006*.

111 See, e.g., S. Siphana, 'Trade and Poverty Eradication through Millennium Development Goals (MDG)', Keynote Speech – Secretary of State for Commerce, Cambodia, at AITCH/ACP Secretariat Symposium on the Trade Dimension of International Development Initiatives, São Paulo, Brazil, 13 June 2004, p. 1.

112 UNDP, *Human Development Report 2005*, p. 9.

113 Siphana, 'Trade and Poverty Eradication through Millennium Development Goals', p. 2.

114 C. George and C. Kirkpatrick, 'Trade and Development: Assessing the Impact of Trade Liberalisation on Sustainable Development', *Journal of World Trade* 38:3, 2004, 468.

115 UNDP, *Human Development Report 2005*, p. 9.

116 George and Kirkpatrick, 'Trade and Development', 468.

117 P. Wapner, 'World Summit on Sustainable Development: Toward a Post-Jo'burg Environmentalism', *Global Environmental Politics* 3:1, 2003, 2.

118 UN, 'The Johannesburg Summit Test: What Will Change?', Johannesburg Summit 2002. Online. Available HTTP: <http://www.un.org/jsummit/index.html> (accessed 13 March 2007).

119 *Johannesburg Declaration on Sustainable Development*, adopted at the 17th plenary meeting of the World Summit on Sustainable Development, 4 September 2002, UN Doc. A/Conf.199/L.6/Rev.2 (2002).
120 *Plan of Implementation of the World Summit on Sustainable Development/Johannesburg Plan of Implementation* ('JPOI'), Report of the World Summit on Sustainable Development, 17th plenary meeting, resolution 2, para. 58, UN Doc. A/CONF. 199/20 (4 September 2002).
121 J. Strachan and M. Roberts, 'Poverty, Environment and Sustainable Development: How the Commonwealth Supports Implementation of the World Summit on Sustainable Development', *Round Table* 92:371, 2003, 542.
122 *Johannesburg Declaration on Sustainable Development*, para. 11.
123 Ibid., para. 14.
124 JPOI, para. 1 (citations omitted).
125 Ibid., para. 47.
126 Ibid., para. 96.
127 Ibid., para. 49.
128 H. French, 'Assessing the summit', *People and Planet*, 22 October 2002 cited in L.A. Swatuk, 'From Rio to Johannesburg and Beyond: Ways Forward for the Post-WSSD Commonwealth', *Round Table* 92:371, 2003, 465.
129 Strachan and Robert, 'Poverty, Environment and Sustainable Development', 543.
130 Swatuk, 'From Rio to Johannesburg and Beyond', 466.
131 Ibid., 467.
132 Ibid., 468.
133 Ibid., 474.
134 See, e.g., G. Eweje, 'Strategic Partnerships between MNEs and Civil Society: The Post-WSSD Perspectives', *Sustainable Development* 15, 2007, 15.
135 Ibid., 23.
136 Ibid., 24.
137 See *Agenda 21*, para. 38.11.
138

> To ensure the effective follow up of the [Rio] Conference as well as to enhance international co-operation and rationalize the inter-governmental decision-making capacity for the integration of environment and development issues and to examine the progress of the implementation of *Agenda 21* at the national, regional and international levels, a high-level Commission on Sustainable Development should be established.
>
> *Agenda 21*, para. 38.11

139 Doran, 'The UN Commission on Sustainable Development', 101.
140 UN General Assembly, 'Institutional arrangements to follow up the United Nations Conference on Environment and Development', Resolution Adopted by the General Assembly [on the report of the second Committee (A/47/719)], 29 January 1993, UN Doc. A/Res/47191.
141 Hunter, *et al.*, *International Environmental Law and Policy*, p. 399.
142 JPOI, para. 145.
143 Ibid., para. 147(e).
144 CSD, *CSD-11: Multi-year Programme of Work for CSD: 2004/2005 to 2016/2017*, 2005. Online. Available HTTP: <http://www.un.org/esa/sustdev/csd/csd11/CSD_mulit year_prog_work.htm> (accessed 12 March 2007).
145 Ibid.
146 Ibid.
147 Hunter *et al.*, *International Environmental Law and Policy*, p. 402.
148 N. Desai, the Under-Secretary General of the United Nations, comment in the Third Session of CSD cited in Doran, 'The UN Commission on Sustainable Development', 103.

149 See B.W. Boer, 'The Globalisation of Environmental Law: the Role of the United Nations', *Melbourne University Law Review* 20:1, 1995, 103.

150 See Elliot, *The Global Politics of the Environment*, p. 169.

151 I. Ghandi, address to the UN Conference on Human Environment, Stockholm, Sweden, 14 June 1972.

152 C. Raghavan, 'Third World Takes Unified Position on Environment for Earth Summit' *Third World Network Features*, 1991 (copy on file with author).

153 Ibid.

154 The World Commission on Environment and Development, *Our Common Future*, London: Oxford University Press, 1987, pp. 364–6.

155 R.J. Prudencio, 'Why UNCED Failed on Trade and Environment', *Journal of Environment and Development* 2:2, 1993, 104.

156 L. Campiglio, *The Environment after Rio: International Law and Economics*, London: Martinus Nijhoff, 1994, p. 36.

157 During the UNCED PrepCom IV, the US proposed to remove the Chapter in *Agenda 21* which states that the elimination or avoidance of unsustainable patterns of production and consumption are a necessary component of sustainable development.

158 *Beijing Declaration*, cited in Raghavan, 'Third World Takes Unified Position on Environment for Earth Summit'.

159 Elliott, *The Global Politics of the Environment*, p. 174.

160 See Campiglio, *The Environment after Rio*, p. 36.

161 Khosla, *The Road from Rio to Johannesburg*, p. 20.

162 M.F. Strong, 'From Stockholm to Rio: A Journey Down a Generation', *Earth Summit 9 –* A *Reference Booklet about UNCED*, 1991, p. 21.

163 C. Raghavan, 'The United Nations at the Cross-roads', Third World Network feature. Online. Available HTTP: <http://www.twnside.org.sg/title/un-ch.htm> (accessed 13 March 2007).

164 See C.Y. Ling and M. Khor, 'International Environmental Governance: Some Issues from a Developing Country Perspective', Third World Network working paper, September 2001. Online. Available HTTP: http://www.twnside.org.sg/title/ieg.htm (accessed 26 March 2007).

165 J. Cameron, 'GATT and the Environment' in P. Sands (ed.), *Greening International Law*, London: Earthscan, 1993, pp. 100–21.

166 Khosla, *The Road from Rio to Johannesburg*, p. 20.

3 GATT/WTO approaches to trade, the environment and sustainable development

I would like to acknowledge the following sources for granting copyright permission to reproduce my earlier works with substantial revisions 'Trade, the Environment, and the World Trade Organization: A Developing Country Perspective on WTO Agreements Concerning Standards, Regulations and Non-tariff Barriers to Trade', published in *New Zealand Yearbook of International Law* 3 (2006), 17–42 and ''Trade–Environment Nexus in GATT Jurisprudence: Pressing Issues for Developing Countries' published in (2005) 17:2 *Bond Law Review* 17:2 (2005), 1–26.

1 M. Halle, 'Trade and Environment: Looking beneath the Sands of Doha?', *Journal for European Environmental and Planning Law* 2006:2, 2006, 114.

2 GATT 1947, 55 UNTS 194, entered into force 1 January 1948.

3 D. Hunter, J. Salzman, and D. Zaelke, *International Environmental Law and Policy*, New York: Foundation Press, 1998, p. 1180.

4 GATT, *Report by Ambassador H. Ukawa (Japan), Chairman of the Group Environmental Measures and International Trade, to the 49th Session of the Contracting Parties*, GATT Doc. L/7402, Geneva: GATT, 1994.

5 *Marrakesh Agreement Establishing the World Trade Organization*, 15 April 1994, 1867 UNTS 154 ('WTO Agreement').
6 Hunter *et al.*, *International Environmental Law and Policy*, p. 1181.
7 *Agreement on Technical Barriers to Trade* ('TBT'), see World Trade Organization, *The Legal Texts: The Results of the Uruguay Round of Multilateral Trade Negotiations* ('*WTO Legal Text*'), New York: Cambridge University Press, 1999, p. 121.
8 *Agreement on the Application of Sanitary and Phytosanitary Measures* ('SPS'), see *WTO Legal Text*, p. 59.
9 *Agreement on Trade-related Aspects of Intellectual Property Rights* ('TRIPS'), see *WTO Legal Text*, p. 321.
10 The preamble to the WTO Agreement clearly states the objective of sustainable development as well as the need to preserve and protect natural environment. See M.A. Cole, *Trade Liberalisation, Economic Growth and the Environment*, Cheltenham: Edward Elgar, 2000, p. 19.
11 M.R. Islam, *International Trade Law*, Pyrmont NSW: Lawbook Company, 1999, p. 440.
12 P. Krugman and M. Obstfeld, *International Economics: Theory and Policy*, 5th edn, Boston MA: Addison-Wesley, 2000, p. 12.
13 P. Samuelson, 'Where Ricardo and Mill Rebut and Confirm Arguments of Mainstream Economists Supporting Globalisation', *Journal of Economic Perspectives* 18:3, 2004, 137.
14 Ibid., 137–9.
15 Hunter *et al.*, *International Environmental Law and Policy*, p. 1182.
16 GATT Article III.
17 GATT Article XI, para. I.
18 OECD, *Analysis of Non-tariff Measures: The Case of Export Restrictions*, 4 April 2003, OECD Doc. TD/TC/WP (2003)7/FINAL. Online. Available HTTP: <http://www.oecd.org/trade> (accessed 26 March 2007).
19 GATT Doc. L/6268, GATT B.I.S.D. 35S/98, adopted 22 March 1988.
20 GATT Doc. MTN/SB/3.
21 J. McDonald, 'Greening the GATT: Harmonizing Free Trade and Environmental Protection in the New World Order', *Environmental Law* 23, 1993, 397.
22 *Agreement on Implementation of Article VI of the General Agreement on Tariffs and Trade 1994*, Article 2.6. See *WTO Legal Text*, p. 150.
23 See, e.g., *Panel Report on United States – Restrictions on Imports of Tuna* ('*Tuna–Dolphin I*'), Final Version Transmitted to the Parties 16 August 1991. The report was submitted to GATT member countries on 3 September 1991 and was made public on 16 September 1991. GATT Doc. DS21/R Sept. 3, 1991.
24 Ibid.
25 McDonald, 'Greening the GATT', 14.
26 Hunter *et al.*, *International Environmental Law and Policy*, p. 1184.
27 Ibid.
28 Halle, 'Trade and Environment', 108.
29 *Tuna–Dolphin I*, GATT Panel Report GATT Doc. DS 21/R: GATT, 30 ILM 1594 (1991).
30 Ibid., para. 6.2.
31 GATT Council, *United States – Restrictions on Imports of Tuna, Report of the Panel*, DS21/R-39S/155, 1991, para. 5.15.
32 *Thailand – Restriction on Importation of and Internal Taxes on Cigarettes*, GATT BISD 38 Supp. 200, 201 (1990).
33 *Panel Report on Prohibition of Imports of Tuna Fish and Tuna Products from Canada*, GATT BISD 29 Supp. 91 (1983).
34 *EC Commission v. Kingdom of Denmark* [1989] 2 CEC 167.

35 *United States – Standards for Reformulated and Conventional Gasoline*, 35 ILM 274 (1996) 280.
36 McDonald, 'Greening the GATT', 27.
37 *Tuna–Dolphin I*, GATT Council, para. 5.15.
38 For details see D.J. Black, 'International Trade v. Environmental Protection: The Case of the US Embargo on Mexican Tuna', *Law and Policy in International Business* 24:1, 1992, 136.
39 *Tuna–Dolphin I*, GATT Council, para. 5.28.
40 *United States – Section 337 of the Tariff Act of 1930* (*'US Section 337 case'*), 7 November 1989, GATT BISD 36 Supp. 345, 1990, para. 5.26.
41 Ibid.
42 *Thailand – Restrictions on Importation of and Internal Taxes on Cigarettes*, Report of the Panel, GATT BISD 37 Supp. 200, 201 (1990).
43 Ibid.
44 GATT, *GATT Activities 1989*, 1990, p. 100, cited in McDonald, 'Greening the GATT', 41.
45 McDonald, 'Greening the GATT', 42.
46 *Commission v. Denmark*, Case 302/86 [1988] ECR 4607.
47 McDonald, 'Greening the GATT', 41.
48 S. Charnovitz, 'Exploring the Environmental Exceptions in GATT Article XX', *Journal of World Trade* 25:5, 1991, 49.
49 Hunter *et al.*, *International Environmental Law and Policy*, p. 1192.
50 *United States – Restrictions on Import of Tuna ('Tuna–Dolphin II')*, 1994, GATT Doc. DS29/R, Geneva: GATT, 1994.
51 *United States – Taxes on Petroleum and Certain Imported Substances*, GATT BISD 34.5/136; GATT Doc. L/6175 (17 June 1987).
52 *Canada – Measures Affecting Exports of Unprocessed Herring and Salmon*, GATT BISD, 35 Supp. 98 (1984).
53 McDonald, 'Greening the GATT', 46.
54 Ibid., 55.
55 S. Charnovitz, 'Trade Negotiations and the Environment', *International Environment Reporter*, 11 March 1992, pp. 144–5.
56 *United States – Prohibition of Shrimps and Certain Shrimp Products*, WTO Doc. WT/DS58/AB/R (98–000) (12 October 1998).
57 *Panel Report on Prohibition of Imports of Tuna Fish and Tuna Products from Canada*, GATT BISD 29 Supp. 91 (1983).
58 E.U. Petersmann, *International and European Trade and Environmental Law after the Uruguay Round*, Boston MA: Kluwer, 1995, p. 30.
59 GATT Secretariat, *International Trade in 1990–91* I, 1992, p. 19.
60 *Tuna–Dolphin I*, GATT Panel Report GATT Doc. DS 21/R.
61 *Tuna–Dolphin II*, paras 5–29.
62 McDonald, 'Greening the GATT', 56.
63 *Agreement on Technical Barriers to Trade*, see *WTO Legal Text*, p. 121; *Agreement on the Application of Sanitary and Phyto-sanitary Measures*, see *WTO Legal Text*, p. 59.
64 *WTO Agreement on Textiles and Clothing*, see *WTO Legal Text*, p. 73; *Agreement on Agriculture*, see *WTO Legal Text*, p. 33, *Agreement on Subsidies and Countervailing Measures*, see *WTO Legal Text*, p. 231; *General Agreement on Trade in Services*, see *WTO Legal Text*, p. 284; *Agreement on Trade-related Investment Measures*, see *WTO Legal Text* p. 143; *Agreement on Trade-related Aspects of Intellectual Property Rights (TRIPS)*, see *WTO Legal Text*, p. 321.
65 V. Jha, 'Overview of the SPS and TBT Agreements and its Possible Implications for India', Discussion Papers for the Havana Workshop on Trade and the Environment,

30 May–2 June 2000. Online. Available HTTP: <http://r0.unctad.org/trade_env/discpapers2.htm> (accessed 6 January 2006).

66 *TBT Agreement*, Preamble.

67 Ibid., Annex 1.

68 *European Communities – Measures Affecting Asbestos and Asbestos-containing Products*, 2001, WTO Doc. WT/DS135/AB/R (2001) (Report of the Appellate Body), para. 67.

69 S. Gaines, 'Products and Production Methods: How to Produce Sound Policy for Environmental PPM-based Trade Measures', *Columbia Journal of Environmental Law* 27, 2002, 397.

70 Ibid., 399.

71 A.A. Ostrovsky, 'The European Commission's Regulations for Genetically Modified Organisms and the Current WTO Dispute: Human Health or Environmental Measures? Why the Deliberate Release Directive is More Appropriately Adjudicated in the WTO Under the TBT Agreement', *Colorado Journal of International Environmental Law and Policy* 15, 2004, 209; N.L.W. Wilson, 'Clarifying the Alphabet Soup of the TBT and the SPS in the WTO', *Drake Journal of Agricultural Law* 8, 2003, 703; A. Okubo, 'Environmental Labelling Programs and the GATT/WTO Regime', *Georgetown International Environmental Law Review* 11, 1999, 599; Hunter *et al.*, *International Environmental Law and Policy*, p. 1208.

72 B. Schwartz, 'WTO and GMOs: Analyzing the European Community's Recent Regulations Covering the Labelling of Genetically Modified Organisms', *Michigan Journal of International Law* 25, 2004, 801.

73 Ibid.

74 WTO Committee on Technical Barriers to Trade, *Decisions and Recommendations adopted by the Committee since 1 January 1995*, WTO Doc. G/TBT/1/Rev.8, 23 May 2002, Section IX – 'Decision of the Committee on Principles for the Development of International Standards, Guides and Recommendations with relation to Articles 2, 5 and Annex 3 of the Agreement'.

75 Ibid.

76 A. Thomas, C. Folke and S. Nystrom (eds), *Trading with the Environment: Ecology, Economics, Institutions and Policy*, London: Earthscan, 1995, p. 92.

77 *SPS Agreement*, Article 1.1.

78 Ibid., Article 2.3.

79 Ibid., Article 5.6.

80 The term 'precautionary restriction' is not referred to in the Agreement. However, in *EC-Hormones*, the Appellate Body held that the article reflects the meaning of the precautionary principle; S. Charnovitz, 'The Supervision of Health and Biosafety Regulation by World Trade Rules', *Tulane Environmental Law Journal* 13, 2000, 271.

81 *Rio Declaration on Environment and Development* (14 June 1992), UN Doc. A/CONF.151/5/Rev.1 (1992).

82 H. Ward, 'WTO Rules and the Application of the Precautionary Principle', *Bridges* (International Centre for Trade and Sustainable Development monthly publication), January–February 2000, p. 15.

83 Jha, 'Overview of the SPS and TBT Agreements and their Possible Implications for India'.

84 World Trade Organization, 'Understanding the WTO – Least Developed Countries'. Online. Available HTTP: <http://www.wto.org/english/thewto_e/whatis_e/tif_e/org7_e.htm> (accessed 31 October 2005).

85 S. Henson, R. Loader, A. Swinbank and M. Bredahl, 'The Impact of Sanitary and Phytosanitary Measures on Developing Country Exports of Agricultural and Food Products (draft for discussion)', paper presented at the conference on *Agriculture*

and the New Trade Agenda in the WTO 2000 Negotiations, 1–2 October 1999, Geneva (Section 6: 'Problems with the SPS Agreement encountered by Developing Countries'). Online. Available HTTP: <http://www.cid.harvard.edu/cidtrade/issues/spstbtpaper.html> (accessed 31 October 2005).

86 Ibid., section 6.1: 'Participation in the SPS Agreement'.

87 The national notification agency is responsible for all procedures associated with the notification of new and/or amended SPS measures.

88 Henson *et al.*, 'The Impact of Sanitary and Phytosanitary Measures', section 6.1; 'Participation in the SPS Agreement'.

89 While many developing countries do not have permanent missions in Geneva, those that do typically only have one person who is responsible for all WTO matters. It is unsurprising, given the importance of matters within the WTO itself, that attendance at SPS committee meetings is so poor. See ibid.

90 Ibid.

91 A. Afilalo and S. Foster 'The World Trade Organization's Anti-discrimination Jurisprudence: Free Trade, National Sovereignty, and Environmental Health in the Balance', *Georgetown International Environmental Law Review* 15, 2003, 633.

92 As required under the SPS Agreement, Article 4.1; A.M. Donahue, 'Comment: Equivalence: Not Quite Close Enough For the International Harmonisation of Environmental Standards', *Environmental Law* 30, 2000, 363.

93 Under Article 4 of the SPS Agreement, importing countries are permitted to inspect the sanitary and phytosanitary measures of the exporting country in order to ensure that they reach the necessary standards; Gaines, 'Processes and Production Methods', 383.

94 R. Ferris Jr and Z. Hongjun, 'The Challenges of Reforming an Environmental Legal Culture: Assessing the *Status Quo* and Looking at Post-WTO Admission Challenges for the People's Republic of China', *Georgetown International Environmental Law Review* 14, 2002, 429; Henson *et al.*, 'The Impact of Sanitary and Phytosanitary Measures', section 4: 'Problems experienced by developing countries due to SPS measures'.

95 Henson *et al.*, 'The Impact of Sanitary and Phytosanitary Measures', section 4.

96 Cato and Lima dos Santas, 'European Union 1997 Seafood Safety Ban: The Economic Impact on Bangladesh Shrimp Processing', *Marine Resource Economics*, 13, 1998, pp. 215–25, in ibid.

97 Ibid.

98 Henson *et al.*, 'The Impact of Sanitary and Phytosanitary Measures', section 2: 'SPS measures as barriers to trade'.

99 *SPS Agreement*, Article 4.2; Donahue, 'Equivalence: Not Quite Close Enough for the International Harmonisation of Environmental Standards', 363.

100 *SPS Agreement*, Article 9.1.

101 Ibid., Article 9.2.

102 Henson *et al.*, 'The Impact of Sanitary and Phytosanitary Measures', section 6.2: 'Concerns about the operation of the SPS Agreement'; Wilson, 'Clarifying the Alphabet Soup of the TBT and the SPS in the WTO', p. 703.

103 Henson *et al.*, 'The Impact of Sanitary and Phytosanitary Measures', section 6.2.

104 Ibid.

105 Ibid., section 6.1: 'Participation in the SPS Agreement'.

106 Ibid., section 3: 'Survey of SPS-related problems associated with developing country exports'.

107 Center for International Development, 'Sanitary and Phytosanitary Measures and Technical Barriers to Trade Summary', Harvard University. Online. Available HTTP: <http://www.cid.harvard.edu/cidtrade/issues/spstbt.html> (accessed 31 October 2005).

108 V. Rege, 'GATT Law and Environment-related Issues Affecting the Trade of Developing Countries', *Journal of World Trade* 28:3, 1994, 95–169.

109 Center for International Development, 'Sanitary and Phytosanitary Measures and Technical Barriers to Trade Summary'.

110 Ibid.

111 Rege, 'GATT Law and Environment-related Issues', 95–169.

112 *Agenda 21*, UN Conference on Environment and Development, UN Doc. A/CONF.151/26/Rev.1 (1992). See also ibid.

113 The United Nations Environment Programme and International Institute for Sustainable Development, *Environment and Trade: A Handbook*, Toronto: IISD, 2000, p. 51.

114 M. Buch-Hansen, 'The WTO Agreement on Agriculture and its impact on developing countries', November 2001, p. 3. Online. Available HTTP: <http://www.ruc.dk/inst3/IDS/Public/workpapers/no29.pdf/> (accessed 6 January 2006).

115 UNEP and IISD, *Environment and Trade: A Handbook*, p. 56.

116 Ibid.

117 Ibid.

118 The World Conservation Union, 'Balancing Imbalances in the WTO: Agreement on Agriculture', p. 1, Online. Available HTTP: <http://www.iucn.org/en/news/archive/2001_2005/press/mtgwtovilm.pdf> (accessed 3 April 2006).

119 Ibid.

120 United Nations Development Programme, *Human Development Report 2003*, New York: Oxford University Press, 2003.

121 World Conservation Union, 'Balancing Imbalances in the WTO', p. 2.

122 UNEP and IISD, *Environment and Trade: A Handbook*. For example, the 2002 US *Farm Bill* and the Doha Round induced qualitative and quantitative shifts in domestic support policies. The impact of these two documents on world agricultural production and trade included the provision of incentives for increased agricultural output through an intensification of production. The result was a significant increase in agricultural production beyond the levels that would normally characterize free markets. The flow-on effect of this was support for export credit and food aid programmes, the depression of commodity prices and the distortion of agricultural trade flows. See K. Maryand, S. Dionne, M. Paquin and I. Pageot-LeBel, 'The Economic and Environmental Impacts of Agricultural Subsidies: An Assessment of the 2002 US Farm Bill and Doha Round', paper prepared for the *Second North American Symposium on Assessing the Environmental Effects on Trade*, Mexico, 26 March 2003, 1. Online. Available HTTP: <http://www.cec.org/files/pdf/ECONOMY/-Session-4-3-Mayrand-Dionne_en.pdf> (accessed 6 April 2006).

123 OECD, *The Environmental Effects of Trade*, Paris: OECD, 1994; L. Karp, 'Internalisation of Environmental Damages in Agriculture', 25 April 1995, UN Doc. UNCTAD/CON/35.

124 WTO, *Report of the Committee on Trade and Environment to Ministers in Singapore*, WTO. Doc. WT/CTE/1, 12 November 1996.

125 UNEP and IISD, *Environment and Trade: A Handbook*, p. 52.

126 G8, 'Trade Statement', 2005. Online. Available HTTP: <http://www.fco.gov.uk/Files/kfile/PostG8_Gleneagles_Trade.pdf > (accessed 16 April 2007).

127 World Conservation Union, 'Balancing Imbalances in the WTO', p. 2.

128 WTO, *Ministerial Declaration*, Doha Work Programme, 22 December 2005, WTO Doc. WT/MIN(05)/DEC, para. 6 (emphasis added). For more detail on the Hong Kong Ministerial Conference, see Chapter 4.

129 Ibid.

130 S.R. Khan, 'Environmental Impacts and Mitigation Costs of Cloth and Leather

Exports from Pakistan'. Online. Available HTTP: <http://www.ictsd.org/dlogue/2001–03–29/RafiKhan.doc> (accessed 31 October 2005).

131 S. Siphana, 'Trade and Poverty Eradication through Millennium Development Goals ('MDGs')', keynote speech at AITIC/ACP Secretariat Symposium on the *Trade Dimension of International Development Initiatives*, São Paulo, Brazil, 13 June 2004.

132 A. Hyvarinen, 'Introduction of the Agreement on Textiles and Clothing and its Implications on Developing Country Producers/Exporters: Eco-labelling and environmentally friendly products and production methods affecting the international trade in textiles and clothing', p. 7. Online. Available HTTP: <http://www. intracen.org/worldtradenet/docs/information/referencemat/ecolabatc.pdf> (accessed 31 October 2005).

133 M. Knappe, 'Textiles and Clothing: What Happens after 2005?' Reprinted from *International Trade Forum*, 2003, No. 2, 16–20. Online. Available HTTP: <http://www.cacci.org.tw/membership/Textiles%20and%20Clothing.PDF> (accessed 6 April 2006).

134 SGIA, 'The End of Textile Quotas: Impact on the World Textile Industry', 2005. Online. Available HTTP: <http://www.sgia.org/feature_articles/pdfs/fa_0205_quotas.pdf> (accessed 31 October 2005).

135 Hyvarinen, 'Introduction of the Agreement on Textiles and Clothing', p. 6.

136 Knappe, 'Textiles and Clothing', p. 5.

137 United Nations Conference on Trade and Development, *A Positive Agenda for Developing Countries: Issues for Future Trade Negotiations*, New York: United Nations, 2000, p. 217.

138 Hyvarinen, 'Introduction of the Agreement on Textiles and Clothing', p. 2.

139 Ibid., p. 3.

140 Ibid., p. 4.

141 Ibid., p. 6.

142 G.P. Sampson, *The WTO and Sustainable Development*, Tokyo: United Nations University Press, 2005, p. 167.

143 M.R. Islam, *International Trade Law of the WTO*, Melbourne: Oxford University Press, 2006, p. 369.

144 Ibid., p. 370.

145 M.R. Islam, 'Pressing Issues of Global Free Trade in Services' in J. Chen and G. Walker (eds), *Balancing Act: Law, Policy and Politics in Globalisation and Global Trade*, Sydney: Federation Press, 2004, p. 260.

146 J.A. Kim, 'Opportunities and Challenges in Liberalizing the Environmental Goods and Services Market: The Case of Developing Countries in Asia', *Journal of World Trade* 40:3, 2006, 528.

147 M. Halle, 'Trade and Environment', 112.

148 Friends of the Earth, *A Disservice to the Earth: The Environmental Impact of the General Agreement on Trade in Services*, Friends of the Earth Feature. Online. Available HTTP: <http://www.citizenstrade.org/pdf/services_foe_2pg.pdf> (accessed 16 February 2007).

149 J. Butkeviciene, 'GATS Negotiations and Issues for Consideration in the Area of Environmental Services from a Development Perspective', paper prepared for the UNEP–UNCTAD Workshop on *Post Doha Negotiating Issues on Trade and Environment in Paragraph 31*. Singapore, 16 May 2002. Online. Available HTTP: <http://www.unep-unctad.org/cbtf/cbtf2/meetings/singapore/environmentalservices.doc> (accessed 16 February 2007).

150 E. Su, 'The Winners and the Losers: The Agreement on Trade Related Aspects of Intellectual Property Rights and its Effects on Developing Countries', *Houston Journal of International Law* 23, 2000, 169.

151 M. Khor (ed.), 'The Multilateral Trading System: A Development Perspective',

Report prepared by the Third World Network for the United Nations Development Programme, December 2001, p. 9. Online. Available HTTP: <http://www.twnside.org.sg/title2/par/mk001.doc> (accessed 16 February 2007).

152 J.M. Finger, 'Implementing the Uruguay Round Agreements: Problems for Developing Countries', *The World Economy* 24:9, 2003, 1103.

153 A. Capling, *Australia and the Global Trade System: From Havana to Seattle*, Oakleigh VIC: Cambridge University Press, 2001, p. 200.

154 Finger, 'Implementing the Uruguay Round Agreements: Problems for Developing Countries', 1103.

155 Khor, 'The Multilateral Trading System: A Development Perspective', chapter 4.

156 Preamble to TRIPs Agreement.

157 V. Jha and R. Vossenaar, *Breaking the Deadlock: A Positive Agenda on Trade, Environment and Development?* UNCTAD, 19 October 1999, p. 15. Online. Available HTTP: <http://r0.unctad.org/trade_env/test1/publications/positive.pdf> (accessed 16 February 2007)

158 Ibid.

159 Su, 'The Winners and the Losers', 169.

160 *Convention on Biological Diversity*, 5 June 1992, 1760 UNTS 79, entered into force 29 December 1993.

161 The relationship of the *TRIPS Agreement* to the *Convention on Biological Diversity* will be discussed further in Chapter 4.

162 Ibid., Article 8.2, p. 239.

163 Third World Network, 'Executive Summary: The Multilateral Trading System: A Development Perspective', Report prepared by the Third World Network for the United Nations Development Programme, December 2001. Online. Available HTTP: <http://www.twnside.org.sg/title/undpsum.htm> (accessed 26 March 2007).

164 *United States – Standards for Reformulated and Conventional Gasoline*, WTO Doc. WT/DSS/AB/R (20 May 1996), 35 ILM 603 (1996).

165 J. McDonald, 'The WTO's Response to the Trade–Environment Debate: A Preliminary Report Card', *International Trade Law Conference* 23, Attorney General's Department, Canberra, 29 May 1997, p. 8 (copy on file with author).

166 M.R. Mendoza, 'Venezuela and the United States: The Evolving Bilateral Relationship', in M.R. Mendoza, P. Correa and B. Kotschwar (eds), *The Andean Community and the United States: Trade and Investment Relations in the 1990s*, Organization of American States, 1998, p. 144.

167 WTO *Report of the Panel in United States – Standards for Reformulated and Conventional Gasoline*, 35 ILM 274 (1996), WTO Doc. WT/DS2/R.

168 Ibid.

169 This approach was established for the first time by the interpretation of the Appellate Body in the *Herring and Salmon* Panel. *Canada – Measures Affecting Exports of Unprocessed Herring and Salmon*, GATT Doc. L/6268, GATT BISD. 35S/98 (adopted 22 March 1988).

170 McDonald, 'The WTO's Response to the Trade–Environment Debate', 12.

171 WTO *Report of the Panel in United States – Standards for Reformulated and Conventional Gasoline*, 35 ILM 274 (1996), WTO Doc. WT/DS2/R.

172 *EC Measures Concerning Meat and Meat Products (Hormones)*, 1996, WTO Doc. WT/DS26/R/USA.

173 McDonald, 'The WTO's Response to the Trade–Environment Debate', 121.

174 *United States – Prohibition of Shrimps and Certain Shrimp Products*, WTO Doc. WT/DS58/AB/R (98–000) (12 October 1998).

175 Ibid.

176 Halle, 'Trade and Environment', 115.

177 Hunter *et al.*, *International Environmental Law and Policy*, p. 1210.

178 Ibid., p. 1213.
179 Ibid., p. 1214.
180 Ibid.
181 The option would mean that a panel which became aware of the environmental dimension of a case before it could ask the International Court of Justice (Chamber for Environmental Affairs) to give an advisory opinion. See ibid., p. 1215.
182 Ibid.
183 Halle, 'Trade and Environment', 114.
184 Ibid., 108.
185 Friends of the Earth International Press Release. Online. Available HTTP: <http://www.foe.co.uk/foei/tes/link12.htm> (accessed 27 June 2005).
186 Ibid.
187 S. Vaughan, 'Trade and Environment: Some North–South Considerations', *Cornell International Law Journal* 27:3, 1994, 602.
188 Halle, 'Trade and Environment', 109–10.
189 B. Jagdish, 'On thinking Clearly about the Linkage between Trade and the Environment', *Environment and Development Economics* 5:4, 2000, 485–96, cited in D.C. Esty, 'Bridging the Trade–Environment Divide', *Journal of Economic Perspectives* 15:3, 2001, 118.
190 Hunter *et al.*, *International Environmental Law and Policy*, p. 1189.
191 Rege, 'GATT Law and Environment Related Issues', 114.
192 Hunter *et al.*, *International Environmental Law and Policy*, p. 1188.
193 K. Anderson and J. Drake-Brockman, 'The World Trade Organization and the Environment' in B.W. Boer, R. Fowler and N. Gunningham (eds), *Environmental Outlook No 2: Law and Policy*, Sydney: Federation Press, 1996, p. 145.
194 Ibid.
195 Hunter *et al.*, *International Environmental Law and Policy*, p. 1186.
196 See the chapters on regional approaches for an in-depth discussion on the issue of harmonization.
197 It was recognized at the UNCED that national environmental standards and laws should be allowed to differ and may reflect different stages of economic development. For detail see Chapter 2.
198 'States should cooperate to promote a supportive and open international economic system that would lead to economic growth and sustainable development in all countries, to better address the problems of environmental degradation'. *Rio Declaration*, Principle 12. For more detail see Chapter 2.
199 P.A.G. van Bergeijk, 'International Trade and the Environmental Challenge', *Journal of World Trade* 25:6, 1991, 109.
200 Various issues relating to MEAs are the focus of Chapter 8.
201 Van Bergeijk, 'International Trade and the Environmental Challenge', 106.

4 The trade–environment linkage in the post-Uruguay round context

I would like to acknowledge the following source for granting copyright permission to reproduce my earlier work 'Trade and Environment Linkage in the Post-Uruguay Round Context' with substantial revisions: *James Cook University Law Review* 11 (2004), 36–62.

1 V. Jha and R. Vossenaar, *Breaking the Deadlock: A Positive Agenda on Trade, Environment and Development?* 1999. Online. Available HTTP: <http://r0.unctad.org/trade_env/test1/publications/positive.pdf> (accessed 16 February 2007).
2 There have been a number of Ministerial Conferences to date. They are: the Singapore Ministerial Meeting, held in Singapore 9–13 December 1996; the Geneva Ministerial Meeting, held in Geneva 18–20 May 1998; the Seattle Ministerial Meeting, held

in Seattle 30 November–3 December 1999; the Doha Ministerial Meeting, held in Doha 9–13 November 2001; and the Cancun Ministerial Meeting, held in Cancun 10–14 September 2003. In late July 2004 a special Ministerial meeting was held in Geneva to discuss only agricultural trade liberalization issues raised in the 2001 Doha Ministerial Conference. Most recently there has been the 2005 Hong Kong ministerial conference which was held from 13 to 18 December 2005.

3 The structure of the Ministerial Conference was set up in Article IV para. 1 of the *Marrakesh Agreement Establishing the World Trade Organization*, 15 April 1994, 33 ILM 1125 (1994), entered into force 1 January 1994.

4 *Ministerial Declaration*, Singapore WTO Ministerial 1996, Adopted 13 December 1996, WTO Doc. Wt/Min(96)/Dec, para. 2. Online. Available HTTP: <http://www.wto.org/English/thewto_e/minist_e/min96_e/wtodec_e.htm> (accessed 25 March 2007).

5 Ibid., para. 13.

6 The International Centre for Trade and Sustainable Development ('ICTSD'), 'A Brief Analysis of the Ministerial Conference' 1996. Online. Available HTTP: <http://www.ictsd.org/ministerial/singapore/story9-13-12-96.htm> (accessed 25 March 2007).

7 Ibid.

8 Ibid.

9 ICTSD, '*Bridges* Weekly Trade News Digest Coverage of the Ministerial', 2:18 (18 May 1998). Online. Available HTTP: <http://www.ictsd.org/ministerial/geneva/story17-05-98.htm> (accessed 25 March 2007).

10 *Ministerial Declaration*, Geneva WTO Ministerial 1998, adopted 20 May 1998. Online. Available HTTP: <http://www.wto.org/english/thewto_e/minist_e/min98_e/mindec_e.htm> (accessed 25 March 2007).

11 ICTSD, '*Bridges* Weekly Trade News Digest Coverage of the Ministerial'.

12 Address by the Director General, Mr Renato Ruggiero, Geneva WTO Ministerial Conference, 1998. Online. Available HTTP: <http://www.wto.org/english/thewto_e/minist_e/min98_e/anniv_e/dg_e.htm> (accessed 25 March 2007).

13 D.K. Das, 'Debacle at Seattle: the Way the Cookie Crumbled', *Journal of World Trade* 34:5, 2000, 186.

14 M. Halle, 'Seattle and Sustainable Development', International Institute for Sustainable Development website ('IISDnet'). Online. Available HTTP: <http://www.iisd.org/trade/wto/seattleandsd.htm> (accessed 25 March 2007).

15 Ibid.

16 Ibid.

17 For more detail see Chapter 3.

18 ICTSD, '*Bridges* Weekly Trade News Digest Coverage of the Ministerial', 3:46 (24 November 1999). Online. Available HTTP: <http://www.ictsd.org/ministerial/seattle/story24-11-99.htm#Environment> (accessed 25 March 2007).

19 For details see ICTSD, *Bridges* Daily Update, 30 November 1999. Online. Available HTTP: <http://www.ictsd.org/ministerial/seattle/wto_daily/991130_eng.htm> (accessed 25 March 2007).

20 WTO Doc. WT/GC/W/233.

21 WTO Doc. WT/GC/W/251.

22 WTO Doc. WT/GC/W/126.

23 WTO Doc. WT/GC/W/255.

24 WTO Doc. WT/GC/W/163.

25 WTO Doc. WT/GC/W/387.

26 A. Najam, 'Trade and Environment after Seattle: A Negotiation Agenda for the South', *Journal of Environment and Development* 9:4, 2000, 410.

27 WTO Doc. WT/GC/W/304.

28 ICTSD, '*Bridges* Daily Update on the Third Ministerial Conference', 1 December 1999. Online. Available HTTP: <http://www.ictsd.org/ministerial/seattle/ wto_daily/991201_eng.htm> (accessed 25 March 2007).
29 '3/12-05.45' Draft Ministerial Text, Seattle Ministerial Conference 1999.
30 Ibid.
31 K. von Moltke, 'Trade and the Environment: The Linkages and the Politics', paper presented at the *Roundtable on Trade and Environment*, Canberra, Australia, 25 August 1999, pp. 7–8, cited in Najam, 'Trade and Environment after Seattle', 405–6.
32 Najam, 'Trade and Environment After Seattle', 410.
33 V. Jha, G. Hewison and M. Underhill (eds), *Trade, Environment and Sustainable Development: A South Asian Perspective*, London: Macmillan, 1997.
34 ICTSD, 'New Trade Round Postponed; Ministerial Meeting Suspended', *Bridges* Daily Update, 3 December 1999. Online. Available HTTP: <http://www.ictsd.org/ministerial/seattle/wto_daily/final.htm> (accessed 25 March 2007).
35 M. Khor, 'The Revolt of Developing Nations', Reports on Seattle, 6 December 1999. Online. Available HTTP: <www.twnside.org.sg/title/revolt-cn.htm> (accessed 25 March 2007).
36 E.H. Preeg, 'The South Rises in Seattle', *Journal of International Economic Law* 3, 2000, 184.
37 *Ministerial Declaration*, Doha WTO Ministerial 2001, adopted 14 November 2001, WTO Doc. WT/MIN(01)/DEC/1 ('*Doha Declaration*'). Online. Available HTTP: <http://www.wto.org/english/thewto_e/minist_e/min01_e/mindecl_e.htm> (accessed 25 March 2007).
38 United Nations, 'Key Points Arising out of the 4th WTO Ministerial Conference from a Development Perspective', Discussion Paper from the United Nations Institute for Training and Research. Online. Available HTTP: <http://www.un.int/unitar/trade_campus/doha_key_points.htm> (accessed 10 January 2004) (copy on file with author).
39 Ibid., p. 6; *Agreement Establishing the WTO ('Marrakesh Agreement')*, preamble.
40 *Doha Declaration*, para. 6.
41 Ibid.
42 *Agenda 21*, UN Conference on Environment and Development, UN Doc. A/CONF.151/26/Rev.1 (1992).
43 *Rio Declaration on Environment and Development*, 14 June 1992, 31 ILM 874 (1992).
44 *Doha Declaration*, para. 2. See M. Stilwell, 'Environment, Trade and Sustainable Development: An Overview of Key Issues Arising from the World Summit on Sustainable Development and the WTO Doha Work Programme', UNEP Background Paper, 2003. Online. Available HTTP: <http://www.unep-unctad.org/cbtf/cbtf2/meetings/capetown/GenpapDohaWSSD.doc> (accessed 27 March 2007).
45 *Doha Declaration*, para. 33.
46 Ibid., para. 37.
47 Ibid., para. 38.
48 H. Mann and S. Porter, 'The State of Trade and Environment Law, 2003: Implications for Doha and Beyond', research paper published by the International Institute for Sustainable Development and the Center for International Environmental Law, 2003. p. 37. Online. Available HTTP: <http://www.iisd.org/pdf/2003/trade_enviro_law_2003.pdf> (accessed 27 April 2007).
49 *United Nations Convention on Biological Diversity*, Rio de Janeiro, 5 June 1992. 31 ILM 818 (1992). For more detail on the Convention see Chapter 8.
50 Ibid., Article 1.
51 G. Dutfield, 'Sharing the Benefits of Biodiversity: Is there a Role for the Patent System?', *Journal of World Intellectual Property* 5:6, 2002, 901.

52 See Chapter 3 for details.
53 Dutfield, 'Sharing the Benefits of Biodiversity', 905.
54 V. Shiva, 'Biodiversity and Intellectual Property Rights', in R. Nader *et al.* (eds), *The Case against "Free Trade": GATT, NAFTA and the Globalisation of Corporate Power*, San Francisco: Earth Island Press, 1993, p. 120.
55 Dutfield, 'Sharing the Benefits of Biodiversity', 928–9.
56 D. Vivas and E. Turek, 'Preliminary Comments on the Revised Documents for the Doha Ministerial Conference', November 2001. Cited in Mann and Porter, 'The State of Trade and Environment Law 2003'.
57 F.M. Abbott, 'The Enduring Enigma of TRIPS: A Challenge for the World Economic System', *Journal of International Economic Law* 1:4, 1998, 497.
58 Dutfield, 'Sharing the Benefits of Biodiversity', p. 930.
59 T. Cottier and M. Panizzon, 'Legal Perspectives on Traditional Knowledge: The Case for Intellectual Property Protection', *Journal of International Economic Law* 7:2, 2004, 371.
60 P.S. Mehta, 'The Doha Development Agenda: The Road Ahead', *Canadian Development Report 2003*, p. 15. Online. Available HTTP: <http://www.nsi-ins.ca/english/pdf/cdr2003_e_3.pdf> (accessed 26 March 2007).
61 M. Khor, 'The WTO, the Post-Doha Agenda and the Future of the Trade System', Third World Network paper prepared for a seminar on WTO held at the annual meeting of the Asian Development Bank held in Shanghai, China, on 10 May 2002. Online. Available HTTP: <http://www.twnside.org.sg/title/mkadb.htm> (accessed 26 March 2007).
62 *Doha Declaration*, para. 16.
63 Mann and Porter, 'The State of Trade and Environment Law 2003', p. 18.
64 *Doha Declaration*, para. 31(i).
65 F. Jawara and A. Kwa, *Behind the Scenes at the WTO: the Real World of International Trade Negotiations*, London: Zed Books, 2003, p. 127.
66 *Doha Declar*ation, para. 32(ii)–(iii).
67 See, e.g., *European Communities – Measures Concerning Meat and Meat Products (Hormones)* WT/DS26/ARB, 12 July 1999.
68 K. Malhotra, 'Doha: Is It Really a Development Round?', *Trade, Environment and Development* 1, 2002, 4.
69 UN Millennium Project Task Force, *The Interim Report of the Millennium Project Task Force 9 on Open, Rule-based Trading Systems*, commissioned by the UN Secretary General, 2004, p. 11. Online. Available HTTP: <http://www.unmillenniumproject.org> (accessed 26 March 2007).
70 Malhotra, 'Doha: Is It Really a Development Round?', 7.
71 Third World Network, 'Cancun: Fundamental Differences over the content of Draft Ministerial Declaration'. Online. Available HTTP: <http://www.choike.org/nuevo_eng/informes/1319.html> (accessed 26 March 2007).
72 S.J. Evenett, 'The Failure of the WTO Ministerial Meeting in Cancun: What Implications for Future Research on the World Trading System?', *CESifo Forum* 4:3, 2003, 11. Online. Available HTTP: <http://www.fordschool.umich.edu/rsie/acit/TopicsDocuments/Evenett031009.pdf> (accessed 26 March 2007). The Singapore Issues included four matters, namely the relationship between trade and investment policy, the interaction between trade and competition policies, transparency in government procurement practices, and trade facilitation practices. They are called the Singapore Issues because they were raised for the first time at the Singapore Ministerial in 1996 by the developed economies.
73 D.K. Das, 'The Doha Round of Multilateral Trade Negotiations: Causal Factors behind the Failure in Cancun', Research Paper, October 2003. Online. Available

HTTP: <http://www.cid.harvard.edu/cidtrade/Papers/das2003.pdf> (accessed 26 March 2007).

74 S.J. Evenett, 'The World Trade Organisation Ministerial Conference in Hong Kong: What next?' *Journal of World Trade* 40:2, 2006, 221.

75 *Ministerial Declaration*, Doha Work Programme, adopted 18 December 2005, WTO Doc. WT/MIN(05)/W/3/Rev.2, para. 1.

76 Ibid., paras 30–2.

77 Indian Ambassador K.M. Chandrasekhar expressed this view in a press briefing criticizing the Cancun Draft. For details see the Third World Network, *Report of WTO Heads of Delegation Meeting on Revised Cancun Draft*, 27 August 2003. Online. Available HTTP: <http://www.twnside.org.sg/title/twninfo69.htm> (accessed 29 March 2007).

78 Jawara and Kwa, *Behind the Scenes at the WTO*, p. 306.

5 Regional approaches to free trade and sustainable development: the European Union

1 J. McDonald, 'Greening the GATT: Harmonizing Free Trade and Environmental Protection in the New World Order', *Environmental Law* 23:2, 1993, 82.

2 A.S. Bhalla and P. Bhalla (eds), *Regional Blocs: Building Blocks or Stumbling Blocks?* London: Macmillan, 1997, p. 196.

3 *Commission's Sixth General Report*, 1972, p. 8, cited in A. Syngellakis, 'The Concept of Sustainable Development in European Community Law and Policy', *Cambrian Law Review* 24, 1993, 65.

4 First Environmental Action Programme, 20 December 1973.

5 Third Environmental Action Programme, section I, 8. 17 December 1983.

6 Article 130 R (2) (now Article 174) of the *Treaty Establishing the European Community*, Rome, 25 March 1957, 298 UNTS 3 ('*Treaty of Rome*').

7 On 1 May 1999 the *Treaty of Amsterdam* came into force. One feature of this treaty was the renumbering of the entire *Rome* and *Maastricht* treaties. Where the article number has changed, the new *Treaty of Amsterdam* number will appear in this book in brackets after the original number, in the first reference to an article in each subsection of the chapter.

8 The argument for introducing environmental legislation under 'harmonization' provisions was that proper environmental control was necessary to secure fair competition and a level economic playing field. For details see A.G.W. Jackson, 'Environmental Law in the European Community: Greek Tragedy or Epic Tale?', *Natural Resources and Environment* 8:2, 1993, 21.

9 M. Wheeler, 'Greening the EEC Treaty' in P. Sands (ed.), *Greening International Law*, London: Earthscan, 1993, p. 88.

10 Ibid. For details see Case 300/89 *Commission v. Council* and Case 155/91 *Commission v. Council.* For more on the problem of the dividing line between Article 130S (now Article 175) and Article 100A (now Article 95), see J. Cameron *et al.* (eds), *Trade and the Environment: The Search for Balance* I, London: Cameron May, 1994, p. 217.

11 Article 3 provides that the activities of the Community shall include a policy in the sphere of the environment; See also Commission for the European Communities, Communication from the Commission Council, the European Parliament and the European Social and Economic Committee, 'Integration of Environmental Aspects into European Standardisation' SEC (2004) 206.

12 A similar instruction was lacking in Title VII of the *Single European Act* of 1986, reprinted in 25 ILM 506 (1986). Also see H. Somsen, 'The European Union and the

OECD' in J. Werksman (ed.), *Greening International Institutions*, London: Earthscan, 1996, p. 194.

13 Somsen, 'The European Union and the OECD', p. 194.

14 S. Bronitt, F. Burns and D. Kinley, *Environmental Law and Policy in Principles of European Community Law: Commentary and Materials*, North Ryde NSW: LBC, 1995, p. 550.

15 European Commission, *Communication on Impact Assessment*, 2002, COM/2002/276.

16 European Commission, *Handbook for Trade Sustainability Impact Assessment*, 2006, 7.

17 Decision No. 1600/2002/EC.

18 *Treaty of Rome*, Article 30 (now Article 28).

19 Case 8/74 *Dassonville*, [1974] ECR 837.

20 P. Oliver, 'Measures having Equivalent Effect: A Reappraisal', *Common Market Law Review*, 19, 1982, 223 in Cameron *et al.* (eds), *Trade and the Environment*, p. 235.

21 For details see J. Steiner, 'Drawing the Line: Uses and Abuses of Article 30 EEC', *Common Market Law Review* 29, 1992, 749 and E. White, 'In Search of the Limits of Article 30 of the EEC Treaty', *Common Market Law Review* 26, 1989, 235.

22 Case 172/82 *Syndicat National des Fabricants Raffineurs d'Huile de Graissage and Others v. Groupement d'Intérêt Economique 'Inter-huiles' and Others;* ('*Inter-huiles Case*'), (1983) ECR 566.

23 *Treaty of Rome*, Article 36 (now Article 30).

24 For examples see Case 229/83, *Leclerq* [1985] ECR 1, 35; Case 95/81, *Commission v. Italy* [1982] ECR 2, 187, 2, 204; Case 113/80, *Commission v. Ireland* [1981] ECR 1, 625, 1, 638; Case 13/68, *Salgoil* [1968] ECR 453, 463, Case 7/68, *Commission v. Italy* [1968] ECR 423, 431.

25 Case 120/78, *Cassis de Dijon* [1979] ECR 649.

26 D. Hunter, J. Salzman and D. Zaelke, *International Environmental Law and Policy*, New York: Foundation Press, 1998, p. 1285.

27 Ibid.

28 Case 240/83 [1984] ECR 548.

29 Bronitt *et al.*, *Environmental Law and Policy in Principles of European Community Law*, p. 535.

30 For detailed analysis of this principle see G. de Burca, 'The Principle of Proportionality and its Application in EC Law,' *Yearbook of European Law*, 13, 1993, 105.

31 *Fromancais v. Forma* [1983] ECR 395, para. 8.

32 D. Geradin, *Trade and the Environment: A Comparative Study of EC and US Law*, Melbourne: Cambridge University Press, 1996, p. 16.

33 *Commission v. Denmark*; Case 302/86 [1988] *ECR* 4607.

34 Article 169 (now Article 226) provides that if the Commission considers that a member state has failed to fulfil an obligation under the Treaty, the Commission may give its reasonable opinion on that matter. If the failure still persists then the Commission may bring the matter before the ECJ.

35 *Commission v. Denmark*, 4607.

36 Ibid., 4608.

37 1979 E. Comm. J. Rep. 2555 [1979–81], *Common Market Report* (CCH) at section 8601.

38 Ibid., 2567.

39 Case 788/79 *Gilli and Andres* [1980] ECR 2071, Case 104/75 *De Peiper* [1976] *ECR* 613.

40 McDonald, 'Greening the GATT', 44.

41 The *Treaty of Accession 2003*, 23 September 2003, Article 38; and *Treaty of Accession 2005*, 25 April 2005, Article 38.

42 K. Inglis, 'Enlargement and the Environment Acquis', *Review of European Community and International Environmental Law* 13:2, 2004, 144.
43 A. Vikhlyaev, 'The Use of Trade Measures for Environmental Purposes – Globally and in the EU Context' UNCTAD Working Paper, September 2001, p. 37. Online. Available HTTP: <http://r0.unctad.org/trade_env/test1/publications/feem.pdf> (accessed 17 April 2007).
44 Ibid.
45 Bronitt *et al.*, *Environmental Law and Policy in Principles of European Community Law*, p. 539.
46 T. Sexton, 'Enacting National Laws More Stringent than Other States' Laws in the European Community', *Cornell International Law Journal* 24, 1991, 590.
47 Inglis, 'Enlargement and the Environment Acquis', 147, 149.
48 L. Kramer, 'Environmental Protection and Article 30 EEC Treaty', *Common Market Law Review* 30, 1993, 120–7.
49 E.U. Petersmann, *International and European Trade and Environmental Law after the Uruguay Round*, London: Kluwer, 1995, p. 70.
50 Case C-2/90, *Commission v. Belgium* [1992] *ECR* 4431.
51 *Commission v. Belgium*, para. 30.
52 Petersmann, *International and European Trade and Environmental Law after the Uruguay Round*, p. 72.
53 *The Basel Convention on the Control of the Transboundary Movements of Hazardous Wastes and their Disposal*, 1989, reprinted in 28 ILM 649 (1989).
54 Organisation for Economic Co-operation and Development, *Environmental Requirements and Market Access*, OECD Trade Policy Studies, 2006, p. 43.
55 Also known as Comité Européen de Normalisation ('CEN').
56 Commission of the European Communities, Communication from the Commission Council, the European Parliament and the European Social and Economic Committee, 'Integration of Environmental Aspects into European Standardisation', SEC (2004) 206, p. 3.
57 'European Policy Principles on International Standardization', SEC (2001) 1296; note this is consistent with the WTO appellate body, which has ruled that 'Members are free to adopt their own policies aimed at protecting the environment as long as, in so doing, they fulfil their obligations and respect the rights of other Members under the WTO Agreements', *United States-Gasoline case*, para. 30 of the Appellate Body Report; *Shrimp-Turtle case*, para. 186 of the Appellate Body Report (see Chapter 3).
58 Government Regulations Affecting Trade in Products of Organic Agriculture, COM/ENV/TD (2002) 86/FINAL, p. 6; See also Traceability regulations promulgated by the *Codex Alimentarius Commission.*
59 For example, the process requirements established by The Standard on Good Agricultural Practice of the Euro Retailer Produce Working Group (EurepGAP) and Council Regulation (EEC) No. 2092/91 on the legal framework for the importation of organic agriculture.
60 Government Regulations Affecting Trade in Products of Organic Agriculture, p. 5.
61 Vikhlyaev, 'The Use of Trade Measures for Environmental Purposes – Globally and in the EU Context', 24.
62 Government Regulations Affecting Trade in Products of Organic Agriculture, p. 7.
63 One example of the challenge of harmonization can be seen in the case of Romania, which made significant efforts for accession to the EU with regard to the adoption of legislation on environmental protection. The failure to properly take account of the costs of implementation of these laws led the Commission to comment in 2002 that the laws may be impossible to enforce and may have to be amended.

64 Government Regulations Affecting Trade in Products of Organic Agriculture, p. 5; OECD, *Environmental Requirements and Market Access*, p. 200.
65 Ibid., pp. 23–4.
66 Article 11(1), Council Regulation (EEC) No. 2092/91.
67 Council Regulation (EEC) No. 1788/2001.
68 M. Soveroski, 'EC Enlargement and the Development of European Environmental Policy: Parallel Histories, Divergent Paths?', *Review of European Community and International Environmental Law* 13:2, 2004, 129.
69 Council Directive 88/609/EEC.
70 Soveroski, 'EC Enlargement and the Development of European Environmental Policy', 130.
71 Directive 98/70/EC.
72 Soveroski, 'EC Enlargement and the Development of European Environmental Policy', 131.
73 European Commission, 'A New Regional Agreement to Develop South Eastern Europe', 2006. Online. Available HTTP: <Trade.ec.europa.eu/doclib/docs/2006/december/tradoc_131840.pdf> (accessed 2 April 2007).
74 Ibid.
75 Ibid.
76 D.C. Esty and D. Geradin, 'Market Access, Competitiveness, and Harmonization: Environmental Protection in Regional Trade Agreements', *Harvard Environmental Law Review* 21, 1997, 284.
77 Cases C-401/92 and C-402/92, *Criminal Proceedings against Tankstation 't Heuske vof and J.B.E. Boermans*, 1994 ECR I-2199, 2215. Cited ibid., 270.
78 Soveroski, 'EC Enlargement and the Development of European Environmental Policy', 133.
79 R.H. Steinberg, 'Trade–Environment Negotiations in the EU, NAFTA, and WTO: Regional Trajectories of Rule Development', *American Journal of International Law* 91:2, 1997, 231.
80 Ibid., 259.
81 Ibid.
82 A. Weale, 'European Environmental Policy by Stealth: the Dysfunctionality of Functionalism?' *Environment and Planning C: Government and Policy* 17, 1999, 44.
83 Steinberg, 'Trade–Environment Negotiations in the EU, NAFTA, and WTO', 231
84 Inglis, 'Enlargement and the Environment Acquis', 146.
85 Weale, 'European Environmental Policy by Stealth', 49.
86 For details about implementation and enforcement problems see G. Pridham and M. Cini, 'Enforcing Environmental Standards in the European Union: Is there a Southern Problem?' in M. Faure *et al.* (eds), *Environmental Standards in The European Union in an Interdisciplinary Framework*, Antwerp: Maklu, 1994, p. 251.
87 Soveroski, 'EC Enlargement and the Development of European Environmental Policy', 134.
88 A. Jordan, 'The Implementation of EU Environmental Policy: A Policy Problem Without a Political Solution?' *Environment and Planning C: Government and Policy* 17, 1999, 69.
89 Weale, 'European Environmental Policy by Stealth', 44.
90 Ibid.
91 Ibid.
92 Vikhlyaev, 'The Use of Trade Measures for Environmental Purposes – Globally and in the EU Context', 34.
93 Esty and Geradin, 'Market Access, Competitiveness, and Harmonization', 276.

94 For example, the European Community fur seal ban (1983) and the European Community whale ban (1981).
95 *Dutch Red Grouse* Case, Case 169/89. For details see Steinberg, 'Trade–Environment Negotiations in the EU, NAFTA, and WTO', 254 .
96 P. Low (ed.), *International Trade and the Environment*, World Bank Discussion Paper, No. 159, Washington DC: World Bank, 1992.
97 The *Lomé Convention* was first signed in February 1975 ('*Lomé I*'). There have since been subsequent renegotiations and renewals of the Convention: *Lomé II* (January 1981–February 1985), *Lomé III* (March 1985 expired in 1990) and *Lomé IV* (December 1989–99). The *Lomé Convention* has since been replaced by the *Cotonou Agreement* discussed below.
98 R. Safadi, *Building Trade Capacity Behind the Broader Agenda*, World Bank Discussion Paper. Online. Available HTTP: <http://www.worldbank.org/ mdf/mdf4/ papers/raed.pdf> (accessed 3 April 2007).
99 International Monetary Fund and the World Bank, 'Market Access for Developing Country Exports – Selected Issues', 2002. Online. Available HTTP: <http://www.imf.org/external/np/pdr/ma/2002/eng/092602.pdf> (accessed 17 April 2007).
100 M. Holland, 'Europe's Changing Development Agenda: Implications for the Pacific', *New Zealand International Review* 22:4, 1997, 11.
101 Ibid., 12.
102 European Commission, 'Economic Partnership Agreements – Means and Objectives', 2003, p. 2. Online. Available HTTP: <http://trade.ec.europa.eu/doclib/ docs/ 2003/december/tradoc_115007.pdf> (accessed 3 April 2007).
103 The rules of origin on imports into the customs of the territory are contained in European Commission Regulation No. 2454/93.
104 For example, the European Directive 2065/2001 requires fishery products to be labelled with the origin.
105 ICTSD, *Fisheries, International Trade and Sustainable Development*, 'Natural Resources, International Trade and Sustainable Development Series', Geneva: International Centre for Trade and Sustainable Development, 2006, p. 44. Online. Available HTTP: <http://www.trade-environment.org/output/ictsd/resource/Fish_intro. pdf> (accessed 3 April 2007).
106 S.K.B. Asante, 'The Lomé Convention: Towards Perpetuation of Dependence or Promotion of Interdependence?' *Third World Quarterly*, 1981, 666.
107 S.K.B. Asante, 'The European Union–Africa-Caribbean-Pacific (ACP), Lomé Convention: Expectations, Reality and the Challenges of the 21st Century', *Africa Insight* 26:4, 1996, 383.
108 Ibid.
109 B. Hoekman Groupe and S. Prowse, 'Policy Responses to Preference Erosion: From Trade as Aid to Aid for Trade', paper presented at the international symposium *Preference Erosion: Impacts and Policy Responses*, Geneva, 13–14 June 2005. Online. Available HTTP: <http://www.uneca.org/atpc/documents/May/preference-erosion. pdf> (accessed 17 April 2007).
110 Ibid.
111 Ibid.
112 See European Council Decision of 21 June 2005 concerning the signing, on behalf of the European Community, of the Agreement amending the Partnership Agreement between the members of the African, Caribbean and Pacific Group of States ('ACP'), of the one part, and the European Community and its Member States, of the other part, signed in Cotonou on 23 June 2000 [Official Journal L 209, 11 August 2005]. Online. Available HTTP: <http://europa.eu/scadplus/leg/en/lvb/ r12101.htm> (accessed 4 April 2007); see also European Commission, *Green Paper*

on Relations between the European Union and ACP Countries on the Eve of the 21st Century, Luxembourg: Office for Official Publications of the European Communities, 1996. Online. Available HTTP: <http://ec.europa.eu/development/body/publications/l-vert/lv_en.htm> (accessed 4 April 2007). See also European Commission, *Guidelines for the Negotiation of new Co-operation Agreements with African, Caribbean and Pacific (ACP) Countries*, Luxembourg: Office for Official Publications of the European Communities, 1997.

113 Ibid.

114 Asante, 'The European Union–Africa-Caribbean-Pacific (ACP), Lomé Convention', 384.

115 The *Cotonou Partnership Agreement*. Online. Available HTTP: <http://ec.europa.eu/development/body/cotonou/index_en.htm> (accessed 4 April 2007).

116 The first formal negotiations commenced in 2002 with Central Africa (CEMAC and Sao Tomé and Principe), *Overview of the regional EPA negotiations: Central Africa–EU Economic Partnership Agreement* (ECDPM InBrief 14A), Maastricht: ECDPM. Online. Available HTTP: <http://www.ecdpm.org/inbrief14a> (accessed 4 April 2007)); and Western Africa (ECOWAS and Mauritania).

117 Private Sector Foundation Uganda, *Economic Partnership Agreements*, 2007. Online. Available HTTP: <http://www.psfuganda.org/modules/PDdownloads/singlefile.php?cid=6&lid=26> (accessed 4 April 2007).

118 Article 1 of the *Cotonou Agreement* states specifically that 'this Partnership shall be centred on the objective of reducing and eventually eradicating poverty.'

119 *Cotonou Partnership Agreement*, Article 19.

120 S. Hurt, 'Cooperation and Coercion? The Cotonou Agreement between the European Union and ACP states and the end of the Lomé Convention', *Third World Quarterly* 24:1, 2003, 162.

121 *Cotonou Partnership Agreement*, Article 20.

122 Hurt, 'Cooperation and Coercion?', 163.

123 D. O'Brien, 'Trade Relations', *European Policy Analyst* 31, 2005, 31.

124 Department of Trade and Industry, United Kingdom, 'Economic Partnership Agreements (EPAs) and Cotonou'. Online. Available HTTP: <http://www.dti.gov.uk/europeandtrade/developing-countries/epas-agreement/page8946.html> (accessed 4 April 2007).

125 The HDI is one of the more useful measures of development levels and is based on life expectancy, education and income levels.

126 Hurt, 'Cooperation and Coercion?', 166.

127 See European Commission, *EU Generalised System of Preferences*, 2005. Online. Available HTTP: <http://www.europa-eu-un.org/articles/en/article_5520_en.htm> (accessed 2 April 2007).

128 Hurt, 'Cooperation and Coercion?', 168.

129 Ibid., 170.

130 Ibid., 169.

131 Ibid.

132 Ibid., 170; Article 9(1) of *Cotonou Agreement* lists democratic principles. The principles of good governance are defined in Article 9.3 of the *Cotonou Partnership Agreement*, and contained in the Preamble as well as Articles 6, 9 and 20.

133 E. Morgera and G.M. Duran, 'Enlargement and EU Development Policy: An Environmental Perspective', *Review of European Community and International Environmental Law* 13:2, 2004, 160.

134 *Cotonou Agreement*, Article 9(2). The principles of civil society are mentioned in Articles 6, 7, 8, 9, 10, 11, 15, 17, 19. Democratic participation is mentioned in Articles 2, 23, 25, 31, 50, 70, 75.

135 Hurt, 'Cooperation and Coercion?', 172.

136 Ibid., 171.
137 Ibid., 172.
138 Ibid., 161.
139 Ibid., 175, 161.
140 'Goods on the GSP list are also subject to quality restrictions which curtail developing countries' market access even further': M.R. Islam, *International Trade Law*, Sydney: LBC Information Services, 1999, p. 168.
141 Steinberg, 'Trade–Environment Negotiations in the EU, NAFTA, and WTO', 254.

6 Regional approaches to free trade and sustainable development: the North American Free Trade Agreement

1 See *North American Free Trade Agreement* ('NAFTA'), 17 December 1992, 32 ILM 289 (1993).
2 See *Canada–US Free Trade Agreement*, 22–3 December 1987 and 2 January 1988, 27 ILM 28 (1988).
3 'NAFTA creates a free trade zone of 8.2 million square miles, 364 million consumers, and economic activity of 7 trillion – the largest free trade zone in history'. See N. Kublicki, 'The Greening of Free Trade: NAFTA, Mexican Environmental Law, and Debt Exchanges for Mexican Environmental Infrastructure Development', *Columbia Journal of Environmental Law* 19:1, 1994, 60.
4 C. Schatan, 'Lessons from the Mexican Environmental Experience: First Results from NAFTA' in D. Tussie (ed.), *The Environment and International Trade Negotiations*, London: Macmillan, 2000, p. 167.
5 'Under "fast-track", Congress statutorily limits its own discretion, agreeing to act on certain specified types of agreements within a specific period, usually sixty days, and approve or reject the agreement as a whole, without amendment or modification.' For details see D. Hunter, J. Salzman and D. Zaelke, *International Environmental Law and Policy*, New York: Foundation Press, 1998, p. 1224.
6 D.C. Esty, 'Making Trade and Environmental Policies Work Together: Lessons from NAFTA', in J. Cameron *et al.* (eds) *Trade and Environment: The Search for Balance* I, London: Cameron May, 1994, p. 373.
7 *North American Agreement on Environmental Cooperation*, 14 September 1993, 32 ILM 1480 (1993).
8 Schatan, 'Lessons from the Mexican Environmental Experience', p. 170.
9 A.L.C. de Mestral, 'The Significance of the NAFTA Side Agreements on Environmental and Labour Cooperation', *Arizona Journal of International and Comparative Law* 15:1, 1998, 174.
10 Among the environmental organizations, some, such as the Sierra Club, Friends of the Earth and the Human Society, were very vocal and active.
11 B. Hogenboom, *Mexico and the NAFTA Environmental Debate: the Transnational Politics of Economic Integration*, Utrecht: International Books, 1998, p. 163.
12 See Memorandum from Rep. David Dreier to Member of the House of Representatives, NAFTA Fact No. 17 (18 October 1993).
13 J.I. Garvey, 'Trade Law and Quality of Life: Dispute Resolution under the NAFTA Side Accords on Labour and the Environment', *American Journal of International Law* 89:2, 1995, 440.
14 J.E. Bailey, 'Free Trade and the Environment: Can NAFTA Reconcile the Irreconcilable?' *American Journal of International Law and Policy* 8:4, 1993, 846.
15 NAFTA Preamble, 32 ILM 297 (1993).
16 According to Article 31.1 of the *Vienna Convention* 'A treaty shall be interpreted in good faith in accordance with the ordinary meaning to be given to the terms of the treaty in their context and in the light of its object and purpose.' Article 31.2 says,

'The context for the purpose of the interpretation of a treaty shall comprise, in addition to the text, including its preamble and annexes.' See United Nations, Treaty Series, vol. 1155, 331. See also the International Law Commission's Commentary on what was then Article 27(3)(a), which stated that 'an agreement as to the interpretation of a provision reached after the conclusion of the treaty represents an authentic interpretation by the parties which must be read into the treaty for purposes of its interpretation', *Yearbook of the International Law Commission*, 1966, II, p. 221, para. 14. This interpretation was cited with approval by the International Court of Justice in *Kasikili/Sedudu Island* 1999, ICJ Rep. 1, para. 49.

17 B. Appleton, *Navigating NAFTA*, Toronto: Carswell, 1994, p. 192.

18 *Mondev International v. United States*, ICSID (W. Bank) Case No. ARB(AF)/99/2, ¶ 127 (Award) (Oct. 11, 2002), paras 120–1.

19 R.A. Middletown, 'NAFTA and the Environmental Side Agreement: Fusing Economic Development with Ecological Responsibility', *San Diego Law Review* 31, 1994, 1043.

20 NAFTA, Article 1106.6.

21 Failed attempts to protect the environment include: the European food-safety measures (*Beef Hormone* cases); the US clean air regulations (*Reformulated Gasoline Case*); marine mammal conservation laws (*Tuna–Shrimp* cases). See Chapter 3 for details on these decisions.

22 For details see Chapter 3.

23 R. Housman, 'The North American Free Trade Agreement's Lessons for Reconciling Trade and the Environment', *Stanford Journal of International Law* 30, 1994, 400.

24 NAFTA Chapter 7, section B.

25 Ibid., Chapter 9.

26 Ibid., Article 712 (1); see also Articles 754.1, 755.3 and 905.3.

27 Ibid., Article 712 (2).

28 See *In the Matter of an International Arbitration under Chapter 11 of the North American Free Trade Agreement and the UNCITRAL Arbitration Rules between Methanex Corporation and United States of America*, Part IV, Chapter B, para. 3. Online. Available HTTP: <http://www.state.gov/s/l/c5818.htm> (accessed 10 April 2007).

29 Housman, 'The North American Free Trade Agreement's Lessons for Reconciling Trade and the Environment', 401.

30 Schatan, 'Lessons from the Mexican Environmental Experience', p. 171.

31 Housman, 'The North American Free Trade Agreement's Lessons for Reconciling Trade and the Environment', 403.

32 NAFTA, Article 3.

33 Middletown, 'NAFTA and the Environmental Side Agreement', 1048.

34 NAFTA, Article 713 (3).

35 Middletown, 'NAFTA and the Environmental Side Agreement', 1045.

36 Ibid.

37 NAFTA, Article 904.4. See Housman, 'The North American Free Trade Agreement's Lessons for Reconciling Trade and the Environment', 402.

38 Bailey, 'Free Trade and the Environment', 854.

39 Ibid.

40 Housman, 'The North American Free Trade Agreement's Lessons for Reconciling Trade and the Environment', 406.

41 Ibid.

42 *Commission v. Denmark*; Case 302/86 [1988] *ECR* 4607.

43 I. McConnell, 'North American Free Trade Agreement: Trading Natural Resource Goods and Protecting the Environment', *Journal of Energy and Natural Resources Law* 12:1, 1994, 171.

44 NAFTA, Article 915, gives the definition of standard and technical regulations.

45 D. Robertson, 'Trade and Environment: Harmonization and Technical Standards' in P. Low (ed.), *International Trade and the Environment*, World Bank Discussion Paper No. 159, Washington DC: World Bank, 1992, p. 309.
46 Ibid.
47 See Chapter 3 for examples.
48 Housman, 'The North American Free Trade Agreement's Lessons for Reconciling Trade and the Environment', 407.
49 The *Montreal Protocol on Substances that Deplete the Ozone Layer*, the *Basel Convention on the Control of Transboundary Movements of Hazardous Wastes and their Disposal* and the *Convention on International Trade in Endangered Species* take precedence over NAFTA if a conflict arises, and if the relevant MEA is implemented in such a manner as to be least inconsistent with NAFTA provisions. See Chapter 8 for a discussion of these MEAs.
50 Final Report, Canada–United States Trade Commission Panel, 16 October 1989, 2 TCT 7162.
51 McConnell, 'North American Free Trade Agreement', 169.
52 *Thailand – Restrictions on Importation of and Internal Taxes on Cigarettes*, 1990, 37 GATT BISD 223 (1990).
53 Investors and investment are broadly defined under Article 1139.
54 NAFTA, Article 1102.
55 Ibid., Article 1103.
56 Ibid., Articles 1104–5.
57 Ibid., Article 1120(1).
58 In 2000 S.D. Myers was granted a partial award under Articles 1102 and 1105 against the Canadian government on its ban on the export of PCBs – highly toxic substances that harm both human and animal health. Online. Available HTTP: <http://ita.law.uvic.ca/documents/SDMeyers-1stPartialAward.pdf> (accessed 12 April 2007).
59 In *Ethyl Corporation v. Canada*, 38 ILM 708 (1999), Ethyl Corporation successfully forced the Canadian government to repeal its legitimate ban on the inter-provincial and international trade in MMT or ethanol (a gasoline additive).
60 NAFTA Article 201(1) defines 'measure' as including 'any law, regulation, procedure, requirement or practice'.
61 *Metalclad Corporation v. United Mexican States* ('*Metaclad*'), Case No. ARB(AF)/97/1 (30 August 2000).
62 Ibid., 104–7.
63 Ibid., 99–101.
64 In a NAFTA Arbitration under the UNCITRAL Arbitration Rules S.D. Myers (claimant) and Government of Canada (respondent) Partial Award, para. 280. Online. Available HTTP: <http://ita.law.uvic.ca/documents/SDMeyers-1stPartialAward.pdf> (accessed 16 April 2007).
65 In a NAFTA Arbitration under the UNCITRAL Arbitration Rules S.D. Myers (claimant) and Government of Canada (respondent) Partial Award, para. 282. Online. Available HTTP: <http://ita.law.uvic.ca/documents/SDMeyers-1stPartialAward.pdf> (accessed 12 April 2007).
66 *Waste Management v. United Mexican States*, 2000, Case No. ARB (AF)/98/2 (2 June 2000).
67 Ibid., para. 98.
68 *In the Matter of an International Arbitration under Chapter 11 of the North American Free Trade Agreement and the UNCITRAL Arbitration Rules between Methanex Corporation and United States of America*. Online. Available HTTP: <http://www.state.gov/s/l/c5818.htm> (accessed 10 April 2007).
69 Ibid., Part IV, Chapter D, para. 7.

70 Schatan, 'Lessons from the Mexican Environmental Experience', p. 173.
71 See D.C. Esty, 'Integrating Trade and Environmental Policy Making: First Steps in the North American Free Trade Agreement', in D. Zaelke, P. Orbuch and R.F. Housman *et al.* (eds), *Trade and the Environment: Law, Economics, and Policy*, Washington DC: Island Press, 1993.
72 See, e.g., J. Pauwelyn, 'Adding Sweeteners to Softwood Lumber: The WTO–NAFTA "Spaghetti Bowl" is Cooking', Duke Law School Legal Studies, Research Paper Series, No. 93, January 2006, p. 6.
73 Ibid., pp. 5–6.
74 Most notable are the US–Canada softwood lumber cases. See WTO Panel Report on *United States – Investigation of the International Trade Commission in Softwood Lumber from Canada, Recourse to Article 21.5 of the DSU by Canada*, WT/DS277/RW, circulated on 15 November 2005; cf. NAFTA Opinion and Order of the Extraordinary Challenge Committee, *In the Matter of Certain Softwood Lumber Products from Canada*, Secretariat File No. ECC-2004-1904-01USA, 10 August 2005 (hereafter ECC Opinion). For more detail see ibid. See also G. Anderson, 'Can Someone Please Settle this Dispute? Canadian Softwood Lumber and the Dispute Settlement Mechanisms of the NAFTA and the WTO', *The World Economy* 29:5, 2006, 585–610.
75 Ibid.
76 S. Charnovitz, 'The NAFTA Environmental Side Agreement: Implications for Environmental Cooperation, Trade Policy and American Treaty Making', *Temple International and Comparative Law Journal* 8, 1994, 266.
77 Bailey, 'Free Trade and the Environment', 860.
78 Charnovitz, 'The NAFTA Environmental Side Agreement', 266.
79 The *Tuna–Dolphin* case illustrates the secrecy maintained by the GATT dispute panel. See Chapter 3 for detail of the case.
80 Housman, 'The North American Free Trade Agreement's Lessons for Reconciling Trade and the Environment', 410.
81 NAFTA, Article 2012.
82 B. Coote, *NAFTA Poverty and Free Trade in Mexico*, Oxford: Oxfam Publications, 1995, p. 12.
83 Ibid., p. 13.
84 J.M. Sheehan, 'Two Years after NAFTA: A Free Market Critique and Assessment', 1996. Online. Available HTTP: <http://www.cei.org/pdf/1624.pdf> (accessed 12 April 2007).
85 Red Mexicana de Accion Frente al Libre Comercio (Mexican Action Network on Free Trade), 'Ten Reasons for Suspending the Free Trade Agreement Negotiations', *Press Release*, 7 July 1992. For details see Hunter *et al.*, *International Environmental Law and Policy*, p. 1235.
86 Coote, *NAFTA Poverty and Free Trade in Mexico*, 39.
87 Sheehan, 'Two Years after NAFTA: A Free Market Critique and Assessment'.
88 Schatan, 'Lessons from the Mexican Environmental Experience', p. 185.
89 Ibid., p. 172.
90 J. Delgado *et al.*, 'The Environment: or How Social Issues Affect the Commitment of Environmental Tasks' in L. Randall (ed.), *Changing Structure of Mexico: Political, Social and Economic Prospects*, 2nd edn, New York: Columbia University, 2006, p. 299.
91 Ibid., p. 327.
92 Kublicki, 'The Greening of Free Trade', 120.
93 Ibid., 124–5.
94 NAFTA, Article 904.
95 Coote, *NAFTA Poverty and Free Trade in Mexico*, 36.

96 Ibid.
97 Ibid.
98 International Monetary Fund, 'How Has NAFTA Affected the Mexican Economy? Review and Evidence', Working Paper WP/04/59, 2004, pp. 12–13. Online. Available HTTP: <http://www.imf.org/external/pubs/ft/wp/2004/wp0459.pdf> (accessed 12 April 2007).
99 I. Morales, 'NAFTA Revisited: Expectations and Realities: The Mexican Crisis and the Weakness of the NAFTA Consensus', *Annals of the American Academy of Political and Social Science* 550, 1997, 130–52.
100 Ibid., 140.
101 Ibid.
102 F. Lazar, 'Investing in the NAFTA: Just Cause for Walking Away', *Journal of World Trade* 27:5, 1993, 23.
103 Morales, 'NAFTA Revisited: Expectations and Realities', 141.
104 Sheehan, 'Two Years after NAFTA: A Free Market Critique and Assessment'.
105 Article 5(1) of the *Environmental Side Agreement* states that 'each party shall effectively enforce its environmental laws.'
106 Middletown, 'NAFTA and the Environmental Side Agreement', 1025.
107 Ibid.
108 Ibid.
109 Ibid., 1051.
110 M.J. Kelly, 'Bringing a Complaint under the NAFTA Environmental Side Accord: Difficult Steps under a Procedural Paper Tiger, but Movement in the Right Direction', *Pepperdine Law Review,* 24:71, 1996, 82.
111 Sheehan, 'Two Years after NAFTA: A Free Market Critique and Assessment'.
112 'Rules of Origin is a non-tariff barrier which is used as a mechanism to differentiate imported goods on the basis of their origins for the purpose of determining the applicable tariff rates.' See M.R. Islam, *International Trade Law*, Sydney: LBC, 1999, p. 131.
113 M. Wilder and S. Whiteford, 'Flowing Uphill toward Money: Groundwater Management and Ejidal Producers in Mexico's Free Trade Environment', in Randall, *Changing Structure of Mexico*, p. 350.
114 Ibid.
115 Ibid.
116 D.B. Bray, S.R. Murphy and M. Cornejo, 'Beyond Islands? Sustainable Rural Development in Mexico' in Randall, *Changing Structure of Mexico*, p. 331.
117 Ibid., p. 337.
118 Details of the tensions between international trade law and Multilateral Environmental Agreements are examined in Chapter 8.
119 Housman, 'The North American Free Trade Agreement's Lessons for Reconciling Trade and the Environment', 394.
120 NAFTA, Article 104.1.
121 Housman, 'The North American Free Trade Agreement's Lessons for Reconciling Trade and the Environment', 409.
122 Schatan, 'Lessons from the Mexican Environmental Experience', 185.
123 Kublicki, 'The Greening of Free Trade', 65.
124 Ibid, 66–7.

7 Regional approaches to free trade and sustainable development: the Asia-Pacific economic cooperation

1 *Seoul APEC Ministerial Declaration*, 14 November 1991. Online. Available HTTP: <http://www.apecsec.org.sg/apec/ministerial_statements/annual_ministerial/1991_3th_apec_ministerial/annex_b___seoul_apec.html> (accessed 22 June 2005).

2 *APEC Economic Leaders' Declaration of Common Resolve* ('*Bogor Declaration*'), Bogor, Indonesia, 15 November 1994. Online. Available HTTP: <http://www.apecsec.org.sg/apec/leaders__declarations/1994.html> (accessed 22 June 2005).
3 Ibid.
4 Ibid.
5 See J. Hunter, 'APEC: Promise or Peril in the Asia Pacific', *Ecological Economics Bulletin* 2:3, 1997. Online. Available HTTP: <http://www.nautilus.org/archives/papers/enviro/hunter_apec.html#II> (accessed 22 June 2005).
6 Ibid.
7 Hunter, 'APEC: Promise or Peril in the Asia Pacific'.
8 Ibid.
9 'The implementation of IAP by each member within a given time frame is viewed as a concerted unilateralism.' See M.R. Islam, *International Trade Law*, Sydney: LBC Information Services, 1999, p. 143.
10 L. Zarsky and J. Hunter, 'Environmental Co-operation at APEC: The First Five Years', Nautilus Institute. Online. Available HTTP: <http://www.nautilus.org/archives/papers/enviro/TEPP/zarsky_hunterTEPP.html> (accessed 22 June 2005).
11 APEC, *Committee on Trade and Investment*. Online. Available HTTP: <http://www.apec.org/apec/apec_groups/committees/committee_on_trade.html> (accessed 22 June 2005).
12 APEC, *Economic Committee*. Online. Available HTTP:<http://www.apec.org/apec/apec_groups/committees/economic_committee.html> (accessed 22 June 2005).
13 Zarsky and Hunter, *Environmental Co-operation at APEC.*
14 Hunter, 'APEC: Promise or Peril in the Asia Pacific'.
15 Ibid.
16 *APEC Leaders' Economic Vision Statement*. Blake Island, Seattle WA, November 1993. Online. Available HTTP: <http://www.apec.org/apec/leaders__declarations/1993.html> (accessed 22 June 2005).
17 The *Bogor Declaration*, Article 8, emphasis added.
18 Ibid.
19 *APEC Environment Ministerial Meeting on Sustainable Development*, Vancouver, Canada, March 1994. Online. Available HTTP: <http://www.apecsec.org.sg/apec/ministerial_statements/sectoral_ministerial/environment/1994_environment.html> (accessed 22 June 2005).
20 *APEC Environmental Vision Statement*. Online. Available HTTP: <www.iie.com/publications/chapters_preview/37/aiie2504.pdf> (accessed 22 June 2005).
21 Ibid.
22 *Rio Declaration on Environment and Development*, 14 June 1992, UN Doc. A/CONF.151/5/Rev.1 (1992).
23 APEC Ministers responsible for the Environment, *Framework of Principles for Integrating Economy and Environment in APEC*, Vancouver, British Columbia, 1994. Online. Available HTTP: <http://www.iisd.org/sd/principle.asp?pid=88&display=1> (accessed 22 June 2005).
24 G. Maggio, 'Inter/Intra-generational Equity: Current Applications under International Law for Promoting the Sustainable Development of Natural Resources', *Buffalo Environmental Law Journal* 4, 1997, 206.
25 Joint Working Party on Trade and Environment, *The Polluter Pays Principle as it Relates to International Trade*, 2001, OECD Doc. COM/ENV/TD (2001) 44/Final, pp. 11–15. Online. Available HTTP: <http://www.olis.oecd.org/olis/2001doc.nsf/linkto/com-env-td(2001)44-final> (accessed 22 June 2005).
26 *Agenda 21: Programme of Action for Sustainable Development*, UN GAOR, 46th Session, Agenda item 21, UN Doc. A/Conf.151/26 (1992). Online. Available HTTP:

<http://www.un.org/esa/sustdev/documents/agenda21/english/agenda21toc.htm> (accessed 15 February 2007).

27 *European Communities – Measures Concerning Meat and Meat Products (Hormones)* WTO Doc. WT/DS26/ARB 12 July 1999.

28 For example, under the WTO measures taken by countries to control exploitation of their natural resources may violate Article XI of the *General Agreement on Tariffs and Trade* (1994). See for details OECD, *Analysis of Non-tariff Measures: the Case for Export Restrictions*, 4 April 2003, OECD Doc. TD/TC/WP (2003)7/Final.

29 *APEC Economic Leaders' Declaration for Action*, Osaka, Japan, 19 November 1995. Online. Available HTTP: <http://www.apec.org/apec/leaders__declarations/1995.html> (accessed 22 June 2005).

30 *APEC Economic Leaders' Declaration: Connecting the APEC Community*, Vancouver, Canada, 25 November 1997. Online. Available HTTP: <http://www.apec.org/apec/leaders__declarations/1997.html> (accessed 22 June 2005).

31 *APEC Leaders Declarations: Strengthening the Foundation for Growth*, Kuala Lumpur, Malaysia, 18 November 1998. Online. Available HTTP: <http://www.apecsec.org.sg/apec/leaders__declarations/1998.html> (accessed 22 June 2005).

32 *APEC Joint Ministerial Statement*, Santiago, Chile, 17–18 November 2004. Online. Available HTTP: <http://www.apec.org/apec/ministerial_statements/annual_ministerial/2004_16th_apec_ministerial.html> (accessed 22 June 2005).

33 APEC, 'New APEC Fund for Supporting Capacity Building Approved' (press release, 2 June 2005). Online. Available HTTP: <http://www.apec.org/apec/news___media/media_releases/030605_supportfund.html> (accessed 22 June 2005).

34 L. Zarsky, 'APEC, Citizen Groups and the Environment', Berkeley CA: Nautilus Institute, May 1995, p. 11. Online. Available HTTP: <http://nautilus.org/archives/papers/enviro/apecenv.html> (accessed 22 June 2005).

35 Twenty-eighth Industrial Science and Technology Working Group, 'APEC Climate Centre for Climate Information', 2005/ISTWG/009. Online. Available HTTP: <http://www.apec.org/apec/documents_reports/industrial_science_technology_working_group/2005.MedialibDownload.v1.html?url=/etc/medialib/apec_media_library/downloads/workinggroups/istwg/mtg/2005/pdf.Par.0004.File.v1.1> (accessed 13 January 2007).

36 Thirty-first Industrial Science and Technology Working Group, 'Progress Report – APEC Climate Centre'. Online. Available HTTP: <http://www.apec.org/apec/documents_reports/industrial_science_technology_working_group/2006.MedialibDownload.v1.html?url=/etc/medialib/apec_media_library/downloads/workinggroups/istwg/mtg/2006/word.Par.0014.File.v1.1> (accessed 13 January 2007).

37 High Level Meeting on Sustainable Development, 'Sustainable Development in APEC: From 1996 to 2006 – Time for Assessment and Some Recommendations', 2006. Online. Available HTTP: <http://www.apec.org/apec/documents_reports/sustainable_development/2006.MedialibDownload.v1.html?url=/etc/medialib/apec_media_library/downloads/otherfora_initiatives/sustdev/mtg/2006/word.Par.0004.File.v1.1 > (accessed 13 January 2007).

38 High Level Meeting on Sustainable Development, 'Conclusions and Recommendations – High Level Meeting on Sustainable Development', 2006. Online. Available HTTP: <http://www.apec.org/apec/documents_reports/sustainable_development/2006.MedialibDownload.v1.html?url=/etc/medialib/apec_media_library/downloads/otherfora_initiatives/sustdev/mtg/2006/word.Par.0007.File.v1.1> (accessed 13 January 2007).

39 Ibid.

40 M.J. Spalding, 'Lessons of NAFTA for APEC', *Journal of Environment and Development* 6:3, 1997, 253.

41 Zarsky and Hunter, *Environmental Co-operation at APEC.*

42 The *Bogor Declaration*, Article 6.
43 See P. Keating, 'Australia, Asia and the New Regionalism', lecture presented at the Institute of Southeast Asian Studies, Singapore, 17 January 1996. Cited in C. See and J.B. Williams, 'APEC and the Environment: is Free Trade Sustainable?', *Current Affairs Bulletin* 73:6, 1997, 23.
44 B. Nagara, 'The Trade–Environment Nexus: Whence, Wither, Why and Wherefore', paper presented at the Nautilus Institute Workshop on *Trade and Environment in Asia-Pacific: Prospects for Regional Cooperation*, East–West Center, Honolulu, 23–25 September 1994. Online. Available HTTP: <http://www.nautilus.org/archives/papers/enviro/trade/wwww.html> (accessed 22 June 2005).
45 Ibid.
46 Ibid.
47 *APEC Environment Ministerial Meeting on Sustainable Development*, Article 34.
48 Zarsky and Hunter, *Environmental Co-operation at APEC.*
49 Ibid.
50 D.C. Esty, 'Trade and Environment in APEC', Global Environment and Trade Study, 1998. Online. Available HTTP: <http://www.gets.org/gets/library/admin/uploadedfiles/showfile.cfm?FileName=Trade_and_Environment_in_APEC.htm> (accessed 22 June 2005).
51 Ibid.
52 Islam, *International Trade Law*, p. 151.
53 Ibid.
54 J. McDonald, 'APEC and ESD: Turning Sustained Economic Growth into Ecologically Sustainable Development' in P. Leadbeter, N. Gunningham and B. Boer (eds), *Environmental Outlook No. 3, Law and Policy*, Sydney: Federation Press, 2000, p. 91.
55 Ibid.
56 Islam, *International Trade Law*, p. 149
57 J. Atkinson, 'APEC: Winners and Losers', Australian Council for Overseas Aid, Development Dossier 34, 1995, p. 89.
58 See Zarsky and Hunter, *Environmental Co-operation at APEC.*
59 APEC–WTO Capacity Building Group, *APEC Environmental Impact Assessment Workshop*, 2004/SOMIII/WCBG/004. Online. Available HTTP: <http://www.apec.org/apec/documents_reports/wto_capacity_building_group/2004.html> (accessed 22 June 2005).
60 Ibid.
61 Spalding, 'Lessons of NAFTA for APEC'.
62 B. Coote, *NAFTA Poverty and Free Trade in Mexico*, Oxford: Oxfam Publications, 1995, p. 13.
63 For a detailed discussion of this issue, see R. Jha, 'Alleviating Environmental Degradation in the Asia-Pacific Region: International Co-operation and the Role of Issue-linkage', February 2005. Online. Available HTTP: <http://ssrn.com/abstract=677881> (accessed 27 April 2007).
64 Asia-Pacific Economic Cooperation Forum, *Achieving the APEC Vision, Second Report of the Eminent Persons Group*, Singapore, August 1994, p. 20. Online. Available HTTP: <http://www.apecsec.org.sg/apec/ministerial_statements/annual_ministerial/1994_6th_apec_ministerial.html#second> (accessed 16 April 2007).
65 J. Drake-Brockman and K. Anderson, 'The Entwining of Trade and Policy in Environmental Issues: Implications for APEC', paper presented at the Nautilus Institute Workshop on *Trade and Environment in Asia-Pacific: Prospects for Regional Cooperation*, East–West Center, Honolulu, 23–5 September 1994.
66 Zarsky, 'APEC, Citizen Groups and the Environment'.
67 Ibid., 7.

68 This is implicitly recognized in Principle 7 of the *Rio Declaration*, which states that 'in view of the different contributions to global environmental degradation, States have common but differentiated responsibilities'.

69 L. Zarsky, 'APEC, Globalization and the "Sustainable Development Agenda" ', Draft Text for Asian Perspectives, Nautilus Institute Publications, October 1998, p. 2. Online. Available HTTP: <http://www.nautilus.org/archives/papers/enviro/zarsky_apec98.html> (accessed 16 April 2007).

70 Ibid., p. 2.

71 Esty, 'Trade and Environment in APEC'.

72 Zarsky, 'APEC, Globalization and the "Sustainable Development Agenda" ', p. 2.

73 Atkinson, 'APEC: Winners and Losers', p. 75.

74 Zarsky, 'APEC, Globalization and the "Sustainable Development Agenda" ', p. 2.

8 Trade restrictions pursuant to multilateral environmental agreements

I would like to acknowledge the following source for granting copyright permission to reproduce my earlier work, 'Trade Restrictions Pursuant to Multilateral Environmental Agreements: Developmental Implications for Developing Countries', with substantial revision: *Journal of World Trade* 41:5 (2007).

1 U. Hoffmann, 'Specific Trade Obligations in Multilateral Environmental Agreements and their Relationship with the Rules of the Multilateral Trading System: A Developing Country Perspective' in UNCTAD, *Trade and Environment Review 2003*, New York and Geneva: United Nations, 2004, UN Doc. UNCTAD/DITC/TED/2003/4, p. 1. Online. Available HTTP: <http://r0.unctad.org/trade_env/TER> (accessed 21 April 2007).

2 United Nations Environment Programme, *Register of International Treaties and Other Agreements in the Field of Environment*, Nairobi: UNEP, 1999; WTO, *Matrix on Trade Measures Pursuant to Selected MEAs*, 2001, WTO Doc. WT/CTE/W/160/Rev.1, p. 55.

3 Hoffmann, 'Specific Trade Obligations in Multilateral Environmental Agreements and their Relationship with the Rules of the Multilateral Trading System'.

4 Opened for signature 3 March 1973, 993 UNTS 243, entered into force 1 July 1975.

5 Opened for signature 16 September 1987, 26 ILM 1550, entered into force 1 January 1989.

6 Opened for signature 22 March 1989, 1673 UNTS 126, entered into force 5 May 1992.

7 Opened for signature 5 June 1992, 1760 UNTS 79, entered into force 29 December 1993.

8 Opened for signature 9 May 1992, 1771 UNTS 107, entered into force 21 March 1994.

9 Opened for signature 10 September 1998, 38 ILM 1, entered into force 24 February 2004.

10 Opened for signature 29 January 2000, 39 ILM 1027, entered into force 11 September 2003. This agreement is the first to deal with modern biotechnology. It is primarily concerned with the trade in agricultural commodities produced using modern biotechnology, establishing the framework of rules for limiting their importation. The potential for protectionist influences as well as the lack of ratification by many major producers and exporters of such crops may signal a credibility problem for this MEA, although it is too early to make a conclusive judgement. Protectionist concerns could be partly based on the inclusion of the 'precautionary principle' in the Protocol which has been controversial and is not yet fully developed. Article 26 permits socio-economic considerations to be taken into account in decision making, especially with regard to the value of biodiversity to indigenous and local

communities. This is qualified, however, by a requirement that such decisions are consistent with international obligations, which leaves some ambiguity around conflicting obligations.

11 Opened for signature 22 May 2001, 40 ILM 532, entered into force 17 May 2004.

12 E. Neumayer, 'Multilateral Environmental Agreements, Trade and Development: Issues and Policy Options Concerning Compliance and Enforcement', A Report for the Consumer Unity and Trust Society, Jaipur, India, funded by the Department for International Development, London, 2002, p. 12. Online. Available HTTP: <www.lse.ac.uk/collections/geographyAndEnvironment/whosWho/profiles/neumayer/pdf/CUTS.pdf> (accessed 21 April 2007).

13 V. Jha and U. Hoffmann, *Achieving Objectives of Multilateral Environmental Agreements: A Package of Trade Measures and Positive Measures*, 2000, UN Doc. UNCTAD/ITCD/TED/6, p. 11.

14 C. Osakwe, 'Finding New Packages of Acceptable Combinations of Trade and Positive Measures to Improve the Effectiveness of MEAs: A General Framework' in A. Fijalkowski and J. Cameron (eds), *Trade and the Environment: Bridging the Gap*, Great Britain: Cameron May, 1998, p. 48.

15 R.G. Tarasofsky, 'Ensuring Compatibility between Multilateral Environmental Agreements and GATT/WTO', *Yearbook of International Environmental Law* 7, 1996, 56.

16 A. Naghavi, 'Multilateral Environmental Agreements and Trade Obligations: A Theoretical Analysis of the Doha Proposal', *The Fondazione Eni Enrico Mattei Note di Lavoro Series Index*, 2005. Online. Available HTTP: <http://www.feem.it/Feem/Pub/Publications/WPapers/default.htm> (accessed 21 April 2007).

17 Jha and Hoffman, *Achieving Objectives of Multilateral Environmental Agreements*, p. 11.

18 OECD, *Trade Measures in Multilateral Environmental Agreements*, Paris: OECD, 1999, p. 41; W.B. Chambers, 'Towards an Improved Understanding of Legal Effectiveness of International Environmental Treaties', *Georgetown International Environmental Law Rev*iew 16, 2004, 501.

19 Sachiko, Morita and Durwood, Zaelke, 'A Review of Empirical Studies on Environmental Compliance', *Seventh International Conference on Environmental Compliance and Enforcement*, 2006. Online. Available HTTP: <http://www.inece.org/conference/7/vol1/19_Morita_Zaelke.pdf> (accessed 21 April 2007); J. Werksman, *Five MEA's, Five Years Since Rio: Recent Lessons on the Effectiveness of Multilateral Environmental Agreements*, Rio+5 Special Focus Report prepared by Foundation for International Environmental Law & Development ('FIELD'), 1997.

20 United Nations University and the South Pacific Regional Environment Programme, *Inter-linkages: Synergies and Coordination among Multilateral Environmental Agreements: Case Study Pacific Island Countries*, 2002. Online. Available HTTP: <http://geic.hq.unu.edu/env/project1.cfm?type=1&ID=254> (accessed 21 April 2007).

21 E. Petroka and K.A. Baumert, 'Making Joint Implementation Work: Lessons from Central and Eastern Europe', World Resources Institute, Climate Energy and Pollution Program, *Climate Notes*, November 2000, p. 2.

22 T. Swanson and S. Johnston, *Global Environmental Problems and International Environmental Agreements: the Economics of Institution Building*, Cheltenham: Edward Elgar, published in association with UNCTAD, 1999, p. 106.

23 Ibid., p. 162.

24 M. Rolen, H. Sjoberg and U. Svedin (eds), *International Governance on Environmental Issues*, Dordrecht: Kluwer, 1997, p. 13.

25 J. Cameron, J. Werksman and P. Roderick (eds), *Improving Compliance with International Environmental Law*, London: Earthscan, 1996, p. 49.

26 R.B. Mitchell, 'Compliance Theory: An Overview', in J. Cameron, J. Werksman and P. Roderick (eds), *Improving Compliance with International Environmental Law*, London: Earthscan, 1996, pp. 3–28; cited in Neumayer, 'Multilateral Environmental Agreements, Trade and Development', 15.
27 R.J. Herring and E. Bharucha, 'India: Embedded Capacities', in Edith Brown Weiss and Harold K. Jacobson (eds), *Engaging Countries: Strengthening Compliance with International Environmental Accords*, Cambridge MA: MIT Press, 2000, p. 409.
28 Neumayer, 'Multilateral Environmental Agreements, Trade and Development', pp. 35 and 52.
29 Ibid., 27.
30 E.B. Weiss and H.K. Jacobson (eds), *Engaging Countries – Strengthening Compliance with International Environmental Accords*, Cambridge MA: MIT Press, 2000, p. 40.
31 C. Barton *et al.*, 'Civil Society Perspectives on the *Millennium Development Goals*', *United Nations Development Program*. Online. Available HTTP: <www.undp.org/cso/resource/CSO_perspectives/CSO%20perspectives%20on%20the%20MDGs%20FINAL.doc> (accessed 21 April 2007). See Chapter 2 for details on the Millennium Development Goals.
32 WTO, *Report of the WTO Committee on Trade and Environment*, 1996, WTO Doc. PRESS/TE 014, para. 110. Online. Available HTTP: <http://www.ictsd.org/ministerial/singapore/envtracom.htm> (accessed 21 April 2007).
33 OECD, *Trade Measures in Multilateral Environmental Agreements*, p. 10.
34 CITES, Article IX.
35 Ibid., Article IX.
36 Ibid., Article II, para. 2.
37 OECD, *Trade Measures in Multilateral Environmental Agreements*, p. 24.
38 CITES, Article IV.2.
39 Ibid., Article IV.3.
40 Ibid., Article II, para. 3.
41 Ibid., Article VIII.
42 Ibid., Article XIV para. 1(a) (b).
43 OECD, *Trade Measures in Multilateral Environmental Agreements*, p. 13.
44 Jha and Hoffman, *Achieving Objectives of Multilateral Environmental Agreements*; European Commission Directorate General for the Environment, *1997–2002. Five Years of New Wildlife Trade Regulations: The European Union's Contribution to Sustainable Trade and Species Conservation*, Luxembourg: Office for Official Publications of the European Communities, 2002, p. 33.
45 T. Swanson, 'International Regulation for Environmental Protection: Learning From CITES', *Economic Affairs*, 11, winter 1996.
46 Jha and Hoffmann, *Achieving Objectives of Multilateral Environmental Agreements*, p. 13; Swanson and Johnston, *Global Environmental Problems and International Environmental Agreements*, p. 178.
47 I. Arroyo-Quiroz, R.Perez-Gil and N. Leader-Williams, 'Developing Countries and the Implementation of CITES: The Mexican Experience', *Journal of International Wildlife Law and Policy* 8, 2005, 47.
48 Jha and Hoffman, *Achieving Objectives of Multilateral Environmental Agreements*.
49 Ibid., p. 76.
50 Ibid.
51 IIED and TRAFFIC, 'Making a Killing or Making a Living? Wildlife Trade, Trade Controls and Rural Livelihoods, Biodiversity and Livelihoods', *Issues* No. 6, 2002. Available HTTP: <http://www.traffic.org/livelihoods/> (accessed 22 April 2007).
52 Jha and Hoffman, *Achieving Objectives of Multilateral Environmental Agreements*, p. 76.

53 OECD, *Trade Measures in Multilateral Environmental Agreements*, pp. 33–4.
54 Jha and Hoffman, *Achieving Objectives of Multilateral Environmental Agreements*, p. 82.
55 Ibid., p. 90.
56 World Bank Report, *Indonesia Country Strategic Paper 2002–2006*, Washington DC: World Bank, 2001, p. 13. Online. Available HTTP: <http://www.eu.int/comm/external_relations/indonesia/csp/02_06_en.pdf> (accessed 22 April 2007).
57 Ibid.
58 R. Hofrichter (ed.), *Toxic Struggles: The Theory and Practice of Environmental Justice*, Salt Lake City UT: University of Utah Press, 2002, p. 188.
59 Jha and Hoffman, *Achieving Objectives of Multilateral Environmental Agreements*, p. 81.
60 Ibid., p. 91.
61 C. Chanrithy, 'Findings of the Country case study: National Policy Co-ordination in Cambodia for Implementing and Further Developing the Basel Convention, Convention on International Trade in Endangered Species, Convention on Biological Diversity, and Montreal Protocol', *National Training Workshop in Enhancing Policy Co-ordination on Trade and Environmental Issues: Implementation of Multilateral Environmental Agreements Containing Trade-related Measures*, 2004, p. 3.
62 OECD, *Trade Measures in Multilateral Environmental Agreements*, p. 44.
63 OECD, *Experience with the Use of Trade Measures in the Convention on International Trade in Endangered Species of Wild Fauna and Flora (CITES)*, OECD Doc. OCDE/GD(97)106, 1997. Online. Available HTTP: <http://www.oecd.org/ech/tradedoc.htm/> (accessed 22 April 2007).
64 Ibid.
65 Ibid., p. 33.
66 C. de Klemm, *Guidelines for Legislation to Implement CITES*, IUCN Environmental Policy and Law Paper No. 26, 1993.
67 For example, tigers in Resolution Conf. 9.13, or the GEF in particular (e.g. Resolution Conf. 9.14 on conservation of rhinoceros in Asia and Africa – see OECD, *Trade Measures in Multilateral Environmental Agreements*, p. 37).
68 The GEF has provided grants for more than 1,300 in 140 countries to a total value of US$4.5 billion since 1991. See details, online. Available HTTP: <http://www.thegef.org/What_is_the_GEF/what_is_the_gef.html> (accessed 22 April 2007).
69 They are the *Convention on Biological Diversity*, the *United Nations Framework Convention on Climate Change*, the *United Nations Convention to Combat Desertification* and the *Stockholm Convention on Persistent Organic Pollutants.* While the GEF is not the financial mechanism for the *Montreal Protocol per se*, its operational policies concerning ozone layer depletion are consistent with those of the *Montreal Protocol*. Online. Available HTTP: <http://www.gefweb.org/public/opstrat/fw.htm> (accessed 22 April 2007).
70 J. Gupta, 'The Global Environment Facility in its North–South Context', *Environmental Politics* 4:1, 1995, 19–43.
71 O. Tickell and N. Hildyard, 'Green Dollars, Green Menace', *The Ecologist* 22:3, 1992, 82, cited in M.A.L. Miller, *The Third World in Global Environmental Politics*, Buckingham: Open University Press, 1995, p. 140.
72 Miller, *The Third World in Global Environmental Politics*, p. 141.
73 OECD, *Experience with the Use of Trade Measures in the Convention on International Trade in Endangered Species of Wild Fauna and Flora*, p. 50. Eighty-six per cent and 82 per cent, respectively, of respondents gave a high ranking to 'training and other activities' and 'special projects' as to priority for increased funding. Eighty-eight per cent of respondents answered in the affirmative to whether an international plan should be drawn up to identify and mobilize additional revenues. 95

per cent of replies supported more use being made of the GEF for CITES-related activities.

74 I.H. Rowlands, 'The Fourth Meeting of the Parties to the Montreal Protocol: Report and Reflection', *Environment* 35:6, 1993, 25–34. Online. Available HTTP: <http://www.ciesin.org/docs/003–077/003–077.html> (accessed 22 April 2007).
75 OECD, *Experience with the Use of Trade Measures in the Convention on International Trade in Endangered Species of Wild Fauna and Flora*, p. 39.
76 Ibid.
77 *Montreal Protocol*, Article 4.
78 Ibid., Article 4.1.
79 Ibid., Article 4.2.
80 Ibid., Article 2.
81 Ibid., Article 4.8.
82 Ibid., Article 4.3.
83 Ibid., Article 4.4.
84 This article was adopted in 1997. It would appear that the requirement to license was fully in force in 2000.
85 *Montreal Protocol*, Article 4.5.
86 Ibid., Article 4.6.
87 Ibid., Article 4.7.
88 Ibid., Article 5.5.
89 OECD, *Trade Measures in Multilateral Environmental Agreements*, p. 29.
90 *Montreal Protocol*, Article 10.
91 An Article 5 country is '[a]ny party that is a developing country and whose annual calculated level of consumption of the controlled substances in Annex A is less than 0.3 kilograms per capita on the date of the entry into force of the Protocol for it, or at any time thereafter until 1 January 1999'.
92 OECD, *Experience with the Use of Trade Measures in the Montreal Protocol on Substances that Deplete the Ozone Layer*, 1997, OECD Doc. OCDE/GD(97)230, p. 15.
93 UNEP, 'Assessment of the Funding Requirement for the Replenishment of the Multilateral Fund for the Period 2006–2008', *Montreal Protocol on Substances that Deplete the Ozone Layer Report of the UNEP Technology And Economic Assessment Panel* II, May 2005. Online. Available HTTP: <http://www.unep.org/ozone/teap/Reports/teap-rtf-report-may2005.pdf> (accessed 22 April 2007).
94 OECD, *Trade Measures in Multilateral Environmental Agreements*, p. 21.
95 *Montreal Protocol*, Article 10A.
96 M. Khor, *IPRS Blocking Access to Eco-friendly Technology*, 1996. Online. Available HTTP: <http://www.sunsonline.org/trade/areas/services/08050196.htm> (accessed 22 April 2007).
97 OECD, *Experience with the Use of Trade Measures in the Montreal Protocol on Substances that Deplete the Ozone Layer*, p. 17.
98 Ibid., p. 34.
99 *Montreal Protocol*, Article 5.5.
100 Z.A. Sanusi, 'Technology Transfer under Multilateral Environmental Agreements: Analyzing the Synergies', UNU-IAS Working Paper No. 134, 2005, 4; U. Hoffmann, 'An Analysis of Effective Operationalization of Provisions on Transfer of Environmentally Sound Technologies to Developing Countries in Multilateral Environmental Agreements, Pursuant to Agenda 21', *Strengthening Research And Policy-making Capacity on Trade and Environment in Developing Countries* Second Workshop, 1999, p. 5; E. Puustjärvi, M. Katila and M. Simula, 'Transfer of Environmentally Sound Technologies from Developed Countries to Developing Countries', *Background Document for the Ad Hoc Expert Group on Finance and*

Environmentally Sound Technologies. The Secretariat of the United Nations Forum on Forests Prepared by INDUFOR, 2004, p. 6; see also Chapter 34 *Agenda 21*, UN Doc. A/CONF.151/26/Rev.1 (1992), ESTs are not just 'individual technologies, but total systems which include know-how, procedures, goods and services, and equipment as well as organizational and managerial procedures'.

101 OECD, *Trade Measures in Multilateral Environmental Agreements*, p. 68.

102 Neumayer, 'Multilateral Environmental Agreements, Trade and Development', p. 35.

103 J. Zhao, 'Implementing International Environmental Treaties in Developing Countries: China's Compliance with the Montreal Protocol', *Global Environmental Politics* 5:1, 2005, 71.

104 Sanusi, 'Technology Transfer under Multilateral Environmental Agreements', 2.

105 Hoffmann, 'An Analysis of Effective Operationalization of Provisions on Transfer of Environmentally Sound Technologies to Developing Countries in Multilateral Environmental Agreements', p. 5.

106 P. Roffe and T. Tesfachew, 'Revisiting the Technology Transfer Debate: Lessons for the New WTO Working Group', *Bridges Between Trade and Sustainable Development*, International Centre for Trade and Sustainable Development, Year 6, Vol. 2, 2002, p. 12.

107 *Montreal Protocol*, Article 10.1.

108 Hoffmann, 'An Analysis of Effective Operationalization of Provisions on Transfer of Environmentally Sound Technologies to Developing Countries in Multilateral Environmental Agreements', p. 7.

109 Ibid.

110 A. Damodaran, *Implications of International Conventions and Opportunities for Transfer of Environmentally Sound Technologies to Developing Countries*, Bangalore: Indian Institute of Plantation Management, 2002, p. 107. Online. Available HTTP: <http://www.unescap.org/tid/publication/Chap3b_2127.pdf> (accessed 22 April 2007).

111 Jha and Hoffman, *Achieving Objectives of Multilateral Environmental Agreements*, p. 11. See also Neumayer, 'Multilateral Environmental Agreements, Trade and Development', p. 35.

112 Jha and Hoffman, *Achieving Objectives of Multilateral Environmental Agreements*, p. 15.

113 E. Blaustein and A. Shanker, 'Technology Co-operation in the Environmentally Sound Technologies', Working paper for the Scientific and Technological Options Assessment ('STOA') Panel, Directorate A Division Industry, Research, Energy, Environment and STOA, Luxembourg, PE 297.572/Fin.St. (2001), p. 13.

114 Sanusi, 'Technology Transfer Under Multilateral Environmental Agreements', 6.

115 Damodaran, *Implications of International Conventions and Opportunities for Transfer of Environmentally Sound Technologies to Developing Countries*, p. 107.

116 Ibid., pp. 112 and 14.

117 Ibid., p. 114.

118 Jha and Hoffman, *Achieving Objectives of Multilateral Environmental Agreements*, p. 54.

119 Ibid.

120 Ibid., p. 43.

121 Ibid., p. 39.

122 Ibid.

123 Jha and Hoffman, *Achieving Objectives of Multilateral Environmental Agreements*, p. 56.

124 Ibid., p. 62.

125 Ibid., p. 68.

126 Ibid., p. 67.
127 Ibid., p. 60.
128 Ibid.
129 Zhao, 'Implementing International Environmental Treaties in Developing Countries', 66.
130 Ibid., 71.
131 Ibid.
132 According to Article 2 of the *Basel Convention*, 'Wastes are substances or objects which are disposed of or are intended to be disposed of or are required to be disposed of by the provisions of national law'. Categories of wastes are defined in Annex I and characteristics of hazardous wastes in Annex III of the Convention. A party can also determine what it considers to be hazardous waste in its domestic legislation.
133 *Basel Convention*, Article 1.
134 UNEP Press Release, 27 February 1998; Jonathan Krueger, *The Basel Convention and Transboundary Movements of Hazardous Wastes*, Briefing No. 45, Royal Institute of International Affairs Energy and Environmental Programme, May 1998. Online. Available HTTP: <http://www.ciaonet.org/wps/krj02/#txt6> (accessed 22 April 2007).
135 *Basel Convention*, Preamble, para. 6.
136 *Basel Convention*, Preamble, para. 20.
137 OECD, *Experience with the Use of Trade Measures in the Montreal Protocol on Substances that Deplete the Ozone Layer*, p. 16.
138 *Basel Convention*, Article 6.
139 Second Conference of the Parties to the Basel Convention, *Decision II/12*, adopted at the Second Conference of the Parties to the Basel Convention, Geneva, Switzerland, 25 March 1994. Online. Available HTTP: <http://www.ban.org/about_basel_ban/copsII_12.html> (accessed 22 April 2007).
140 Francis O. Adeola, 'Environmental Injustice and Human Rights Abuse: The States, MNCs, and Repression of Minority Groups in the World System', *Human Ecology Review* 8:1, 2001, 45.
141 OECD, *Trade Measures in the Basel Convention on the Control of Transboundary Movements of Hazardous Wastes and their Disposal*, OECD Doc. COM/ENV/TD (97) 41/FINAL, 1997, p. 10. Online. Available HTTP: <http://www1.oecd.org/ech/docs/envi.htm> (accessed 22 April 2007).
142 Ibid.
143 M. Shultz, 'Trading Waste: Environmental Transfers between Nations', *Harvard International Review* 21, summer 1999, 11.
144 R. Anand, *International Environmental Justice: A North–South Dimension*, Aldershot: Ashgate, 2004, p. 63.
145 *Basel Convention*, Article 4.5.
146 Ibid., Article 11.
147 Ibid., Article 4.8.
148 Ibid., Article 8.
149 Ibid., Article 4.10.
150 Ibid., Article 4.7.
151 D. Hunter, J. Salzman and D. Zaelke (eds), 'Hazardous Wastes and Materials', *International Environmental Law and Policy*, New York: Foundation Press, 2002, p. 847.
152 E.B. Ristroph, 'How Can the US Correct Multinational Corporations' Environmental Abuses Committed in the Name of Trade?' *Indiana International and Comparative Law Review* 15, 2004–5, 52.
153 M. Cusack, 'International Law and the Transboundary Shipment of Hazardous

Waste to the Third World: Will the Basel Convention Make a Difference?', *American University Journal of International and Policy* 5, 1990, 420.

154 J. Pluckett, 'The Basel Plan: A Triumph over Business as Usual', *Basel Action Network*, 1997. Online. Available HTTP: <http://www.ban.org/about_basel_ban/jims_article.htm> (accessed 23 April 2007).

155 Ibid., pp. 420–2, cited in Hunter *et al.*, *International Environmental Law and Policy*, p. 851.

156 Ibid.

157 OECD, *Experience with the Use of Trade Measures in the Montreal Protocol on Substances that Deplete the Ozone Layer*, p. 26.

158 Hunter *et al.*, *International Environmental Law and Policy*, p. 859.

159 *Bamako Convention on the Ban on the Import into Africa and the Control of Transboundary Movement and Management of Hazardous Wastes within Africa ('Bamako Convention')*, Organization of African Unity, adopted 30 January 1991, Bamako, Mali.

160 K. Gray, 'Multilateral Environmental Agreements in Africa: Efforts and Problems in Implementation', *International Environmental Agreements: Politics, Law and Economics* 3, 2003, 121.

161 *Bamako Convention*, Article 4(3)(d).

162 Ibid., Article 4(3)(b).

163 Ibid., Article 6 (6).

164 Ibid., Article 10.

165 E.C. Eguh, 'The Bamako Convention and the First Meeting of the Parties: A Glance at Implementation Strategies', *RECIEL* 7:3, 2000, 257.

166 Ibid., 262.

167 Adelphi Consult, Friends of the Earth Europe and Greenpeace, 'Is the WTO the Only Way? Safeguarding Multilateral Environmental Agreements from International Trade Rules and Settling Trade and Environment Disputes outside the WTO', Briefing Paper, 2005, p. 7. Online. Available HTTP: <http://www.foeeurope.org/publications/2005/alternatives_wto.pdf> (accessed 23 April 2007).

168 M. Knigge, 'Report on Trade and Multilateral Environmental Agreements', *Concerted Action on Trade and Environment*, sponsored by the European Commission, Research Directorate General, under Contract No. EVK2-CT-2002-20017 CAT&E, 2005, p. 4. Online. Available HTTP: <http://www.ecologic.de/download/projekte/1800–1849/1800/3_1800_cate_meas.pdf> (accessed 23 April 2007); 'The Relationship between Existing WTO Rules and Specific Trade Obligations Set Out in Multilateral Environmental Agreements (MEAs)', Japan's paper TN/TE/W/10, 3 October 2002.

169 W.A. Kerr, 'Who Should Make the Rules of Trade? The Complex Issue of Multilateral Environmental Agreements', *The Estey Centre Journal of International Law and Trade Policy* 3:2, 2002, 163–75.

170 K.R. Gray, 'Accommodating MEAs in Trade Agreements', paper presented at the *International Environmental Governance Conference*, Paris, 15–16 March 2004. Online. Available HTTP: <http://www.iddri.org/iddri/telecharge/gie/communications/4e_gray.pdf> (accessed 23 April 2007).

171 Center for International Environmental Law, 'Clarifying the Relationship between Economic and Environmental Governance: Some Key Challenges', Center for International Environmental Law Issue Brief for the World Summit on Sustainable Development, 26 August–4 September 2002. Online. Available HTTP: <http://www.iucn.org/themes/pbia/themes/trade/training/Clarify%20Relationship%20Economic%20and%20Env%20Governance.pdf> (accessed 23 April 2007).

172 *Agenda 21*, Chapter 2.22(j).

173 *Rio Declaration on Environment and Development*, Principle 12, UN Doc. A/CONF.151/5/Rev.1 (1992).

174 *Agenda 21*, Chapter 2.20.

175 WTO, *Report of the WTO Committee on Trade and Environment*, para. 101.

176 Empirical studies suggest that approximately one-third of the exports of developing countries originate in sectors covered in MEAs: see '"MEAs Should Use Positive Measures" says UNCTAD', 1995. Online. Available HTTP: <http://www.sunsonline.org/trade/areas/environm/11070095.htm> (accessed 23 April 2007). The result is that the cost of the implementation of MEAs is imposed on a greater proportion of developing countries' industries, as compared with developed countries. Examples of essential developing country industries covered by MEAs include fishery products, textiles and clothing, leather and footwear, tea, timber and timber products (see UNCTAD, *Train for Trade 2000: Environmental Requirements and Market Access – Module 3*, 2001. Online. Available HTTP: <r0.unctad.org/trade_env/rene/mod3entext.doc> (accessed 23 April 2007)).

177 See A. Oxley, K. Osborne and L. Marty, *European Unilateralism: Environmental Trade Barriers and the Rising Threat to Prosperity through Trade*, Melbourne: Australian APEC Study Centre, Monash University, 2003, p. 5. Online. Available HTTP: <http://www.apec.org.au/docs/tradebarriers2003.pdf> (accessed 23 April 2007).

178 R. Paris, 'Capacity Building, and Multilateral Environmental Agreements, Development Co-operation Directorate'. Online. Available HTTP: <http://www.geic.or.jp/interlinkages/docs/oecd.PDF> (accessed 23 April 2007); UNEP, 'Developing Responses to Factors Inhibiting Implementation and Enforcement of Multilateral Environment Agreements', *High-Level Meeting Envisioning the Next Steps for Compliance with and Enforcement of Multilateral Environmental Agreements*, 2006. Online. Available HTTP: <http://www.unep.org/DEC/Events/mdg_meeting_col.asp> (accessed 23 April 2007).

179 N. McCulloch, A.L. Winters and X. Cirera, *Trade Liberalization and Poverty: A Handbook*, London: Centre for Economic Policy Research, 2002, p. 321. Online. Available HTTP: <http://www.ids.ac.uk/ids/global/pdfs/tlpov.pdf> (accessed 23 April 2007).

180 World Trade Organization, *CTE: Trade Measures in MEAs (1)*, 2003. Online. Available HTTP: <http://www.wto.org/english/thewto_e/whatis_e/eol/e/wto09/wto9_9.htm> (accessed 23 April 2007).

181 Neumayer, 'Multilateral Environmental Agreements, Trade and Development', p. 12.

182 GATT, Article 1. See discussion of principle in Chapter 3.

183 For details of the trade restrictions see CITES, Appendix I, II, *Basel Convention*, Article. 4(2) (e), *Montreal Protocol*, Article 4.

184 GATT, Article 3.

185 CITES, Article III, Article IV and Article V: Regulation of Trade in Specimens of Species Included in Appendix I-III; see OECD, *Experience with the Use of Trade Measures in the Convention on International Trade in Endangered Species of Wild Fauna and Flora*, 34.

186 Ibid.

187 Ibid., Article XX(g).

188 It is important to acknowledge that there have been some important developments in the WTO Appellate Body's jurisprudence concerning the interaction of the Article XX exceptions with various international environmental law issues. See Chapter 3 for a discussion of these issues.

189 Hunter *et al.*, *International Environmental Law and Policy*, p. 859.

190 Ibid.

191 See for example, *Doha Round Briefing Series* 4, 2005, pp. 34 f. Online. Available HTTP: <http://www.ictsd.org/pubs/dohabriefings/Hong_Kong_Update/9-environment.pdf> (accessed 23 April 2007).
192 K. Heydon, 'After the WTO Hong Kong Ministerial Meeting: What is at Stake?', OECD Trade Policy Working Paper No. 27, 2006.
193 D.C. Esty, 'Greening the GATT: Trade, Environment and the Future', Washington DC: Institute for International Economics, 1994, pp. 9–32; WTO, *Report of the WTO Committee on Trade and Environment*, para. 102; Chris Wold, 'Multilateral Environmental Agreements and the GATT: Conflict and Resolution?' *Environmental Law* 26:3, 1996, 841–921; Erik Beukel, *Multilateralism vs. Unilateralism: The International Political Economy of the Trade/Environment Nexus*, Working Paper No. 22, Vancouver: Institute of International Relations, University of British Columbia, 1998, p. 2.
194 G.P. Sampson and W.B. Chambers (eds), *Trade, Environment, and the Millennium*, 2nd edn, Tokyo: United Nations University Press, 2002, pp. 4–5.
195 M.R. Islam, *International Trade Law*, Sydney: LBC Information Services, 1999, p. 398.
196 It has been estimated that up to half of all environmental protection methods may in fact be disguised protectionism. See L. Fontagne, *Protection(ism): the Environment and the WTO*, Storrs CT: Department of Economics, University of Connecticut, 2001, p. 206. Online. Available HTTP: <http://www.cepii.fr/anglaisgraph/publications/lettre/pdf/2001/206ang.pdf> (accessed 23 April 2007); Sampson and Chambers, *Trade, Environment, and the Millennium*, pp. 4–5.
197 D. Brack, 'Commentaries on Article 1: The Relationship between MEAs and WTO Rules' in UNCTAD, *Trade and Environment Review 2003*, Geneva: United Nations, 2004, UNCTAD Doc. UNCTAD/DITC/TED/2003/4. Online. Available HTTP: <http://r0.unctad.org/trade_env/test1/publications/TER2003eversion/openTERF1.htm> (accessed 23 April 2007).
198 A. Oxley, 'Commentaries on Article 1: The Relationship between MEAs and WTO Rules' in UNCTAD, *Trade and Environment Review 2003*.
199 Islam, *International Trade Law*, p. 409.
200 A. Najam, 'Trade and Environment after Seattle: A Negotiation Agenda for the South', *Journal of Environment and Development* 9:4, 2000, 410.
201 Oxley, 'Commentaries on Article 1', p. 96.
202 E. Weiss and H. Jacobson, 'Getting Countries to Comply with International Agreements', *Environment* 41, July–August 1999, 16.
203 Hoffmann, 'Specific Trade Obligations in Multilateral Environmental Agreements and their Relationship with the Rules of the Multilateral Trading System'.
204 M. Khor, *The Proposed New Issues in the WTO and the Interests of Developing Countries*. Online. Available HTTP: <http://www.twnside.org.sg/title/mk10.htm> (accessed 23 April 2007).
205 P. Uimonen and J. Whalley, *Environmental Issues in the New World Trading System*, London: Macmillan, 1997, p. 63.
206 B. Boyer, 'Institutional Coordination, Multi-stakeholder Participation and the Implementation of MEAS: National Experiences of Thailand and Malaysia', 2001, p. 27. Online. Available HTTP: <http://www.unu.edu/inter-linkages/docs/DiscussionP/2001_03_Brook.pdf> (accessed 23 April 2007).
207 Global Environment Information Centre, *Sri Lanka Case Study on Interlinkages Among Multilateral Environmental Agreements (MEAs): Results of the Questionnaire Survey*, 2004. Online. Available HTTP: <http://geic.hq.unu.edu/ENV/active1.cfm?type=1&ID=535> (accessed 23 April 2007).
208 Global Environment Information Centre, *Pakistan Case Study on Inter-linkages: Synergies and Coordination among Multilateral Environmental Agreements (MEAs)*

Questionnaire Report, 2005. Online. Available HTTP: <http://geic.hq.unu.edu/ENV/active1.cfm?type=1&ID=536> (accessed 23 April 2007).

209 Ibid., p. 19.

210 Ibid., p. 16.

211 Ibid., p. 25.

212 OECD, *Trade Measures in Multilateral Environmental Agreements*, p. 5.

213 R. Vossenaar and V. Jha, 'Implementation of MEAs at the National Level and the Use of Trade and Non Trade Measures: Results of Developing Country Case Studies', in A. Fijalkowski and J. Cameron (eds), *Trade and the Environment: Bridging the Gap*, London: Cameron May, 1998, p. 74.

9 Free trade and sustainable development: challenges ahead

1 L. Elliott, *The Global Politics of the Environment*, London: Macmillan, 1998, p. 249.

2 *Rio Declaration on Environment and Development*, Principle 12, UN Doc. A/CONF.151/5/Rev.1 (1992).

3 *Agenda 21, UN Conference on Environment and Development*, Annex II, UN Doc. A/CONF.151/26/Rev.1 (1992), para. 2.2.

4 See for details Gregory F. Maggio, 'Inter/intra-generational Equity: Current Applications under International Law for Promoting the Sustainable Development of Natural Resources', *Buffalo Environmental Law Journal* 4, 1997, 206.

5 C. Raghavan, 'Third World Takes Unified Position on Environment for Earth Summit', *Third World Network Features*, 1991 (copy on file with author).

6 T. Panayotou, 'Economic Growth and the Environment', Harvard University Center for International Development, Working Paper No. 56, July 2000, 76–7.

7 Ruggiero, speech in Bonn, 7.

8 K. Anderson and J. Drake-Brockman, 'The World Trade Organisation and the Environment', *Environmental Outlook: Law and Policy No 2*, Sydney: Federation Press, 1996, 149.

9 P.A.G. van Bergeijk, 'International Trade and the Environmental Challenge', *Journal of World Trade* 25:6, 1991, 106.

10 M.R. Islam, *International Trade Law*, Sydney: LBC Information Services, 1999, p. 442.

11 *Agenda 21*, para. 2.8.

12 World Commission on Environment and Development, *Our Common Future*, Oxford: Oxford University Press, 1987, p. 79; see also Elliott, *The Global Politics of the Environment*, p. 209.

13 The World Bank, with Paul Collier and David Dollar (eds), *Globalization, Growth, and Poverty: Building an Inclusive World Economy*, A World Bank Policy Research Report, New York: Oxford University Press, 2002, p. 9.

14 *The Agreement on Trade Related Aspects of Intellectual Property Rights* ('TRIPs Agreement') 33 ILM. 81 (1994).

15 *General Agreement on Trade in Services*, see World Trade Organization, *The Legal Texts: The Results of the Uruguay Round of Multilateral Trade Negotiations* ('*WTO Legal Text*'), New York: Cambridge University Press, 1999, p. 284.

16 The South Centre, 'The South, the North and Sustainable Development: The Continuity of Basic Issues'. Online. Available HTTP: <http://www.southcentre.org/publications/conundrum/conundrum-03.htm#divide> (accessed 23 April 2007).

17 The South Centre, *The Founex Report on Development and Environment, 1971*. Online. Available HTTP: <http://www.southcentre.org/publications/conundrum/-conundrum-04.htm> (accessed 23 April 2007).

18 Third World Network, 'Dangers of increasing WTO's scope through "TREMs"', *Comments on the WTO Work Programme: Third World Network Position Paper*,

1993. Online. Available HTTP: <http://www.twnside.org.sg/title/env2-ch.htm> (accessed 23 April 2007).

19 Islam, *International Trade Law*, p. 443.

20 The International Centre for Trade and Sustainable Development ('ICTSD'), 'Environment', *Bridges Weekly Trade News Digest*, 24 November 1999. Online. Available HTTP: <http://www.ictsd.org/ministerial/seattle/story24-11-99.htm#Environment> (accessed 23 April 2007).

21 *Agreement on Trade-related Investment Measures* ('TRIMs'), see *WTO Legal Text*, p. 143.

22 U. Hoffmann, 'Specific Trade Obligations in Multilateral Environmental Agreements and their Relationship with the Rules of the Multilateral Trading System: A Developing Country Perspective' in UNCTAD, *Trade and Environment Review 2003*, New York and Geneva: United Nations, 2004, p. 12.

23 South Centre, 'The South, The North and Sustainable Development'.

24 Briefing from Birdlife International on Trade and Environment Issues of the Doha Development Round. Online. Available HTTP: <http://www.euractiv.com/ndbtext/trade/birdlife-cancun2.pdf> (accessed 27 April 2007).

Bibliography

28th Industrial Science and Technology Working Group, 'APEC Climate Centre for Climate Information', 2005/ISTWG/009.

31st Industrial Science and Technology Working Group, 'Progress Report – APEC Climate Centre'. Online. Available HTTP: <http://www.apec.org/apec/ documents_reports/industrial_science_technology_working_group/2006.MedialibDownload.v1.html?url=/etc/medialib/apec_media_library/downloads/workinggroups/istwg/mtg/2006/word.Par.0014.File.v1.1> (accessed 13 January 2007).

Abbott, F.M., 'The Enduring Enigma of TRIPS: A Challenge for the World Economic System', *Journal of International Economic Law* 1:4, 1998, 497–522.

Adeola, F.O., 'Environmental Injustice and Human Rights Abuse: The States, MNCs, and Repression of Minority Groups in the World System', *Human Ecology Review* 8:1, 2001, 39–59.

Afilalo, A. and Foster, S., 'The World Trade Organization's Anti-discrimination Jurisprudence: Free Trade, National Sovereignty, and Environmental Health in the Balance', *Georgetown International Environmental Law Review* 15, 2003, 633–76.

Anand, R., *International Environmental Justice: A North–South Dimension*, Aldershot: Ashgate, 2004.

Anderson, B., 'Unilateral Trade Measures and Environmental Protection Policy', *Temple Law Review* 66, 1993, 751–84.

Anderson, G., 'Can Someone Please Settle This Dispute? Canadian Softwood Lumber and the Dispute Settlement Mechanisms of the NAFTA and the WTO', *The World Economy* 29:5, 2006, 585–610.

Anderson, K. and Drake-Brockman, J. 'The World Trade Organisation and the Environment' in B. Boer, R. Fowler and N. Gunningham (eds), *Environmental Outlook No. 2: Law and Policy*, Sydney: Federation Press, 1996.

Anderson, T., Folke, C. and Nystrom, S., *Trading with the Environment*, London: Earthscan, 1995.

APEC Ministers responsible for the Environment, *Framework of Principles for Integrating Economy and Environment in APEC*, Vancouver, BC, 1994.

Appleton, B., *Navigating NAFTA*, Toronto: Carswell, 1994.

Arroyo-Quiroz, I., Perez-Gil, R. and Leader-Williams, N., 'Developing Countries and the Implementation of CITES: The Mexican Experience', *Journal of International Wildlife Law and Policy* 8, 2005, 13–50.

Asante, S.K.B., 'The Lomé Convention: Towards Perpetuation of Dependence or Promotion of Independence?' *Third World Quarterly*, 1981.

—— 'The European Union–Africa-Caribbean-Pacific (ACP), Lomé Convention: Expectation, Reality and the Challenges of the 21st Century, *Africa Insight* 26:4, 1996.

Asia-Pacific Economic Cooperation Forum, *Achieving the APEC Vision, Second Report of the Eminent Persons Group*, Singapore, August 1994. Online. Available HTTP: <http://www.apecsec.org.sg/apec/ministerial_statements/annual_ministerial/1994_6th_apec_ministerial.html#second> (accessed 16 April 2007).

Atkinson, J., *APEC: Winners and Losers*, Development Dossier 34, Deakin ACT: Australian Council for Overseas Aid, 1995.

Bailey, J.E., 'Free Trade and the Environment: Can NAFTA Reconcile the Irreconcilable?' *American Journal of International Law and Policy* 8:4, 1993, 839–53.

Beukel, E., *Multilateralism vs. Unilateralism: The International Political Economy of the Trade/Environment Nexus*, Institute of International Relations, University of British Columbia Working Paper No. 22, 1998.

Bhagwati, J. (ed.), *The Next Trade Negotiating Round: Examining the Agenda for Seattle*, proceedings of the conference held at Columbia University, 23–4 July 1999.

Bhalla, A.S., and Bhalla, P. (eds), *Regional Blocs: Building Blocks or Stumbling Blocks*? London: Macmillan, 1997.

Birnie, P., 'Environmental Protection and Development', *Melbourne University Law Review* 20, 1995, 66–100.

Black, D.J., 'International Trade v. Environmental Protection: The Case of the US Embargo on Mexican Tuna', *Law and Policy in International Business* 24:1, 1992, 123–56.

Blaustein, E. and Shanker, A., 'Technology Co-operation in the Environmentally Sound Technologies', Working Paper for the Scientific and Technological Options Assessment ('STOA') Panel, Directorate A Division Industry, Research, Energy, Environment and STOA, Luxembourg, PE 297.572/Fin.St. (2001).

Boas, M., 'The Trade–Environment Nexus and the Potential of Regional Trade Institutions', *New Political Economy* 5:3, 2000, 415–33.

Boer, B., 'The Globalisation of Environmental Law,' *Melbourne University Law Review* 20, 1995, 101–25.

Boudeville, N. *et al.*, 'Sustainability Impact Assessment (SIA) of the EU–ACP Economic Partnership Agreements – Regional SIA: West African ACP countries', Report prepared for the European Commission under Framework Contract, EC TRADE 02-F3-02, Specific Agreement No. 1 (2004). Online. Available HTTP: <http://www.odi.org.uk/IEDG/Publications/report_riwa.pdf> (accessed 4 April 2007).

Boyer, B., 'Institutional Coordination, Multi-stakeholder Participation and the Implementation of MEAS: National Experiences of Thailand and Malaysia', 2001. Online. Available HTTP: <http://www.unu.edu/inter-linkages/docs/DiscussionP/2001_03_Brook.pdf> (accessed 23 April 2007).

Brack, D., 'Commentaries on Article 1: The Relationship between MEAs and WTO Rules' in UNCTAD, *Trade and Environment Review 2003*, Geneva: United Nations, 2004.

Bray, D.B., Murphy, S.R. and Cornejo, M., 'Beyond Islands? Sustainable Rural Development in Mexico' in L. Randall (ed.), *Changing Structure of Mexico: Political, Social and Economic Prospects*, 2nd edn, New York: Columbia University, 2006.

Bretherton, C. and Vogler, J., *The European Union as a Global Actor*, London: Routledge, 1999.

Bronitt, S., Burns, F. and Kinley, D., *Environmental Law and Policy in Principles of*

European Community Law: Commentary and Materials, North Ryde NSW: LBC, 1995.

Buch-Hansen, M., 'The WTO Agreement on Agriculture and its impact on developing countries', November 2001. Online. Available HTTP: <http://www.ruc.dk/inst3/IDS/Public/workpapers/no29.pdf/> (accessed 6 January 2006).

Butkeviciene, J., 'GATS Negotiations and Issues for Consideration in the Area of Environmental Services from a Development Perspective', paper prepared for the UNEP–UNCTAD Workshop on *Post-Doha Negotiating Issues on Trade and Environment in Paragraph 31*, Singapore, 16 May 2002. Online. Available HTTP: <http://www.unep-unctad.org/cbtf/cbtf2/meetings/singapore/environmentalservices.doc> (accessed 16 February 2007).

Caldwell, L.K., *International Environmental Policy: Emergence and Dimensions*, Durham, NC: Duke University Press, 1984.

Cameron, J., 'GATT and the Environment' in P. Sands (ed.), *Greening International Law*, London: Earthscan, 1993.

—— 'The Precautionary Principle' in G.P. Sampson and B. Chambers (eds), *Trade, Environment and the Millennium*, Tokyo: United Nations University, 1999.

Cameron, J., Demaret, P. and Geradin, D. (eds), *Trade and the Environment: The Search for Balance* I, London: Cameron May, 1994.

Cameron, J., Werksman, J. and Roderick, P. (eds), *Improving Compliance with International Environmental Law*, London: Earthscan, 1996.

Campiglio, L., *The Environment after Rio: International Law and Economics*, London: Martinus Nijhoff, 1994.

Capling, A., *Australia and the Global Trade System: From Havana to Seattle*, Oakleigh VIC: Cambridge University Press, 2001.

Center for International Environmental Law, 'Clarifying the Relationship between Economic and Environmental Governance: Some Key Challenges', Center for International Environmental Law Issue Brief for the World Summit on Sustainable Development, 26 August–4 September 2002.

Chambers, W.B., 'Towards an Improved Understanding of the Legal Effectiveness of International Environmental Treaties, *Georgetown International Environmental Law Review* 16, 2004, 501–32.

Chanrithy, C., 'Findings of the Country Case Study: National Policy Co-ordination in Cambodia for Implementing and Further Developing the Basel Convention, Convention on International Trade in Endangered Species, Convention on Biological Diversity, and Montreal Protocol', National Training Workshop in Enhancing Policy Co-ordination on Trade and Environmental Issues: *Implementation of Multilateral Environmental Agreements Containing Trade related Measures*, 2004.

Charnovitz, S., 'Exploring the Environmental Exceptions in GATT Article XX', *Journal of World Trade* 25:5, 1991, 37–55.

—— 'Trade Negotiations and the Environment', *International Environment Reporter*, 11 March 1992, 144–5.

—— 'The NAFTA Environmental Side Agreement: Implications for Environmental Cooperation, Trade Policy and American Treaty Making', *Temple International and Comparative Law Journal* 8, 1994, 257–314.

—— 'The Supervision of Health and Biosafety Regulation by World Trade Rules', *Tulane Environmental Law Journal* 13, 2000, 271–302.

Cole, M.A., *Trade Liberalisation, Economic Growth and the Environment*, Cheltenham: Edward Elgar, 2000.

Commission on Sustainable Development, *Trade, Environment and Sustainable Development: Report of the Secretary-General*, Fourth Session, 18 April–3 May 1996, UN Doc. E/CN.17/1996/8.

Coote, B., *NAFTA Poverty and Free Trade in Mexico*, Oxford: Oxfam Publications, 1995.

Cottier, T. and Panizzon, M., 'Legal Perspectives on Traditional Knowledge: The Case for Intellectual Property Protection', *Journal of International Economic Law* 7:2, 2004, 371–99.

Cusack, M., 'International Law and the Transboundary Shipment of Hazardous Waste to the Third World: Will the Basel Convention Make a Difference?' *American University Journal of International Law and Policy* 5, 1990, 393–422.

Damodaran, A., *Implications of International Conventions and Opportunities for Transfer of Environmentally Sound Technologies to Developing Countries*, Bangalore: Indian Institute of Plantation Management, 2002. Online. Available HTTP: <http://www.unescap.org/tid/publication/Chap3b_2127.pdf> (accessed 22 April 2007).

Das, D.K., 'Debacle at Seattle: the Way the Cookie Crumbled', *Journal of World Trade* 34:5, 2000, 181–201.

—— 'The Doha Round of Multilateral Trade Negotiations: Causal Factors behind the Failure in Cancun', Research Paper, October 2003. Online. Available HTTP: <http://www.cid.harvard.edu/cidtrade/Papers/das2003.pdf> (accessed 26 March 2007).

de Burca, G., 'The Principle of Proportionality and its Application in EC Law', *Yearbook of European Law*, 13, 1993, 105–50.

de Klemm, C., 'Guidelines for Legislation to Implement CITES', *IUCN Environmental Policy and Law Paper* No. 26, 1993.

de Mestral, A.L.C., 'The Significance of the NAFTA Side Agreements on Environmental and Labour Cooperation', *Arizona Journal of International and Comparative Law* 15:1, 1998, 169–86.

Delgado, J. *et al.*, 'The Environment: Or How Social Issues Affect the Commitment of Environmental Tasks' in L. Randall (ed.), *Changing Structure of Mexico: Political, Social and Economic Prospects*, 2nd edn, New York: Columbia University, 2006.

Dervis, K., 'Bridging the Gap: How the Millennium Development Goals are Uniting the World in the Fight against Global Poverty', *Sustainable Development Law and Policy* 6, 2005–6, 2–3, 7.

Donahue, A.M., 'Comment: Equivalence: Not Quite Close Enough for the International Harmonisation of Environmental Standards', *Environmental Law* 30, 2000, 363–86.

Doran, P., 'The UN Commission on Sustainable Development', *Environmental Politics* 5:1, 1996, 100–7.

Drake-Brockman, J. and Anderson, K., 'The Entwining of Trade and Policy in Environmental Issues: Implications for APEC', paper presented at the Nautilus Institute workshop on *Trade and Environment in Asia-Pacific: Prospects for Regional Cooperation*, East–West Center, Honolulu, 23–5 September 1994.

Duhot, S.S.M., 'Implementation of Community Environmental Policy', in *Environment and Europe*, Dordrecht: Kluwer, 1994.

Durbin, A.C., 'Trade and the Environment: the North–South Divide' *Environment* 37:7, 1995, 16–26.

Dutfield, G., 'Sharing the Benefits of Biodiversity: Is there a Role for the Patent System?' *Journal of World Intellectual Property* 5:6, 2002, 899–931.

Eguh, E.C., 'The Bamako Convention and the First Meeting of the Parties: A Glance at Implementation Strategies, *RECIEL* 7:3, 2000, 256–63.

Elliot, L., *The Global Politics of the Environment*, London: Macmillan, 1998.

Esty, D.C., 'Integrating Trade and Environmental Policy Making: First Steps in the North American Free Trade Agreement', in D. Zaelke, P. Orbuch and R.F. Housman *et al.* (eds), *Trade and the Environment: Law, Economics, and Policy*, Washington DC: Island Press, 1993.

—— 'Greening the GATT: Trade, Environment and the Future', *Institute for International Economics*, 1994, 9–32.

—— 'Making Trade and Environmental Policies Work Together: Lessons from NAFTA', in J. Cameron *et al.* (eds), *Trade and Environment: The Search for Balance* I, London: Cameron May, 1994.

—— 'Trade and Environment in APEC', *Global Environment and Trade Study*, 1998. Online. Available HTTP: <http://www.gets.org/gets/library/admin/uploadedfiles/showfile.cfm?FileName=Trade_and_Environment_in_APEC.htm> (accessed 22 June 2005).

—— 'Bridging the Trade–Environment Divide', *Journal of Economic Perspectives* 15:3, 2001, 113–30.

Esty, D.C. and Geradin, D., 'Market Access, Competitiveness, and Harmonization: Environmental Protection in Regional Trade Agreements', *Harvard Environmental Law Review* 21, 1997, 265–336.

European Commission, *Green Paper on Relations between the European Union and ACP Countries on the Eve of the 21st Century*, Luxembourg: Office for Official Publications of the European Communities, 1996.

—— *Guidelines for the Negotiation of new Co-operation Agreements with African, Caribbean and Pacific (ACP) Countries*, Luxembourg: Office for Official Publications of the European Communities, 1997.

—— 'Economic Partnership Agreements – Means and Objectives', 2003. Online. Available HTTP: <http://trade.ec.europa.eu/doclib/docs/2003/december/tradoc_115007.pdf> (accessed 3 April 2007).

—— 'A New Regional Agreement to Develop South Eastern Europe', 2006. Online. Available HTTP: <Trade.ec.europa.eu/doclib/docs/2006/december/tradoc_131840.pdf> (accessed 2 April 2007).

—— *Handbook for Trade Sustainability Impact Assessment*, Luxembourg: Office of Official Publications of the European Communities, 2006.

European Commission Directorate General for the Environment, *1997–2002. Five Years of New Wildlife Trade Regulations: The European Union's Contribution to Sustainable Trade and Species Conservation*, Luxembourg: Office for Official Publications of the European Communities, 2002.

Evenett, S.J., 'The Failure of the WTO Ministerial Meeting in Cancun: What Implications for Future Research on the World Trading System?', *CESifo Forum* 4:3, 2003, 11–17. Online. Available HTTP: <http://www.fordschool.umich.edu/rsie/acit/Topics-Documents/Evenett031009.pdf> (accessed 26 March 2007).

—— 'The World Trade Organisation Ministerial Conference in Hong Kong: What next?' *Journal of World Trade* 40:2, 2006, 221–39.

Eweje, G., 'Strategic Partnerships between MNEs and Civil Society: The Post-WSSD Perspectives', *Sustainable Development* 15, 2007, 15–27.

Ferris, R. Jr and Hongjun, Z., 'The Challenges of Reforming an Environmental Legal Culture: Assessing the Status Quo and Looking at Post-WTO Admission Challenges for the People's Republic of China', *Georgetown International Environmental Law Review* 14, 2002, 429–60.

Finger, J.M., 'Implementing the Uruguay Round Agreements: Problems for Developing Countries', *The World Economy* 24:9, 2003, 1103.

Fontagne, L., *Protection(ism): the Environment and the WTO*, Storrs CT: Department of Economics, University of Conneticutt, 2001, p. 206. Online. Available HTTP: <http://www.cepii.fr/anglaisgraph/publications/lettre/pdf/2001/ 206ang.pdf> (accessed 23 April 2007).

Food and Agriculture Organization of the United Nations, *The State of Agricultural Commodity Markets 2004*, Rome: FAO, 2004.

Friends of the Earth, *A Disservice to the Earth: The Environmental Impact of the General Agreement on Trade in Services*, Friends of the Earth Feature. Online. Available HTTP: <http://www.citizenstrade.org/pdf/services_foe_2pg.pdf> (accessed 16 February 2007).

Gaines, S., 'Products and Production Methods: How to Produce Sound Policy for Environmental PPM-based Trade Measures', *Columbia Journal of Environmental Law* 27, 2002, 383–432.

Garvey, J.I., 'Trade Law and Quality of Life: Dispute Resolution under the NAFTA Side Accords on Labour and the Environment', *American Journal of International Law* 89:2, 1995, 439–53.

GATT, *GATT Law and the Environment*, GATT Doc. 1529, 13 February 1992.

—— *Report by Ambassador H. Ukawa (Japan), Chairman of the Group Environmental Measures and International Trade, to the 49th Session of the Contracting Parties*, GATT Doc. L/7402, Geneva: GATT, 1994.

George, C., and Kirkpatrick, C., 'Trade and Development: Assessing the Impact of Trade Liberalisation on Sustainable Development', *Journal of World Trade* 38:3, 2004, 441–69.

Geradin, D., *Trade and the Environment: A Comparative Study of EC and US Law*, Melbourne: Cambridge University Press, 1996.

Ghina, F. 'Sustainable Development in Small Island Developing States: The Case of the Maldives', *Environment, Development and Sustainability* 5, 2003, 139–65.

Gibbs, M., 'The Positive Agenda and the Seattle Conference' in UNCTAD, *Positive Agenda and Future Trade Negotiations*, New York: United Nations, 2000.

Global Environment Information Centre, *Sri Lanka Case Study on Interlinkages among Multilateral Environmental Agreements (MEAs): Results of the Questionnaire Survey*, 2004. Online. Available HTTP: <http://geic.hq.unu.edu/ENV/active1.cfm?type=1&ID=535> (accessed 23 April 2007).

—— *Pakistan Case Study on Inter-linkages: Synergies and Coordination among Multilateral Environmental Agreements (MEAs) Questionnaire Report*, 2005. Online. Available HTTP: <http://geic.hq.unu.edu/ENV/active1.cfm?type=1&ID=536> (accessed 23 April 2007).

Granville-West, C., 'Special Report 2: The WTO and EU policy towards GMOs', *European Policy Analyst*, May 2006.

Gray, K., 'Multilateral Environmental Agreements in Africa: Efforts and Problems in Implementation', *International Environmental Agreements: Politics, Law and Economics* 3, 2003, 97–135.

—— 'Accommodating MEAs in Trade Agreements', paper presented at the *International Environmental Governance conference*, Paris, 15–16 March 2004. Online. Available HTTP: <http://www.iddri.org/iddri/telecharge/gie/communications/4e_gray.pdf> (accessed 23 April 2007).

Group of 77, *The Group of 77 at Forty: Championing Multilateralism, a Democratic and*

Equitable World Order, South–South Cooperation and Development, Geneva: South Centre, 2004.

Gupta, J., 'The Global Environment Facility in its North–South Context', *Environmental Politics* 4:1, 1995, 19–43.

Guruswamy, L.D., 'The Convention on Biological Diversity: Exposing the Flawed Foundations', *Environmental Conservation* 26:2, 1999, 79–82.

Halle, M., 'Trade and Environment: Looking beneath the Sands of Doha?' *Journal for European Environmental and Planning Law* 2006:2, 2006, 107–16.

—— 'Seattle and Sustainable Development', International Institute for Sustainable Development web site ('IISDnet'). Online. Available HTTP: <http://www.iisd.org/trade/wto/seattleandsd.htm> (accessed 25 March 2007).

Henson, S., Loader, R., Swinbank, A. and Bredahl, M., 'The Impact of Sanitary and Phytosanitary Measures on Developing Country Exports of Agricultural and Food Products (draft for discussion)', paper presented at the Conference on *Agriculture and the New Trade Agenda in the WTO 2000 Negotiations*, 1–2 October 1999, Geneva (Section 6: 'Problems with the SPS Agreement encountered by Developing Countries'). Online. Available HTTP: <http://www.cid.harvard.edu/cidtrade/issues/spstbtpaper.html> (accessed 31 October 2005).

Herring, R.J. and Bharucha, E., 'India: Embedded Capacities', in Edith Brown Weiss and Harold K Jacobson (eds), *Engaging Countries: Strengthening Compliance with International Environmental Accords*, Cambridge MA: The MIT Press, 2000.

Heydon, K., 'After the WTO Hong Kong Ministerial Meeting: What is at Stake?' OECD Trade Policy Working Paper No. 27, 2006.

High Level Meeting on Sustainable Development, 'Conclusions and Recommendations: High Level Meeting on Sustainable Development', 2006. Online. Available HTTP: <http://www.apec.org/apec/documents_reports/sustainable_development/2006.MedialibDownload.v1.html?url=/etc/medialib/apec_media_library/downloads/otherfora_initiatives/sustdev/mtg/2006/word.Par.0007.File.v1.1> (accessed 13 January 2007).

—— 'Sustainable Development in APEC, from 1996 to 2006: Time for Assessment and Some Recommendations', 2006. Online. Available HTTP: <http://www.apec.org/apec/documents_reports/sustainable_development/2006.MedialibDownload.v1.html?url=/etc/medialib/apec_media_library/downloads/otherfora_initiatives/sustdev/mtg/2006/word.Par.0004.File.v1.1> (accessed 13 January 2007).

Hoekman Groupe, B. and Prowse, S., 'Policy Responses to Preference Erosion: From Trade as Aid to Aid for Trade', paper presented at the international symposium *Preference Erosion: Impacts and Policy Responses*, Geneva, 13–14 June 2005. Online. Available HTTP: < http://www.uneca.org/atpc/documents/May/preference-erosion.pdf> (accessed 17 April 2007).

Hoffmann, U., 'An Analysis of Effective Operationalization of Provisions on Transfer of Environmentally Sound Technologies to Developing Countries in Multilateral Environmental Agreements, Pursuant to Agenda 21', *Strengthening Research And Policy-making Capacity on Trade And Environment in Developing Countries Second Workshop*, 1999.

—— 'Specific Trade Obligations in Multilateral Environmental Agreements and their Relationship with the Rules of the Multilateral Trading System: A Developing Country Perspective' in UNCTAD, *Trade and Environment Review 2003*, New York and Geneva: United Nations, 2004.

Hofrichter, R. (ed.), *Toxic Struggles: The Theory and Practice of Environmental Justice*, Salt Lake City UT: University of Utah Press, 2002.

Hogenboom, B., *Mexico and the NAFTA Environmental Debate: the Transnational Politics of Economic Integration*, Utrecht: International Books, 1998.

Holland, M., 'Europe's Changing Development Agenda: Implications for the Pacific', *New Zealand International Review* 22:4, 1997.

Housman, R., 'The North American Free Trade Agreement's Lessons for Reconciling Trade and the Environment', *Stanford Journal of International Law* 30, 1994, 379–422.

Hunter, D., Salzman, J. and Zaelke, D., *International Environmental Law and Policy*, New York: Foundation Press, 1998.

—— 'Hazardous Wastes and Materials', *International Environmental Law and Policy*, New York: Foundation Press, 2002.

Hunter, D., Sommer, J. and Vaughan, S., *Concepts and Principles of International Law: An Introduction*, Nairobi: United Nations Environment Programme, 1994.

Hunter, J., 'APEC: Promise or Peril in the Asia Pacific', *Ecological Economics Bulletin* 2:3, 1997. Online. Available HTTP: <http://www.nautilus.org/archives/papers/enviro/hunter_apec.html#II> (accessed 22 June 2005).

Hurt, S., 'Cooperation and Coercion? The Cotonou Agreement between the European Union and ACP states and the End of the Lomé Convention', *Third World Quarterly* 24:1, 2003, 161–76.

Hyvarinen, A. 'Introduction of the Agreement on Textiles and Clothing and its Implications on Developing Country Producers/Exporters: Eco-labelling and environmentally friendly products and production methods affecting the international trade in textiles and clothing'. Online. Available HTTP: <http://www.intracen.org/worldtradenet/docs/information/referencemat/ecolabatc.pdf> (accessed 31 October 2005).

Imber, M., 'The Impasse in UN Reform', *Global Environmental Change* 9, 1999, 329–32.

Inglis, K., 'Enlargement and the Environment Acquis', *Review of European Community and International Environmental Law* 13:2, 2004, 135–51.

International Centre for Trade and Sustainable Development, 'A Brief Analysis of the Ministerial Conference', 1996. Online. Available HTTP: <http://www.ictsd.org/ministerial/singapore/story9-13-12-96.htm> (accessed 25 March 2007).

—— *Fisheries, International Trade and Sustainable Development*, Natural Resources, International Trade and Sustainable Development Series, Geneva: International Centre for Trade and Sustainable Development, 2006.

International Institute for Sustainable Development, *Rio+5 Special Focus Report on Trade and Sustainable Development*, 13–19 March 1997. Online. Available HTTP: <http://iisd1.iisd.ca/trade/tradedoc.htm> (accessed 27 April 2007).

International Monetary Fund, 'The Truth about Industrial Country Tariffs', *Finance and Development* 39:3, 2002. Online. Available HTTP: <http://www.imf.org/external/pubs/ft/fandd/2002/09/smith.htm> (accessed 16 February 2007).

—— 'How Has NAFTA Affected the Mexican Economy? Review and Evidence', Working Paper WP/04/59, 2004. Online. Available HTTP: <http://www.imf.org/external/pubs/ft/wp/2004/wp0459.pdf> (accessed 12 April 2007).

International Monetary Fund and the World Bank, 'Market Access for Developing Country Exports: Selected Issues', 2002. Online. Available HTTP: <http://www.imf.org/external/np/pdr/ma/2002/eng/092602.pdf> (accessed 17 April 2007).

Islam, M.R., *International Trade Law*, Pyrmont NSW: Lawbook Company, 1999.

—— Pressing Issues of Global Free Trade in Services' in J. Chen and G. Walker (eds), *Balancing Act: Law, Policy and Politics in Globalisation and Global Trade*, Sydney: Federation Press, 2004.

—— *International Trade Law of the WTO*, Melbourne: Oxford University Press, 2006.

Jackson, A.G.W., 'Environmental Law in the European Community: Greek Tragedy or Epic Tale?', *Natural Resources and Environment* 8:2, 1993.

Jawara, F. and Kwa, A., *Behind the Scenes at the WTO: the Real World of International Trade Negotiations*, London: Zed Books, 2003.

Jha, R., 'Alleviating Environmental Degradation in the Asia-Pacific Region: International Co-operation and the Role of Issue-linkage', February 2005. Online. Available HTTP: <http://ssrn.com/abstract=677881> (accessed 27 April 2007).

Jha, V., 'Overview of the SPS and TBT Agreements and their Possible Implications for India', *Discussion Papers for the Havana Workshop on Trade and the Environment*, 30 May–2 June, 2000. Online. Available HTTP: <http://r0.unctad.org/trade_env/discpapers2.htm> (accessed 6 January, 2006).

Jha, V. and Hoffmann, U., *Achieving Objectives of Multilateral Environmental Agreements: A Package of Trade Measures and Positive Measures*, 2000, UN Doc. UNCTAD/ITCD/TED/6.

Jha, V. and Vossenaar, R., *Breaking the Deadlock: A Positive Agenda on Trade, Environment and Development?* 1999. Online. Available HTTP: <http://r0.unctad.org/trade_env/test1/publications/positive.pdf> (accessed 16 February 2007).

Jha, V., Hewison, G. and Underhill, M. (eds), *Trade, Environment and Sustainable Development: A South Asian Perspective*, London: Macmillan, 1997.

Johnson, S.P. (ed.), *The Earth Summit: The United Nations Conference on Environment and Development (UNCED)*, London: Martinus Nijhoff, 1993.

Joint Working Party on Trade and Environment, 'Uncertainty and Precaution: Implications for Trade and Environment', OECD Doc. COM/ENV/TD (2002) 114/FINAL, 5 September 2002.

—— *The Polluter Pays Principle as it Relates to International Trade*, 2001, OECD Doc. COM/ENV/TD (2001) 44/FINAL, 22 December 2002.

Jordan, A., 'The Implementation of EU Environmental Policy: A Policy Problem without a Political Solution?' *Environment and Planning C: Government and Policy* 17, 1999, 69–90.

Kelly, M.J., 'Bringing a Complaint under the NAFTA Environmental Side Accord: Difficult Steps under a Procedural Paper Tiger, but Movement in the Right Direction', *Pepperdine Law Review*, 24:71, 1996, 72–97.

Kerr, W.A., 'Who Should Make the Rules of Trade? The Complex Issue of Multilateral Environmental Agreements', *Estey Centre Journal of International Law and Trade Policy* 3:2, 2002, 163–75.

Khan, S.R., 'Environmental Impacts and Mitigation Costs of Cloth and Leather Exports from Pakistan'. Online. Available HTTP: <http://www.ictsd.org/dlogue/2001-03-29/RafiKhan.doc> (accessed 31 October 2005).

Khor, M., *IPRS Blocking Access to Eco-friendly Technology*, 1996. Online. Available HTTP: <http://www.sunsonline.org/trade/areas/services/08050196.htm> (accessed 22 April 2007).

—— 'The Revolt of Developing Nations', *Reports on Seattle*, 6 December 1999. Online. Available HTTP: <www.twnside.org.sg/title/revolt-cn.htm> (accessed 25 March 2007).

—— (ed.), 'The Multilateral Trading System: A Development Perspective', Report prepared by the Third World Network for the United Nations Development Programme, December 2001. Online. Available HTTP: <http://www.twnside.org.sg/title2/par/mk001.doc> (accessed 16 February 2007).

—— 'The WTO, the Post-Doha Agenda and the Future of the Trade System', Third World Network paper prepared for a seminar on WTO held at the annual meeting of the Asian Development Bank held in Shanghai, China, on 10 May 2002. Online. Available HTTP: <http://www.twnside.org.sg/title/mkadb.htm> (accessed 26 March 2007).

Khosla, A., *The Road from Rio to Johannesburg*, Millennium Papers, No. 5, UNED Forum, 30 April 2001.

Kim, J.A., 'Opportunities and Challenges in Liberalizing the Environmental Goods and Services Market: The Case of Developing Countries in Asia', *Journal of World Trade* 40:3, 2006.

Knappe, M. 'Textiles and Clothing: What Happens after 2005?' Reprinted from *International Trade Forum*, 2003, No. 2, 16–20. Online. Available HTTP: <http://www.cacci.org.tw/membership/Textiles%20and%20Clothing.PDF> (accessed 6 April 2006).

Knigge, M., 'Report on Trade and Multilateral Environmental Agreements', *Concerted Action on Trade and Environment*, sponsored by the European Commission, Research Directorate-General, under Contract No. EVK2-CT-2002-20017 CAT&E, 2005. Online. Available HTTP: <http://www.ecologic.de/download/projekte/1800–1849/1800/3_1800_cate_meas.pdf> (accessed 23 April 2007

Kramer, L., 'Environmental Protection and Article 30 EEC Treaty', *Common Market Law Review* 30, 1993, 111–43.

Krueger, J., *The Basel Convention and Transboundary Movements of Hazardous Wastes*, Briefing No. 45, Royal Institute of International Affairs Energy and Environmental Programme, May 1998. Online. Available HTTP: <http://www.ciaonet.org/wps/krj02/#txt6> (accessed 22 April 2007).

Krugman, P. and Obstfeld, M., *International Economics: Theory and Policy*, 5th edn, Boston MA: Addison-Wesley, 2000.

Kublicki, N., 'The Greening of Free Trade: NAFTA, Mexican Environmental Law, and Debt Exchanges for Mexican Environmental Infrastructure Development', *Columbia Journal of Environmental Law* 19:1, 1994, 59–140.

Kütting, G., 'Globalisation, Poverty and the Environment in West Africa: Too Poor to Pollute?' *Global Environmental Politics* 3:4, 2003, 42–60.

Lang, W., 'Environmental Protection: The Challenge for International Law', *Journal of World Trade Law* 20:5, 1986, 490.

Lazar, F., 'Investing in the NAFTA: Just Cause for Walking Away', *Journal of World Trade* 27:5, 1993, 19–35.

Levy, R.E., 'International Law and the Chernobyl Accident: Reflections on an Important but Imperfect System', *University of Kansas Law Review* 36, 1987–8, 81–132.

Ling, C.Y. and Khor, M., 'International Environmental Governance: Some Issues from a Developing Country Perspective', *Third World Network Working Paper*, September 2001. Online. Available HTTP: <http://www.twnside.org.sg/title/ieg.htm> (accessed 26 March 2007).

Low, P. (ed.), *International Trade and the Environment*, World Bank Discussion Paper No. 159, Washington DC: World Bank, 1992.

McConnell, I., 'North American Free Trade Agreement: Trading Natural Resource Goods and Protecting the Environment', *Journal of Energy and Natural Resources Law* 12:1, 1994, 151–74.

McCulloch, N., Winters, A.L. and Cirera, X., *Trade Liberalization and Poverty: A Hand-*

book, London: Centre for Economic Policy Research, 2002. Online. Available HTTP: <http://www.ids.ac.uk/ids/global/pdfs/tlpov.pdf> (accessed 23 April 2007).

McDonald, J., 'Greening the GATT: Harmonizing Free Trade and Environmental Protection in the New World Order', *Environmental Law* 23, 1993, 397–474.

—— 'The WTO's Response to the Trade–Environment Debate: A Preliminary Report Card', *International Trade Law Conference* 23, Attorney General's Department, Canberra, 29 May 1997 (copy on file with author).

—— 'APEC and ESD: Turning Sustained Economic Growth into Ecologically Sustainable Development' in P. Leadbeter, N. Gunningham and B. Boer (eds), *Environmental Outlook No. 3: Law and Policy*, Sydney: Federation Press, 2000.

Maggio, G.F., 'Inter/Intra-generational Equity: Current Applications under International Law for Promoting the Sustainable Development of Natural Resources', *Buffalo Environmental Law Journal* 4, 1997, 161–224.

Malhotra, K., 'Doha: Is it Really a Development Round?' *Trade, Environment, and Development* 1, 2002, 1–7.

Mann, H. and Porter, S., 'The State of Trade and Environment Law 2003: Implications for Doha and Beyond', Research Paper published by the International Institute for Sustainable Development and the Center for International Environmental Law, 2003. Online. Available HTTP: <http://www.iisd.org/pdf/2003/trade_enviro_law_2003.pdf> (accessed 27 April 2007).

Maryand, K., Dionne, S., Paquin, M. and Pageot-LeBel, I., 'The Economic and Environmental Impacts of Agricultural Subsidies: An Assessment of the 2002 US Farm Bill and Doha Round', paper prepared for the *Second North American Symposium on Assessing the Environmental Effects on Trade*, Mexico, 26 March 2003. Online. Available HTTP: <http://www.cec.org/files/pdf/ECONOMY/Session-4–3-Mayrand-Dionne_en.pdf> (accessed 6 April 2006).

Mehta, P.S., 'The Doha Development Agenda: The Road Ahead', *Canadian Development Report, 2003*, 2003. Online. Available HTTP: <http://www.nsi-ins.ca/english/pdf/cdr2003_e_3.pdf> (accessed 26 March 2007).

Mendoza, M.R., 'Venezuela and the United States: The Evolving Bilateral Relationship', in M.R. Mendoza, P. Correa and B. Kotschwar (eds), *The Andean Community and the United States: Trade and Investment Relations in the 1990s*, Organization of American States, September 1998.

Middletown, R., 'NAFTA and the Environmental Side Agreement: Fusing Economic Development with Ecological Responsibility', *San Diego Law Review* 31, 1994, 1025–56.

Miller, M.A.L., *The Third World in Global Environmental Politics*, Buckingham: Open University Press, 1995.

Miranda, K. and Muzondo, T.R., 'Public Policy and the Environment', *Finance and Development* 28:2, 1991, 25.

Morales, I., 'NAFTA Revisited: Expectations and Realities: The Mexican Crisis and the Weakness of the NAFTA Consensus', *Annals of the American Academy of Political and Social Science* 550, 1997, 130–52.

Morgera, E. and Duran, G.M., 'Enlargement and EU Development Policy: An Environmental Perspective', *Review of European Community and International Environmental Law* 13:2, 2004, 152–63.

Nagara, B., 'The Trade–Environment Nexus: Whence, Wither, Why and Wherefore', paper presented at the Nautilus Institute workshop on *Trade and Environment in Asia-Pacific: Prospects for Regional Cooperation*, East–West Center, Honolulu, 23–5

September 1994. Online. Available HTTP: <http://www.nautilus.org/archives/papers/enviro/trade/wwww.html> (accessed 22 June 2005).

Naghavi, A., 'Multilateral Environmental Agreements and Trade Obligations: A Theoretical Analysis of the Doha Proposal', *Fondazione Eni Enrico Mattei Note di Lavoro Series Index*, 2005. Online. Available HTTP: <http://www.feem.it/Feem/Pub/Publications/WPapers/default.htm> (accessed 21 April 2007).

Najam, A., 'Trade and Environment after Seattle: A Negotiation Agenda for the South', *Journal of Environment and Development* 9:4, 2000, 405–25.

Najam, A. and Robins, N., 'Seizing the Future: the South, Sustainable Development and International Trade', *International Affairs* 77:1, 2001, 49–68.

Nanda, V., 'Trends in International Environmental Law', *California Western International Law Journal* 20, 1989–90, 187–206.

Nath, K., 'Trade, Environment and Sustainable Development' in V. Jha, G. Hewison and M. Underhill (eds), *Trade, Environment and Sustainable Development: A South Asian Perspective*, London: Macmillan, 1997.

Neumayer, E., 'Multilateral Environmental Agreements, Trade and Development: Issues and Policy Options Concerning Compliance and Enforcement', Report for the Consumer Unity and Trust Society, Jaipur, India, funded by the Department for International Development, United Kingdom, 2002. Online. Available HTTP: <www.lse.ac.uk/collections/geographyAndEnvironment/whosWho/profiles/neumayer/pdf/CUTS.pdf> (accessed 21 April 2007).

O'Brien, D., 'Trade Relations', *European Policy Analyst* 31, 2005.

Okubo, A., 'Environmental Labelling Programs and the GATT/WTO Regime', *Georgetown International Environmental Law Review* 11, 1999, 599–646.

Organization for Economic Co-operation and Development, *Recommendation of the OECD Council on Guiding Principles concerning International Economic Aspects of Environmental Policies*, OECD Doc. C (72) 128, 1972.

—— *The Environmental Effects of Trade*, Paris: OECD, 1994.

—— *Trade Principles and Concepts*, OECD Doc. OCDE/GD (95) 141, 1995. Online. Available HTTP: <http://www.oecd.org/dataoecd/4/22/36784663.pdf> (accessed 2 April 2007).

—— *Experience with the Use of Trade Measures in the Convention on International Trade in Endangered Species of Wild Fauna and Flora (CITES)*, OECD Doc. OCDE/GD (97) 106, 1997. Online. Available HTTP: <http://www.oecd.org/ech/tradedoc.htm/> (accessed 22 April 2007).

—— *Experience with the Use of Trade Measures in the Montreal Protocol on Substances that Deplete the Ozone Layer*, OECD Doc. OCDE/GD (97) 230, 1997.

—— *Trade Measures in the Basel Convention on the Control of Transboundary Movements of Hazardous Wastes and their Disposal*, OECD Doc. COM/ENV/TD (97) 41/FINAL, 1997. Online. Available HTTP: <http://www1.oecd.org/ech/docs/envi.htm> (accessed 22 April 2007).

—— *Trade Measures in Multilateral Environmental Agreements*, Paris: OECD, 1999.

—— *Analysis of Non-tariff Measures: The Case of Export Restrictions*, 4 April 2003, OECD Doc. TD/TC/WP (2003)7/FINAL. Online. Available HTTP: <http://www.oecd.org/trade> (accessed 26 March 2007).

—— *Environmental Requirements and Market Access*, OECD Trade Policy Studies, Paris: OECD, 2006.

Osakwe, C., 'Finding New Packages of Acceptable Combinations of Trade and Positive Measures to Improve the Effectiveness of MEAs: A General Framework' in Agata

Fijalkowski and James Cameron (eds), *Trade and the Environment: Bridging the Gap*, London: Cameron May, 1998.

Ostrovsky, A.A., 'The European Commission's Regulations for Genetically Modified Organisms and the Current WTO Dispute: Human Health or Environmental Measures? Why the Deliberate Release Directive is More Appropriately Adjudicated in the WTO under the TBT Agreement', *Colorado Journal of International Environmental Law and Policy* 15, 2004, 209–44.

Oxley, A., 'Commentaries on Article 1: The Relationship between MEAs and WTO Rules' in UNCTAD, *Trade and Environment Review 2003*.

Oxley, A., Osborne, K. and Marty, L., *European Unilateralism: Environmental Trade Barriers and the Rising Threat to Prosperity through Trade*, Australian APEC Study Centre, 2003. Online. Available HTTP: <http://www.apec.org.au/docs/tradebarriers2003.pdf> (accessed 23 April 2007).

Pallamaerts, M., 'International Environmental Law from Stockholm to Rio: Back to the Future?' in P. Sands (ed.), *Greening International Law*, London: Earthscan, 1993.

Panayotou, T., 'Economic Growth and the Environment', Harvard University Centre for International Development, Working Paper No. 56, July 2000.

Panjabi, R.L., 'From Stockholm to Rio: A Comparison of the Declaratory Principle of International Environmental Law', *Denver Journal of International Law and Policy* 21, 1993, 215–88.

Paris, R., 'Capacity Building, and Multilateral Environmental Agreements, Development Co-operation Directorate'. Online. Available HTTP: <http://www.geic.or.jp/interlinkages/docs/oecd.PDF> (accessed 23 April 2007).

Patterson, E., 'International Trade and the Environment: Institutional Solutions', *Environmental Law Reporter* 21, 1991, 10599–604.

Pauwelyn, J., 'Adding Sweeteners to Softwood Lumber: The WTO–NAFTA "Spaghetti Bowl" is Cooking', Duke Law School Legal Studies, Research Paper Series, No. 93, January 2006.

Pearson, C.S., 'The Trade and Environment Nexus: what is new since '72?' in D. Zaelke, P. Orbuch and R.F. Housman (eds), *Trade and the Environment, Law, Economics and Policy*, Washington DC: Island Press, 1993.

Petersmann, E.U., *International and European Trade and Environmental Law after the Uruguay Round*, Boston MA: Kluwer, 1995.

Petroka, E. and Baumert, K.A., 'Making Joint Implementation Work: Lessons from Central and Eastern Europe', World Resources Institute, Climate Energy and Pollution Program, *Climate Notes*, November 2000.

Pluckett, J., 'The Basel Plan: A Triumph over Business as Usual', *Basel Action Network*, 1997. Online. Available HTTP: <http://www.ban.org/about_basel ban/jims_article.htm> (accessed 23 April 2007).

Preeg, E.H., 'The South Rises in Seattle', *Journal of International Economic Law* 3, 2000, 183–6.

Pridham, G. and Cini, M., 'Enforcing Environmental Standards in the European Union: Is there a Southern Problem?' in M. Faure *et al.* (eds), *Environmental Standards in the European Union in an Interdisciplinary Framework*, Antwerp: Maklu, 1994.

Private Sector Foundation Uganda, *Economic Partnership Agreements*, 2007. Online. Available HTTP: <http://www.psfuganda.org/modules/PDdownloads/singlefile.php?cid=6&lid=26> (accessed 4 April 2007).

Prudencio, R.J., 'Why UNCED Failed on Trade and Environment', *Journal of Environment and Development* 2:2, 1993, 103–9.

Puustjärvi, E., Katila, M. and Simula, M., 'Transfer of Environmentally Sound Technologies from Developed Countries to Developing Countries', *Background Document for the Ad Hoc Expert Group on Finance and Environmentally Sound Technologies*. Secretariat of the United Nations Forum on Forests, prepared by INDUFOR, 2004.

Raghavan, C., 'Third World Takes Unified Position on Environment for Earth Summit', *Third World Network Features*, 1991 (copy on file with author).

—— 'The United Nations at the Cross-roads', *Third World Network Feature*. Online. Available HTTP: <http://www.twnside.org.sg/title/un-ch.htm> (accessed 13 March 2007).

Rajamani, L., *Developing Country Resistance to Linking Trade and Environment: The Perceptions of Inequity and the Politics of Autonomy*, Global and Environment Trade Study: North–South Series, No. 1, August 2000. Online. Available HTTP: <http://www.gets.org/library/listcontent.cfm> (accessed 16 February 2007).

Rauscher, M., *International Trade, Factor Movements, and the Environment*, Oxford: Clarendon Press, 1997.

Rege, V., 'GATT Law and Environment-related Issues Affecting the Trade of Developing Countries', *Journal of World Trade* 28:3, 1994, 95–169.

Ricupero, R., 'UNCED and Agenda 21: Chronicle of a Negotiation', *Colorado Journal of International Environmental Law and Policy* 4:1, 1993, 81–102.

Ristroph, E.B., 'How Can the US Correct Multinational Corporations' Environmental Abuses Committed in the Name of Trade?' *Indiana International and Comparative Law Review* 15, 2004–05, 51–88.

Robertson, D., 'Trade and Environment: Harmonization and Technical Standards' in P. Low (ed.), *International Trade and the Environment*, World Bank Discussion Paper No. 159, Washington DC: World Bank, 1992.

Roffe, P. and Tesfachew, T., 'Revisiting the Technology Transfer Debate: Lessons for the New WTO Working Group', *Bridges between Trade and Sustainable Development*, International Centre for Trade and Sustainable Development, Year 6, Vol. 2, 2002.

Rolen, M., Sjoberg, H. and Svedin, U. (eds), *International Governance on Environmental Issues*, Dordrecht: Kluwer, 1997.

Rowland, S., 'Failure at the Earth Summit', *Science* 256:5060, 1992, 1109.

Rowlands, I.H., 'The Fourth Meeting of the Parties to the Montreal Protocol: Report and Reflection', *Environment* 35:6, 1993, 25–34. Online. Available HTTP: <http://www.ciesin.org/docs/003–077/003–077.html> (accessed 22 April 2007).

Safadi, R., *Building Trade Capacity: Behind the Broader Agenda*, World Bank Discussion Paper. Online. Available HTTP: <http://www.worldbank.org/mdf/mdf4/papers/raed.pdf> (accessed 3 April 2007).

Sampson, G.P., *The WTO and Sustainable Development*, Tokyo: United Nations University Press, 2005.

Sampson, G.P. and Chambers, W.B. (eds), *Trade, Environment, and the Millennium*, 2nd edn, Tokyo: United Nations University Press, 2002.

Samuelson, P., *Economics*, 11th edn, New York: McGraw-Hill, 1989.

—— 'Where Ricardo and Mill Rebut and Confirm Arguments of Mainstream Economists Supporting Globalisation', *Journal of Economic Perspectives* 18:3, 2004, 135–47.

Sands, P. (ed.), *Greening International Law*, London: Earthscan, 1993.

—— *Principles of International Environmental Law* I, New York: Manchester University Press, 1995.

Sanusi, Z.A., 'Technology Transfer under Multilateral Environmental Agreements:

Analyzing the Synergies', UNU-IAS Working Paper No. 134, 2005, Yokohama: UNU-IAS.

Schatan, C., 'Lessons from the Mexican Environmental Experience: First Results from NAFTA' in D. Tussie (ed.), *The Environment and International Trade Negotiations*, London: Macmillan, 2000.

Schwartz, B., 'WTO and GMOs: Analyzing the European Community's Recent Regulations Covering the Labelling of Genetically Modified Organisms', *Michigan Journal of International Law* 25, 2004, 771–812.

See, C. and Williams, J.B., 'APEC and the Environment: Is Free Trade Sustainable?' *Current Affairs Bulletin* 73:6, 1997, 20–5.

Sexton, T., 'Enacting National Laws More Stringent than Other States' Laws in the European Community', *Cornell International Law Journal* 24, 1991, 563–94.

Shahin, M., 'Developing Country Perspective' in D. Brack (ed.), *Trade and Environment: Conflict or Compatibility?* London: Earthscan/Royal Institute of International Affairs, 1998.

Sheehan, J.M., 'Two Years after NAFTA: A Free Market Critique and Assessment', 1996. Online. Available HTTP: <http://www.cei.org/pdf/1624.pdf> (accessed 12 April 2007).

Shiva, V., 'Biodiversity and Intellectual Property Rights', in R. Nader *et al.* (eds), *The Case against "Free Trade": GATT, NAFTA and the Globalisation of Corporate Power*, San Francisco: Earth Island Press, 1993.

Shultz, M. 'Trading Waste: Environmental Transfers between Nations', *Harvard International Review* 21, summer 1999, 11–13.

Simpson, T. and Jackson, V., 'Human Rights and the Environment', *Environment and Planning Law Journal* 14, 1997, 268–81.

Siphana, S., 'Trade and Poverty Eradication through Millennium Development Goals (MDG)', keynote speech, Secretary of State for Commerce, Cambodia, at AITCH/ACP Secretariat Symposium on the *Trade Dimension of International Development Initiatives*, São Paulo, Brazil, 13 June 2004.

Snape, W.J. III and Lefkovitz, N.B., 'Searching for GATT's Environmental Miranda: Are Process Standards Getting Due Process?' *Cornell International Law Journal* 27, 1994, 777–816.

Somsen, H., 'The European Union and the OECD' in J. Werksman (ed.), *Greening International Institutions*, London: Earthscan, 1996.

Soto, A., 'The Global Environment: A Southern Perspective', *International Journal* 47, 1992, 679–705.

South Centre, The, *The Founex Report on Development and Environment, 1971*. Online. Available HTTP: <http://www.southcentre.org/publications/conundrum/conundrum-04.htm> (accessed 23 April 2007).

—— 'The South, the North and Sustainable Development: The Continuity of Basic Issues', South Centre Publication. Online. Available HTTP: <http://www.southcentre.org/publications/conundrum/toc.htm> (accessed 16 April 2007).

Soveroski, M., 'EC Enlargement and the Development of European Environmental Policy: Parallel Histories, Divergent Paths?' *Review of European Community and International Environmental Law* 13:2, 2004, 127–34.

Spalding, M.J., 'Lessons of NAFTA for APEC', *Journal of Environment and Development* 6:3, 1997, 252–75.

Steinberg, R.H., 'Trade–Environment Negotiations in the EU, NAFTA, and WTO:

Regional Trajectories of Rule Development', *American Journal of International Law* 91:2, 1997, 231–67.

Steiner, J., 'Drawing the Line: Uses and Abuses of Article 30 EEC', *Common Market Law Review* 29, 1992, 749–74.

Stevens, C., 'The OECD Guiding Principle Revisited', *Environmental Law* 23:2, 1993, 607–19.

—— 'Interpreting the Polluter Pays Principle in the Trade and Environment Context', *Cornell International Law Journal* 27:3, 1994, 577–90.

Stilwell, M., 'Environment, Trade and Sustainable Development: An Overview of Key Issues Arising from the World Summit on Sustainable Development and the WTO Doha Work Programme', UNEP Background Paper, 2003. Online. Available HTTP: <http://www.unep-unctad.org/cbtf/cbtf2/meetings/capetown/GenpapDohaWSSD.doc> (accessed 27 March 2007).

Strachan, J. and Roberts, M., 'Poverty, Environment and Sustainable Development: How the Commonwealth Supports Implementation of the World Summit on Sustainable Development', *The Round Table* 92:371, 2003, 541–59.

Strong, M.F., 'From Stockholm to Rio: A Journey Down a Generation', *Earth Summit 9: A Reference Booklet about UNCED*, 1991.

Su, E., 'The Winners and the Losers: The Agreement on Trade Related Aspects of Intellectual Property Rights and its Effects on Developing Countries', *Houston Journal of International Law* 23, 2000, 169–218.

Subedi, S.P., 'The Road from Doha: The Issues for the Development Round of the WTO and the Future of International Trade', *International and Comparative Law Quarterly* 52:2, 2003, 425–46.

Swanson, T., 'International Regulation for Environmental Protection: Learning from CITES', *Economic Affairs*, 11, winter 1996.

Swanson, T. and Johnston, S., *Global Environmental Problems and International Environmental Agreements: the Economics of Institution Building*, Cheltenham: Edward Elgar, published in association with UNCTAD, 1999.

Swatuk, L.A., 'From Rio to Johannesburg and Beyond: Ways Forward for the Post-WSSD Commonwealth', *The Round Table* 92:371, 2003, 465–75.

Syngellakis, A., 'The Concept of Sustainable Development in European Community Law and Policy', *Cambrian Law Review* 24, 1993, 59–77.

Tarasofsky, R.G., 'Ensuring Compatibility between Multilateral Environmental Agreements and GATT/WTO', *Yearbook of International Environmental Law* 7, 1996, 52–74.

Tay, S.S.C., *International Trade and Environment in Asia: A Survey of the Issues*, monograph commissioned for the Asia Conference on Trade and the Environment, Singapore, June 1996.

Third World Network, 'Dangers of increasing WTO's scope through "TREMs"', *Comments on the WTO Work Programme: Third World Network Position Paper*, 1993. Online. Available HTTP: <http://www.twnside.org.sg/title/env2-ch.htm> (accessed 26 March 2007).

—— 'After the Uruguay Round: Third World Resurgence', *Third World Network Features*, May 1994. Online. Available HTTP: <http://www.twnside.org.sg/> (accessed 16 February 2007).

—— 'Executive Summary: The Multilateral Trading System: A Development Perspective', Report prepared by the Third World Network for the United Nations Development Programme, December 2001. Online. Available HTTP: <http://www.twnside.org.sg/title/undpsum.htm> (accessed 26 March 2007).

—— *Report of WTO Heads of Delegation Meeting on Revised Cancun Draft*, 27 August 2003. Online. Available HTTP: <http://www.twnside.org.sg/title/twninfo69.htm> (accessed 29 March 2007).

Thomas, A., Folke, C. and Nystrom, S. (eds), *Trading with the Environment: Ecology, Economics, Institutions and Policy*, London: Earthscan, 1995.

Thomas, C., 'Where is the Third World now?' *British International Studies Association*, 1999. Online. Available HTTP: <http://journals.cambridge.org/download.php?file=%2FRIS%2FRIS 25_05%2FS026021059900225Xa.pdf&code=e32e8bbf267c9182d990e75cf703ee45> (accessed 2 April 2007).

Trouwborst, *Evolution and Status of the Precautionary Principle in International Law*, Boston MA: Kluwer, 2002.

Uimonen, P. and Whalley, J., *Environmental Issues in the New World Trading System*, London: Macmillan, 1997.

United Nations, *Millennium Development Goals Report 2006*, New York: United Nations, 2006. Online. Available HTTP: <http://unstats.un.org/unsd/mdg/ Resources/Static/Products/Progress2006/MDGReport2006.pdf> (accessed 15 February 2007).

—— *World Economics Situation and Prospects 2007*, New York: United Nations, 2007.

United Nations Conference on Trade and Development, 'UN Recognition of the Least Developed Countries'. Online. Available HTTP: <http://www.unctad.org/Templates/Page.asp?intItemID=3618&lang=1> (accessed 16 February 2007).

—— *Trade and Development Report 1986*, New York: UNCTAD, 1986.

—— *Trade and Development Report 1999*, New York: UNCTAD, 1999. Online. Available HTTP: <http://www.unctad.org/en/docs/tdr1999_en.pdf> (accessed 2 April 2007).

—— *A Positive Agenda for Developing Countries: Issues for Future Trade Negotiations*, New York: United Nations, 2000.

—— *Train for Trade 2000: Environmental Requirements and Market Access, Module 3*, 2001. Online. Available HTTP: <r0.unctad.org/trade_env/rene/mod3entext.doc> (accessed 23 April 2007).

United Nations Development Programme, *Human Development Report 1998*, New York: United Nations, 1998. Online. Available HTTP: <http://hdr.undp.org/reports/global/1998/en/> (accessed 2 April 2007).

—— *Human Development Report 2003 – Millennium Development Goals: a compact among nations to end human poverty*, New York: Oxford University Press, 2003.

—— 'Policy Statement on Trade Issues', Fifth World Trade Organization Ministerial Meeting held in Cancun, Mexico, 10–14 September 2003, 2 (copy on file with author).

—— *Human Development Report 2005*, New York: United Nations, 2005.

United Nations Environment Programme, *Register of International Treaties and Other Agreements in the Field of Environment*, Nairobi: UNEP, 1999.

—— 'Assessment of the Funding Requirement for the Replenishment of the Multilateral Fund for the Period 2006–2008', *Montreal Protocol on Substances that Deplete the Ozone Layer: Report of the UNEP Technology And Economic Assessment Panel* II, May 2005. Online. Available HTTP: <http://www.unep.org/ozone/teap/Reports/teap-rtf-report-may2005.pdf> (accessed 22 April 2007).

—— 'Developing Responses to Factors Inhibiting Implementation and Enforcement of Multilateral Environment Agreements', *High Level Meeting Envisioning the Next Steps for Compliance with and Enforcement of Multilateral Environmental Agreements*, 2006. Online. Available HTTP: <http://www.unep.org/DEC/Events/mdg_meeting_col.asp> (accessed 23 April 2007).

United Nations Environment Programme and International Institute for Sustainable Development, *Environment and Trade: A Handbook*, Winnipeg: IISD, 2000.

United Nations Millennium Project Task Force, *The Interim Report of the Millennium Project Task Force 9 on Open, Rule-based Trading Systems*, commissioned by the UN Secretary General, 2004. Online. Available HTTP: <http://www.unmillenniumproject.org> (accessed 26 March 2007).

United Nations University and the South Pacific Regional Environment Programme, *Inter-linkages: Synergies and Coordination among Multilateral Environmental Agreements: Case Study Pacific Island Countries*, 2002. Online. Available HTTP: <http://geic.hq.unu.edu/env/project1.cfm?type=1&ID=254> (accessed 21 April 2007).

van Bergeijk, P.A.G., 'International Trade and the Environmental Challenge', *Journal of World Trade* 25:6, 1991, 105–15.

Vaughan, S., 'Trade and Environment: Some North–South Considerations', *Cornell International Law Journal* 27:3, 1994, 591–606.

Vikhlyaev, A., 'The Use of Trade Measures for Environmental Purposes – Globally and in the EU Context' UNCTAD Working Paper, September 2001. Online. Available HTTP: <http://r0.unctad.org/trade_env/test1/publications/feem.pdf> (accessed 17 April 2007).

Vossenaar, R. and Jha, V., 'Implementation of MEAs at the National Level and the Use of Trade and Non-trade Measures: Results of Developing Country Case Studies', in Agata Fijalkowski and James Cameron (eds), *Trade and the Environment: Bridging the Gap*, London: Cameron May, 1998.

Wapner, P., 'World Summit on Sustainable Development: Toward a Post-Jo'burg Environmentalism', *Global Environmental Politics* 3:1, 2003, 1–10.

Ward, H., 'WTO Rules and the Application of the Precautionary Principle', *Bridges* (International Centre for Trade and Sustainable Development Monthly Publication), 2000, January–February, 15.

Watkins, K., 'Eight Broken Promises: Why the WTO is Not Working for the World's Poor', Oxfam Briefing Paper 9, 2001. Online. Available HTTP: <http://www.oxfam.org.uk/what_we_do/issues/trade/bp09_8broken.htm> (accessed 16 February 2007).

Weale, A., 'European Environmental Policy by Stealth: the Dysfunctionality of Functionalism?' *Environment and Planning C: Government and Policy* 17, 1999, 37–51.

Weiss, E.B. and Jacobson, H.K., 'Getting Countries to Comply with International Agreements', *Environment* 41, July–August 1999, 16–31.

—— (eds), *Engaging Countries – Strengthening Compliance with International Environmental Accords*, Cambridge MA: MIT Press, 2000.

Werksman, J.D., 'Greening Bretton Woods' in J. Kirkby, P. O'Keefe and L. Timberlake (eds), *The Earthscan Reader in Sustainable Development*, London: Earthscan, 1995.

—— *Five MEA's, Five Years since Rio: Recent Lessons on the Effectiveness of Multilateral Environmental Agreements*, Rio+5 Special Focus Report prepared by Foundation for International Environmental Law and Development ('FIELD'), 1997.

Wheeler, M., 'Greening the EEC Treaty' in P. Sands (ed.), *Greening International Law*, London: Earthscan, 1993.

White, E., 'In Search of the Limits of Article 30 of the EEC Treaty', *Common Market Law Review* 26, 1989, 235–80.

Wilcox, C., *A Charter for World Trade*, New York: Macmillan, 1949.

Wilder, M. and Whiteford, S., 'Flowing Uphill toward Money: Groundwater Management and Ejidal Producers in Mexico's Free Trade Environment', in L. Randall (ed.), *Changing Structure of Mexico: Political, Social and Economic Prospects*, 2nd edn, New York: Columbia University, 2006.

Wilson, N.L.W., 'Clarifying the Alphabet Soup of the TBT and the SPS in the WTO', *Drake Journal of Agricultural Law* 8, 2003, 703–24.

Wold, C., 'Multilateral Environmental Agreements and the GATT: Conflict and Resolution?' *Environmental Law* 26:3, 1996, 841–921.

Wolfowitz, P., 'Doha's Last Chance', President of the World Bank Group Special to *The Wall Street Journal*, 1 July 2006. Online. Available HTTP: <http://www.worldbank.org/> (accessed 16 February 2007).

World Bank, *Indonesia Country Strategic Paper 2002–2006*, 2001. Online. Available HTTP: <http://www.eu.int/comm/external_relations/indonesia/csp/02_06_en.pdf> (accessed 22 April 2007).

World Bank, with P. Collier and D. Dollar (eds), *Globalization, Growth, and Poverty: Building an Inclusive World Economy (A World Bank Policy Research Report)*, New York: Oxford University Press, 2002.

World Commission on Environment and Development, *Our Common Future*, London: Oxford University Press, 1987.

—— *Our Common Future*, Australian edition, Sydney: Oxford University Press, 1990.

World Conservation Union, 'Balancing Imbalances in the WTO: Agreement on Agriculture'. Online. Available HTTP: <http://www.iucn.org/en/news/archive/2001_2005/press/mtgwtovilm.pdf> (accessed 3 April 2006).

World Trade Organization, *Report of the Committee on Trade and Environment to Ministers in Singapore*, WTO Doc. WT/CTE/1, 12 November 1996.

—— *Report of the WTO Committee on Trade and Environment*, 1996, WTO DOC. PRESS/TE 014. Online. Available HTTP: <http://www.ictsd.org/ministerial/singapore/envtracom.htm> (accessed 21 April 2007).

—— *The Legal Texts: The Results of the Uruguay Round of Multilateral Trade Negotiations*, New York: Cambridge University Press, 1999.

—— *Matrix on Trade Measures Pursuant to Selected MEAs*, 2001, WTO Doc. WT/CTE/W/160/Rev.1.

—— *CTE: Trade Measures in MEAs (1)*, 2003. Online. Available HTTP: <http://www.wto.org/english/thewto_e/whatis_e/eol/e/wto09/wto9_9.htm> (accessed 23 April 2007).

Yoder, A.J., 'Lessons from Stockholm: Evaluating the Global Convention on Persistent Organic Pollutants', *Indiana Journal of Global Legal Studies* 10:2, 2003, 113–56.

Zarsky, L., 'APEC, Citizen Groups and the Environment', Berkeley CA: Nautilus Institute, May 1995. Online. Available HTTP: <http://nautilus.org/archives/papers/enviro/apecenv.html> (accessed 22 June 2005).

—— 'APEC, Globalization and the "Sustainable Development Agenda"', Draft Text for Asian Perspectives, Berkeley CA: Nautilus Institute, October 1998. Online. Available HTTP: <http://www.nautilus.org/archives/papers/enviro/zarsky_apec98.html> (accessed 16 April 2007).

Zarsky, L. and Hunter, J., 'Environmental Co-operation at APEC: The First Five Years', Berkeley CA: Nautilus Institute. Online. Available HTTP: <http://www.nautilus.org/archives/papers/enviro/TEPP/zarsky_hunterTEPP.html> (accessed 22 June 2005).

Zhao, J., 'Implementing International Environmental Treaties in Developing Countries: China's Compliance with the Montreal Protocol', *Global Environmental Politics* 5:1, 2005, 58–81.

Index

accession countries, EU 133–4, 135
African, Caribbean and Pacific (ACP) countries 125, 138–42, 241–2n112
African Development Fund 44
Agenda 21: assessment of 41–6; programme areas 38–41
Agreement on Agriculture, WTO 11–12, 83–5, 107, 113
Agreement on Subsidies and Countervailing Measures, WTO 18, 91
Agreement on Textiles and Clothing, WTO 86–7, 107, 140
Agreement on Trade-related Aspects of Intellectual Property Rights (TRIPS), WTO 89–91; and biodiversity 113–14; and indigenous peoples 46
agriculture 83–5, 112–13, 230n122
aid, under Cotonou Agreement 142
animal protection 68–71, 78–83, 149, 201; *see also* endangered species
Arun Hydro-project 189
Asia-Pacific Economic Cooperation (APEC): achievements of 174; continuing issues/recommendations for reform 174–80; emergence of sustainable development 169–72; institution structure 167–8; recent developments 172–4
automobile taxes case 72
AZO dyes 86–7

Bamako Convention 198–9
Bangladesh: clothing/textiles industry 86; shrimp dispute 81
Basel Convention (1989): comparison with Bamako Convention 198–9; implications for developing countries 196–8; self–sufficiency/proximity principles 132; trade measures 195–6, 201–2
beef hormone dispute 94–5
Beijing Ministerial Conference (1991), WTO 57
biodiversity and TRIPS 113–14
biotechnology 251–2n10
Bogor Declaration (1984) 169
Brazil, gasoline dispute 92–3
Brundtland Report 2, 4–5, 206
Budget and Management Committee, APEC 168

Canada, herring and salmon case 65, 72, 154
Cancun Ministerial Conference (2003), WTO 116–17
capacity building: and Agenda 21/Rio Principle 44–5; APEC 171; and Doha Declaration 111–12; for sustainable development 209–10
capacity building fund, APEC 172–3
Cassis de Dijon case 126–7, 128
China, technologies 192–4
chlorofluorocarbons (CFCs) 190–4
Climate Centre, APEC 173
clothing 86–7
Codex Alimentarius 80, 82, 83
coffee production 43
colonial trade patterns 42
Committee on Trade and Development, GATT/WTO 108, 113
Committee on Trade and Environment (CTE), GATT/WTO: and *Doha Declaration* 111, 113; and eco-labelling

16, 18; objectives 108; work programme 98–9, 117
Committee on Trade and Investment (CTI), APEC 168
commodity markets 38–40; and Agenda 21 42–3
commodity prices 13–14, 31
common but differentiated responsibility principle 6–7, 25–6, 37, 57–8, 171–2, 179–80
Commonwealth Secretariat 139
comparative advantage model 62–3, 76, 77, 79–80, 83
compensation issues 32, 178
consensus-building approach, APEC 167
consumption patterns 14–15, 42
Convention on Biodiversity (CBD), WTO 113–14
Convention on International Trade in Endangered Species of Wild Fauna and Flora (CITES): implications for developing countries 187–9; trade measures under 185–7
corporate social responsibility (CSR) 52, 53
cost internalization principle 27–8
Cotonou Convention (2000) 140–1; trade pillar of 141–2
cotton production 43
countervailing measures 91

Danish bottles case 71, 128–30, 131, 152–3
Dassonville case 125–6
debt 44
debt exchange 161
Declaration for Action (1995), APEC 172
Declaration on a New International Economic Order (UN) 32
developed countries: EU 135–7; exploitation by 222n73
developing countries: concerns of 99–101; definition of 216n22; economic realities in 8–20; in EU 135–7; implications of Basel Convention 196–8; implications of CITES 187–9; implications of Montreal Protocol 191–4; and MEAs 183–5, 259n176; in NAFTA 159–64; need for open/equitable trading system 207; outside EU 137–42; special needs of 31; UNEP as captive of 34–5
development: economic policies for 41; right to 30, 36–7, 56; making trade mutually supportive with environment 40
discrimination, arbitrary/unjustifiable 72–3
dispute resolution, NAFTA 156–9, 176–7
dispute settlement system, GATT/WTO 92–8, 157–9
Doha Declaration: instruction to CTE 111; and LDCs 118; negotiations on trade/environment 111; recognition of technical assistance/capacity building 111–12; rhetoric and reality 114–16; trade and environment provisions 110, 112–13; and TRIPS/biodiversity 113–14
Drake-Brockman, J. 100

eco-imperialism 100
eco-labelling 16–18, 86–7
economic benefits, distribution of 9–10
Economic Committee, APEC 168
economic growth, trade as means of 1–3
Economic Leaders' Vision Statement, APEC 169
Economic Partnership Agreements (EPAs), EU 140–2
economic policies, promotion of 41
economic realities, developing countries 8–20
Eminent Persons Group, APEC 178–9
endangered species 185–9
enforcement of standards 137, 162–3, 201
environment: and APEC institutional structure 167–8; economic policies for 41; impacts of free trade 3–4; implications of GATT principles 66–7; interface with trade 8–20; interlinkages with trade/sustainable development 206–7; mainstreaming of 19–20; mutually supportive with trade 40; principles and concepts 25–8; relationship with trade 4; WTO negotiations 111
Environment Fund, UNEP 33–4
Environmental Action Programmes, EU 121–2, 124–5
environmental funds 189

environmental goods/services, definition of 88–9
environmental groups 108–9
environmental issues, APEC 174–80
Environmental Law (1988), Mexico 160–1
environmental policies, EU 122–3
environmental protection, NAFTA 147–56
environmental provisions, *Doha Declaration* 110, 112–13
environmental regulation, EU 123
environmental services 89
Environmental Side Agreement, NAFTA 147, 150, 156, 158, 162
Environmental Vision Statement (1994), APEC 169–70, 176
environmentalism: GATT 68–74; WTO 74–99
environmentally sound technologies (ESTs) 191–4
Equator Principles 35
equity 6–7, 27, 207
European Commission 124–5, 131–2, 136–7, 171
European Commission v. Denmark 138
European Commission v. Republic of Germany 130
European Committee for Standardization 133
European Court of Justice (ECJ) 125–32, 137, 138, 152–3
European Development Fund (EDF) 142
European Free Trade Agreement (2006) 134
European Union (EU): beef hormone dispute 94–5; compensatory mechanisms 178; developed/developing countries within 135–7; developing countries outside 137–42; development of sustainable development concept 121–5; harmonization of environmental standards 133–4; labelling requirements 76; Regulation 3626/82 186; at Seattle Ministerial Conference 107–8; shrimp dispute 81; trade–environment interface 125–32
exhaustible natural resources 71–2
extraterritoriality 73–4

fair trade, unfairness of 208–9
finance, UNEP 33–5
financial assistance 12, 30, 100
financial cooperation 191–4
financial resources 18, 21, 41, 43, 171, 184–5
food safety 78–83
food security 45
Framework of Principles for Integrating Economy and Environment (1994), APEC 170–2
free trade, environmental impacts of 3–4
Fromançais v. Forma 128

G8 Ministerial Conference (2005) 85
G15 Ministerial Conference (1999) 85
Gaines, S. 75
gasoline imports 92–3
General Agreement on Tariffs and Trade (GATT): Article XX 68–74, 148, 151; core principles 64–7, 200–2; dispute settlement system 92–8; genesis of 60–1
General Agreement on Trade in Services (GATS), WTO 18, 87–9
Generalized System of Preferences (GSP), EU 10–11, 134, 139
Geneva Declaration (1998), WTO 105–6
Germany: domination of trade–environment disputes 135; dyes case 86–7; meat case 130
Ghandi, Indira 56
global economic policy making, and developing countries 8–9
Global Environmental Facility (GEF) 189, 209
global financial system, unfairness of 56
globalization 50–2
green protectionism 15–16, 45, 99–100
gross national product (GNP) 2
Group on Environmental Measures and International Trade (EMIT), GATT 61
Guruswamy, L.D. 6

Halle, M. 9, 36
harmonization of standards: APEC 178–9; challenges 239n63; EU 121–5, 133–4; GATT/WTO 100–1; NAFTA 160–1
hazardous waste, transboundary movement of 195–9

heavily indebted poor countries (HIPCs) 44
herring and salmon case 65, 72, 154
High Level Meeting on Sustainable Development (2006), APEC 173–4, 176
Hong Kong Declaration 85, 117–18
Human Development Report 2005 48
human protection 68–71, 149, 201
Hunter, David 201
Hunter, Jason 175

India: shrimp–turtle dispute 73, 95–7; technologies 192–4
individual action plans (IAPs), APEC 167; incorporation of environmental considerations 177–8
Indonesia: and CITES 188; export of rattan 65
innovation models 91
institutional structure, APEC 167–8, 176–7
intellectual property rights (IPRs) 18, 46, 89–91, 113–14
intergenerational equity principle 27
Inter-governmental Conference (1996), EU 135
Inter-Huiles case 126
International Centre for Trade and Sustainable Development (ICTSD) 202
International Court of Justice 98
International Institute for Sustainable Development (IISD) 202
International Monetary Fund 44
International Organization for Standardization (ISO) 16–17, 83
international standards organizations: focus of 83; WTO membership of 80–1
International Trade Centre (ITC), Geneva 87
IPPC 82

Johannesburg Declaration on Sustainable Development 19, 50
Johannesburg Plan of Implementation (JPOI) 50–3
Jubilee Debt Campaign 44

Kher, Rajeev 15
Khor, Martin 35, 107, 109
Khosla, A. 7, 13, 19, 38
Kirkpatrick, C. 49
Korea, technologies 192–4
Kyoto Protocol 134

labour-intensive services 88
Large Combustion Plants Directive, EU 133–4
least developed countries (LDCs) 106, 118, 141–2
Leutwiler Commission 1–2
liability issues 32
liberal trade theory 62–3, 76, 77, 79–80, 83
'like products' 66–7
Ling, C.Y. 35
Lomé Convention 138–40

Maastricht Treaty 124–5, 135
Madelin, Robert 108
Malaysia, shrimp–turtle dispute 73, 95–7
market access 10–13, 115, 134, 162, 209
Marrakesh Agreement 110
Mehra, Malini 109
Metalclad Corporation v. United Mexican States 155
Methanex case 155–6
Mexican Action Network on Free Trade 159–60
Mexican Confederation of Chambers of Industry 160
Mexico: as NAFTA member 155, 159–64; tuna–dolphin dispute 67, 69–71, 73–4
Millennium Development Goals 46–9; implementation of 18, 185; report 2006 11, 44
Montreal Protocol: compliance with 200–1; implications for developing countries 191–4; trade measures under 190
most favoured nations (MFNs) 64, 66–7, 140, 154, 200
Multi-Fibre Agreement (MFA) 12
multilateral environmental agreements (MEAs): and Basel Convention 195–9; and CITES 185–9; and Montreal Protocol 190–4; sectors covered by 259n176; and technology transfer 255–6n100; trade measures and developing countries 183–5;

multilateral environmental agreements (MEAs) *continued*
trade-related provisions 114–15; trade restrictive measures in 212; and WTO free trade regime 199–202
Multilateral Fund 191–2, 193, 194
multinational corporations 88–9, 197
Mutual Recognition Agreements (MRAs) 81–2
mutual recognition principle 137

Najam, Adil 27, 107
National Agency for the Protection of the Environment (NAPE), Denmark 129–30
National Treatment obligations 64, 66–7, 154, 200–1
necessary tests principle, GATT 68–70
non–discrimination principle: EU 131–2; NAFTA 151
North American Free Trade Agreement (NAFTA): developing countries within 159–64; dispute resolution 156–9; Preamble 147–8; precautionary principle 152–3; process and production methods 153; standards regime 148–51; technical barriers to trade 151; trade-related environmental measures 148; unnecessary obstacles to trade 152, 153–6
North–South approach: APEC 167–8; UN 55–8
North–South consensus 209–10
North–South dynamics, APEC 167–8
North–South tensions: APEC 168, 174–5; SPS/TBT Agreements 82–3

Official Development Assistance (ODA) 43, 209
OIE 80, 82
Organization for Economic Cooperation and Development (OECD) countries: agricultural sector 84; and CITES 186; hazardous wastes 195–7; and polluter pays principle 28; studies by 10
Organization of African Unity (OAU) 198
Our Common Future see *Brundtland Report*
OxonAction programme, UNEP 192
ozone-depleting substances (ODS) 190–4

Packaging Waste Directive, EU 134
Pakistan, shrimp–turtle dispute 73, 95–7
Paris Summit (1972) 121
plant protection 58–71, 78–83, 149, 201; *see also* endangered species
pollutants, identification and control 29–30
polluter pays principle 27–8, 171, 180
precautionary principle 26, 79–80, 115, 152–3, 171, 180
preferential trade arrangements, EU 138–40
process and production methods (PPMs) 15–17, 66–7, 75–6, 100, 114, 153
product standards 16–18
production processes, technical know-how in 197
proportionality and necessity principle, EU 128–31
proportionality test, GATT 70–1
protectionism 9–13, 37, 84–5, 99–100, 104–5, 162, 175, 210–11

qualified majority voting (QMV), EU 123
quantitative restrictions elimination, EU 126–32; GATT 64–5, 201

Rauscher, M. 15
reformulated gasoline dispute 92–3
Ricardo, David 62–3, 76, 77, 79–80, 83
Rio Declaration (*Earth Charter*) 36–8; assessment of 42, 44–5; common but differentiated responsibility principle 25–6; intergenerational equity principle 27; polluter pays principle 28; precautionary principle 26, 171–2
Roberts, M. 49
Ruggiero, Renato 106
rules of origin 139–40, 162

Salzman, James 201
Sanitary and Phytosanitary (SPS) Agreement, WTO 17, 78–83, 94
sanitary and phytosanitary measures, NAFTA 149
Seattle Declaration 106–9
Secretariat Trade and Environment Report 1992, GATT 14
services, trade in 18, 87–9

shrimp dispute 81
shrimp–turtle dispute 73, 95–7
Singapore Declaration 104–5
Single European Act (1986) 122–3, 124, 135
Siphana, Sok 48, 86
Small Island Developing States (SIDS) 2
'smart partnership' 52–3
Social Development Fund, EU 159, 178
special and differential treatment 9–10
standards regimes, NAFTA 148–51; *see also* harmonization of standards
standards-related measures (SRMs) 151, 152; as unnecessary obstacles to trade 153–6
state sovereignty 32
Steinberg, Richard H. 135
Stockholm Declaration 29–32, 220n22
Strachan, J. 49
Subramanian, Arvind 90
subsidies 18, 84, 91; removal of 209
sustainable development: emergence of 4–6; equity and responsibility 6–7
Swatuk, Larry A. 52

tariffs, removal of 209
technical assistance 12
Technical Barriers to Trade (TBT) Agreement, WTO 17, 75–8
technical barriers to trade, NAFTA 151
technical cooperation 191–4
technical know-how, production processes 197
technical standard setting 161–2
technological assistance 30, 82, 111–12, 179
technology transfer 18, 44, 88, 89–90, 100, 255–6n100
terms of trade 13–14
textiles 12, 86–7, 107
Thailand: cigarette case 70; and CITES 187, 188, 189; shrimp–turtle dispute 73, 95–7
trade: core principles of GATT 64–7; and Cotonou Agreement 141–2; and economic growth 1–3; interlinkages with environment/sustainable development 206–7; as means of economic growth 1–3; North–South aspects of UN approach 55–8; principles and concepts 25–8; relationship with environment 4; SRMs as obstacles to 153–6; sustainable development through 38–40; WTO negotiations 111
trade–environment interface, developing countries 8–20; EU 125–42; NAFTA 159–64; WTO Ministerial Conferences 103–18
trade environment nexus, challenges ahead 213–14
trade issues, APEC 174–80
trade measures: Basel Convention 195–6; CITES 185–7; MEAs 183–5; Montreal Protocol 190; primarily aimed at 72
trade obstacles, NAFTA 152, 153–6
trade provisions, *Doha Declaration* 110, 112–13
trade-related environmental measures (TREMS) 15–16, 45
trade restrictive measures, MEAs 212
Trade Sustainability Impact Assessment (TSIA), EU 124–5
trade theory and WTO 62–3
traditional methods/knowledge 46
transboundary movement, hazardous waste 195–9
Treaty of Rome 121–3, 124, 125–32, 138
Treaty of the European Union *see* Maastricht Treaty
tuna–dolphin dispute 67, 69–71, 73–4
Turtle Excluder Devices (TEDs) 95–7

United Nations: Charter 29, 53; environment in 28–35; future developments 58; Millennium Summit 11, 18, 44, 46–9, 185; North–South approach of 55–8; World Summit on Sustainable Development (WSSD) 49–53
United Nations Commission on Sustainable Development (UNCSD) 53–5
United Nations Conference on Environment and Development (UNCED) 55–7, 206–7; *see also* Agenda 21; Rio Declaration
United Nations Conference on the Human Environment (UNCHE) 29–32, 220n22

United Nations Conference on Trade and Development (UNCTAD) 16, 45
United Nations Development Programme (UNDP) 14–15
United Nations Environment Programme (UNEP): creation of 29; financing issues 33–5; legitimacy of 35
United Nations University 184
upward harmonization, NAFTA 160–1
Uruguay Round: concessions to developing countries 9–10, 85, 106–7, 116; key objectives 8; market access 11–13
US: automobile taxes case 72; beef hormone dispute 94–5; reformulated gasoline dispute 92–3; at Seattle Ministerial Conference 107–8; shrimp–turtle dispute 73, 95–7; technical standard setting 161–2; Thai cigarette case 70; tuna–dolphin dispute 67, 69–71, 73–4
US Clean Air Act 92
US Endangered Species Act (1973) 95
US Environmental Protection Agency 92–3, 162
US Marine Mammal Protection Act (1972) 67, 69
US Tariff Act (1930) 69–70

Venezuela, gasoline dispute 92–3
Vienna Convention on the Law of Treaties (1969) 147–8, 243–4n16
Voluntary Indicative Scale of Contributions (VISC) 34

Wallonian Waste case 131–2
Waste Management v. Mexico 155
Waste Oil case 127–8
World Bank 10, 35, 44, 48, 138, 193
World Trade Organization (WTO): asymmetries/imbalances within Agreements 211–12; Beijing Ministerial Conference (1991) 57; Cancun Ministerial Conference (2003) 116–17; core principles of GATT—WTO regime 200–2; dispute settlement system 92–8; Doha Ministerial Conference (2001) 109–16, 118; environmentalism in 74–99; genesis of GATT–WTO 60–1; Geneva Ministerial Conference (1998) 105–6; Hong Kong Ministerial Conference (2005) 85, 117–18; mainstreaming of environment 19–20; relationship with MEAs 199–202; Seattle Ministerial Conference (1999) 106–9; Singapore Ministerial Conference (1996) 104–5; trade negotiations 213; and trade theory 62–3; Treaty establishing 110

Zaelke, Durwood 201
Zarsky, Lyuba 175